LUFTWAFFE GENERALS

LUFTWAFFE GENERALS

THE KNIGHT'S CROSS HOLDERS • 1939-1945

Jeremy Dixon

Schiffer Military History
Atglen, PA

Acknowledgements

This is my second book and it's dedicated to my sister and my two nephews Josh and Max who have given me support throughout this project, and along with my parents my sincere thanks go to all of them. Without the support of family, friends and work colleagues this book would not have been written, and it's now that I take this opportunity to thank all those who have supported and encouraged me.

I have so many people to thank and I just hope I don't miss anyone out. First I would like to thank those people who have contributed photographs that are essential in any book. My thanks go to publisher and author Roger James Bender who, although extremely busy himself, took the trouble in sending me photographs to my exact specification. I would also like to thank Ian Sayer, Eric Stahel and the owners of the Wehrkundearchiv who gave me permission to use photographs from their collection.

As I said support and encouragement is so important when working on a project like this, and sometimes I thought it would never get finished, but interest and encouragement from friends always help. I would like to thank the following: John Preece and Graham Harris for lending me various books, Pauline Forgie for helping me proof read various pages, Michelle Pearce for coming up with a working title and Dan Fraser for help in scanning various negatives into useable photographs. I would also like to thank Alex Curran, Rob Sales, Matt Lockie, Colin Harris, Matt Jackman, James Hunter, Jared Gregory, Rob French, Scott Blake, Julie Cheetham, Sue Grimwood, Phil Cooke, Malcolm Card, Bob Lynn, Moira Moore, Lorraine Horsnell, Karen Fowler, Kim Botting, and all my friends and work colleagues. Finally I would like to thank two friends who have helped and encouraged me right from the start and have continued to take an interest throughout, my thanks to David Ross and Nathan Pearce.

Jeremy Dixon
Dartford, 2008

Dedication

To Joanna, Josh and Max

Book design by Robert Biondi.

Library of Congress Catalog Number: 2008943543.

Printed in China.
ISBN: 978-0-7643-3243-2

We are always looking for people to write books on new and related subjects. If you have an idea for a book, please contact us at the address below.

Published by Schiffer Publishing Ltd.
4880 Lower Valley Road
Atglen, PA 19310
Phone: (610) 593-1777
FAX: (610) 593-2002
E-mail: Info@schifferbooks.com.
Visit our web site at: www.schifferbooks.com
Please write for a free catalog.
This book may be purchased from the publisher.
Please include $5.00 postage.
Try your bookstore first.

In Europe, Schiffer books are distributed by:
Bushwood Books
6 Marksbury Ave.
Kew Gardens, Surrey TW9 4JF
England
Phone: 44 (0)20 8392-8585
FAX: 44 (0)20 8392-9876
E-mail: info@bushwoodbooks.co.uk
www.bushwoodbooks.co.uk

CONTENTS

Dedication
To Joanna, Josh and Max

ACKNOWLEDGEMENTS

This is my second book and it's dedicated to my sister and my two nephews Josh and Max who have given me support throughout this project, and along with my parents my sincere thanks go to all of them. Without the support of family, friends and work colleagues this book would not have been written, and it's now that I take this opportunity to thank all those who have supported and encouraged me.

I have so many people to thank and I just hope I don't miss anyone out. First I would like to thank those people who have contributed photographs that are essential in any book. My thanks go to publisher and author Roger James Bender who, although extremely busy himself, took the trouble in sending me photographs to my exact specification. I would also like to thank Ian Sayer, Eric Stahel and the owners of the Wehrkundearchiv who gave me permission to use photographs from their collection.

As I said support and encouragement is so important when working on a project like this, and sometimes I thought it would never get finished, but interest and encouragement from friends always help. I would like to thank the following: John Preece and Graham Harris for lending me various books, Pauline Forgie for helping me proof read various pages, Michelle Pearce for coming up with a working title and Dan Fraser for help in scanning various negatives into useable photographs. I would also like to thank Alex Curran, Rob Sales, Matt Lockie, Colin Harris, Matt Jackman, James Hunter, Jared Gregory, Rob French, Scott Blake, Julie Cheetham, Sue Grimwood, Phil Cooke, Malcolm Card, Bob Lynn, Moira Moore, Lorraine Horsnell, Karen Fowler, Kim Botting, and all my friends and work colleagues. Finally I would like to thank two friends who have helped and encouraged me right from the start and have continued to take an interest throughout, my thanks to David Ross and Nathan Pearce.

Jeremy Dixon
Dartford, 2008

INTRODUCTION

The Knight's Cross of the Iron Cross is one of the most famous decorations of World War II, and was instituted on 1st September 1939 by Adolf Hitler, the first award was presented on 30th September 1939.[1] It was a unique award since it had not been in existence prior to that time. Hitler had ordered that the Knight's Cross was to be awarded to all ranks, in fact 1,676 NCOs and enlisted men won the award.

The Knight's Cross was awarded for acts of ultimate bravery and was awarded to all the services which included the Luftwaffe, the Army, the Navy and Waffen-SS and was also extended to Foreign Nationals[2] who had been fighting alongside the German forces. It was different to the very famous Victoria Cross or the U.S. Medal of Honor which was strictly received for valor. The Knight's Cross could also be awarded on a point basis. A pilot for example could have received the Knight's Cross in 1940 for downing twenty-six aircraft. A U-boat commander could get the Knight's Cross for sinking 100,000 tons of shipping. It could also be awarded for a successful command during a battle, or even for a successful withdrawal and in some cases it was given for services rendered and as a result approx. 7,200 were awarded. There were 688 Luftwaffe officers who held the rank of general during World War II and 115 were awarded the Knight's Cross about 17%, and this illustrates just how special this award was in Germany during the war. There is a misconception that the Knight's Cross was awarded more to generals than any other rank, but this is not true, only 6.9% of the German generals received the award, that's 502 out of 7,200.

As the war went on more and more awards were presented and in June 1940 Hitler instituted the Oakleaves, it took the form of two oakleaves overlapping each other and was presented in a small presentation case. This was awarded to a person, who had already been awarded the Knight's Cross, and in September 1941 two other higher grades of the Knight's Cross were introduced, the Swords and the Diamonds, and real diamonds were used. (These awards will be discussed further in the next chapter.) There was one additional grade to the Knight's Cross that was only awarded to one person, the Knight's Cross with Golden Oakleaves, Swords and Diamonds was awarded to the Stuka pilot Hans-Ulrich Rudel.

However the highest award instituted during the war in Germany was the Grand Cross of the Iron Cross which had been in existence during World War I and Hitler was responsible for reintroducing it. Again only one was ever awarded in Nazi Germany and the recipient was Hitler's Deputy *Reichsmarschall* Hermann Göring who was presented this high award for his successful command of the Luftwaffe during the campaign in France and the Low Countries.

There have been many books written about the Knight's Cross and its recipients. This study brings together the highest ranking recipients of this coveted award from the Luftwaffe, the German air force. There were one hundred and fifteen generals in the Luftwaffe who won this most prestigious award, and inside you will find mini biographies of all these recipients. This book also uses information from a recently published title *Ritterkreuzträger 1939-1945 by Veit Scherzer*, the author has meticulously researched all the recipients and found that mistakes had been made and he has completed his study using original documents and files, and has identified those recipients who were awarded the Knight's Cross illegally and some who never were actually awarded it in the first place. He is the first author not to have been a member of the Award Association of Knight's Cross Recipients, (*Ordensgemeinschaft der Ritterkreuzträger*) and has studied the evidence without being hindered by arrogance or beholden to personal relationships with other members. Some who read this might be surprised by his findings with regard to the Oakleaves and Swords recipients. For example: Eugen Meindl who is reported to have been the 155th recipient of the Swords on 8th May 1945, Scherzer explains that his award hadn't been endorsed or forwarded in the usual manner and with the Commander-in-Chief of the Armed Forces (Hitler) dead all awards were deemed unofficial

Willrich postcards showing Adolf Galland, and General Eugen Meindl. (Author's Collection)

after this time. A few were endorsed by Hitler's successor Karl Dönitz[3] but not Meindl's and because he became a member of the Award Association after the war his name was added to the list of Swords recipients. The other Luftwaffe general whose award is unofficial is Hermann Plocher who was according to his own statement awarded the Oakleaves on 8th May 1945 making him the 867th recipient and again he was a member of the Award Association after the war. His award is deemed unofficial and therefore illegal.

The Nazis were fast to capitalize on the Knight's Cross popularity. During World War II postcards were produced by Hitler's photographer Heinrich Hoffmann, and the war artists Willrich.

They featured portraits of Knights Cross holders of all ranks and featured members of the Luftwaffe, Kriegsmarine (Navy), Heer (Army) and the Waffen-SS. These cards proved to be very popular with German citizens and were avidly collected by adults and children alike. These cards are widely collected even today. The Knight's Cross is still a popular award for collectors and those interested in reading about the award and its recipients.

What follows is a brief look at the Knight's Cross and it's higher grades, the Oakleaves, the Swords, the Diamonds and the very rare Grand Cross. I then take a brief look at the Iron Cross 1st and 2nd Classes together with the Bar to Iron Cross for both classes and finally the German Cross in Gold. All further awards are listed in alphabetical order to make it easier for the reader and I have included some of the decorations rendered during World War I.

Hoffmann postcards showing one of each of the four different branches of Germany's Armed Forces. Left to right: Oberst Werner Mölders of the Luftwaffe; Kapitänleutnant Wolfgang Lüth of the Kriegsmarine; Generalfeldmarschall Wilhelm List of the Heer and SS-Obergruppenführer Josef Sepp Dietrich of the Waffen-SS. (Author's Collection)

THE KNIGHT's CROSS - OTHER AWARDS AND DECORATIONS

The Knight's Cross was basically the same design as the Iron Cross except it was larger. It measured 48mm x 48mm with a silver ring on top which measured 6mm. At the top of the cross there was an elongated ribbon top which went through the silver ring and this is where the ribbon went that was used to hold it into position around the recipients' neck. The award was presented in an elongated black leather-like case, which contained the award and a folded length of neck ribbon. Most were awarded to each recipient by their divisional commanders, corps commanders, army group commanders and equivalents in the case of Luftwaffe and Kriegsmarine personnel. On some special occasion Hitler would present the award. With the award came an impressive looking citation presented in a red leather binder and stamped in gold with a German eagle on the front cover and signed by Hitler.

The Knight's Cross with Oakleaves

Instituted by Hitler on 3rd June 1940 the Knight's Cross with Oakleaves was worn above the original Knight's Cross and held in place by means of a silver loop that would also secure the neck ribbon. The Oakleaves, as it was known, was the next higher grade of the Knight's Cross and was as such even more highly regarded. The first Oakleaves was awarded on 19th July 1940 to *Generalleutnant* Eduard Dietl as Commanding General of the Mountain Corps Norway. During the course of the war a total number of 843 were officially awarded, the last one being awarded to *Oberst* Hans-Peter Knaust on 17th April 1945. Other sources give a different figure; they give the number as 882 with the last awarded being made to *Generalleutnant* Joseph von Radowitz on 9th May 1945. But according to Veit Scherzer's study all Oakleaves recipients after 17th April 1945 were unofficial and therefore illegal. This author has used this study throughout but some may still consider all the awards as legal, so I leave it to the individual reader and their beliefs.

The Oakleaves were presented to the recipient in a presentation case not unlike the Knight's Cross. A new length of neck ribbon measuring 45mm wide was presented with the award. The award document was signed by Hitler and on most occasions was presented by Hitler personally during a special ceremony.

The Knight's Cross with Oakleaves and Swords

Instituted by Hitler on 28th September 1941, the Knight's Cross with Oakleaves and Swords was the next higher grade and could only be awarded to previous winners of the Oakleaves. The Swords was presented to each recipient in a case similar to that of the Oakleaves. The Swords was attached below the Oakleaves crossed at a forty degree angle, with the right sword overlapping the left. Each sword measured 24mm in length. The first Swords were awarded on 21st June 1941 to *Oberstleutnant* Adolf Galland and it was presented to Galland by Hitler personally. It's interesting to note that the Swords were awarded three times before it was officially instituted by Hitler. The last award was made to *Generalmajor* Hellmuth Mader on 18th April 1945, according to Scherzer. Again other sources make a different claim, they claim that the last recipient was Josef Bremm awarded on 9th May 1945 being the 159th recipient. There was a single case when the Swords were awarded to a recipient on the same day as the award of the Oakleaves was rendered, that person was *Oberst* Hermann Graf on 2nd May 1942.

The Knight's Cross with Oakleaves, Swords, and Diamonds

The Knight's Cross with Oakleaves, Swords and Diamonds was instituted by Hitler on 15th July 1941. The Diamonds could only be awarded to previous winners of the Swords. The first Diamonds were awarded the day after it was instituted to *Oberstleutnant* Werner Mölders. All the awards of the Diamonds were awarded personally by Hitler and all were won by officers, the award came with a lavish document. It was printed by hand on high grade parchment in gold. The Diamonds were hand crafted by a jeweller with real diamonds set in the Oakleaves and on the handles of the swords.

Just like the Swords there was one recipient who was awarded the Diamonds on the same day as the Swords. *General der Fallschirmtuppe* Bernhard-Hermann Ramcke was that person, he became the 99th recipient of the Swords and the 20th recipient of the Diamonds on 19th September 1944. There were twenty-seven recipients of the Diamonds, the last being awarded to *General der Panzertruppe* Dietrich von Saucken on 8th May 1945.

The Grand Cross of the Iron Cross

On 1st September 1939 Hitler reinstituted the Grand Cross of the Iron Cross. It had been awarded during World War I, and was Germany's highest military award. It was only awarded to generals. There were five recipients during World War I: Kaiser Wilhelm II, *Generalfeldmarschall* Paul Ludwig von Hindenburg, *General der Infanterie* Erich Ludendorf, *Generalfeldmarschall* Prinz Leopold Maximilian Joseph Maria Arnulf and *Generalfeldmarschall* August von Mackensen.

On the 19th July 1940 Hitler presented the Grand Cross to *Reichsmarschall* Hermann Göring, the only recipient during World War II. The Grand Cross was larger than the Knight's Cross; it measured 63.3mm across and required a 57mm wide neck ribbon. The award document was very elaborate, and was held in a blue-grey leather case, hand constructed with the national emblem and border design in gold and diamonds. The Swastika of the national emblem was studded with diamonds, surrounded by small diamonds and emeralds.

Other Awards and Decorations

The Iron Cross

The Iron Cross was originally instituted in 1813 and was reinstituted in 1870 without change. When Germany entered World War I the Kaiser reinstituted the award again on 5th August 1914. The award could be rendered to all ranks for bravery in the field or service to the war effort. It was awarded in two classes 1st and 2nd Class. The total number awarded during the period of 1914-1918 was: 2nd Class 5,009,645 and 1st Class 163,000.

In World War II Hitler reinstituted the Iron Cross once more on 1st September 1939. Its basic design remained unchanged and it was still awarded to all ranks. The only changes were instead of the oakleaves the swastika now appeared on the front and the date was changed from 1914 to 1939. The Iron Cross 2nd Class was given out with a ribbon attached and during World War II the colour changed from black and white to the same as the Knight's Cross, black, white and red. The number awarded during World War II remains unclear but approx. figures put the number for the 2nd Class award: 3,000,000 and for 1st Class: 450,000.

Bar to the Iron Cross 2nd Class

The Bar to the Iron Cross was awarded to those who had received the 1914 Iron Cross 2nd Class for actions during World War I. The award was fixed to black ribbon with two white stripes rather than be given a second cross. Its design was that of the national eagle with outstretched wings mounted on a bar bearing the date "1939". It measured 29mm to 31.4mm across and 30.5mm to 31.5mm high. It was worn in the second button hole of the tunic.

Bar to the Iron Cross 1st Class

The Bar to the Iron Cross 1st Class was awarded to those who had received the 1914 Iron Cross 1st Class. It was given a pin-back clasp identical in design to the 2nd Class Bar but was slightly larger. It measured 43.8mm to 45mm across the wing-span, and 30mm to 31mm high. It was worn on the left breast pocket immediately above the 1914 Iron Cross 1st Class.

German Cross in Gold

Introduced by Hitler to bridge the gap that existed between the Iron Cross 1st Class and the Knight's Cross. The German Cross was instituted on 28th September 1941. There were two grades: Gold and Silver. The Silver was awarded for leadership not directly involving combat operations. The German Cross in Gold was a completely independent award, many who received the German Cross never got the Knight's Cross while there were Knight's Cross winners who never received the German Cross. The German Cross in Gold and Silver are identical in appearance, the only exception being that the wreath of laurel leaves around the swastika is gold on one and silver of the other.

There was a cloth version made but only in gold. It was introduced because the original being heavy and bulky would stick out especially in the confined spaces of a U-boat, aircraft cockpit or a tank. The cloth version would be sewn on in exactly the same place on the tunic as the original and was officially introduced on 5th June 1942.

The German Cross was worn in the center of the pocket on the right hand side of the uniform tunic. It took precedence over all other decorations on the tunic except the Blood Order. There were individuals who were award both the silver and gold but these were rare cases. Altogether there were 24,190 recipients of the German Cross in Gold and 1,114 Silver were awarded. These numbers are only approximate figures and as a result the silver award is highly prized by collectors today, more so than the German Cross in Gold.

AFRIKA Cufftitle

Instituted on 15th January 1943.

This was an award made from cloth and worn around the cuff of the recipients tunic, and was awarded for at least one of the following: six months service in North Africa; invalided out as a result of a tropical disease and served at least three months in North Africa and if the recipient had won an award whilst serving in North Africa.

Aircrew Badge
Instituted on 19th January 1935.
Awarded to pilots and observers.

Anti-aircraft or Flak Badge
Instituted on 19th July 1940.
Awarded for an act of bravery while on anti-aircraft duty or being a commander of a battery when half of the men have received the award.

Baltic Cross
Instituted in the summer of 1919.
Awarded for service in the Freikorps during the fighting in the Baltic region against the Communist insurgents between 1919-1921. The award was allowed to be worn after the general ban on Freikorps awards in late 1935.

Blood Order
Instituted on 15th March 1934.
Awarded to those who took part during the Munich Putsch of 9th November 1923 or for special merits after May 1938. The Medal itself was only worn on very special occasions but the ribbon was worn through the button hole of the right breast pocket on the recipient's tunic.

Cholm Shield
Instituted on 1st July 1942.
Awarded for participation of the defence of the besieged Fortress Cholm from January-May 1942.

Close Combat Clasp of the Luftwaffe
Instituted on 3rd November 1944.
Awarded in three grades. Bronze awarded for the participation in 15 days of hand-to-hand combat or taking part in 10 days of close-combat. Silver awarded for 30 days hand-to-hand combat or participation in 20 days of close-combat. Gold awarded for 50 days hand-to-hand combat or participation in 40 days of close-combat.

Combined Pilot and Observers Badge
Instituted on 26th March 1936.
Awarded to those who held both pilot's and observer's certificates.

Combined Pilot and Observers Badge in Gold with Diamonds
It was officially awarded from 19th October 1939 as an honorary award given to deserving Germans and non-Germans.

Commemorative Medal of 13th March 1938
Instituted on 1st May 1938.
Awarded to those who participated in the march into Austria (Anschluss).

Commemorative Medal of 1st October 1938
Instituted on 18th October 1938.
Awarded to those who took part in the annexation of the Sudetenland or Bohemia and Moravia.

Crimea Shield
Instituted on 7th July 1942.
Recipients had to have participated in the German advance into the Crimea.

Cross of Honor for Frontline Combatants
Instituted on 13th July 1934.
Awarded for service during World War I.

Demjansk Shield
Instituted on 25th April 1943.
Recipients had to have participated in the fighting of the Demjansk Pocket in 1942.

German Defences Medal (West Wall)
Instituted on 2nd August 1939.
This was awarded to those who took part in the building of the fortifications along Germany's border or being stationed on the border before May 1940. It was reissued on 10th October 1944 when the defences along Germany's border were being strengthened.

Golden Party Badge of the NSDAP
Instituted on 13th October 1933.
Awarded to those members of the Nazi Party with membership numbers between 1-100,000 or having been a member since February 1925. The most notable recipient was Adolf Hitler.

Ground Assault Badge
Instituted on 31st March 1942.
Awarded for participation in three assaults, or having been wounded or having earned an award during an assault.

Honor Goblet of the Luftwaffe
Established in February 1940 and was awarded by the authority of *Reichsmarschall* Hermann Göring to Luftwaffe personnel "for special achievements in the air war." This was an award for aircrew or pilots only. The recipients' details were etched into the stem of the goblet.

Honor Roll Clasp of the Luftwaffe
Instituted on 5th July 1944.
Recipients had to have already been awarded the Iron Cross 1st Class, and were required to have performed acts of bravery beyond the call of duty, that didn't justify the award of the Knight's Cross or German Cross.

Knight's Cross of the Military Order of Maximilian Joseph
Instituted on 1st January 1806.
This award was bestowed upon Bavarian soldiers for bravery in combat. A knighthood entitled the recipient to a lifelong pension and the right to append "Ritter von" to his surname. Most notable recipient was *Generalfeldmarschall* Robert Ritter von Greim. (as far as this publication is concerned)

KRETA Cufftitlev
Instituted on 16th October 1942.
Awarded for one of the following: Taken part in a parachute or glider landing on Crete between 20th-27th May 1941; taken part in air operations over Crete or seen active service in the sea around Crete.

Kuban Shield
Instituted on 21st September 1943.
The recipient had to have participated in the fighting to preserve the Kuban Bridgeheads from February-October 1943.

Long Service Awards of the Wehrmacht (Armed Forces)
Instituted on 16th March 1936 in four grades:
Silver Medal – member of the Wehrmacht for 4 years
Gold Medal – member of the Wehrmacht for 12 years
Silver Cross – member of the Wehrmacht for 18 years
Gold Cross – member of the Wehrmacht for 25 years

Medal for the Winter Campaign in Russia 1941/1942
Instituted on 26th May 1942.
Awarded to those who participated in 14 days of combat or performed 30 combat sorties or served 60 days in the combat zone or were wounded in line of duty between 15th November 1941 and 26th April 1942.

Narvik Shield
Instituted on 19th August 1940.
Awarded for the participation in the Battle of Narvik (9 April – 9 June 1940)

Observer's Badge
Instituted on 27th November 1935.
Awarded after two months service in a non-operational squadron or five operational sorties.

Operational Flying Clasp
This was awarded in three grades 3rd Class for 20 operational flights, 2nd Class for 60, and 1st Class for 110 flights. There were various types for different operational flights, detailed below with the date of their introduction.
Day fighters – 30th January 1941
Heavy, medium and dive-bombers – 30th January 1941
Reconnaissance, air/sea rescue – 30th January 1941
Transport and gliders – 19th November 1941
Long-range day fighters – 13th May 1942
Night fighters – 14th August 1942
Long-range night fighters – 14th August 1942
Air to ground support – 12th April 1944
On 26th June 1942 a pendant with a gold star was worn for the following number of flights:
Fighter and transport – 500; Dive-bomber and Long-range fighters – 400; Bombers, air-sea rescue – 300 and Reconnaissance and night fighters – 250.

Parachutist Badge
Instituted on 1st January 1935.
Awarded after having completed the instruction course for paratroopers or having made five qualifying jumps.

Pilot's Badge
Instituted on 19th January 1936.
Worn after the completion of a pilot's course.

Pour le Mérite
First founded in 1740 by King Frederick II of Prussia, and given a French name as this was the language of the Prussian Royal Court at the time. Until 1810 it was awarded to both civilian and military. Although by World War I the *Pour le Mérite* had been around for over 170 years it wasn't until World War that it gained international fame and became known as the "Blue Max". In aerial warfare a fighter pilot was initially awarded the *Pour le Mérite* after shooting down eight enemy aircraft. Aces Max Immelmann and Oswald Boelcke were the first to receive the ward on 12th January 1916. The number of aerial victories necessary to receive the award continued to increase during the war; by early 1917, it generally required destroying sixteen enemy airplanes, and by war's end the approximate figure was thirty. However, other aviation recipients included Zeppelin commanders, bomber and observation aircrews, and at least one balloon observer.

Although many of its famous recipients were junior officers, especially pilots, more than a third of all awards in World War I went to generals and admirals. Junior officers (army captains and lieutenants and their navy equivalents) accounted for only about 25% of all awards. Senior officer awards tended to be more for outstanding leadership in combat than for individual acts of bravery.

Most notable recipients were: Otto von Bismarck, Paul von Hindenburg, Manfred von Richthofen the Red Baron, Hermann Göring, Werner von Blomberg, Fedor von Bock, Robert Ritter von Greim, Erwin Rommel and Ernst Udet.

Prussian Observer's Badge
This was not strictly an achievement award and was only issued after an observer had completed his full training which was far more rigorous than pilot training. It features an enamelwork Prussian "signal flag" in the center and is surrounded by a red

border and fixed to a background piece with a starburst design and a spray of laurels and oak leaves. The Prussian crown surmounts the design.

Prussian Pilot's Badge
Just like the Observers Badge this was more a skills insignia rather than an award and wasn't automatically issued to a new pilot upon completion of his training. During the war the pilot had to have completed actual combat flying before he was awarded the Pilot's Badge.

Radio Operator/Air Gunner Badge
Instituted in 1936 and was awarded after two months service in a non-operational squadron or having made five operational sorties.

Return of Memel Commemorative Medal
Instituted on 1st May 1939.
Awarded for the participation in the annexation of Memel on 23rd March 1939.

Royal Hohenzollern House Order
This was an award that was given by the Prussian ruling family, the Hohenzollerns. It was presented in the form of Knight's Cross and became a bridge to the considerable gap between the Iron Cross 1st Class and the Pour le merite for recognizing heroism. There was also a "member's cross" of the order which was awarded to NCOs. There were over 8,000 awards made during World War I, the vast majority of these were Knight's Crosses.

Silesian Eagle
Instituted on 16th June 1919.
Awarded for taking part in the defence of Silesia. It was awarded in two grades, 2nd Class for three months service and 1st Class for six months service. It was one of the few Freikorps awards, along with the Baltic Cross that was allowed to be worn on the uniforms during the Third Reich period.

Spanish Cross
Instituted on 14th April 1939.
Awarded in various grades for acts of bravery beyond the call of duty whilst serving in the Spanish Civil War.
Spanish Cross with Gold and Diamonds – 28 awarded
Gold with Swords – 1,126 awarded
Silver with Swords – 8,304 awarded
Silver without Swords – 8,327 awarded
Bronze with Swords – 8,462 awarded
Bronze without Swords – 7,869 awarded

Wehrmacht Daily Report (*Wehrmachtberichte*)
This was the Official Wehrmacht reports made daily between September 1939 and May 1945 reporting on the military situations at all fronts. The reports were often heard on German radio and often individual commanders or soldiers were mentioned if they had achieved special recognition, such as a high award or in the case of Luftwaffe fighter pilots, their number of victories might be mentioned. It was a special honour to be mentioned.

Wound Badge
Instituted on 1st September 1939.
Black Wound Badge – awarded for being wounded once or twice or being injured during an air raid or by frostbite in the line of duty.
Silver Wound Badge – for being wounded 3 or 4 times in fighting or in an air raid or serious injury in the line of duty.
Gold Wound Badge – for being wounded 5 times or more during combat or during an air raid or being wounded extremely seriously in the line of duty.

Wound Badge, 20th July 1944
Instituted on 2nd September 1944.
Being injured during the attempt on Hitler's life at the Wolfsschanze 20 July 1944.
Notable recipients were: *Oberst* Klaus von Below; *General der Flieger* Karl Bodenschatz; *SS-Gruppenführer* Hermann Fegelein; *SS-Hauptsturmführer* Otto Günsche; *Generaloberst* Alfred Jodl; *Generalfeldmarschall* Wilhelm Keitel; *General der Flieger* Günther Korten; *General der Infanterie* Rudolf Schmundt and *General der Artillerie* Walther Warlimont.

Wound Badge - World War I
Instituted on 3rd March 1918.
It was awarded in three grades: Black – for less than three wounds; Silver – for three or more wounds; Gold – for severe wounds that permanently injured or disfigured the recipient.

THE KNIGHT's CROSS RECIPIENTS

Grand Cross of the Knight's Cross
Hermann Wilhelm Göring

Knight's Cross with Oakleaves, Swords and Diamonds
Adolf Galland
Albert Kesselring
Hermann Bernhard Ramcke

Knight's Cross with Oakleaves and Swords
Robert Ritter von Greim
Richard Heidrich
Ludwig Heilmann
Hans Kroh
Dietrich Peltz
Karl-Lothar Schulz
Rainer Stahel
Erich Walther

Knight's Cross with Oakleaves
Ernst Bormann
Paul Conrath
Otto Deßloch
Oskar Dinort
Martin Fiebig
Walter Hagen
Martin Harlinghausen
Hubertus Hitschhold
Alexander Löhr
Eugen Meindl
Kurt Leopold Pflugbeil
Wolfgang Pickert
Wolfram Freiherr von Richthofen
Wilhelm Schmalz
Ludwig Schulz
Hans Seidemann
Walter Storp
Kurt Student
Heinrich Trettner

Knight's Cross
Kurt Andersen
Karl Angerstein
Werner Anton
Walther Axthelm
Walter Boenicke
Rudolf Bogatsch
Bruno Bräuer
Alfred Bülowius
Ernst Buffa
Wolfgang von Chamier-Glisczinski
Joachim Coeler
Gerhard Conrad
Paul Deichmann
Ullrich Diesing
Johann-Wilhelm Doering-Manteuffel
Wolfgang Erdmann
Johannes Fink
Helmuth Förster
Gotthard Frantz
Stefan Fröhlich
Robert Fuchs
Hans Geisler
Walter Grabmann
Ulrich Grauert
Fritz Grieshammer
Johannes Hintz
Walter von Hippel
Otto Höhne
Otto Hoffmann von Waldau
Alexander Holle
Joachim-Friedrich Huth
Max-Josef Ibel
Hans Jeschonnek
Werner Junck
Josef Kammhuber
Alfred Keller
Ulrich Kessler
Friedrich Kless
Fritz Koehler
Karl Koller
Hans Korte
Gunther Korten
Hermann Lichtenberger
Bruno Loerzer
Alfons Luczny
Rudolf Meister
Erhard Milch
Friedrich-Wilhelm Morzik
Gottlob Müller
Hanns-Horst von Necker
Georg Neuffer
Job Odebrecht
Theodor Osterkamp
Hermann Plocher
Maximilian Ritter von Pohl
Johann Raithel
Heino von Rantzau
Hans-Joachim Rath
Hans Rauch
Richard Reimann
Franz Reuss
Herbert Rieckhoff
Ernst-August Roth
Günther Sachs
Richard Schimpf
Alfred Schlemm
Joseph Schmid
August Schmidt
Karl-Heinrich Schulz
Carl-August Schumacher
Günther Schwarzkopff
Hugo Sperrle
Hans-Jurgen Stumpff
Alfred Sturm
Wolf von Stutterheim
Otto Sydow
Ernst Udet
Klaus Uebe
Oskar Vorbrugg
Hubert Weise
Paul Weitkus
Gustav Wilke
Adolf Wolf
Alwin Wolz

GRAND CROSS OF THE IRON CROSS

Herman Wilhelm GÖRING
(1893-1946)
Reichsmarschall

Knight's Cross: Awarded on 30th September 1939 as *Generalfeldmarschall* and Commander-in-Chief of the Luftwaffe for his part in the defeat of Poland.

Grand Cross of the Iron Cross: Awarded on 19th July 1940 as *Generalfeldmarschall* and Commander-in-Chief of the Luftwaffe for his part in the defeat of France.

Ranks:
Leutnant – 20th January 1914
Oberleutnant – 18th August 1917
Hauptmann – 8th June 1920
SA-Gruppenführer – 18th December 1931
SA-Obergruppenführer – 1st January 1933
General der Infanterie – 31st August 1933
General der Flieger – 1st March 1935
Generaloberst – 20th April 1936
Generalfeldmarschall – 4th February 1938
Reichsmarschall – 19th July 1940

Awards:
Royal Prussian Observers Badge – 15th November 1914
Royal Prussian Pilots Badge – 12th October 1915
Wound Badge in Silver – World War I
Turkish Iron Half-Moon Badge (The Gallipoli Star)
Iron Cross 2nd Class – 15th September 1914
Iron Cross 1st Class – 22nd March 1915
Knight's Cross First Class of the Order of the Zähringen Lion with Oakleaves and Swords – 8th July 1915
Knight's Cross of the Royal Prussian Hohenzollern House Order with Swords – 20th October 1917
Knight's Cross of the Grand Baden Military Karl-Friedrich Order of Merit – 11th February 1918
Honour Goblet for aerial combat – 15th April 1918
Pour le Mérite – 2nd June 1918
Blood Order of the NSDAP – 9th November 1933
Golden Party Badge of the NSDAP – 1st December 1933
Luftwaffe Air Crew Badge – 19th January 1935
Pilot's Badge with Diamonds
Combined Pilot's and Observers Badge in Gold with Diamonds
Luftwaffe Cuff-title "Jagdgeschwader Frhr. v. Richthofen Nr.1 1917/1918"
Cross of Honour for Frontline Combatants
Silver Gau Eagle of the NSDAP "Gau Thüringen"
Golden Honour Badge of the Berlin NSDAP
Civil Defence Award 1st & 2nd Class – 20th April 1938
Bar to Iron Cross 2nd Class

Hermann Göring wearing his full Reichsmarschall uniform, and holding his Marshall's Baton. Around his neck he wears the Pour le Mérite, the Grand Cross of the Iron, and the Knight's Cross. (Author's Collection)

Bar to Iron Cross 1st Class
Danzig Cross 2nd & 1st Classes – October 1939
U-Boat Badge with Diamonds
Wehrmacht Daily Report: 8 September 1940

Herman Göring was the Commander-in-Chief of Hitler's Luftwaffe during the Second World War and Hitler's designated successor, he was also founder and first head of the Gestapo; the inventor of the Concentration Camp System; the architect of the "Final Solution of the Jewish Question"; Prussian Prime Minister; Reichstag President and Head of the Four Year Plan as well as being a World War One fighter ace. Göring was born on 12th January 1893 in Rosenheim, Upper Bavaria. His mother, Franziska Tiefenbrunn was a Bavarian from Austrian descent and his father, Heinrich Ernst Göring was the first Governor-General of the German Protectorate of South West Africa as well as being a former cavalry officer.

In 1905 Göring was sent to the Cadet School at Karlsruhe, four years later he transferred to the Cadet Academy at Lichterfelde where he enjoyed life and decided to pursue a military career. In January 1914 he joined the Imperial Army as a *Leutnant* and served with the 112th Infantry Regiment. At the beginning of World War I he served as a battalion adjutant on the Western Front against the French and in August he won the Iron Cross 2nd Class. However his military career was almost cut short when in October he contracted serious rheumatism in his legs and was made unfit for military service. He had to leave his regiment and go into hospital and he feared he would never be able to distinguish himself in battle again. But his friend Bruno Loerzer (who would later serve under Göring in World War II), found the ideal solution. Göring became an airman.

On 13th October Göring flew as an observer and won the Iron Cross 1st Class, in September 1915 he became a fighter pilot serving with the 5th Fighter Squadron. He was later shot down and spent most of 1916 recovering from his injuries, returning to active duty in 1917 with the 26th Fighter Squadron. In May 1917 Göring got his first command and went on to claim twenty-one air victories and won several awards and was promoted to *Oberleutnant* in August. On 2nd June 1918 he was awarded the coveted *Pour le Mérite*, one of the highest German military award of World War I. On 7th July he was named commander of the 1st Fighter Wing "Richthofen", the fighter wing that had once been commanded by the famed "Red Baron" – Manfred von Richthofen who had been killed in action on 21st April 1918.

When Germany surrendered Göring felt betrayed, he became depressed and found civilian life almost intolerable and took several jobs as a pilot. On a winters day in 1920 he flew an important businessman home in heavy snow and lost his way and his passenger was airsick. However Göring managed to land on a frozen lake near the businessman's home, Rockelstad castle. It was too late for Göring to go back so he stayed the night and it was here that he met his future wife Baroness Karin von Kantzow. They married on 3rd January 1923 in Stockholm and set up home together near Bayrischzell about fifty miles from Munich.

In 1922 Göring joined the Nazi Party and briefly commanded the SA and proved to be a good organiser. On 9th November 1923 Göring was with Hitler during the Munich Putsch and they marched side by side. When the Bavarian police fired upon the crowd Göring was seriously wounded when a splinter of granite block struck him in the groin and he collapsed. He

Göring as Reichsminister, and Prussian Minister of the Interior. (Author's Collection)

Göring in 1933 as the Reich Chief Hunter. (Author's Collection)

managed with the help of friends to leave the scene and make his way to Austria to avoid arrest. He was admitted to hospital and given morphine for his pain and this was the beginning of his morphine addiction. In 1927 President von Hindenburg issued a general amnesty and all those who took part in the Putsch were pardoned and Göring returned to Germany to resume his political work for Hitler. He became the Party's representative in upper class circles and as a *Pour le Mérite* winner and former fighter ace he was a bit of a "celebrity" and was therefore able to drum-up support for Hitler.

In October 1931 Göring's wife suddenly died of tuberculosis, he was at her bedside when she died. Göring soon returned to work, he needed something to occupy his mind, and on 30th August 1932 he was elected President of the German Parliament, the Reichstag. When Hitler became Chancellor in January 1933 he appointed Göring to his cabinet as Minister without portfolio, Commissioner for air, and Prussian Minister of the Interior. As Interior Minister Göring controlled the police forces of Prussia and through his efforts the Nazis quickly began to crush their opponents, such as the Social Democrats, Communists and the Jews. On 28th February 1933 the Reichstag building was burned down and the Communists got the blame, Göring made sure of that.

This one act led to the "Reichstag Fire Decree", signed by von Hindenburg which suspended all civil liberties and enabled the police to arrest anyone they wanted and in March 1933 it led to the establishment of the first concentration camp at Dachau. An ex-communist radical called van der Lubbe was arrested and charged with the fire but many people were convinced that the Nazis were responsible. In fact Franz von Papen[4] at Nuremberg Trials in 1946, stated that he had heard Göring at an evening reception in 1942 admit to setting fire to the building himself. Göring denied all knowledge and it still remains unclear as to who actually started the fire.

In June 1934 Göring played a vital role in the removal of the SA leadership during the Blood Purge in which many SA leaders, including its commander Ernst Röhm, were murdered. Göring's own police force had participated in the murders and his underground monitoring service, the "*Forschungsamt*" was connected to the SS. In March 1935 Germany's new air force, the Luftwaffe was officially revealed to the world and Göring was named as its commander. In April 1935 Göring had married again, he married Emmy Sonnemann a well-known actress and a divorcée, they had one daughter Edda.

Göring was by this time one of Hitler's most powerful lieutenants and after Hjalmar Schacht[5] resigned as Minister of Economics in November 1937 and Göring took over himself and became the head of the Four Year Plan for the German rearmament. He gained great influence with Hitler who had placed a high value on rearmament and Göring opened his own steel works, the Reichswerke Hermann Göring and made a small fortune. Also at this time he plotted the downfall of the War Minister von Blomberg[6] and the army commander-in-chief von Fritsch.[7] With the help of his police Göring found out that

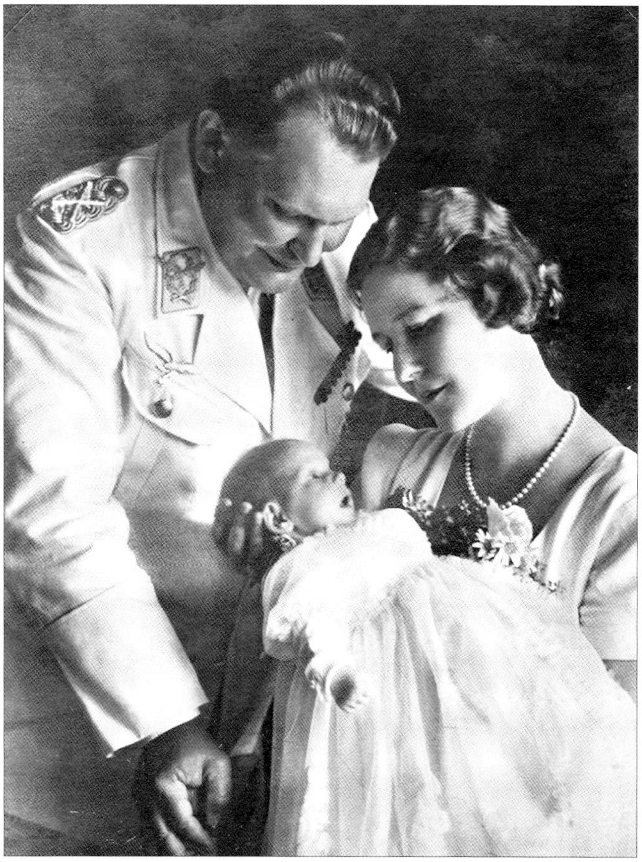

Göring with his wife and daughter Edda at her christening. (Author's Collection)

von Blomberg's wife had been a prostitute and forced the War Minister to resign. However Göring couldn't find anything on von Fritsch so he fabricated a story and again with the help of his police evidence and witnesses were produced after a false charge was made against him. It was said that von Fritsch had been meeting with a man and was having a homosexual affair and he was forced to resign. He naturally denied the charges but the scandal was enough for him to lose his job. He was later cleared of all charges by a military court but remained a civilian. Göring now wanted to take over the armed forces himself but Hitler took over the leadership himself and scrapped the office of War Minister. He thanked Göring by giving him the rank of *Generalfeldmarschall* and naming him officially as his deputy and legal heir.

By 1939 Göring's Luftwaffe was the most advanced and the most powerful air force in the world, it had already been tested in battle during the Spanish Civil War and Göring believed it to be invincible. In fact Göring said in August, "The Ruhr will not be subjected to a single bomb … if a bomb reaches the Ruhr … you can call me Meier!"[8] Göring's Luftwaffe also included ground troops that became Göring's private army that eventually grew into around thirty divisions. There was also a Parachute-Panzer Division, which had originally been a special police battalion but when Himmler, head of the SS took over

Göring with his daughter, c.1940, clearly showing hes Reichsmarschall rank insignia and Grand Cross. (Author's Collection)

all police units, Göring insisted on keeping these troops. His new army fought alongside the armies as a panzer force but came under the direct command of Göring himself. However many of these divisions were led by officers with little or no training for ground combat, and some performed very badly as a result.

Göring was at first sceptical about Hitler's war plans and felt that Germany wasn't ready for another war, in particular he felt that his Luftwaffe were not ready to beat the British Royal Air Force. However once Hitler decided on war Göring stood by him. In September 1939 the Luftwaffe destroyed the Polish Air Force in two weeks, Göring was awarded the Knight's Cross for his leadership and after the defeat of France he was awarded the Grand Cross of the Iron Cross, he would become the only recipient. On 19th July 1940 to celebrate the defeat over France Hitler gave out promotions on mass, he promoted over ten generals to the rank of *Generaloberst* and another twelve generals to the rank of *Generalfeldmarschall* and he made Göring a *Reichsmarschall*, the highest military rank of the Third Reich.

Göring now turned his attention to Britain and he promised Hitler that he could smash the RAF and break British morale in a matter of weeks. He personally directed the first attacks on Britain but his pilot's were no match for the determination and skill of the RAF. Germany's first defeat came when they failed to secure control of the skies during the Battle of Britain and the invasion of Britain was indefinitely postponed. In April 1941 the Luftwaffe destroyed Belgrade and Göring's paratroopers captured Crete from the British and Göring was at his peak of popularity and prestige with Hitler.

However things were to change when Hitler decided to attack the Soviet Union. Göring had been against the attack from the outset and he tried to convince Hitler to cancel the attack but failed. Instead he told Hitler he was committed to the campaign and at first the Luftwaffe had many victories, they destroyed thousands of aircraft and tanks. However the Soviet resistance grew and the weather would play a major role and the Luftwaffe itself became overstretched and exhausted. Göring himself became disinterested in the administration of the Luftwaffe and left his subordinates to take care of the day-to-day running, men like Hans Jeschonnek and Ernst Udet. The aircraft industry began to lag behind and Udet committed suicide through pressure of work and later Jeschonnek followed when he shot himself in August 1943. When the Soviets surrounded the 6th Army at Stalingrad Göring encouraged Hitler to fight on and promised that his Luftwaffe could deliver 500 tons per day of supplies to the trapped 6th Army. In fact less than 100 tons were ever delivered in a day and the troops trapped in Stalingrad were slowly starving and freezing to death, and those who survived went into Russian captivity.

It was now that Göring's reputation and influence with Hitler began to decline and Göring withdrew more and more away from the military scene. He was hardly ever seen at Hitler's headquarters and would more often than not send a representative instead. Göring spent more time at his home

Opposite
Top left: Göring with Generaloberst Wilhelm Keitel. Göring's adjutant, Karl Bodenschatz, can be seen over his shoulder. (Author's Collection)

Top right: Göring wearing Generalfeldmarschall uniform with Knight's Cross, and clearly showing his rank insignia.

Bottom left: Göring in Reichsmarschall uniform with Pour le Mérite and Grand Cross. (Author's Collection)

Bottom right: Göring with his RSD bodyguard during an inspection tour in the Eiffel region of France, May 1940. (Author's Collection)

This page: Göring inspecting Luftwaffe troops somewhere on the Western Front. (Author's Collection)

Opposite
Top: Göring with Hitler looking unhappy during a meeting late in the war – at this time the two men were hardly talking to each other. (Private source)

Bottom: Göring cheated the hangman by taking poison. The Reichsmarschall maintained throughout his trial that he would never let the Allies hang him. In the background is the coffin waiting for von Ribbentrop who was the first Nazi war criminal to hang at Nuremberg. (Private source)

enjoying the pleasures of life, he was a very wealthy man and his reputation for extravagance made him unpopular with other Nazi leaders and the ordinary German person when most had lost their homes and suffering so much.

Göring met with Hitler for the last time in April 1945 and the two hardly said a word to one another, Göring then fled Berlin with his art treasures for the Nazi alpine retreat at Berchtesgaden. He urged Hitler to leave Berlin and join him but Hitler refused. Göring then decided to act, on 25th April he sent a message to Hitler in the Bunker stating that if he did not hear back from Hitler by 10pm he would assume Hitler was either dead or unable to communicate and he Göring would assume the leadership of the Reich as Hitler's designated successor. Hitler was furious when he learnt of this and after goading by Bormann[9] he ordered Göring arrested and dismissed him as Commander-in-Chief of the Luftwaffe and expelled him from the Nazi Party. Göring was arrested by the SS at Berchtesgaden and kept under house arrest along with his wife and daughter.

On 8th May 1945 Göring surrendered to the U.S. 36th Infantry Division near Mauterndorf. He was at first treated like a VIP and even gave a press conference. A few days later however he was stripped of his medals and insignia and confined as a war criminal. In September 1945 he was sent to Nuremberg along with other top Nazis, including the commander of the German Navy and Hitler's successor *Großadmiral* Karl Dönitz, *Generalfeldmarschall* Wilhelm Keitel, Hitler's most senior military advisor and Albert Speer Armaments Minister. At Nuremberg Göring defended himself well and during the early stages of the trial scored well against his accusers and even made jokes and built up his popularity not only with his fellow defendants but also with the court. However it soon became apparent that Göring had been involved with the murder of the Jews and prisoners of war. One such charge Göring was held accountable was the murder of fifty Allied airmen during the "Great Escape."

On 15th October 1946 Göring was found guilty and sentenced to death by hanging. The judgement said: "There is nothing to be said in mitigation … Göring was often, indeed almost always, the moving force, second only to his Führer. He was the leading war aggressor … he was director of the slave labour program and the creator of the oppressive programme against the Jews … All of these crimes he has admitted."[10]

Göring filed an appeal with the court, he had accepted the death sentence but had asked to be shot as a soldier instead of being hanged like a common criminal. The court refused. Two hours before his execution was due to take place Göring committed suicide in his cell, taking a capsule of poison that he had succeeded in hiding from his guards. Where Göring obtained the cyanide, and how he concealed it during his entire imprisonment at Nuremberg, remains unknown. There is strong speculation that Göring befriended U.S. Army Lieutenant Jack G. "Tex" Wheelis, who was stationed at Nuremberg and helped Göring obtain cyanide which had been hidden among Göring's personal effects when they were confiscated by the Army. In

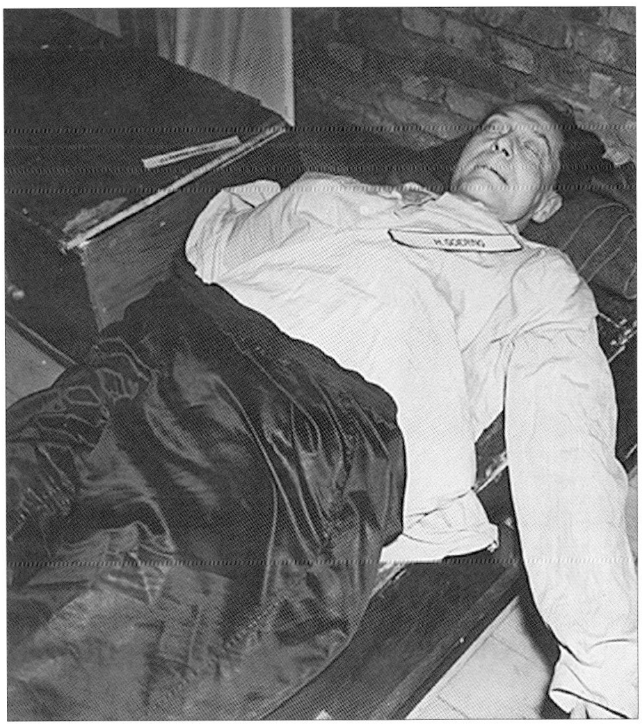

2005, former U.S. Army Private Herbert Lee Stivers claimed he gave Göring "medicine" hidden inside a fountain pen from a German woman the private had met and flirted with. Stivers served in the 1st Infantry Division's 26th Regiment, who formed the honour guard for the Nuremberg Trials. Stivers claims to have been unaware of what the "medicine" he delivered actually was until after Göring's death. After his death, Hermann Göring was cremated and his ashes were scattered in the Conwentzbach in Munich, which runs into the Isar River.

KNIGHT'S CROSS WITH OAKLEAVES, SWORDS AND DIAMONDS

Adolf Josef Ferdinand GALLAND
(1912-1996)
Generalleutnant

Knight's Cross: Awarded on 29th July 1940 as *Major* and Commander of 3rd Group, 26th Fighter Wing "Schlageter" after his 17th aerial victory.

Oakleaves: Galland was the 3rd recipient of the Oakleaves on 24th September 1940 as Commander of the 26th Fighter Wing "Schlageter" after achieving his 40th aerial victory.

Swords: Awarded the Swords on 21st June 1941 as *Oberstleutnant* and still Commander of the 26th Fighter Wing, he was the 1st recipient of this award after his 69th aerial victory.

Diamonds: The 2nd recipient of this award on 28th January 1942 as *Oberst* and still as Commander of the 26th Fighter Wing, awarded after his 94th aerial victory.

Ranks:
Fahnenjunker-Unteroffizier – 1st May 1934
Fähnrich – 1st September 1934
Leutnant – 1st January 1935
Oberleutnant – 1st August 1937
Hauptmann – 1st October 1939
Major – 19th July 1940
Oberstleutnant – 1st November 1940
Oberst – 4th December 1941
Generalmajor – 1st November 1942
Generalleutnant – 1st November 1944

Awards:
Iron Cross 2nd Class – 15th September 1939
Iron Cross 1st Class – 22nd May 1940
Armed Forces Long Service Award 4th Class
Spanish Cross in Gold with Diamonds – 7th June 1939
Pilot's Badge with Diamonds
Combined Pilot's and Observer's Badge in Gold with Diamonds – August 1940

Adolf Galland, wearing the Knight's Cross with Oakleaves, shown here as an Oberstleutnant in late 1940. (Author's Collection)

Combat Clasp for Fighters in Gold with pendant for 400 missions
"Jagdgeschwader Schlageter" cufftitle
Wehrmacht Daily Report: 16 August 1940; 25 September 1940; 2 November 1940; 18 April 1941; 22 June 1941; 30 October 1941; 15 February 1942

Probably the most famous and highest ranking Luftwaffe fighter pilot of World War II, and one of the youngest German officers to achieve the rank of general. Adolf Galland was born on 19th March 1912 in Westerholt, Recklinghausen, the son of an estate manager of French descent.

He first began flying for Lufthansa[11] after graduating from the German Commercial Air Transport School at Brunswick in April 1934. He joined the army and served with the 10th Infantry regiment until September 1935 when he transferred to the Luftwaffe with the rank of *Leutnant*. He served as a flying instructor at the Flying School in Schleißheim and was transferred to the Fighter Wing "Richthofen" in October. In May 1937 he volunteered for service with the Condor Legion in Spain where he commanded the 3rd Squadron of J/88 which was equipped with He 51 biplanes. Here he distinguished himself in the use of ground attack against the enemy and in support of the ground troops. He served on the Asturias, Teruel and Ebro fronts and flew 280 combat missions before being recalled to Germany being succeeded by his good friend Werner Mölders in June 1938. Once back in Germany he found himself assigned to a desk in the Air Ministry, then in August he was appointed adjutant to the Fighter Wing "Richthofen", and by November he had been made a Squadron Leader.

When World War II started Galland was assigned as a Squadron Leader with the 4th Squadron of the 2nd Group while attached to 2nd Instruction Wing, equipped with Henschel Hs 123, a biplane Stuka. He took part in the invasion of Poland where he won Iron Cross 2nd Class, and where he flew more than fifty ground attack missions. In October 1939 he was promoted to *Hauptmann* and was appointed adjutant of the 27th Fighter Wing at Krefeld. On 12th May 1940 he scored his first aerial victory over Liege, Belgium, it was followed by another two victories that same day, all three were RAF Hurricanes. His fifth victory was a Spitfire over Dunkirk, and now Galland had become an official ace. After his eighth kill on 22nd May 1940 Galland was awarded the Iron Cross 1st Class, presented to him personally by *Generaloberst* Erhard Milch. By the end of the French Campaign Galland had accumulated fourteen victories, in June 1940 he was appointed Commander of the 3rd Group of 26th Fighter Wing "Schlageter". On 24th July Galland led his Group over the Thames Estuary and engaged RAF Spitfires, he shot down the British ace Johnny Allen who was killed when he crash landed. On 28th July Galland shot

Galland as an Oberst wearing the Knight's Cross with Oakleaves and Swords. Clearly seen on his right breast pocket is the Spanish Cross in Gold with Diamonds. On his sleeve is the "Jagdgeschwader Schlageter" cufftitle of his old fighter wing, JG 26 – he wore this throughout his career. (Wehrkundearchiv)

down another Spitfire near Dover this was another British ace, *Leutnant* Francis Dawson-Paul, a Royal navy pilot on loan to the RAF. He crash landed in the channel and was picked up by a German E-Boat but later died of his wounds in hospital. The next day in recognition of his success as a fighter pilot Galland was awarded the Knight's Cross, a few days after he was promoted to *Major*.

Galland was the most successful German fighter pilot during the Battle of Britain and his 40th aerial victory came on 20th September 1940 when he shot down a Hurricane over Rochester, another notable RAF fighter ace Harold Bird-Wilson who managed to bail out near Chatham but was badly burned. On 25th September Galland was awarded the Oakleaves to his Knight's Cross, becoming the 3rd recipient, in recognition of his 40th aerial victory. On 1st November Galland was promoted to *Oberstleutnant* and was now the Commander of the 26th Fighter Wing, and he had scored his 50th victory. On 21st June 1941 Galland scored his 68th and 69th aerial victories, both Spitfires and both over Boulogne. That same day Galland was shot down himself by the Polish ace Boleslaw Drobinski, he baled out wounded. Shortly afterwards he receives the news that he is to become the first recipient of the much desirable Swords to his Knight's Cross in recognition of his leadership and his skill as a fighter pilot. On 9th August the British ace Douglas Bader is shot down, Galland took part in the same aerial battle. Bader was later invited to dinner with Galland and the two aviators become good friends after the war.

In December 1941 Galland was promoted to *Oberst* and ordered by Göring and by Hitler not to fly anymore combat missions, he ignored their orders and continues to fly. On 5th December 1941 Galland was named as the new General of Fighters, after his good friend Werner Mölders was killed. Before settling into his new command he was responsible for the fighter protection of the battleships *Scharnhorst* and *Gneisenau*, and the heavy cruiser *Prinz Eugen*, during the Channel dash. It was a great success and for his part he was awarded the Diamonds on 28th January 1942, becoming the 2nd recipient. It was during this time as the new General of Fighters that Galland had his most serious skirmish with *Reichsmarschall* Göring and Hitler when he told them both that Germany needed more fighters if it was going to win the air war over Europe. Göring was furious with Galland and jealous of his popularity with his men, and wanted him replaced. Hitler refused, he knew who was to blame for the Luftwaffe's failures, but wouldn't sack Göring either. Göring on the other hand blamed Galland for the failure and sacked him as General of the Fighters in January 1945.

Galland now a *Generalleutnant* was appointed commander of a newly formed squadron, the 44th Fighter Formation, made up of Messerschmitt 262 jet-fighters. He managed to gain another seven aerial victories as a jet-fighter pilot, and

Well known propaganda pose of Oberst Adolf Galland wearing the Knight's Cross with Oakleaves and Swords. He was the first recipient of the Swords and the award was presented to him personally by Hitler during a private ceremony. (Author's collection)

Grave of Generalleutnant a.D. Galland, in the churchyard cemetery at St. Laurentius Church, in Remagen-Oberwinter. (Private Source)

on 26th April 1945 Galland led a formation of Me 262 fighters against a formation of B-26 medium bombers targeting an airfield at Lechfeld and claimed two more victories. However during the attack Galland was hit by returning fire and broke off his attack and was then attacked by a U.S. P-47 fighter and his aircraft received more damage and Galland wounded his knee. He was able to bring his aircraft back to Munich-Reim airfield and landed it successfully; he had to scramble out of the cockpit to safety as U.S. fighters were attacking his aircraft while on the ground. Gallands' wounds were serious and they were enough to ground him for the rest of the war, he had shot down 104 enemy aircraft.

He surrendered to the Americans at Tegernesee on 5th May 1945, and went into captivity. He was held in military custody for two years and released in May 1947. In October 1948, he took a position with the Argentine Air Force. He was offered many jobs, one as a consultant to an armaments firm who were to equip the new West German Air force. He spent the remaining years as a successful businessman and spent the last years of his life at home in Germany or at his home by the Alicante coast of Spain. During his final years he suffered from heart trouble and in early 1996 he was admitted to hospital and perhaps sensing that the end was near, he returned home. He died on 9th February 1996 and at his request he was buried in the churchyard cemetery at St. Laurentius Church in Remagen-Oberwinter.

Albert KESSELRING
(1885-1960)
Generalfeldmarschall

Knights Cross: Awarded on 30th September 1939 as the commander of the 1st Air Fleet for actions during the invasion of Poland.

Knights Cross with Oakleaves: On 25th February 1942 he became the 78th recipient of the Oakleaves as the Commander-in-Chief South.

Knights Cross with Oakleaves and Swords: Kesselring became the 15th recipient of the Swords on 15th July 1942 while still serving as C-in-C South for actions in North Africa.

Knight's Cross with Oakleaves, Swords and Diamonds: Awarded the Diamonds for actions in Italy while serving as Commander-in-Chief South on 19th July 1944 and was the 14th recipient.

Ranks:
Fähnrich – 4th February 1905
Leutnant – 8th March 1906
Oberleutnant – 25th October 1913
Hauptmann – 19th May 1916

Albert Kesselring wearing the Knight's Cross in late 1940, with the rank insignia of Generalfeldmarschall. (Author's collection)

Major – 1st April 1925
Oberstleutnant – 1st February 1930
Oberst – 1st October 1932
Generalmajor – 1st October 1934
Generalleutnant – 1st April 1936
General der Flieger – 1st June 1937
Generaloberst – skipped
Generalfeldmarschall – 19th July 1940

Awards:
Prussian Iron Cross 2nd Class – World War I
Prussian Iron Cross 1st Class – World War I
Cross of Honour for Frontline Combatants
Grand Cross of the Royal Italian Order with Crown
Royal Bavarian Military Service Order 4th Class with Swords
Royal Bavarian Prince Regent Leopold Jubilee Medal
Knight's Cross 2nd Class of the Royal Sachsburg Albrecht Order with Swords
Bar to the Iron Cross 2nd Class – 12th September 1939

Bar to the Iron Cross 1st Class – 25th September 1939
Armed Forces Long Service Award 1st Class
Commemorative Medal 1st October 1938
Pilot's Badge with Diamonds
Combined Pilots and Observers Badge in Gold with Diamonds
Italian Pilot's Badge
AFRIKA Cufftitle
Wehrmacht Daily Report: 8 October 1940; 26 October 1940; 9 November 1940; 15 November 1940; 20 November 1940; 19 June 1941; 6 August 1941; 7 August 1941; 19 September 1941; 18 October 1941; 17 June 1942; 10 September 1943

Kesselring photographed shortly after receiving the Knight's Cross, with the rank of General der Flieger. (Author's collection)

One of the most outstanding generals of the Third Reich and possibly the most capable of all the Luftwaffe generals. Albert Kesselring was born on 30th November 1885, in Lower Franconia in the small village of Marksteft near Kitzingen, the son of a town official who was also the local schoolmaster. After completing his education he joined the army in July 1904 as an officer candidate or *Fahnenjunker* with 2nd Bavarian Fusilier Regiment. In March 1905 he was assigned to the Munich War School where amongst other things he learnt about the importance of light artillery in battle.

On 4th June 1912 he trained as an observer with the Bavarian Airship and Motor Transport Battalion before returning to his unit two weeks later. He had won his commission in March 1906, and in October 1913 had been promoted to *Oberleutnant* while assigned as adjutant to 1st Battalion of his old artillery regiment. While serving with this unit war broke out and Kesselring saw action in France where he gained valuable experience and was able to make good use of his artillery training. Promoted to *Hauptmann* in May 1916 he continued to serve as a field officer until November 1917 when he was transferred to the General Staff. He spent the rest of the war assigned to 2nd Bavarian Army Corps Headquarters. Kesselring remained in the army after the Armistice, serving in the Reichswehr as a staff officer and then with an artillery regiment.

Summoned to Berlin in October 1922 where he was appointed an advisor with the Reich War Ministry. In April 1924 he was promoted to *Major* and within eighteen months had been appointed as a member of the *Truppenamt*,[12] the forerunner of the German General Staff. He spent the next few years as a staff officer with 3rd and 7th Division and by February 1930 had been promoted to *Oberstleutnant*. In August 1930 he was transferred to the Army Personnel Office and remained there until February 1932 when he was appointed commander of 3rd Battalion, 4th Artillery Regiment; this was to be his last army command.

In January 1933 the Nazis came to power and one of the first priorities for Hitler was the expansion of the German armed forces which was to include an air force. Kesselring had already struck up a friendship with the new commander of Germany's Luftwaffe, Hermann Goring. In October, now an *Oberst*, Kesselring transferred to the newly created Luftwaffe and was immediately attached to the Reich Air Ministry where he was made responsible for the administration of food, clothing, finance and air-field construction. In October 1934 Kesselring was promoted to *Generalmajor* after a recommendation from Goring himself. He joined the staff of *Generalleutnant* Erhard Milch, the head of the Air Ministry in 1935, and became an effective administrator. In April 1936 Kesselring was promoted to *Generalleutnant*, and on 3rd June was named as the new Chief of Staff of the Luftwaffe, after the death of General Walter Wever. The appointment had been made by Goring who had ignored all objections from Milch who had felt that Kesselring lacked operational experience. For almost twelve months Kesselring put up with the pressure of serving under a boss who disliked him and who cut him out of meetings and ignored his advice. Finally Kesselring was transferred and appointed Commander of Air District III, with its headquarters in Dresden. On 1st June 1937 Kesselring was promoted to *General der Flieger* and the following February was appointed as commander of Luftwaffe forces in Berlin.

In September 1939 during the invasion of Poland, Kesselring commanded the 1st Air Fleet which supported *Generaloberst* Fedor von Bock's[13] Army Group North and it was here that Kesselring developed his close tactical air support techniques. It was his command that almost completely destroyed Warsaw and for this role in the defeat in Poland he was awarded the Knight's Cross on 30th September 1939. On 12th January 1940 Kesselring was appointed commander of 2nd Air Fleet, and its first duty was to make itself ready for Hitler's invasion in the West. On 10th May German forces invaded the Low Countries; Kesselring had been greatly involved in the planning, he was responsible for the paratroop forces, for their training, protection and transportation and he was responsible for the anti-aircraft artillery. During the attack against Belgium and Holland Kesselring supported von Bock's Army Group again and with his success in Poland while supporting the ground forces he now felt confident. The idea was to use Blitzkrieg methods, with Kesselring's troops attacking from the air. It wasn't long before both Belgium and Holland capitulated and within a few weeks France fell too. However it wasn't all success, Kesselring was blamed for the failure of the Luftwaffe to knock out the Dunkirk beachhead and prevent the British from evacuating. However once the celebrations for the victory of Belgium, Holland and France began all was soon forgotten. For his role in the defeat, along with twelve other generals, including von Bock, Kesselring was promoted to the rank of *Generalfeldmarschall* and received his Marshal's Baton from Hitler in a lavish ceremony on 19th July 1940.

The next target for Hitler was Britain and Kesselring's Air Fleet took an active role in the Battle of Britain in the summer of 1940. His command took heavy losses and Kesselring fell out with Goring. Kesselring later wrote in his memoirs that his command wasn't defeated by the Royal Air Force, but defeated by being stripped of its aircraft which had been recalled to Poland to make ready for the invasion of Russia. In the summer of 1941 Kesselring's 2nd Air Fleet was re-equipped and made ready for the transfer to the Eastern Front. Here he would again support von Bock's Army Group with over a 1000 aircraft under his command he helped von Bock's army take Smolensk, and took a major role in the attack on Moscow in September.

On 10th January 1942 Kesselring was appointed Commander-in-Chief "South" and moved his headquarters to Rome, he was now the most senior Luftwaffe officer with a field command. He worked closely with Rommel and at first the two men got on well, although Rommel would find Kesselring's optimism annoying. During their time as colleagues they would often clash and Hitler would sometime back Rommel and sometimes back Kesselring, often playing them off at one another. On one occasion when Rommel, after celebrating his victory over the British at Gazala in May, had decided on a further offensive, Kesselring had objected, he argued that the British 8th Army had been reinforced and the Royal Air Force was now no match for the Luftwaffe. Hitler was informed of the plan and supported the plan put forward by Rommel. He sent a telex signal to Kesselring telling him that this planned offensive was "none of his business" Kesselring felt insulted and never forgot this, but he was to have the last laugh when Rommel's troops were defeated by the superior British forces, just as Kesselring had foreseen. However for his leadership skill Kesselring was awarded the Oakleaves on 25th February 1942, followed shortly by the Swords on 18th July of the same year becoming the 15th recipient.

On 8th November 1942 Kesselring was named as Mussolini's military deputy and became commander of all Italian forces along with his own command and Rommel's Panzer Army. Kesselring showed his skill when supervising the German withdrawal from Tunisia; he managed to delay the British and saved 100,000 Italian and German troops from capture. By the end of August 1943 the Allies had completely captured Tunisia, and Rommel had setup his new headquarters in Northern Italy, under the command of Kesselring who was now the Commander-in-Chief of all German forces in Italy.

Kesselring in North Africa along with his adjutant. (Author's collection)

General Kesselring in Brussels in May 1940 on an inspection tour with Göring. (Author's collection)

Kesselring talking to Luftwaffe troops in Italy during a 1944 inspection tour. He is shown here wearing the Knight's Cross with Oakleaves, Swords and Diamonds. (Author's collection)

His brilliant and expert maneuvering and his excellent planned retreat helped to delay the Allied advance by more than a year. Throughout the winter of 1943-1944 Kesselring successfully contained the Anzio beachhead. His forces withdrew to what had become known as the Gustav Line, this included Monte Cassino, a hilltop site of a Benedictine monastery. The Allied offensive resumed on 11th May 1944 and they entered Rome on 4th June. Kesselring's troops tried to delay the Allies and fought well and organized another fortified line, the Gothic Line. Kesselring was still in favour with Hitler and on 19th July he was awarded the Diamonds to his Knight's Cross for his successful command in Italy.

On 25th October 1944 Kesselring was involved in a car accident when his staff car collided with a large gun coming out of a side road and the *Generalfeldmarschall* was seriously injured. He was hospitalized for three months and his command in Italy was taken over by *Generaloberst* Heinrich Vietinghoff,[14] who was given the command permanently in March 1945. That same month the Allies captured the last bridge over the Rhine, the Remagen Bridge and as a result *Generalfeldmarschall* Gerd von Rundstedt[15] was sacked as Commander-in-Chief "West". Kesselring took over with his headquarters in Bayreuth, with orders to hold the Allies back, but the situation was hopeless. A few days before Hitler committed suicide he named Kesselring Commander-in-Chief "South", almost a week later Kesselring was taken prisoner at Saalfelden, near Erfurt in May 1945 by U.S. forces.

Albert Kesselring or "Smiling Albert" as he was known was the only *Generalfeldmarschall* to serve continuously without being relieved by Hitler. Kesselring was a great strategist and military commander, loved by his men and well thought by his divisional commanders, and even well thought of by Hitler. Kesselring should have returned to Germany with his honour intact but for one terrible episode. He was implicated in the Ardeantine cave massacre of March 1944 where 335 Italian civilians were shot as a reprisal for the attack on an SS unit. The order to shoot these Italians came from Hitler himself but the responsibility of carrying out the order fell to the Commander on the spot: Kesselring. As a result he was arrested by the Allies and handed over to the British for trial. Tried by a Military court in Venice on 17th February 1947, for crimes against humanity, Kesselring told the court that he had no power to countermand such an order from Hitler, it was after-all a "Führer Order" and had to be obeyed. He was also charged with other crimes against the Italian population and faced the death penalty if found guilty. On 6th May 1947 the trial ended and Kesselring although found not guilty of complicity in the Ardeantine massacre he was found guilty of crimes against humanity in other areas of his command and was sentenced to death by firing squad. However the sentence was commuted to life imprisonment and Kesselring was moved to Werrl Prison; however he was released on 24th October 1952, suffering from throat cancer, on the orders of Sir Anthony Eden. After his release he wrote his memoirs and lived in quiet retirement in Bad Nauheim until his death on 16th July 1960.

Kesselring was highly regarded by the Allies and his trial and consequent imprisonment was always considered controversial. The troops that carried out the executions in Italy were mainly SS and Gestapo, troops that Kesselring had very little control over. He once said to his British guards while in prison shortly after the death sentence had been announced, "The British are a chivalrous people, and we should never have fought each other. Thank you for your consideration and kindness. With young soldiers like you England has nothing to fear."[16]

"Smiling Albert" was Kesselring's nickname and this photograph shows it perfectly. (Wehrkundearchiv)

Hermann-Bernhard RAMCKE
(1889-1968)
General der Fallschirmtruppe

Knight's Cross: Awarded for his heroic action during the Battle of Crete on 21st August 1941 while serving as *Generalmajor* and Commanding General of the Parachute Assault Regiment.

Oakleaves: He became the 145th recipient of the Oakleaves on 13th November 1942 as Commanding General of the Parachute Assault Regiment "Ramcke" in North Africa.

Swords: For his heroism in the defence of "Fortress Brest" on 19th September 1944 he became the 99th recipient of the Swords as *Generalleutnant*.

Diamonds: Awarded the same day as the Swords, becoming the 20th recipient of the award.

Ranks:
Matrose – 26th September 1907
Obermatrose – 1st July 1909
Bootsmannsmaat – 1st April 1912
Feldwebel – 11th September 1915
Offiziers-Stellvertreter – 5th December 1916
Leutnant – 18th July 1918
Oberleutnant – 15th January 1921
Hauptmann – 1st February 1927
Major – 1st September 1934
Oberstleutnant – 16th March 1937
Oberst – 29th February 1940
Generalmajor – 22nd July 1941
Generalleutnant – 21st December 1942
General der Fallschirmtruppe – 14th September 1944

Awards:
Prussian Golden Military Service Cross – 24th April 1918
Prussian Long Service Award 1st Class – 20th October 1919
Iron Cross 2nd Class – 17th April 1916
Iron Cross 1st Class – 21st January 1917
Baltic Cross 1st & 2nd Class – 5th November 1919
Wound Badge in Gold – 3rd November 1919
Cross of Honour for Frontline Combatants – 26th January 1935
Armed Forces Long Service Award 1st Class
Bar to Iron Cross 2nd Class – 1st October 1939
Bar to Iron Cross 1st Class – 23rd May 1941
Luftwaffe Parachutist Badge – 1st August 1940

Hermann-Bernhard Ramcke wearing the Knight's Cross with Oakleaves in late 1942. (Wehrkundearchiv)

Ramcke as a Generalmajor shortly after being awarded the Knight's Cross on 21st August 1941 for his heroic actions during the Battle of Crete, while serving as the Commanding General of the Parachute Assault Regiment. (Roger James Bender)

Pilot's Badge with Diamonds
Combined Pilot's and Observer's Badge in Gold with Diamonds
Luftwaffe Ground Assault Badge
KRETA Cuff-title
AFRIKA Cuff-title
Wehrmacht Daily Report: 9 June 1941; 9 November 1942; 10 September 1944; 21 September 1944

One of the bravest and most highly decorated German soldiers of World War II, Hermann-Bernhard Ramcke started his career with the Imperial German Navy, then joined the army and finally served in the Luftwaffe. He spent most of the First World War as a NCO and was awarded the Prussian Military Cross in Gold, the highest award for bravery that could be awarded to an enlisted man, the equivalent of the *Pour le Mérite*. Hermann-Bernhard Ramcke was born on 24th January 1889 in Schleswig-Friedrichsberg and he entered military service with the German Navy in April 1905 as a ship's boy. He served aboard the school ships *Stosch* and *Moltke* and in December 1907 he transferred to the light cruiser *Medusa*. In May 1908 he served aboard the armoured cruiser *Prinz Adalbert* and from there was attached to the artillery school at Sonderburg until November 1908. In January 1909 he was transferred back to the *Prinz Adalbert* where he remained until September 1911, he went on to serve in a number of different ships and at the start of the First World War in 1914 he once again was serving aboard the *Prinz Adalbert*.

In September 1915 he was promoted to *Feldwebel* and was attached to a Replacement Battalion in Bruges, Belgium.

In early 1916 he was appointed Platoon Leader in the 12th Company, 2nd Matrosen-Regiment in Flanders. On 26th January he was wounded when a grenade exploded and a fragment struck his right thigh. According to official records he was admitted to hospital but Ramcke's memoirs state that he was treated at the front so he could remain with his men. In July 1917 Ramcke was transferred and made Platoon Leader with the Assault Battalion of the Flanders Naval Corps. In July 1918 he was commissioned as a *Leutnant* and took part in the withdrawal from Flanders and he led his assault battalion in house-to-house fighting along the Ghent-Bruges Canal and for this he was recommended for the Knight's Cross with Swords of the Prussian Royal Hohenzollern House Order but the war ended before the award could be approved.

Ramcke remained in the army after the war serving as a Company Leader with the Freikorps in the Baltic States. In April 1919 he was wounded when he was shot in the shoulder and was evacuated back to Germany. He trained himself to shoot and throw hand grenades with his left hand while simultaneously exercising his right arm until his shoulder healed. He spent the next few years in various different infantry regiments and in January 1921 was promoted to *Oberleutnant*, in February 1927 he was made Hauptman, and by September 1934 he had been promoted to *Major*. In November 1935 he transferred to the Army Command Centre where he became an Instruction Staff Officer in Breslau, training the Silesian Border Defence Units. In July 1936 he joined the infantry and in March 1937 he was promoted to *Oberstleutnant* and transferred to the staff of the Commandant of the Großborn Troop Training Area.

At the outbreak of World War II he was transferred as an observer to the 14th Army, part of General von Kleist's[17] XXII Army Corps. Ramcke was part of the training and planning unit for the campaign and whilst out with his unit during the latter stages of the Polish campaign he came upon a Polish troops and managed to talk them into surrendering. He captured 109 soldiers who included nine officers together with eighteen vehicles and explosives, and drove them all to the German lines, and on 1st October 1939 he was awarded the Bar to the Iron Cross 2nd Class. Between 3rd October and July 1940 Ramcke served in various infantry regiments seeing action in France with the 69th Regiment, and being promoted to *Oberst* in February 1940. In July 1940 he joined the 7th Air Division and started his paratrooper training at the Parachute School in Brauschweig. In August he transferred from the army to the Luftwaffe and was assigned to the 1st Fallschirmjäger Regiment and made responsible for the development and training of parachute troops in the use of heavy weapons.

On 21st May 1941 the airborne invasion of Crete began with the 2nd Air Corps dropping two massive waves of paratroopers and glider troops onto the island. The following day Ramcke, who had been appointed commander of Battle Group West, was dropped by parachute into Crete along with 550 German reinforcements. They landed west of Tavronitis and east of the airfield at Malem, and once landed Ramcke took command of the 1st Fallschirmjäger Assault Regiment after its commander *Generalmajor* Meindl had been seriously wounded upon landing. Advancing with elements of *Generalmajor* Julius Ringel's[18] 5th Mountain Division, Ramcke led his assault group in bitter fighting along the coast road that culminated in the capture of Canea on 27th May. Five days later the last of the British troops who had not already been evacuated surrendered to the Germans. Ramcke was praised by Meindl and other senior commanders and as a result was awarded the Knight's Cross on 21st August 1941 in recognition of his bravery and leadership during the heavy fighting in Crete.

Generalleutnant Ramcke inspecting troops in North Africa wearing the Knight's Cross with Oakleaves and his Afrikakorps cufftitle. (Wehrkundearchiv)

In March 1942 he was transferred to the Headquarters Staff of the Italian Armed Forces to assist with the training of the *Enrico Frattini's Folgore* Parachute Division for the proposed German-Italian invasion of Malta. However the operation to invade was called off by Hitler in May, he had decided to wait until Egypt fell to the Axis before attempting an invasion of Malta which had by then, become a fortress. In July Ramcke was transferred from Greece to Libya and the 1st Parachute Regiment took up defensive positions on the El Alamein front. In October the British 8th Army began its offensive and the German-Italian front almost collapsed. However Ramcke's command held out and without vehicles he began to fight a retreat on foot to the west and by 6th November Ramcke's men high jacked an entire British supply column and captured their vehicles. His command then travelled about 200 miles through enemy held territory, and the 600 survivors of Ramcke's command joined Rommel's Panzer Army. On 13th November

Ramcke was summoned to Berlin where he was presented the Oakleaves to his Knight's Cross personally by Hitler, a week later Ramcke was promoted to *Generalleutnant.*

On 13th February 1943 Ramcke was appointed Commander of the 2nd Fallschirmjäger Division and in the summer he led his division during the occupation of Rome after the Peitro Badoglio's (who had taken over from Mussolini after the Italian dictator had been dismissed) government had tried to defect to the Allies. Ramcke's division had begun to arrive in Rome in July 1943 to seize the government and occupy Italy. After the announcement of Italy's armistice with the Allies on 8th September the Germans took control of the country and Ramcke's command seized the capital along with the 3rd Panzer Grenadier Division and took part in heavy fighting against Italian troops. Finally by the 10th September German troops had taken key positions from the Italian forces and 2,500 prisoners had been taken from one Italian headquarters, Germany controlled Rome again. A few days later Ramcke was seriously injured when his staff car was attacked by an Allied fighter plane, and Ramcke spent several weeks in a military hospital in Dresden. He returned as Commander of the 2nd Fallschirmjäger Division on 17th February 1944 and found that his division had been deployed to the southern sector of the Russian Front. During his absence the 2nd Fallschirmjäger Division had been under the command of *Generalmajor* Gustav Wilke and had been busy helping stop the massive Soviet attacks aimed at reaching the Dniester River. When Ramcke took over the division it was taking part in heavy fighting and fell back across the Bug River and managed, for a while at least, to contain the enemy bridgeheads on the Dniester River until it could hold out no longer and was almost destroyed. On 17th March Ramcke fell ill and returned to Germany where he oversaw the formation and rebuilding of the 2nd Fallschirmjäger Division.

Whilst making ready to return to Russia the division was ordered to France following the Allied invasion in Normandy on 6th June. The 2nd Fallschirmjäger Division arrived in Brittany a few weeks after the invasion and started defending the port of Brest from possible Allied air landings. Then came the breakout by the Americans from the Normandy beachhead in late July 1944 when the U.S. 8th Army Corps captured Avranches at the base of the Cotentin Peninsula. They carried on west and entered Brittany in August their objective being to seize the fortified port of Brest. Ramcke's division arrived in Brest as the U.S. 6th Armoured Division approached the city from the north and it managed to contain the German Garrison at Brest until it was relieved by the 2nd, 8th and 29th Infantry Divisions a month later. On 11th August Ramcke assumed command of what was now "Fortress Brest" and he handed over the command of the 2nd Fallschirmjäger Division to *Oberst* Hans Kroh. Ramcke now had over 35,000 Army, Luftwaffe and Kriegsmarine troops at his disposal and he told his men to defend the city to the "last grenade" in an effort to tie down the American forces for as long as possible. Ramcke's men held on for over a month and then finally on 19th September 1944 Ramcke surrendered his headquarters on the Crozon Penisula, the day after Brest itself capitulated. His bunker was found to contain a vast store of alcohol and large quantities of food and other plunder. On that same day Ramcke was informed that he had not only been awarded the Swords to his Knight's Cross but had in fact also been awarded the Diamonds a rare event. A few days later the award was presented to Ramcke by a representative of the Red Cross while he was a prisoner of war at Trent Park.

In May 1946 Ramcke was transferred to the London District Cage a famous British prison camp and then into French Custody. He was described by his British captives as vain, ruthless but naive. Ramcke also told the British that he wanted to win the highest awards and told the British officers who were guarding him that he would recommend his men for high decorations, knowing full well that the High Command would have to recommend him for a higher award than they had received. He was charged with organising or permitting the murder of French citizens and in taking part in reprisals against French citizens, for plundering private property and for taking part in torture and murder. Most thought the charges were in excess and in March 1951 Ramcke was sentenced to five years imprisonment, but was released just three months later because of time already served. Ramcke returned home and wrote his memoirs, he died on 4th July 1968 in Kappeln, Schlei.

KNIGHT'S CROSS WITH OAKLEAVES AND SWORDS

Robert *Ritter* von GREIM
(1892-1945)
Generalfeldmarschall

Knight's Cross: Awarded on 24th June 1940, as *Generalleutnant* and Commanding General of 5th Air Corps, in recognition for his actions against France and of his part in its defeat.

Knight's Cross with Oakleaves: On 2nd April 1943 von Greim became the 216th recipient of the Oakleaves while serving as *Generaloberst* and Commander of 6th Air Fleet, for actions in Russia.

Knight's Cross with Oakleaves and Swords: Awarded on 28th August 1944, while still commanding the 6th Air Fleet and for further actions in Russia while supporting Army Group Centre, he became the 92nd recipient of the Swords.

Ranks:
Fähnrich – 7th January 1912
Leutnant – 25th October 1913
Oberleutnant – 17th January 1917
Hauptmann – 15th February 1921

Major – 1st January 1934
Oberstleutnant – 1st September 1935
Oberst – 20th April 1936
Generalmajor – 1st February 1938
Generalleutnant – 1st January 1940
General der Flieger – 19th July 1940
Generaloberst – 16th February 1943
Generalfeldmarschall – 25th April 1945

Awards:
Prussian Iron Cross 2nd Class – 26th November 1914
Prussian Iron Cross 1st Class – 26th November 1915
Royal Bavarian Pilots Observers Badge – World War I
Royal Bavarian Pilots Badge – World War I
Royal Bavarian Military Service Order 4th Class with Swords – April 1915
Royal Bavarian Military Service Order 4th Class with Swords and with Crown – 18th May 1917
Knight's Cross with Swords of the Prussian Royal Hohenzollern House Order – 29th April 1918
Knight's Cross of the Royal Bavarian Military Max Joseph Order – 23rd October 1918
Pour le Mérite – 14th October 1918
Cross of Honour for Frontline Combatants
Bar to Iron Cross 2nd Class – 1940
Bar to Iron Cross 1st Class – 1940
Armed Forces Long Service Award 3rd Class
Combined Pilots and Observers Badge
Combined Pilots and Observers Badge in Gold with Diamonds – 17th April 1945
Wehrmacht Daily Report: 20 June 1940; 22 November 1941; 19 January 1942; 3 September 1943; 9 September 1944; 31 October 1944

Generaloberst von Greim wearing the Knight's Cross with Oakleaves and Swords together with his Pour le Mérite. (Author's collection)

The son of a Bavarian army officer, Robert *Ritter* von Greim was born on 22nd June 1892 in Bayreuth. He entered the army in July 1911 as a *Fahnenjunker*, spending the next nine months training as an officer in Munich, before being transferred to 8th Bavarian Field Artillery as a *Leutnant*. In August 1915 he joined the air arm and soon became a successful pilot, being appointed commander of the 34th Fighter Squadron in June 1917. By the end of the war he had twenty-eight air victories to his credit and had been awarded the *Pour le Mérite* on 14th October 1918.

After the Armistice von Greim continued to fly until his aircraft was confiscated by order of the Allies. He worked for the next two years in a local Munich bank, and hated it. In August 1924 he was given the opportunity to help with the training of the military in China. Von Greim could hardly wait to begin his new job and was so successful that he soon moved his family there where he founded a flying school helping with the development of the Chinese Air Force. In May 1927 von Greim returned to Germany where he became the director of the Bavarian Air Sport Society.

On 1st January 1934, von Greim re-entered the German armed forces as a *Major*, he was appointed commander of an air Group located in Döberitz, later becoming the 132nd Fighter Group, part of the Richthofen Squadron equipped with biplanes. In April 1935 von Greim was named by Hitler as Inspector of Fighters and Dive Bombers, shortly afterwards he was promoted to *Oberstleutnant*. Von Greim was a man with talent, he had the experience, the enthusiasm and most importantly he believed in the new Germany and its Führer. His enthusiasm and talent soon paid off when he was named Chief of the Luftwaffe Personnel Office, his position being further ratified by his promotion to *Generalmajor* in February 1938. A year later von Greim was given his first field command when he was appointed commander of the 5th Air Division. He did not take part in the Polish campaign but was nevertheless promoted to *Generalleutnant* on 1st January 1940; soon afterwards his command was upgraded to Corps strength. In May he took part in the Battle for France, his bombers made short work of destroying large parts of the French transportation system which

did so much to prevent the French from gaining vital ground during the campaign. After the fall of France he was awarded the Knight's Cross, which was personally presented to him by Hitler on 24th June 1940, followed shortly by his promotion to *General der Flieger*.

During the Battle of Britain he commanded the 5th Air Corps, when the invasion was cancelled von Greim's command was moved to Russia in May 1941. He was now responsible for supporting *Generalfeldmarschall* von Rundstedt's Army Group South, and it was at this time that he began to make a name for himself. On 1st April 1942 he was appointed Commander-in-Chief of Luftwaffe Command East; now responsible for the air and anti-aircraft support of *Generalfeldmarschall* von Kluge's[19] Army Group Centre. His command was greatly outnumbered by Soviet forces, but he was just about able to win a few tactical air victories, however the sheer number of the Soviet force he was fighting against would soon prove too much.

In November 1942 the battle for Stalingrad had reached its climax and von Greim made efforts to keep the troops on the ground supplied for as long as he could. He continued to attack the Soviet railway system and by February he had shot down 38 Soviet aircraft and was destroying 116 tanks daily until the Soviets gave up the offensive in March 1943. Von Greim had since been promoted to *Generaloberst* and on 2nd April was awarded the Oakleaves to his Knight's Cross, and in May his command was upgraded and became the 6th Air Fleet. On 22nd June 1944 the Soviets attacked Army Group Centre with over 2,500,000 troops, 2,300 fighter aircraft, 1740 ground attack aircraft, 1660 bomber aircraft, 430 night bomber aircraft and almost 180 reconnaissance aircraft. Von Greim had less than

Left: During the French Campaign von Greim commanded the 5th Air Corps. In February 1943 he was promoted to Generaloberst and transferred to Russia where his command became very successful during the early part of the campaign. Von Greim is seen here during an inspection tour in conversation with an Oberleutnant somewhere on the Russian Front. (Author's collection)

Right: Generalleutnant Werner Kreipe was born on 12th April 1904 in Hannover. He entered the German army in April 1922 and was commissioned in August 1925 serving in the artillery. He transferred to the Luftwaffe in October 1934 and served mainly as a staff officer. He rose rapidly and from November 1941 served as Chief of the General Staff of the 1st Air Corps as an Oberstleutnant. Appointed chief-of-staff of the Commander of Training Affairs in the Air Ministry in November 1942, he was promoted to Generalmajor in 1943; Generalleutnant in July 1944; and General der Flieger in September 1944. He was for a brief time appointed acting chief-of-staff of the Luftwaffe and his last command was as Commander of the Air War Academy. Kreipe died in Badenweiler on 7th September 1967. (Private Source)

775 aircraft, with less than 100 ground attack aircraft, and he could do very little while the Soviet force destroyed Army Group Centre. During this time the Germans lost 350,000 troops, as a result the commander of the Army Group, *Generalfeldmarschall* Ernst Busch[20] was sacked.

During the unsuccessful attempt on Hitler's life, on 20th July 1944, the Luftwaffe Chief of Staff Günther Korten was killed and Hitler wanted von Greim to take over as his replacement, and there was even talk that von Greim should take over the running of the Luftwaffe from Göring. But the *Reichsmarschall* who had already learnt of this rumor was keen that his own choice of replacement, *Generalleutnant* Werner Kreipe[21] should take over. It was well known that von Greim was already being called the "number one man in the Luftwaffe," and most saw him as an outstanding officer who his men adored and called "Papa". He was further described as having a commanding and imposing physical presence, but was friendly and approachable, unlike Göring.

On 31st August 1944, much to the surprise of von Greim himself especially after the disastrous campaign in Russia when *Generalfeldmarschall* Busch had been sacked, von Greim felt he had been partly to blame, he was awarded the Knight's Cross with Oakleaves and Swords. Three weeks later in September, von Greim was even more surprised when Hitler offered him the post of deputy Commander of the Luftwaffe, and he was told that Göring would just be the figurehead and he would be the actual commander. When Göring heard about this he confronted von Greim and shouted abuse at him, at one point von Greim thought the *Reichsmarschall* was going to have a heart attack. Von Greim was shocked by Göring's remarks and the post of deputy commander of the Luftwaffe was forgotten, and von Greim was ordered back to command his Air Fleet in Poland.

On 23rd April 1945 Hitler, now inside his bunker, received a telegram from Göring detailing that he intended to take over the command of the Reich as Hitler would soon be unable to communicate outside of Berlin. Hitler was enraged and ordered Göring's immediate arrest, and dismissed him from the Nazi Party. The next day he sent a message to von Greim, he wanted to see him in person in the Bunker as soon as possible. Von Greim was in Munich when he received the message, and although totally baffled as to why Hitler wanted him he made the necessary arrangements to fly to Berlin as soon as he could. With the war almost lost and with very few planes available and the skies over Berlin almost impossible to fly over, von Greim was determined to be by his Führer's side.

On the morning of 25th April, von Greim and his lover the female aviator Hanna Reitsch[22] arrived at the Luftwaffe airbase at Rechlin where they boarded a Focke Wulf 190 and ordered the pilot to fly them to Gatow. The aircraft was only a two-seater fighter and Reitsch had to squeeze into the tail section, the journey was uncomfortable for all concerned especially Reitsch. They were escorted by twenty fighter aircraft, and

An excellent portrait of von Greim as Generaloberst shortly after being presented the Knight's Cross with Oakleaves on 2nd April 1943. Note the high-quality Generaloberst collar insignia, and his Pour le Mérite visible under his Knight's Cross. (Author's collection)

The grave of the last commander-in-chief of Hitler's Luftwaffe. Von Greim is buried in Salzburg, Austria. (Private Source)

during the flight nine were shot down by Soviet anti-aircraft fire, they arrived at Gatow in one piece after some skilful flying by their pilot. The next morning the two intrepid aviators managed to find a Fiesler-Storch aircraft, especially designed to land and take-off in areas with limited space, they then flew at treetop level in the direction of the Bunker. Von Greim was at the controls himself, and over the Tiergarten the plane was hit by a soviet anti-aircraft shell which went through the cockpit and shattered von Greim's right foot, he fainted due to loss of blood. Reitsch immediately reached over across from her seat and grabbed the controls; she managed to land the aircraft in a nearby street not far from the Reich Chancellery.

On landing von Greim was carried to Hitler's Bunker on a stretcher, he was in terrible pain and feared he might lose his foot. He was taken immediately to Hitler's surgeon *SS-Obersturmbannführer* Dr. Ludwig Stumpfegger[23] who operated to save his foot. When the operation was over and von Greim had rested he was taken to Hitler, who told him why he had so urgently summoned him to Berlin. Hitler calmly informed von Greim that Göring was no longer the Commander-in-Chief of the Luftwaffe and von Greim was now appointed as Göring's successor with the rank of *Generalfeldmarschall*. Hitler shook hands with his new *Feldmarschall* and left the room.

In the early hours of 29th April the new Commander-in-Chief of the Luftwaffe with his female companion, his foot bandaged and hobbling on crutches, left the Bunker for the last time. They both were taken by an armoured vehicle to a makeshift landing sight along the Hermann Göring Strasse and onto the Brandenburg Gate. There waiting for them was an Arado 96 light aircraft which would take them out of Berlin. Von Greim was helped into the aircraft and Reitsch climbed in next to him and their pilot took off and flew up towards the Brandenburg Gate and out of Berlin. They landed at the headquarters of *Grossadmiral* Karl Dönitz in Plön, Schleswig-Holstein just before midday. The next day Hitler committed suicide and named Dönitz as his successor. The new head of Germany wanted von Greim to remain as head of the Luftwaffe but he had other plans and declined the offer, he now made his way with Hanna Reitsch to northern Austria. They were both taken prisoner by the Americans on 8th May, and von Greim was admitted to a military hospital in Salzburg.

It was here that the *Generalfeldmarschall* learnt that he would be part of a Soviet-American prisoner exchange program and fearing he might be tortured or executed at the hands of the Soviets he took his own life on 24th May 1945. It was thought that he had used a cyanide capsule given to him by Hitler.

Richard "Arno" HEIDRICH
(1896-1947)
General der Fallschirmtruppe

Knight's Cross: Awarded on 14th June 1941 as *Oberst* and Commander of 3rd Parachute Infantry Regiment for actions in Crete.

Generalleutnant Richard Heidrich wearing the Knight's Cross with Oakleaves as Commander of the 1st Parachute Infantry Division. (Wehrkundearchiv)

Oakleaves: He became the 382nd recipient on 5th February 1944 as *Generalleutnant* and Commanding General of 1st Parachute Infantry Division for actions in Italy.

Swords: Awarded on 25th March 1944, he became the 55th recipient of the Swords as the Commanding General of 1st Parachute Division.

Ranks:
Gefreiter – 17th November 1914
Unteroffizier – 18th May 1915
Fähnrich – 14th July 1915
Leutnant – 20th August 1915
Oberleutnant – 1st April 1925
Hauptmann – 1st February 1931
Major – 18th January 1936
Oberstleutnant – 1st January 1939
Oberst – 20th April 1940

Generalmajor – 4th August 1942
Generalleutnant – 1st July 1943
General der Fallschirmtruppe – 31st October 1944

Awards:
Iron Cross 2nd Class – World War I
Iron Cross 1st Class – World War I
Knight's Cross of the Saxony Order of Albert with Swords
Wound Badge in Black – World War I
Cross of Honour for Frontline Combatants
Armed Forces Long Service Award 1st Class
Commemorative Medal for 1st October 1938 with Bar "Prague Castle"
Bar to Iron Cross 2nd Class – 25th May 1941
Bar to Iron Cross 1st Class – 25th May 1941
German Cross in Gold – 13th April 1942
KRETA Cufftitle
Luftwaffe Parachutist Badge
Wehrmacht Daily Report: 9 June 1941; 24 December 1943; 25 March 1944; 29 June 1944

Heidrich as an Oberst shortly after being awarded the Knight's Cross in June 1941 for actions during the Crete campaign. (Wehrkundearchiv)

Richard Heidrich was born on 27th July 1896 in Lewalde, Saxony and he joined the Imperial Army at the age of eighteen as a war volunteer serving on the Western Front with the 101st Reserve Infantry Regiment. He went on to serve as a Platoon Leader and was awarded the Iron Cross 1st Class, and was commissioned as a *Leutnant* in August 1915. When the war ended he was taken into the Reichswehr where he served as a Platoon Leader in a number of different regiments before becoming a staff officer in August 1924 and was promoted almost a year later to *Oberleutnant*. In February 1931 he was promoted to *Hauptmann* and took over as Company Commander with 10th Infantry Regiment. Appointed a tactics instructor at the Infantry School in Dresden in September 1934, and between October 1935 and October 1937 he served at the War Schools in Potsdam and Munich, where he impressed his superiors and was promoted to *Major* in January 1936.

In June 1938 Heidrich commanded a parachute Battalion that he had formed while an instructor in Munich. In January 1939 he was transferred to the Luftwaffe with the rank of *Oberstleutnant*, and was appointed commander of the 1st *Fallschirmjäger* Regiment. In February he was appointed Operations Officer with 7th Air Division, under the command of *Generalmajor* Kurt Student before being assigned to the staff of Hermann Göring in June. On 1st October 1939 he was transferred back to the army once more and served with 10th Infantry Replacement Battalion in Dresden, and here he trained new recruits.

In February 1940 he commanded the 514th Infantry Regiment, part of the 294th Infantry Division and stayed on reserve during most of the campaign against France and the Low Countries. He hated this time and wanted to get into the war, in April he was promoted to *Oberst* and finally towards the end of May his command was released from the reserve and assigned to the 2nd Army at the front where he saw action in the final stages of the invasion of France. In June 1940 he was transferred back to the Luftwaffe and appointed Commander of the 3rd Parachute Regiment. For the planned invasion of England (Operation Sealion), his division was assigned drop zones in the area of Lyming, Sellinge and Hythe as part of *Generaloberst* Ernst Busch's 16th Army and were tasked with the capture of the high ground around Folkestone. When Operation Sealion was cancelled and after months of training the 7th Air Division was assigned to Greece in the spring of 1941. In May 1941 *General der Flieger* Kurt Student's 11th Air Corps started the invasion of Crete with a large air drop from gliders; Heidrich's regiment drooped southwest of Canea. The landing didn't go well and his command was scattered in a large area, by the end of the day his command had suffered heavy losses and had been surrounded by New Zealand and Greek forces. He was relieved by German mountain troops under the command of *Oberst* Willibald Utz[24] on the night of 24-25th May, and Heidrich's command continued its advance on Canea. However his initial landing and his defence against the strong Allied opposition which secured the landing filed for 5th Mountain Division earned him the Knight's Cross on 20th May. By June the last British troops who had not been evacuated surrendered to the German forces.

In September 1941 the 7th Air Division was transferred to Russia, along with Heidrich's regiment, where it saw heavy combat near Leningrad until January 1942 when it was withdrawn from Russia with the bulk of the division for a rest and refitting in France. On 1st August Heidrich was given temporary command of the 7th Air Division, and was promoted to *Generalmajor*, and in October he returned to Russia and a few weeks later his command was made permanent, after its former commander, *Generalleutnant* Erich Petersen had been promoted and reassigned. The 7th Air Division now found itself in the central sector of the Russian Front seeing action near Smolensk, Rzhev and Orel until its withdrawal to France in early 1943.

On 1st May 1943 the 7th Air Division was re-designated the 1st Fallschirmjäger Division whilst undergoing refitting in the south of France. By mid July 1943, Heidrich now promoted to *Generalleutnant*, led his troops into Sicily to help with the German forces there following the Allied invasion. However following heavy combat the division was evacuated to the mainland, and after the British landed at Taranto on 9th September, Heidrich realising his command was outnumbered and in much need of reinforcements decided to withdrawn his division northwards beyond Foggia. He continued to lead his command along the Adriatic coast until early February 1944 when it was transferred to the critical Monte Cassino sector under *General der Panzertruppe* Fridolin von Senger und Etterlin's[25] 14th Panzer Corps. Over the next few months the Allies suffered heavy casualties while trying to displace the German force in the mountain defences. Heidrich was awarded the Oakleaves on 5th February for his leadership skills and for the part he played in the prevention of the British 8th Army breaking through the German defences. The battle for Cassino went on and on, and Heidrich was mentioned in the Official Wehrmacht Reports on 25th March 1944, they thanked him and the men of 1st Fallschirmjäger Division for their tough defence and awarded Heidrich, on the same day, with the much coveted Swords to his Knight's Cross.

In May 1944 the Allies finally won the battle at Monte Cassino and captured Rome in June, and the Germans started to withdraw. Heidrich was transferred to the Gothic Line defences along the Adriatic Coast and when the Allies broke through these defences his command withdrew to Imola. In October Heidrich was promoted to *General der Fallschirmtruppe* and a month later he was appointed Commanding General of the 1st Fallschirm Corps in Italy, succeeding *General der Fallschirmtruppe* Alfred Schlemm. It wasn't long before the Allies launched their final Italian offensive in April 1945. By the end of the month General der Panzertruppe Traugott Herr's[26] 10th Army, which included the 1st Fallschirm Corps were pushed back by the British 8th Army to the Italian-Yugoslav border. By the beginning of May the end for Germany was in sight and on 3rd May Heidrich surrendered to the British and spent just over two years in Allied captivity. He spent time in various prison camps which included the famous London Cage and the Island Farm Special Camp. On 16th January 1947 he was transferred to hospital where he died on 22nd December 1947 in Hamburg-Bergedorf.

Ludwig Heilmann wearing the Knight's Cross with Oakleaves and Swords, as a Generalmajor in 1944. (Wehrkundearchiv)

Ludwig HEILMANN
(1903-1959)
Generalmajor

Knight's Cross: Awarded on 14th June 1941as Commander of the 3rd Battalion, 3rd Parachute Regiment for actions in Crete.

Oakleaves: For actions in Monte Cassino as *Oberst* and still a battalion commander in 3rd Parachute Regiment on 2nd March 1944.

Swords: He became the 67th recipient of the Swords on 15th May 1944 while still commanding the same unit and for continued actions at Monte Cassino.

Ranks:
Oberschütze – 1st November 1924
Gefreiter – 1st December 1924
Unteroffizier – 1st May 1925
Unterfeldwebel – 1st October 1927
Feldwebel – 1st July 1929
Leutnant – 1st July 1934
Oberleutnant –skipped
Hauptmann – 1st December 1935
Major – 1st August 1940
Oberstleutnant – 1st April 1942
Oberst – 1st December 1943
Generalmajor – 22nd December 1944

Awards:
Iron Cross 2nd Class – 2nd October 1939
Iron Cross 1st Class – 14th June 1941
Armed Forces Long Service Award 3rd Class
Luftwaffe Parachutists Badge
Luftwaffe Ground Assault Badge
Wound Badge in Black
German Cross in Gold – 15th March 1942
KRETA Cufftitle – 20th May 1943
Wehrmacht Daily Report: 16 March 1944

Major Heilmann seen shortly after being awarded his Knight's Cross on 14th June 1941. He was at this time Commander of the 3rd Battalion, 3rd Parachute Regiment in Crete. (Wehrkundearchiv)

Ludwig Heilmann became one of the most famous German parachute commanders of World War II, and one of the most decorated, described as upstanding, straightforward and strong nerved. He was born on 9th August 1903 in Würzburg, Germany and he joined the Reichswehr at the age of seventeen and spent the next twelve years as an enlisted man. Commissioned in July 1934 with the rank of *Oberleutnant* and appointed commander of the 5th Company of the 20th Infantry Regiment. During the fighting in France he won the Iron Cross 1st Class with as part of the 3rd Battalion of the 91st Infantry Regiment.

In June 1940 he was sent on a rifleman course at the Parachute School in Wittstock, a few weeks later he took over as Commander of the 3rd Battalion, 423rd Infantry Regiment. On 1st August 1940 Heilmann transferred to the Luftwaffe with the rank of *Major* and was appointed Commander of the 3rd Battalion, 3rd Parachute Regiment, in May 1941 his battalion took part in the first assault on Crete. His command suffered heavy losses and only one company landed on target, the other three companies were scattered with one company landing in a reservoir and many drowned. However his troops took part in bitter fighting and played a major role in the German success on the island. On 14th June 1941 for his bravery and leadership during the invasion he was awarded the Knight's Cross.

In the autumn of 1941 Heilmann and his unit was sent to Russia, where they fought as infantry. They fought with much bravery and took part in the defence of the blood-soaked Vyborgskaya Bridgehead. In April 1942 Heilmann was promoted to *Oberstleutnant* and in November was appointed commander of the 3rd Parachute Regiment. After the Allies landed in Sicily Heilmann and his regiment parachuted into the Catania Plain to reinforce the German troops there, who were part of the elite Hermann Göring Panzer Division. His command fought near Francoforte and Centuripe near Regalbuto, Bronte and Maletto. Heilmann led his men with great skill and on 1st December 1943 he was promoted to *Oberst*.

In January 1944 Heilmann's regiment saw heavy action in Sicily and Italy including the tough defensive battle at Monte Cassino. On 2nd March Heilmann became the 412th recipient of the Oakleaves, awarded for actions near Monte Cassino. Heilmann's command was considered the anchor of the Cassino defence, and using every resource at his disposal, he managed to support his Battalion commanders with accurate mortar fire and artillery fire. His leadership and bravery was recognised again when he was awarded the Swords to his Knight's Cross, becoming the 67th recipient on 15th May 1944.

In November he was appointed Commander of the 5th Parachute Division and led them during the Ardennes Offensive where it suffered heavy loses while fighting on the German southern flank. In December he was promoted to *Generalmajor* and in January 1945 his unit took part in fierce fighting and in March he was captured by U.S. forces. He spent time in various prisoner of war camps being transferred in May 1946 to the famous London District Cage prison camp, and was described by the British as an ardent Nazi. Heilmann was released from captivity in August 1947, and returned home, where he died in Kempten, Allgäu on 26th October 1959.

Hans KROH
(1907-1967)
Generalmajor

Knight's Cross: Awarded on 21st August 1941 as *Major* and Commander of the 1st Battalion, 2nd Parachute Jäger Regiment during the Battle of Crete.

Oakleaves: Kroh became the 443rd recipient on 6th April 1944 as *Oberstleutnant* and Commander of the 2nd Fallschirmjäger Regiment for actions in Russia.

Swords: He became the 96th recipient on 12th September 1944 as *Oberst* and Commander of the 2nd Fallschirmjäger Division during the Battle of Brest.

Ranks:
Polizei-Leutnant – 1st April 1933
Polizei-Oberleutnant – 1st August 1933
Oberleutnant – 1st October 1935
Hauptmann – 1st October 1937
Major – 1st March 1941
Oberstleutnant – 11th January 1943
Oberst – 6th April 1944
Generalmajor – 13th September 1944

Awards:
Iron Cross 2nd Class – 22nd May 1940
Iron Cross 1st Class – 22nd May 1940
Wound Badge in Black
Armed Forces Long Service Award 4th Class
Luftwaffe Anti-Aircraft Badge
Luftwaffe Paratrooper Badge
German Cross in Gold – 24th December 1942
Combined Pilot's and Observer's Badge
Luftwaffe Ground Assault Badge
Medal for the Winter Campaign in Russia 1941/1942
KRETA Cufftitle
AFRIKA Cufftitle

Hans Kroh started his career as a policeman and later became a paratrooper and highly decorated officer. He was born in Heidelberg on 13th May 1907 and entered the Brandenburg-Havel Police School as a cadet in April 1926. He was commissioned as a *Leutnant* in April 1933 and by August he had been appointed platoon leader with the *Landespolizeigruppe* Wecke as an *Oberleutnant*. In January 1934 he had been transferred to the *Landespolizeigruppe "General Göring"*, and in October 1935 was appointed Commander of the 2nd Company of the *"General Göring"* Regiment.

Kroh wearing the Knight's Cross as Commander of the 1st Battalion, 2nd Parachute Jäger Regiment during the Battle of Crete. (Wehrkundearchiv)

He transferred to the Luftwaffe in April 1936 and after he completed his parachutist-rifle course he was appointed senior trainer at the Stendal Parachute School. Promoted to *Hauptmann* in October 1937 he went on to command a company with the 1st Battalion, 1st Fallschirmjäger Regiment in April 1938. In January 1939 he was transferred to the 7th Air Division and by June 1940 he had been appointed Operations Officer under *Generalleutnant* Kurt Student. Appointed Commander of the 1st Battalion, 2nd Fallschirmjäger Regiment in August 1940, he was promoted to *Major* in March 1941. Kroh led a Battle Group that had been formed from his own command during the invasion of Crete in May, after its commander *Oberst* Alfred Sturm was taken prisoner. He led his unit to an oil refinery near Stavromenos and they managed to hold out against far superior forces. His men fought against Greek and British forces for ten days until troops of the mountain infantry finally relieved them. This battle helped to secure the area and to win the Battle of

Crete and for this Kroh was awarded the Knight's Cross on 21st August 1941.

In January 1943 Kroh was promoted to *Oberstleutnant* and in March he was made Commander of the 2nd Fallschirmjäger Regiment under General Ramcke's 2nd Fallschirmjäger Division in North Africa. He was then transferred to the Russian Front where his forces suffered heavy losses as they weren't trained or designed to stand and fight in such a way, but nevertheless they fought with bravery and tenacity. As a result of his leadership and bravery Kroh was awarded the Oakleaves on the 6th April 1944, becoming the 443rd recipient. On 11th August 1944 Ramcke was made Commandant of Fortress Brest and Kroh took over command of the 2nd Fallschirmjäger Division. On 12th September Kroh was awarded the Swords for actions in the fighting during the Battle of Brest, then just six days later Ramcke surrendered his force at Brest and Kroh was taken prisoner along with his men.

Kroh was released from captivity in 1948, he returned to active service with the Bundeswehr with the rank of *Oberst* in June 1956. In September 1957 he was promoted to *Brigadegeneral* and appointed Commander of the 1st Air Landing Division, and in July 1959 he was promoted to *Generalmajor*. On 30th September 1962 he retired and died five years later in Braunschweig.

Official photograph of Oberst Dietrich Peltz shortly after being awarded the Knight's Cross with Oakleaves and Swords on 23rd July 1943. (Wehrkundearchiv)

Dietrich PELTZ
(1914-2001)
Generalmajor

Knight's Cross: Awarded on 14th October 1940 in recognition of his 130th ground-support mission while serving as *Oberleutnant* and Squadron Leader of the 1st Squadron, 3rd Stuka Wing.

Oakleaves: *Hauptmann* Peltz became the 46th recipient of the Oakleaves on 31st December 1941 having flown 250 tactical missions as Commander of the 2nd Group, 77th Bomber Wing.

Swords: Awarded on 23rd July 1943 after flying 300 tactical missions as *Oberst* and Inspector of Bomber and Stuka aircraft, becoming the 31st recipient of the Oakleaves.

Ranks:
Fahnenjunker-Gefreiter – 1st October 1934
Fahnenjunker-Unteroffizier – 1st December 1934
Fähnrich – 1st June 1935
Oberfähnrich – 1st October 1935
Leutnant – 1st April 1936
Oberleutnant – 1st March 1939
Hauptmann – 1st March 1941
Major – 18th July 1942
Oberstleutnant – 1st December 1942
Oberst – 17th March 1943
Generalmajor – 1st November 1943

Awards:
Armed Forces Long Service Award 4th Class
Iron Cross 2nd Class – 15th September 1939
Iron Cross 1st Class – 22nd May 1940
Pilot's Badge with Diamonds
Combined Pilot's and Observer's Badge in Gold with Diamonds
Combat Clasp for Fighters in Gold with Pendant for 300 missions
Wehrmacht Daily Report: 26 June 1944

The youngest general in the Luftwaffe, Dietrich Peltz was promoted to the rank of *Generalmajor* at the age of twenty-nine in 1943. The son of a factory manager he was born in Gear-Reuß on 9th June 1914 and learnt to fly before he passed his final school exams at the age of eighteen. In April 1934 he joined the German army and was assigned to the 5th Motor Transport Battalion before entering the Munich War School where he trained as an officer.

In October 1935 he entered the Luftwaffe and began his training as a bomber pilot at the flying school in Salzwedel. In April 1936 he was commissioned as a *Leutnant* and was posted to the Fighter Wing "Immelmann" where for a time he served as adjutant. In 1937 he trained as a Stuka pilot with the 162nd Stuka Wing and then in 1938 with the 76th Stuka Wing. He flew first the Hs 123 and then from 1938 he flew the new Ju 87 and was a natural.

In March 1939 he was promoted to *Oberleutnant* and by May he had been appointed Squadron Leader with the 76th Stuka Wing. In September 1939 Peltz took a leading role in the last major exercise before World War II at Neuhammer. There was bad weather and thirteen crew members lost their lives but Peltz didn't lose a single aircraft from his own squadron and his superiors soon learnt that Peltz was a natural bomber pilot with excellent leadership qualities. When war broke out he saw action in Poland where he flew over forty-five missions destroying important railway junctions at Miechow and Kamienna and was soon awarded the Iron Cross 2nd Class. He went onto see action over the skies of France in May 1940 and was awarded the Iron Cross 1st Class. His superiors were impressed by his accuracy and boldness against the enemy targets. He flew against British Spitfires and managed to out manoeuvre them, something that wasn't easy as the Stuka was often slow and cumbersome against the superior British fighters. Peltz took part in fifty-seven combat missions over Dunkirk and Calais and by the end of the French Campaign had flown 102 combat missions, and his squadron hadn't suffered a single loss of aircraft during the campaign.

After the fall of France he took part in the Battle of Britain where he flew the Ju 88 as part of the 77th Bomber Wing, commanded by *Major* Clemens Graf von Schönborn-Wiesentheid[27] with its headquarters in Brugy. Peltz was one of the very few pilots that would bomb targets in solo raids; he would dive out of the clouds at low level and bomb his targets - airfields, factories etc with great accuracy. During one of his solo missions over England Peltz was caught in bad weather and used the cloud cover to approach his target at low-level, however just before he reached his target the weather cleared leaving him vulnerable, undaunted he proceeded to the target, an aircraft production facility near Birmingham, and attacked with his usual accuracy. After the attack he flew again at low-level through the English countryside shaking off British fighters and managed to escape unscathed back to his base. On 14th October 1940 his skills were recognised when he was awarded the Knight's Cross, the official notification of his award stated it was in recognition of his 130 combat missions over Poland, France and Britain. During the attack on Dunkirk he destroyed a fully loaded troop ship and went on to fly seventy daylight and night time missions over England.

In March 1941 Peltz was promoted to *Hauptmann* and appointed a Group Commander with the 77th Bomber Wing. He now developed superior bombing techniques, which allowed his pilots to achieve great success against ground targets during the Russian campaign. In recognition of his new bombing methods and for his highly accurate results against difficult targets and in recognition of his 250th combat mission he was awarded the Oakleaves on 31st December 1941, becoming the 46th recipient of the award. Peltz was then assigned to the Bomber Unit Commanders School in Foggia, Italy where he had to prove himself as a skilful Bomber Wing commander, something that seemed to come naturally. When he left the school he was ordered to form a special unit, the 66th Bomber Wing, where he helped to develop the use of rocket bombs against Allied shipping. Promoted in July 1942 to *Major* this was soon followed by his rise to *Oberstleutnant* in December.

Hauptmann Peltz wearing the Knight's Cross with Oakleaves, seen here during the time he was Commander of the 2nd Group, 77th Bomber Wing. (Author's collection)

In January 1943 he was named as Inspector of Bomber and Dive-bomber aircraft and in March he was promoted to *Oberst*. On 23rd July 1943 Peltz was awarded the much sought-after Swords to his Knight's Cross. The award came in recognition of his contribution to the war effort and for achieving more than 300 combat missions against targets in the Soviet Union, Sardinia and Africa. In August Peltz was named as the "Attack Leader England", with orders to make plans for renewed attacks on Southern England. On 1st November 1943 Peltz was promoted to *Generalmajor* and appointed Commanding

General of the 9th Air Corps, and Göring ordered him to put his plans of attack against England into action. Finally in late December and early January a force of over 500 aircraft of all different types was made ready on French airfields, including Ju 88s, Ju 188s, Do 217s, Me 410s and even the new He 177. All of these aircraft were used in the attacks on England in January 1944. The bomber crews' general lack of night flying experience and the very different performances of the aircraft types required pathfinder aircraft to be used to mark targets within the London area. The raid was a disaster for the Luftwaffe, and only thirty-two tons of bombs of the 282 dropped fell on London that night. For the following four months, further raids were made, resulting in the loss of 329 aircraft, to little effect, and as a result these aircraft were not available to help with the defense against the forthcoming Allied invasion of Europe. Peltz had just 144 operational aircraft left by May 1944 when the raids ceased.

In October 1944 Peltz was made Commanding General of the 2nd Fighter Corps, with its headquarters located near Koblenz, here he used his organizational skills as a fighter commander rather than a bomber commander. In December he led his unit during the Ardennes Offensive, although at first his aircraft had great success against the American forces his aircraft were soon grounded due to lack of fuel and experienced pilots. In January 1945 he took over once again as the Commander of the 9th Air Corps, responsible for the air defence around Prague and then during the final months of the war with his headquarters in Munich. Peltz was captured by U.S. forces on 8th May 1945 and was soon released, he returned to Germany and civilian life and made a career in industry until his retirement. The youngest Luftwaffe general of World War II died in Munich on 10th August 2001.

Karl-Lothar Schulz as an Oberst wearing the Knight's Cross with Oakleaves and Swords in November 1944. (Wehrkundearchiv)

Karl-Lothar SCHULZ
(1907-1972)
Generalmajor

Knight's Cross: Awarded on 24th May 1940 as *Hauptmann* and commander of the 3rd Battalion 1st Fallschirmjäger Regiment for actions in Rotterdam, Holland.

Oakleaves: He became the 459th recipient on 20th April 1944 as *Oberst* and commander of the 1st Fallschirmjäger Regiment for actions in Italy.

Swords: The 112th recipient of the Swords it was awarded on 18th November 1944 as *Oberst* and commander of the 1st Fallschirmjäger Division for actions in Italy.

Ranks:
Polizei-Wachtmeister – 1st April 1927
Polizei-Oberwachtmeister – 1st August 1930
Polizei-Leutnant – 20th April 1934
Polizei-Oberleutnant – 1st September 1935
Oberleutnant – 1st October 1935
Hauptmann – 1st March 1937
Major – 19th July 1940
Oberstleutnant – 26th October 1942
Oberst – 21st October 1943
Generalmajor – 17th January 1945

Awards:
Armed Forces Long Service Award 3rd Class
Iron Cross 2nd Class – 12th May 1940
Iron Cross 1st Class – 12th May 1940
Luftwaffe Parachutist Badge
German Cross in Gold – 26th February 1942
Wound Badge in Black – World War II
KRETA Cufftitle

Karl-Lothar Schulz was a parachute commander who distinguished himself in battle in Holland, Crete, Monte Cassino and the Eastern Front being awarded one of the highest awards for bravery. He was born on 30th April 1907 in Königsberg and on completing his schooling he entered the artillery in June 1924. His time as a soldier was short however and in October 1925 he transferred to the police service and after training he served with the Security Police in Berlin with the rank of *Polizei-Wachtmeister.* In February 1933 he was assigned to the special purpose unit that later became the Hermann Göring Division. He served as a Platoon Leader and as a Company Leader with the State Police Group "General Göring" until September 1935, leaving the police with the rank of *Oberleutnant.*

In October 1935 he transferred to the Luftwaffe and after attending a parachutist-rifleman course he joined the 5th Engineer Company in the Luftwaffe Regiment "Hermann Göring". He was promoted to *Hauptmann* in March 1937 and in September he was appointed commander of the 15th Engineer Company. In January 1940 Schulz was made commander of the 3rd Battalion, 1st Parachute Regiment and during the Western Campaign his battalion captured the airport at Rotterdam which was essential to the campaign, the ground troops could now be supplied with food, ammunition, and troops. For this achievement and in recognition of his leadership Schulz was awarded the Knight's Cross on 24th May 1940.

Schulz was promoted to *Major* on 19th July 1940, after the celebrations of the victory over France. He took part in the aerial invasion of Crete when he was dropped near Heraklion and led his forces into the city. His troops encountered fierce fighting and due to a shortage of ammunition his troops were forced to abandon the city shortly afterwards. Schulz nevertheless held positions near Heraklion and again his leadership skills helped secure a victory. In September 1941 his command was transferred to the Eastern Front where it saw action near Leningrad. His command fought at the Neva River at great cost. In April 1942 he was made temporary Chief of Operations of the 7th Air Division serving under *Generalleutnant* Erich Petersen. In June 1942 he took over as commander of the 1st Paratrooper Regiment and saw action in Russia, seeing action in the areas around Leningrad, Volkhov, Rshev, and Orel. Schulz was promoted to *Oberstleutnant* in October 1942 and to *Oberst* on 21st October 1943. In April 1944 he was awarded the Oakleaves for actions following the Allied landing in Italy, it was after the withdrawal to Bologna that the award was rendered.

On 18th November 1944 Schulz took over as commander of the 1st Paratrooper Division when he succeeded *Generalmajor* Hans Korte. It was while commanding this unit during the Battle of Monte Cassino that Schulz earned the support and respect of his superiors. His command spent November 1944 to April 1945, defending a sector near Imola in Italy under the command of the 10th Army. Schulz fought with great bravery and his troops fought with great skill and determination suffering heavy losses. In recognition of Schulz's bravery and skill he became the 112th recipient of the Swords on 18th November 1944. Promoted to *Generalmajor* in January 1945, Schulz was captured by U.S. forces on 2nd May 1945. He was released on 17th October 1947, and returned to Germany where he lived with his wife in Wiesbaden until his death at the age of sixty-five on 26th September 1972.

A nice studio portrait photograph of Rainer Stahel as a Generalmajor wearing the Knight's Cross with Oakleaves. (Author's collection)

Rainer Joseph Karl August STAHEL (1892-1955) *Generalleutnant*

Knight's Cross: Awarded as *Oberstleutnant* and commander 34th Flak Regiment on 18th January 1942, for his support of Army Group Centre on the Russian Front.

Oakleaves: On 4th January 1943 he became the 169th recipient as *Oberst* and commander of Luftwaffe Combat Group Stahel for actions in Stalingrad.

Swords: Awarded as *Generalmajor* and Commandant Fortress Vilna on 18th July 1944, becoming the 79th recipient for his defence of the Fortress Vilna.

Ranks:
Fahnenjunker-Unteroffizier – 1st August 1911
Fähnrich – 19th December 1911
Leutnant – 18th October 1912
Oberleutnant – 27th January 1916
Charakter als Hauptmann – 11th April 1918
Finnischer Major – 28th February 1918
Finnischer Oberstleutnant – 27th May 1918
Hauptmann – 23rd February 1934
Major – 1st April 1935
Oberstleutnant – 1st November 1939
Oberst – 1st March 1942
Generalmajor – 21st January 1943
Generalleutnant – 22nd July 1944

Awards:
Iron Cross 2nd Class – 12th October 1914
Iron Cross 1st Class – 24th March 1915
Wound Badge in Silver – World War I
Finnish Liberation Cross 3rd Class – 8th May 1918
Finnish Liberation Cross 2nd Class – 29th May 1918
Cross of Honour for Frontline Combatants
Armed Forces Long Service Award 2nd Class
Bar to Iron Cross 2nd Class – 16th July 1941
Bar to Iron Cross 1st Class – 18th September 1941
Medal for the Winter Campaign in Russia 1941/1942
Luftwaffe Anti-Aircraft Badge
Wehrmacht Daily Report: 14 July 1944

Generalmajor Stahel, probably in Italy during an inspection tour in the summer of 1943. (Author's collection)

One of the most notable Luftwaffe officers of the war, he served with the German Army in World War I, during the inter-war period he served with the Finnish Army and during World War II he was a highly decorated Luftwaffe general. Rainer Stahel was born in Bielefeld, Germany on 15th January 1892 and joined the infantry in April 1911. In October 1912 he won his commission and after serving at the War School in Hersfeld he was appointed a company commander with the 130th Infantry Regiment. In February 1917, with the rank of *Oberleutnant* he became an artillery observer on the Eastern Front with the 27th Jäger Battalion. In March 1918 he transferred to the Finnish Army serving as commander of the 2nd Jäger Regiment, then the 3rd Jäger Brigade and in June 1918 with the rank of *Oberstleutnant* he was appointed Chief of Staff of the 1st Finnish Division. In November 1919 he retired from the army and entered service with the Finnish Border Police as commander of the Protection Corps in Turku until July 1925.

From 1925 until 1933 Stahel worked for a local insurance company in his home town of Bielefeld. In November 1933 he worked for the German Army as an advisor and in May 1935 he transferred to the Luftwaffe with the rank of *Hauptmann*. He became an advisor with the Air Ministry and became responsible for the development of German anti-air artillery weapons. Promoted to *Major* in April 1936 he was appointed battery commander in the 73rd Light Flak Battalion on 15th November 1938 in Leipzig. Following his promotion to *Oberstleutnant* in November 1939 Stahel was made commander of the 226th Reserve Flak Battalion in early 1940 and became responsible for the anti-air defence of Augsburg in June the same year. Soon afterwards he was sent to Vichy France as a military advisor where he stayed until January 1941 when he was transferred to the Eastern Front to take command of the 34th Motorised Flak Regiment in Bobrusik, Belarus. Stahel was awarded the Knight's Cross on 18th January 1942, for his personal courage and determination while supporting Army Group Centre near Anissowo Gorodit in Russia. In April Stahel now promoted to *Oberst* took over as commander of the 99th Flak Regiment in Stalino, part of the 17th Flak Division under *Oberst* Karl Veith, and responsible for supporting the 1st Panzer Army.

In September 1942 Stahel established the 4th Luftwaffe Field Division, and went onto command it during the Russian Campaign. He remained as commander until the end of November when he became the commander of an emergency Battle Group that had been formed from Luftwaffe ground personnel in Southern Russia. He led this Battle Group at Stalingrad in January 1943, and managed to get some troops out of the area before it became completely surrounded by the Soviets. Stahel was considered a specialist when it came to forming special units or battle groups, his effective methods and organisation skills earned him the Oakleaves on 4th January, and at the end of the month he was promoted to *Generalmajor*. On 21st May 1943 Stahel was appointed commander of the 22nd Flak Brigade which had been formed to protect the Messina Strait. Following the German retreat from Sicily and Italy's surrender in September he was appointed Military Commander of the city of Rome. It was an important position especially for a newly appointed general, but Stahel was very capable and was probably transferred because of his expertise in a crisis situation. However he did have his problems. When he arrived in Rome he was immediately confronted with an order from Himmler, the head of the SS who wanted to depot the Jews of Rome to Auschwitz Concentration Camp. The Bishop of Rome warned Stahel, that the Pope might take a position against the deportations, so Stahel decided that he wouldn't carry out the deportations without the permission of the Foreign Office. At the same time Mollhausen, the German Consul-General in Rome wrote to Hitler's Foreign Minister Joachim von Ribbentrop[28] recommending that the Jews be interned in Italian labour camps rather than being deported to Auschwitz. Stahel agreed and contacted von Ribbentrop himself. The answer was clear, von Ribbentrop would not intervene and wouldn't go against Himmler. Stahel had no choice he had to follow Himmler's orders and in October 1943 the first deportation of Jews from Rome began.

In July 1944 Stahel was promoted to *Generalleutnant* and transferred to Vilna in German occupied Poland, where he became military commander of the city's garrison. Here he initially commanded 500 troops but because of the Soviets major offensive Operation Bagration, the liberation of Belorussia, Stahel was given reinforcements. The Soviets had torn open the front line between German Army Group Centre and Army Group North in Vilinius. It was imperative for the Germans to hold this line because without it they wouldn't be able to re-establish a sustainable connection between the two German army groups, and wouldn't be able to hold back the Red Army outside East Prussia, and away from the Baltic. Stahel was ordered to hold back the Soviet forces as long as possible. On 12th July the German units made up some ground, and the 6th Panzer Division, under the command of *Generaloberst* Georg-Hans Reinhardt,[29] was able to advance approx. thirty miles to link up with forward elements from the Vilnius garrison. A fierce battle took place and the Germans managed to hold back the Polish Home Army. The next morning the German forces were attacked by the Soviets and they managed to split the Germans into two pockets, around 3,000 Germans managed to escape through the corridor opened by the 6th Panzer Division before the Soviets closed the gap. But 13,000 German troops were lost in the city which was liberated later the same day. The Germans had planned to hold Vilnius and make it a fortress under the command of Stahel but this had failed, but the stubborn defence of the city by the 6th Panzer Division and Stahel's garrison had helped to slow down the Red Army's advance on the west for a few precious days. Hitler was please and recognised the

During his inspection tour Stahel paid a visit to a local hospital and poses with a nurse, 1943. (Author's collection)

achievement of Stahel by awarding him the Swords on 18th July 1944, making Stahel the 79th recipient.

On 25th July Stahel was transferred to Warsaw where he was appointed City Commandant and ordered to defend the city against the advancing Red Army. The Soviet offensive was halted but on 1st August 1944 the Warsaw Uprising was started by the Polish Home Army. Stahel had just over 10,000 German troops under his command as City Commandant but he had seriously underestimated the Poles and on the first day his headquarters was surrounded and he lost control of the situation and on 4th August Stahel handed over command of all forces in Warsaw to *SS-Obergruppenführer* Erich von dem Bach-Zelewski[30] and Stahel became subordinate to the SS general. The next day a major German offensive started and army and Waffen-SS troops attacked the districts of Wola and Ohota, and carried out mass executions. A total of 65,000 civilians were captured and more than 1350 patients and staff of Wola and St. Lazarus hospitals were murdered. In Mokotov female civilians were used as shields in front of tanks that were attacking Polish positions. The Poles managed, with the help of a captured Panther tank to liberate 350 Jewish prisoners from the local concentration camp. On 7th August troops of *SS-Oberführer* Oskar Dirlewanger[31] had managed to reach Stahel's headquarters and rescue him. The fighting continued inside Warsaw and the allies dropped supplies to the fighters inside the Ghetto. However the Germans managed to breakthrough and before then end of 1944 the areas around Wola and Warsaw were completely surrounded and more than 600,000 inhabitants were deported to Auschwitz and other concentration camps.

On 25th August Stahel was transferred out of Warsaw and was sent to Romania, to crush the resistance inside Bucharest. The day before members of the resistance had stopped *Generalleutnant* Alfred Gerstenberg, the Commanding General and Commander-in-Chief of the Luftwaffe in Romania at the Banessa Bridge and had blocked his entrance to the capital. Stahel was sent in with fresh troops to try and re-establish German rule. However on 26th August Romania switched sides and the Red Army entered the city almost unopposed. Stahel had fled the city northwards with 1,900 men, trying to reach the 5th Flak Division at Ploesti. However on 29th August Stahel was arrested by the N.K.V.D (*Narodnyy Komissariat Vnutrennikh Del* or People's Commissariat for Internal Affairs). He was later interrogated about his part in the Warsaw Uprising and was imprisoned in the Soviet Gulag system. In 1955 he was to be freed and returned to Germany but on 30th November of that year he suffered a heart attack and died.

Erich WALTHER
(1903-1947)
Generalmajor

Knight's Cross: Awarded on 24th May 1940 as *Major* and commander 1st Battalion, 1st Fallschirmjäger Regiment, for his part in the victory in Norway.

Oakleaves: He became the 411th recipient of the award on 2nd March 1944 as *Oberst* and commander 4th Fallschirmjäger Regiment for actions in Russia.

Swords: He was the 131st recipient on 1st February 1945 as *Oberst* and commander of the 2nd Fallschirmpanzer Grenadier Division "Hermann Göring".

Ranks:
Polizei-Anwärter – 1st April 1924
Polizei-Wachtmeister – 1st July 1925
Polizei-Leutnant – 16th June 1928
Polizei-Oberleutnant – 21st March 1933
Hauptmann – 1st October 1935
Major – 19th June 1940
Oberstleutnant – 1st January 1942
Oberst – 20th April 1942
Generalmajor – 30th January 1945

Awards:
Armed Forces Long Service Award 3rd Class
Luftwaffe Parachutist Badge
Commemorative Medal for 1st October 1938 with Bar "Prague Castle"
Wound Badge in Black - World War II

Erich Walther, wearing the Knight's Cross with Oakleaves, is seen here in an official studio photograph taken in January 1945 at the time of his promotion to Generalmajor. (Author's collection)

Iron Cross 2nd Class – 18th April 1940
Iron Cross 1st Class – 26th April 1940
Narvik Shield
German Cross in Gold – 31st March 1942
KRETA Cufftitle

Erich Walther served the entire war as a parachute officer attached to the Hermann Göring Division and became one of the most highly decorated Luftwaffe officers. He was born in the small town of Gordon, Liebenwerda in Saxony on 5th August 1903. He joined the Berlin Police in April 1924 as a police cadet and in June 1928 was commissioned as a *Leutnant*. In 1933 he was promoted to *Oberleutnant* and transferred to the Wecke State Police where he served until January 1934 when the Wecke Police Units became known as the *Landespolizeigruppe* "General Göring" and went on to serve as a Platoon Commander until September 1935.

In October 1935 Walther entered the Luftwaffe as a *Hauptmann* and was appointed company commander of the 1st Battalion of the Luftwaffe Regiment "General Göring". In May he passed his parachute training and in April 1938 he was appointed Company Commander in 1st Battalion, 1st Fallschirmjäger Regiment. During the attack on Poland Walther was assigned as Inspector of Parachute Troops in the Air Ministry in Berlin. In November 1939 he was made Battalion Commander of the 1st Fallschirmjäger Regiment and saw action in Holland when he parachuted with his unit near Dordrecht. In May 1940 he fought in Norway in support of the 3rd Mountain Infantry Division, and its commander *Generalleutnant* Eduard Dietl[32] thanked Walther personally for his contribution to the victory in Norway, and his contribution Walther was awarded the Knight's Cross on 24th May 1940.

Promoted to *Major* in June 1940 and almost a year later he led the 3rd Battalion in Heraklion, Crete and he marched into the city at the head of his paratroopers. Walther went on to see action in Russia from September 1941 where he was awarded the German Cross in Gold on 31st March 1942 for actions near Leningrad. On 20th April he was promoted to *Oberst* and in September of the same year he helped to form three new battalions to make up the 4th Fallschirmjäger Regiment and was appointed its first commander in September 1942. He led his troops on the island of Sicily and fought a defensive battle in the area near the Simeto Bridge. At Cassino his regiment defended well and fought bravely on the hills around the area.

Awarded the Oakleaves to his Knight's Cross for his efforts during actions in Russia on 2nd March 1944 he took over command of the 2nd Fallschirm Panzer Grenadier Division "Hermann Göring" in East Prussia in September 1944 and faced the Russian onslaught. He was directly subordinated to the Fallschirm Panzer Corps, under *Generalleutnant* Wilhelm Schmalz who in turn was fighting as part of Army Group Centre. He then saw action as commander of a Battle Group and fought at Arnhem and managed to stop the enemy paratroopers during the ill-fated "Operation Market Garden". By early 1945 Walther was running out of men and supplies but still fought on and was promoted to *Generalmajor*, soon after on 1st February he was awarded the Swords for his outstanding leadership of his division and for his successful attacks against the Red Army which enabled other divisions to move out of the area and gain some ground. However by March 1945 his command had been pushed back into the heart of East Prussia, and it was later transferred south and ended the war east of Prague where it surrendered to Soviet forces on 8th May 1945.

Erich Walther was taken prisoner and after a few months was imprisoned in the former Buchenwald concentration camp where he was forgotten. The Soviets didn't like these Luftwaffe troops who thought themselves elite and fought with such conviction, this could be why Walther was imprisoned in such a place and treated so badly. On 26th December 1947 Walther died in circumstances that have never been fully explained, but it may have been due to malnutrition, bad treatment or even suicide.

KNIGHT'S CROSS WITH OAKLEAVES

Dr. Ing. Ernst BORMANN
(1897-1960)
Generalmajor

Knight's Cross: Awarded on 5th October 1941 as Commander of 76th Bomber Wing and *Oberstleutnant*, for actions on the Russian Front.

Oakleaves: He became the 119th recipient on 3rd September 1942 as *Oberst* and Commander of Combat Group "Bormann" (76th Bomber Wing).

Ranks:
Fahnenjunker – 17th August 1915
Leutnant – 5th November 1916
Oberleutnant – 31st March 1920
Hauptmann – 1st September 1934
Major – 1st January 1938
Oberstleutnant – 19th July 1940
Oberst – 1st April 1941
Generalmajor – 1st October 1944

Awards:
Iron Cross 2nd Class – 24th July 1916
Iron Cross 1st Class – 13th August 1918
Royal Prussian Pilot's Badge
Honour Goblet for aerial combat
Silesian Eagle Order 1st & 2nd Classes
Cross of Honour for Frontline Combatants
Armed Forces Long Service Award 3rd Class
Luftwaffe Pilot's Badge
Bar to Iron Cross 2nd Class – 22nd September 1939
Bar to Iron Cross 1st Class – 10th October 1939
Combat Clasp for Bombers in Gold
Medal for the Winter Campaign in Russia 1941/1942

Born on 5th November 1897 in Kirchbrack, Holzminden, Lower Saxony, Ernst Bormann volunteered for active service during World War I as a *Fahnenjunker* with 82nd Reserve Infantry Regiment in August 1915. He was commissioned as a *Leutnant* in November 1916 and started his pilots training with 7th Air Replacement Battalion in March 1917, and the following year he was a fully trained pilot with 42nd Air Battalion seeing action briefly in France, and ended the war as a pilot attached to the famous Fighter Wing "Boelcke".

When the war was over he returned to school where he earned his engineering doctorate before volunteering as an instructor with the secret training of Germany's future Luftwaffe. From August 1925 to September 1930 he trained pilots at the airbase near Lipezk in Russia, and in September 1934 he was accepted into the new Luftwaffe with the rank of *Hauptmann*. In April 1935 he became a Squadron Leader with the Bomber

Oberst Bormann standing with an unknown Major wearing the Knight's Cross with Oakleaves. (Author's collection)

Bormann at the front during his time as Commander of Combat Group "Bormann", part of Bomber Wing 76. (Author's collection)

Wing "Boelcke" and in June 1938, now a *Major* he was commander of the 3rd Group of the Fighter Wing "Richthofen".

In November 1938 he was appointed commander of the 1st Group of the Bomber Training Wing in Greifswald, and it was with this command that he saw his first action of World War II. He took part in the early days of the Polish Campaign and then took part in the Battle for France in May 1940. When France fell Bormann was delighted and celebrated his promotion to *Oberstleutnant* in July 1940. From August 1940 to February 1941 he served as the Commander of the pilot School in Geblingen near Augsburg.

When Germany invaded Russia in June 1941, now an *Oberst*, Bormann saw action as the commander of the 76th Bomber Wing when he succeeded *Oberst* Stefan Fröhlich. Here he led his bomber wing, of Ju 88 aircraft, with great success. On 5th October 1941 in recognition of his success in bombing enemy targets he was awarded the Knight's Cross, and in fact he was so successful that from November 1941 until April 1942 he led his own unit, Combat Unit "Bormann" over the skies of Russia. On 3rd September 1942 his success was again recognised when he became the 119th recipient of the Oakleaves.

In February 1943 Bormann was appointed Air Leader Crimea while attached to the 4th Air Fleet, under *Generaloberst* Deßloch. In June 1943 he was relieved of his command for reasons unknown and for the next fourteen months he was assigned to various commands as and when needed, probably in a advisory capacity, on bombing techniques. In October 1944 he was promoted to *Generalmajor* and appointed Commandant of 5th Airport Area, operating from Brünn in Germany until May 1945. Bormann was captured by the Soviets on 10th May and remained in captivity until his release on 9th October 1955. He returned to Germany an ill man and died in Düsseldorf on 1st August 1960 at the age of just sixty-two.

Paul CONRATH
(1896-1979)
General der Fallschirmtruppe

Knight's Cross: Awarded on 4th September 1941, while serving as commanding officer of an Flak Regiment "General Göring" for actions in Russia.

Oakleaves: Awarded on 22nd August 1943 as commanding general of the Panzer Division "HG", becoming the 276th recipient, for actions in Sicily.

Ranks:
Gefreiter– 10th August 1914
Leutnant – 1st March 1917
Polizei-Leutnant – 11th January 1920
Polizei-Oberleutnant – 1st April 1924
Polizei-Hauptmann – 1st April 1928
Polizei-Major – 1st December 1934
Major – 1st April 1935
Oberstleutnant – 1st December 1938
Oberst – 1st March 1940
Generalmajor – 11th July 1942
Generalleutnant – 1st September 1943
General der Fallschirmtruppe – 1st January 1945

Paul Conrath as an Oberst wearing the Knight's Cross. On his left breast pocket is the Iron Cross 1st Class, and Bar to the Iron Cross 1st Class. (Wehrkundearchiv)

Oberst Conrath wearing the Knight's Cross, shown here walking with Göring during an inspection of Conrath's Anti-aircraft Regiment "General Göring" on the eastern Front in 1941-1942. (Author's collection)

Awards:
Iron Cross 2nd Class – World War I
Iron Cross 1st Class – World War I
Cross of Honour for Frontline Combatants
Bar to Iron Cross 2nd Class
Bar to Iron Cross 1st Class
Armed Forces Long Service Award 1st Class
German Cross in Gold – 18th May 1944
AFRIKA Cufftitle

Born on 21st November 1896 in Berlin-Rudow, Paul Conrath joined the army as a war volunteer on 10th August 1914, with 4th Artillery Regiment at Potsdam. He saw action at the front with 44th Reserve Artillery Regiment in October 1914, and two years later he served as battery officer and battalion ordnance officer with 4th Bavarian Field Artillery Regiment. In 1917 he was finally commissioned, seeing action in the Verdun area and the Somme and later Flanders where he won the Iron Cross 1st and 2nd Classes.

Conrath joined the Prussian security police in January 1920, where he served as a section leader, ordnance officer, Battalion Adjutant and later served with the security police in Berlin. In April 1928 he was promoted to *Polizei-Hauptmann* and in 1930 he attended the Prussian Police School in Spandau as an instructor. In May 1933 he was transferred to the State Police in Halle and then in Magdeburg where he remained until June 1934 when he was appointed personnel officer on the staff of the Prussian Prime Minister Hermann Göring.

In April 1935 he joined the Luftwaffe with the rank of *Major* and was appointed adjutant to Göring, who was now the Commander-in-Chief of the Luftwaffe. He made a good impression with Göring and they got on well. In October 1936 Conrath became a battery commander with 12th Flak Regiment and a year later he was appointed the commander of 2nd Battalion of the Luftwaffe Regiment "General Göring". In early 1938 he was appointed Chief adjutant to Göring and in October was promoted to *Oberstleutnant*, and in less than eighteen months he had been promoted to *Oberst*.

On 1st June 1940 Conrath assumed command of the Regiment "General Göring" where he saw action in France, and further action in securing the Romanian oil fields of Ploesti. He then led his unit during the campaign in Russia where on 7th July 1941 he was awarded the Knight's Cross for his outstanding leadership during the tank battle at Dubno. On 21st July 1942 his command was upgraded to Brigade strength and he continued to command it now with the rank of *Generalmajor*, and by October his command had been upgraded to divisional level. In July 1943 his command became the Panzer Division "HG" and was transferred to Italy, where he was to play an important role in the counterattack against the U.S. and British forces during the invasion of Sicily. On 10th July elements of the U.S. 7th and the British 8th Armies, about 12 divisions landed in Sicily. The German and Italian forces were caught by complete surprise and the ten Italian and three German divisions, one of which was Conrath's Panzer Division had to make a quick counterattack. Conrath quickly organised his division into two units, one was infantry and the other mainly tanks. He was anxious to move his forces into action as quickly as possible, and by 6am the next morning the attacks began. Conrath's infantry units attacked westward and joined up with the tank battalions near Pian Lupo, his forces then moved onto their objective at Gela Beach. There was a fierce battle and the Allied attacks were strong and by the second counterattack Conrath had lost a third of his strength. In the end, none of his tanks ever got across the highway bordering Gela Beach. U.S. General Bradley later wrote, "... the enemy turned and ran for the hills." However Conrath had managed to pull his troops back to their original starting point, they would at least keep the Allies occupied while the rest of the German forces fell back to recuperate. However Sicily was soon overrun by the Allies and it was only a matter of time before the rest of Italy would fall. For his efforts and leadership in Sicily Conrath was awarded the Oakleaves, becoming the 276th recipient, on 22nd August 1943. In January 1944 his command was known as "Fallschirm-Panzer Division "Hermann Göring" and redeployed to the Eastern Front. In April 1944 Conrath was appointed Inspector of Parachute Troops and in January 1945 was promoted to *General der Fallschirmtruppe*.

Taken prisoner by the Allies on 8th May 1945, Conrath was soon released and returned home. He died in Hamburg on 15th January 1979.

Otto DEßLOCH
(1889-1977)
Generaloberst

Knight's Cross: Awarded on 24th June 1940 as *Generalmajor* and Commanding General of 2nd Flak Corps after his troops had destroyed over 200 tanks.

Otto Deßloch as General der Flieger wearing the Knight's Cross, in a photograph that was published as a Hoffmann postcard in 1940. (Author's collection)

Knight's Cross with Oakleaves: *Generaloberst* Deßloch was the 470th recipient of the award on 10th May 1944, while Commander-in-Chief of 4th Air Fleet for actions in the Caucasus.

Ranks:
Fahnenjunker – 20th July 1910
Fähnrich – 3rd March 1911
Leutnant – 28th October 1912
Oberleutnant – 16th March 1916
Hauptmann – 1st July 1921
Major – 1st June 1932
Oberstleutnant – 1st October 1934
Oberst – 1st April 1936
Generalmajor – 1st January 1939
Generalleutnant – 19th July 1940
General der Flakartillerie – 1st January 1942
Generaloberst – 20th April 1944

Awards:
Iron Cross 2nd Class – 20th August 1914
Iron Cross 1st Class – 29th September 1915
Royal Bavarian Observers Badge – 1st February 1915
Royal Bavarian Military Order of Service 4th Class with Swords – 19th April 1915
Royal Bavarian Pilots Badge – 8th August 1916
Honour Goblet for aerial combat
Royal Bavarian Military Order of Merit 4th Class + Crown and Swords – 9th November 1917
Royal Bavarian Prince Regent Leopold Jubilee Medal
Wound Badge in Black – 15th May 1918
Cross of Honour for Frontline Combatants
Armed Forces Long Service Award 1st Class
Commemorative Medal of 13 March 1938
Pilot's Badge with Diamonds
Combined Pilot's and Observers Badge in Gold with Diamonds
Bar to Iron Cross 2nd Class – 13th May 1940
Bar to Iron Cross 1st Class – 24th May 1940
Medal for the Winter Campaign in Russia 1941/1942
Wehrmacht Daily Report: 4 August 1943; 9 April 1944; 30 October 1944; 29 November 1944

Otto Deßloch was born on 11th June 1889 in Bamburg, Upper Franconia, the son of a forestry official. After passing his exams he entered the Imperial Army in July 1910 as an officer candidate with 5th Bavarian Chevaulegers Regiment. In October 1912 he was commissioned and served as platoon commander and was serving in this capacity when World War I broke out. On 21st August 1914 just days into the war Deßloch was seriously wounded, during the fighting in the Chateau Salins area, and taken to a military hospital in Viviers where he stayed until October 1914.

On 18th October Deßloch returned to his old regiment, and two months later he started training as an aircraft observer with the Bavarian Flying Replacement Battalion in Schleißheim. A year later he trained as a pilot and on 13th February 1916 he crashed his aircraft and lost four front teeth, and was very lucky to escape without serious injury. In March 1916 he was promoted to *Oberleutnant* and a few months later he began to fly single-seater aircraft – he was a fully fledged fighter pilot. However he wasn't very lucky, in October he was caught in fog while out on a sortie and had to make an emergency landing in neutral Switzerland, on landing he was immediately interned. Released in January 1917 he joined the 16th Fighter Squadron before being transferred to the 35th Fighter Squadron where he

Generalleutnant Deßloch in a striking pose taken shortly after the victory of France, and after his promotion to Generalleutnant in July 1940. (Author's collection)

Deßloch as a Generalleutnant and wearing the Knight's Cross. On the right breast pocket of the uniform is his Pilot's Badge, next to the Iron Cross and Bar. (Author's collection)

was appointed Squadron Leader. He spent the rest of the war flying in various different units and helped with the training of new pilots at two flying schools. He ended the war as commander of the Air Base in Gersthofen, still only an *Oberleutnant*.

He remained in the army after the war and from April 1919 until the beginning of September the same year he was the leader of the volunteer Flying Battalion "Deßloch" attached to Freikorps Epp. After brief spells with the Bavarian Flying Troop and the 23rd Bavarian Signals Battalion, he joined the 46th Infantry Regiment as Signals Officer. In July 1921 he was finally promoted to *Hauptmann* and appointed a Squadron Commander with 17th Mounted Regiment where he remained until April 1926 when he took part in secret training as a pilot in Russia at the secret airbase at Lipezk. He returned to Germany in March 1927 as an adviser with 7th Division in Munich, on the use of aircraft while supporting ground troops.

In December 1933 Deßloch now a *Major* joined the Luftwaffe and was appointed commander of the Pilot School and Air Base Commandant at Cottbus. In April 1935 he was made commander of all pilot schools within the Luftwaffe with the rank of *Oberstleutnant*. In October he was appointed to his first operational command when he became commander of Bomber Wing 155, followed in April 1936 with his transfer to Bomber Wing 158 and his promotion to *Oberst*. He served briefly on the staff of the Reich Air Ministry with special duties attached to Göring's office, and was promoted to *Generalmajor* in January 1939.

At the outbreak of World War II he was appointed commander 2nd Flak Corps, supporting the 22nd Army Corps under *General der Kavallerie* von Kleist in France. In June 1940 Deßloch was awarded the Knight's Cross for his support of Kleist's troops and in recognition of his part in destroying over 200 enemy tanks. In April 1942, now with the rank of *General der Flakartillerie* he was appointed Commander of 1st Flak Corps and at the same time was made Commander of all Luftwaffe forces in the Caucasus. In February 1943 he was appointed commander of all forces in the Kuban area of the Soviet Union, and in September was appointed Commander-in-Chief of the 4th Air Fleet.

On 1st March 1944 Deßloch was promoted to *Generaloberst* and while commanding 4th Air Fleet he became the 470th recipient of the Oakleaves on 10th May 1944. The award came for his exemplary command in the defence of the areas of Saporoshje and Dnjepropetrowsk in February 1943; he had destroyed a total of 842 aircraft on the ground as well as 1,168 tanks. In August he took over command of 3rd Air Fleet from *Generalfeldmarschall* Hugo Sperrle who had been placed on the Reserve list by Hitler. His last appointment of the war was as Commander of 6th Air Fleet which he took over from *Generaloberst* Robert *Ritter* von Greim who had been summoned to Hitler's Bunker to be told he was the new commander-in-chief of the Luftwaffe.

Portrait shot showing a relaxed Deßloch shortly after being promoted to Generaloberst in April 1944. (Wehrkundearchiv)

Captured by U.S. forces on 8th May 1945, Deßloch was held in an internment camp until 1948 when he returned home. During his time in post-war Germany he became involved in horse riding, something which he had done as a young officer shortly after the First World War. He was President of the Riding Association in Munich until his death at the age of eighty-seven on 13th May 1977.

Oskar DINORT
(1901-1965)
Generalmajor

Knight's Cross: Awarded on 20th June 1940 as *Major* and Commander of 2nd Stuka Wing "Immelmann", for air support during the French Campaign.

Oakleaves: He became 21st recipient of the Oakleaves on 14th July 1941 as Commander of the same Stuka Wing, for his continued success in supporting ground troops.

Oskar Dinort in official photographs taken shortly after being promoted to Oberst in September 1941, and showing him wearing the Knight's Cross with Oakleaves. (Wehrkundearchiv)

Ranks:
Gefreiter – 1st May 1919
Fahnenjunker-Unteroffizier – 1st March 1921
Fähnrich – 1st October 1921
Oberfähnrich – 1st November 1922
Leutnant – 1st February 1923
Oberleutnant – 1st February 1928
Hauptmann – 1st April 1934
Major – 1st March 1937
Oberstleutnant – 19th July 1940
Oberst – 1st September 1941
Generalmajor – 1st April 1945

Awards:
Iron Cross 2nd Class – 20th September 1939
Iron Cross 1st Class – 11th May 1940
Royal Bulgarian Bravery Medal 3rd Class with 1 Star
Armed Forces Long Service Award 2nd Class
Combat Clasp for Bombers in Gold
Royal Bulgarian Bravery Medal 3rd Class

Born on 23rd June 1901 in Berlin-Charlottenburg Oskar Dinort entered military service in February 1919, as an officer cadet, with an Assault Instruction Regiment, attached to the Guards Rifle Division. He then spent the next few years serving with the 51st Rifle Regiment and the 2nd Infantry Regiment, finally serving the next eighteen months attached to an Infantry School in Munich. He returned to the 2nd Infantry Regiment in October 1922 and in February 1923 was commissioned as a *Leutnant*, and immediately trained as a pilot.

In February 1928 he was promoted to *Oberleutnant* and in May he took part in secret flying training in Lipezk and when he returned he took part in aerobatics training in Würzburg. The following year he established the world endurance record for gliders and in 1931 he won the National Aeroplane Competition, and three years later he was promoted to *Hauptmann*. In May 1934 he transferred to the Luftwaffe, where he was assigned as Chief of Operations to the 1st Group of Fighter Wing "Richthofen" and in March 1935 was transferred as Chief of Operations on the staff of the Inspector of Fighter and Ground Attack Pilots within the Air Ministry.

Dinort went onto serve with two other fighter squadrons and was promoted to *Major* in March 1937 before transferring to dive bombers in September when he assumed command of the 1st Group of 165th Stuka Wing. The same year he established a new world endurance record for gliders and became a minor celebrity. Prior to the outbreak of war he was assigned as commander of the 163rd Stuka Wing "Immelmann" and from May 1939 until the invasion of Poland he commanded the Airbase at Cottbus. In October 1939 he was appointed Wing Commander of the 2nd Stuka Wing "Immelmann" which had been formed in Cologne and he remained as commander until October 1941 seeing action on virtually every front which included France, Romania, Poland, Greece and finally Russia.

He won the Knight's Cross on 20th June 1940, in recognition of his forty missions when attacking targets from 2nd to 6th June 1939 in Piotrkow and from 17th September 1939 for attacks against Warsaw. He helped with the destruction of the remaining sixteen Polish divisions in the forest of Radom. It was also for the part he played during the campaign in the west in 1940 against such targets as Fort Eben Emael, the Fort of Barchon, de Pontisee, and attacks on Arras, Boulogne, Calais and Dunkirk. He was also awarded the Oakleaves on 14th July 1941 for his success against English ports and shipping in the Channel, where his command sank 87,400 tons of shipping and damaged 68,100 tons of British ships from Greece. During the fighting against the British in Crete his command sunk six destroyers and damaged 66,000 tons of shipping. In September 1941 Dinort was promoted to *Oberst* and in October he was transferred to the Air Ministry as Chief of Staff of the General Air Equipment Branch, and he remained here until February 1942 when he became an advisor on bombing to *Generalfeldmarschall* Milch. In September 1943 he was given another combat command when he was named commander of the *Flieger-Zielgeschwader*, a command that controlled and guided aircraft target units. It was formed in Weidenlupnitz, near Hörselberg, Germany, and he remained in this command until September 1944 when he was named Commander of the 3rd Flying School Division, a position he held until the end of the war.

Dinort was captured by Allied forces on 23rd June 1945 and interned, he was released two years later in June 1947 and returned home. He died in Köln-Riehl on 27th May 1965.

Martin FIEBIG
(1891-1947)
General der Flieger

Knight's Cross: Awarded on 8th May 1940 as *Oberst* and Commander of 4th Bomber Wing "General Wever," for his successful bombing of Rotterdam.

Oakleaves: On 23rd December 1942 Fiebig became the 168th recipient of the Oakleaves as Commanding General of 8th Air Corps, for his outstanding leadership near Minsk.

General der Flieger Martin Fiebig wearing the Knight's Cross with Oakleaves. (Wehrkundearchiv)

Ranks:
Fähnrich – 3rd March 1910
Leutnant – 20th March 1911
Oberleutnant – 18th June 1915
Hauptmann – 20th June 1918
Major – 1st May 1934
Oberstleutnant – 1st May 1936
Oberst – 1st June 1938
Generalmajor – 1st April 1941
Generalleutnant – 1st April 1942
General der Flieger – 1st March 1943

Awards:
Iron Cross 2nd Class – World War I
Iron Cross 1st Class –World War I
Royal Prussian Pilot's Badge – World War I
Cross of Honour for Frontline Combatants
Armed Forces Long Service Award 3rd Class
Bar to Iron Cross 2nd Class – 18th September 1939

Bar to Iron Cross 1st Class – 3rd May 1940
Pilot's Badge
German Cross in Gold - 11th May 1942
Medal for the Winter Campaign in Russia 1941/1942
Combat Clasp for Bombers in Gold

The general made responsible for the failure of the Stalingrad airlift, although he had never believed in its success, Martin Fiebig was born on 7th May 1891 in Rösnitz, Upper Silesia. After his schooling he joined the Imperial Army in March 1910 at the age of eighteen, serving with the 18th Infantry Regiment. In August 1914 he was appointed battalion Adjutant and in August 1915 he was promoted to *Oberleutnant* joining the Army Air Corps. He went on to become a Squadron Leader with 3rd Bomber Wing and in August 1918 he became the commander of the 9th Bomber Wing with the rank of *Hauptmann.*

When the war ended he left the armed forces and remained unemployed for some years apart from a few short periods of part-time employment. In 1926 he joined Lufthansa, which had just been founded in Berlin that same year, where he remained until April 1934. In May he joined the Luftwaffe with the rank of *Major* and was appointed Airbase Commander in Greifswald, in 1936 he was promoted to *Oberstleutnant* and appointed commander of the Bomber School at Faßberg. Appointed Commander of the 253rd Bomber Wing in June 1938 he was at the same time promoted to *Oberst* and led his wing successfully during the Polish and French Campaigns. It was aircraft from his command that bombed Rotterdam and forced the Dutch government to capitulate soon afterwards, it was a terrible act and many thousands died. However at the time of the actual bombing of Rotterdam Fiebig himself was a Dutch prisoner of war, having been shot down during a bombing raid on 10th May 1940. He was soon released after the surrender and rejoined his command. For his leadership and in recognition of the successful bombing of Rotterdam he was awarded the Knight's Cross, officially rendered on 8th May 1940.

On his return to Germany he was assigned to special duties while attached to a Battle Group with Panzer Group Guderian, before being appointed as Chief of Air Flight Security in August 1940. In April 1941 he was promoted to *Generalmajor* and appointed Close-Combat Commander with 4th Air Corps, under Bruno Loerzer in Warsaw, then with Kesselring's 2nd Air Corps. In April 1942 he was promoted to *Generalleutnant* and appointed commander of 1st Air Division on the eastern front under the command of Luftwaffe Command East. In July he became the commander of 8th Air Corps, part of 4th Air Fleet under von Richthofen with its headquarters in Tazinskaja, Oblivskaja, Krimskij am Donez and Itschi-Grammatikova. He

Top: Martin Fiebig as an Oberst somewhere in Berlin shortly after returning from a Dutch prisoner of war camp, June 1940. (Author's collection)

Bottom: Wearing the Knight's Cross with Oakleaves, General Fiebig poses for the camera while in the cockpit of a bomber, probably on his way to inspect his troops, somewhere over Russia. (Author's collection)

later became responsible for the Stalingrad airlift, it was his aircraft that was held responsible for trying to save the stricken 6th Army from defeat by flying in ammunition, food, clothing and flying out the wounded. However right from the start, after Göring had told Hitler that the 6th Army could be supplied by air as long as needed, Fiebig had believed it was an impossible task and had given repeated warnings that the airlift would be in vain. He even telephoned Paulus's chief of staff at Stalingrad, *Generalmajor* Arthur Schmidt and told him it was impossible. He told him that all of Germany's heavy transport planes were already committed to North Africa. However the airlift went ahead in November and the first two days of the proposed airlift, the weather was atrocious. Over the next few days very little actually got through to the 6th Army and on 11th December Paulus reproached Fiebig about the failure, all Fiebig could do was tell Paulus that he had warned against such a plan from the outset and never thought it could have succeeded.

On 23rd December Fiebig became the 168th recipient of the Oakleaves, awarded for his outstanding success with taking Brest, during the battle in Minsk and Smolensk in which his command supported the 45th and 134th Infantry Divisions. He was also recognised for his ground-support efforts in Mzensk-Serpuchow-Meydyn areas during the summer offensive on the eastern front and although it failed for his efforts in the air supply of Stalingrad. On 24th December Fiebig left his headquarters in Tatsinskaya and flew out to Rostov in the last Ju 52 to leave the area. He knew that the 6th Army would be lost, he had always known. On 22nd May 1943 Fiebig took over as the Commanding General of the 10th Air Corps and at the same time was named as Commander of Luftwaffe Command Southeast after the death of its former commander *General der Flieger* Otto Hoffmann von Waldau a few days before. He became responsible for all Luftwaffe components in Greece and part of the Balkans until September 1944 when he went on the reserve list. In February 1945 he returned to active service as the Commanding General of 2nd Air Corps, under the command of *Generaloberst* Otto Deßloch with his headquarters in Biesenthal, near Berlin, and became responsible for the air defence of the region. In April 1945 his command was redesignated as Luftwaffe Command Northeast and became responsible for the air support of Army Group Vistula under the command of *Generaloberst* Gotthard Heinrici who had been ordered by Hitler to defend Berlin against the Russians. Fiebig had under his command, at least on paper: the 1st Air Division, 4th Air Division and the 2nd Air Corps but in reality there was almost nothing left and fuel was almost non-existent. The air support for Army Group Vistula never came but neither did the counter-attack against the Soviet forces.

On 8th May 1945 Fiebig surrendered to British forces and on 6th February 1946 he was handed over to Yugoslavian authorities. He was blamed for the air attack on Belgrade in which 1700 civilians were killed, and as a result was found guilty and sentenced to death on 10th September 1947, and he was executed on 24th October the same year.

Oberst Walter Hagen wearing the Knight's Cross with Oakleaves awarded for his continued success against the enemy. His unit had sunk 210,000 tonnes of shipping, heavily damaged another 306,500 tonnes of shipping, and had sunk four destroyers, three light ships and six cruisers. (Wehrkundearchiv)

Walter HAGEN
(1897-1963)
Generalmajor

Knight's Cross: Awarded for attacks on airfields and bridges during the French Campaign on 21st July 1940 as the Commander of 1st Stuka Group of 186th Stuka Wing.

Oakleaves: Hagen became the 77th recipient of the Oakleaves on 17th February 1942 as *Oberst* and Commander of the 1st Stuka Wing for his success during the Balkans Campaign.

Ranks:
Vizewachtmeister der Reserve – 27th January 1917
Hauptmann – 1st April 1935
Major – 1st February 1938
Oberstleutnant – 1st July 1940
Oberst – 1st April 1942
Generalmajor – 1st July 1944

Awards:
Iron Cross 2nd Class – World War I
Iron Cross 1st Class – World War I
Cross of Honour for Frontline Combatants
Armed Forces Long Service Award 2nd Class
Bar to Iron Cross 2nd Class – 17th September 1939
Bar to Iron Cross 1st Class – 9th June 1940
Combat Clasp for Bombers in Gold
AFRIKA Cufftitle
Wehrmacht Daily Report: 10 November 1940

Born in Kiel on 16th March 1897, Walter Hagen entered the Imperial Army Reserves in June 1915 serving with the 13th Hussar Regiment. He made Platoon Leader in January 1917 and in November of the same year he was transferred to the newly formed flying arm and trained as a pilot, attending the Flying School at Holtenau in May 1918. He served with distinction during the war and was awarded the Iron Cross 1st and 2nd Classes for bravery.

When the war ended Hagen spent time unemployed and working where he could, and in September 1924 he took a job with Junkers as a pilot. In July 1928 he became Flight Captain with the Reichs Organisation of German Aviation Industry and was appointed a test pilot for camouflaged aircraft. In April 1935 he joined the Luftwaffe as a test pilot with the rank of *Hauptmann*. In March 1936 he took a position with the Reich Air Ministry as an advisor for flight security, while serving in this position he was recognised for his skill as a instructor and knowledge of most types of aircraft. In January 1938 he was appointed as a Squadron Commander with the new Testing and Instruction Squadron, and a month later he was promoted to the rank of *Major*.

In November 1938 Hagen was recommended as a new Commander of a Stuka Squadron, and trained with the 186th Aircraft Carrier Squadron until early 1940. He took part in the Western Campaign against France and the Low Countries and was made Commander of the 1st Stuka Wing in June 1940, shortly afterwards he was promoted to *Oberstleutnant*. On 21st July 1940 he was awarded the Knight's Cross for his success in attacks against enemy airfields, for the destruction of bridges and ship yards in the Boulogne area, and was also credited with destroying tanks and railway facilities near Dunkirk. On 17th February 1942, Hagen became the 77th recipient of the Oakleaves in recognition of his continued success against the enemy. His unit had sunk 210,000 tons of shipping and had heavily damaged another 306,500 tons of shipping and had sunk four destroyers, three light ships and six cruisers. In January 1943 he was made Air Leader "Croatia" and continued with his success in the Balkans and in the Mediterranean area. In March he was shot down and spent sometime in the naval hospital in Kiel, returning eventually to active duty in September. In April 1944 he was re-appointed Air Leader "Croatia" succeeding *Generalleutnant* Wolfgang Erdmann and shortly after his promotion to *Generalmajor* in July his command was redesignated Air Command North Balkans in where his unit supported ground assault units.

Hagen's command was again redesignated the 17th Air Division and was made up from the remnants of different units that had been almost destroyed. By March 1945 the situation was almost hopeless and Hagen managed to get most of units to the safety of the Western Allies, and in May he surrendered with his unit to U.S. troops. Hagen spent almost two years in Allied captivity, and he returned home to Kiel where he died on 24th November 1963.

Martin HARLINGHAUSEN
(1902-1986)
Generalleutnant

Knight's Cross: Awarded on 4th May 1940 as *Major* i.G and Chief of the General Staff of the 10th Air Corps, for his support during the fighting in Narvik.

Oakleaves: He became the 8th recipient on 30th January 1941 as *Oberstleutnant* i.G and Chief of the General Staff of the 10th Air Corps for actions in support of operations in North Africa.

Ranks:
Leutnant zur See – 1st October 1927
Oberleutnant zur See – 1st July 1929
Hauptmann – 1st July 1934
Major – 1st August 1938
Oberstleutnant – 30th January 1941
Oberst – 1st July 1942
Generalmajor – 1st December 1942
Generalleutnant – 1st December 1944

Awards:
Iron Cross 2nd Class – 30th January 1940
Iron Cross 1st Class – 3rd February 1940
Armed Forces Long Service Award 3rd Class
Spanish Cross in Gold with Diamonds – 31st May 1939
Combined Pilot's and Observer's Badge in Gold with Diamonds – 17th April 1945
Wound Badge in Black – February 1942
Pilot's Badge with Diamonds
AFRIKA Cufftitle
Wehrmacht Daily Report: 3 November 1940

Martin Harlinghausen was born on 17th January 1902 in Rheda, Westphalia, a senior staff officer who became a successful and highly decorated bomber commander during World War II. His military career began in April 1923 when he entered the German Navy. In October 1927 he was commissioned as a *Leutnant* and assigned to the 1st Torpedo Boat Flotilla as a Watch Officer before being promoted to *Oberleutnant* and being transferred to 2nd Torpedo Boat Flotilla in July 1929. He underwent pilot training in 1931 and then transferred to the Baltic Naval Station a few months later.

He transferred to the Luftwaffe in October 1933 and trained as an aerial observer with 1st Sea Flying Squadron and in July the following year he was promoted to *Hauptmann* and attended the Air War Academy in Berlin. Following staff assignments in the Air Ministry he entered military service with the Condor Legion in Spain and saw action during the Spanish Civil War. He was appointed the Commander of the Sea Reconnaissance Squadron, and later was made Commander of the 88th Bomber and Torpedo Squadron. In May 1939 he was awarded the Spanish Cross in Gold with Diamonds in recognition of his leadership and success in Spain.

In January 1939 Harlinghausen returned to Germany and after completing a training course in Berlin he was assigned as Chief of Operations with Luftwaffe Command II. In August he was appointed to a similar position with the 10th Air Division and in October it was upgraded to the 10th Air Corps, under *Generalleutnant* Hans Geisler, and he became responsible for attacking enemy shipping in the North Sea. On 4th May 1940 Harlinghausen was awarded the Knight's Cross for his effort and support during the difficult operation in Narvik. In December he was appointed both Air Leader of Drontheim and Air Leader "Afrika", becoming responsible for all Luftwaffe activities in those areas. He was awarded the Oakleaves on 30th January 1941 in recognition for his support of the ground troops in North Africa, on the same day he was promoted to *Oberstleutnant*.

His aircraft had caused chaos in the North Atlantic after Harlinghausen had developed a tactical system of attacking ships from a low height, he had concluded that the lower an aircraft was when it approached its target, the higher and clearer its victim's silhouette stood against the horizon. As a result of his tactics his pilots sank fifteen vessels in January 1941 and twenty-two more in February. They also guided U-boats to their targets and it was at this time that Great Britain was threatened with starvation. However the aircraft needed for this type of tactic, the Condor, hadn't been produced in great numbers and soon the British were able to counterattack by equipping more of their merchant shipping with anti-aircraft guns. Aircraft losses became so heavy that Harlinghausen had to abandon his tactics. He continued to patrol the North Atlantic himself until November 1941 when his He 111 was hit by anti-aircraft fire over the Irish Sea. He managed to nurse his badly damaged aircraft to the French coast, where he crash-landed and was rescued and he was badly injured and spent almost three months in hospital. He was discharged from hospital in January 1942 and was appointed Plenipotentiary for Air Torpedo Affairs in the Air Ministry and was responsible for the formation of the first Torpedo Wing, deployed to the North Sea. In July 1942 he was promoted to *Oberst* and in December of the same year he was made *Generalmajor* and Air Leader in Tunisia. Here he was responsible for the support of the ground forces under the command of General Walter Nehring,[33] and his command consisted of 140 aircraft, including 109 fighters and dive-bombers.

Oberstleutnant Martin Harlinghausen, shortly after being awarded the Knight's Cross with Oakleaves. (Wehrkundearchiv)

In February 1943 he led the 2nd Air Corps and for the remaining half of that year he was on the reserve list. In September 1944 he was appointed Commanding General of 14th Air Region in Wiesbaden, and in December was promoted to *Generalleutnant*. His last command of the war was as Commander of Luftwaffe Command West. He surrendered to the Allies in May 1945 and was released in September 1947. He entered the Bundeswehr in August 1957 as a *Generalmajor* and in October he was appointed Commanding General of Luftwaffe Group North. In July 1959 he was promoted to *Generalleutnant* and in December 1961 he retired after a difference of opinion with the Secretary of Defence Strauß. He lived in retirement until his death in Gütersloh on 23rd March 1986.

Hubertus HITSCHHOLD
(1912-1966)
Generalmajor

Knight's Cross: Awarded on 21st July 1940 as *Hauptmann* and Commander of the 1st Group of the 2nd Stuka Wing "Immelmann" in recognition of his success as a Stuka pilot in France.

Oakleaves: He became the 57th recipient on 31st December 1941 as *Major* and Commander of the same unit, for his successful sinking of three British destroyers near Crete.

Ranks:
Gefreiter – 1st April 1930
Fähnrich – 1st June 1933
Leutnant – 1st March 1934
Oberleutnant – 1st September 1935
Hauptmann – 1st January 1939
Major – 1st July 1940
Oberstleutnant – 1st February 1943
Oberst – 1st July 1943
Generalmajor – 1st January 1945

Awards:
Armed Forces Long Service Award 4th Class
Pilot's Badge
Commemorative Medal for 1st October 1938 with Bar "Prague Castle"
Iron Cross 2nd Class – 15th September 1939
Iron Cross 1st Class – 11th May 1940
Combat Clasp for Bombers in Gold
Wound Badge in Black

Hubertus Hitschhold was on of the youngest and most successful Luftwaffe Stuka pilots to reach the rank of General during World War II. He was born on 7th July 1912 in Kurwien, East Prussia and volunteered for service in the Reichswehr in April 1930. He had been selected early in his career to take part in the secret flying lessons at the Flying School at Schleißheim

Major Hubertus Hitschhold was the 57th recipient of the Knight's Cross with Oakleaves for his successful sinking of three British destroyers near Crete. (Wehrkundearchiv)

An official photograph taken shortly after Hitschhold was awarded the Oakleaves. This image was used for a postcard sold for propaganda purposes. (Author's collection)

between April 1930 and March 1931, and took part in the secret pilot training in Lipezk, Russia. In March 1934 he was commissioned as a *Leutnant* and by the end of the year had transferred to the newly formed Luftwaffe.

Hitschhold joined the 2nd Stuka Wing "Immelmann" in October 1934 and began his training as a dive-bomber pilot. He soon showed that he was a natural and in September 1935 was promoted to *Oberleutnant* and a year later was appointed Squadron Leader. In September 1939 during the invasion of Poland he became one of the first pilots to engage in combat against ground targets. He was soon appointed as Group Commander and became very successful during the campaigns against France, Belgium and Holland. Promoted to Hauptman in January 1939 he was promoted to *Major* in July 1940 and on the 21st July was awarded the Knight's Cross for his success against ground targets, which had included the destruction of an enemy squadron on the ground and for attacks on the Fort at Ebel Emael. In the area around Gemblaux he had destroyed enemy positions making way for a tank assault.

After seeing action in the English Channel against British shipping he saw action in the Balkans, and then Crete where he became even more successful. On 22nd May 1941 during a breakthrough near Rupelpass against the British evacuation fleet in the Bay of Megera during the Crete Campaign he sank the British destroyer *Greyhound*, and the following day he sank the destroyer *Kelly* and *Kashmir*. In June 1941 he was transferred to the Russian Front, and during the first day of the campaign he was shot down and nearly killed, but he was rescued after a daring mission. In October 1941 he left the frontline to take up a new position as the commander of the Stuka School in Wertheim, where he passed on some of his techniques and experience to the young trainee Stuka pilots. In December he returned to active service at the front and continued with his success against enemy ground targets, he had by this time been responsible for the sinking of three British destroyers, three cruisers, and had heavily damaging ten transport ships and various other shipping, in fact he had sunk a total of 164,000 shipping tons. In recognition of his achievements and for his success he became the 57th recipient of the Oakleaves on 31st December 1941.

In June 1942 Hitschhold was appointed Commander of the 1st Ground Attack Wing, where he flew the Focke Wulf 190 equipped with new close support bombing equipment. In February 1943 he was promoted to *Oberstleutnant* and in June was appointed Air Leader "Sardinia", and shortly afterwards he was promoted to *Oberst*. In November 1943, after the death of Dr. Ernst Küpfer in an air crash, Hitschhold was named as the new Commander of the air-to-ground Support Flyers. He was now responsible for the production of aircraft used in supporting ground troops and under his direction the production of Ju 87, the Stuka dive-bomber was suspended and instead the Focke-Wulf 190 was put into full production. He undertook this new appointment with skill and determination but he really wanted to fly again, but he never would, this would be his last wartime appointment. Promoted to *Generalmajor* on 30th April 1945, he went into Allied captivity when he surrendered to the Americans on 8th May.

Generaloberst Alexander Löhr seen here in an official Hoffmann photograph taken shortly after his promotion. (Wehrkundearchiv)

Released from captivity in June 1947, he returned to Germany where he became a successful businessman. However he died suddenly of a heart attack on 10th March 1966 in Söcking, East Prussia, he was only fifty-three years old.

Alexander LÖHR
(1885-1947)
Generaloberst

Knight's Cross of the Iron Cross: Awarded on 30th September 1939 as *General der Flieger* and Commander of 4th Air Fleet, for his success in supporting the ground troops during the invasion of Poland.

Knight's Cross with Oakleaves: *Generaloberst* Löhr became the 705th recipient of this award on 20th January 1945 as Commander-in-Chief of Army Group E.

Ranks:
Leutnant – 18th August 1906
Oberleutnant – 1st November 1911
Hauptmann – 1st March 1915
Major – 1st July 1920
Oberstleutnant – 1st January 1921
Oberst – 20th July 1928
Generalmajor – 25th September 1934
Generalleutnant – 24th March 1938
General der Flieger – 25th March 1939
Generaloberst – 3rd May 1941

Awards:
Austro-Hungarian Military Jubilee Cross 1848-1908
Austro-Hungarian Commemorative Cross 1912-1913
Knight's Cross of the Austro-Hungarian Order of "Franz Joseph" with War Decoration
Austro-Hungarian Military Service Cross 3rd Class with the War Decoration and Swords
Austro-Hungarian Military Service Medal in Bronze with Swords
Austro-Hungarian Military Service Medal in Silver with Swords
Royal Bavarian Military Service Order 4th Class with Swords
Austro-Hungarian Wound Medal
Austrian Golden Service Badge
Austrian War Commemorative Medal with Swords
Cross of Honour for Frontline Combatants
Armed Forces Long Service Award 4th Class
Wound Badge in Silver
Pilot's Badge with Diamonds
Combined Pilot's and Observer's Badge in Gold with Diamonds
KRIM Shield
Iron Cross 2nd Class – 12th September 1939
Iron Cross 1st Class – 25th September 1939
KRETA Commemorative Shield
Romanian Order of the "Michael the Brave" 3rd Class – 19th September 1941
Romanian Order of the "Michael the Brave" 2nd Class – 29th July 1942
Medal for the Winter Campaign in Russia 1941/1942
Wehrmacht Daily Report: 12 April 1941; 23 April 1941; 8 August 1941; 11 October 1941; 12 October 1941; 19 May 1942; 20 May 1942; 30 May 1942; 26 June 1944; 19 January 1945; 9 May 1945

Photograph taken just before the outbreak of World War II of General der Flieger Alexander Löhr. He was at this time Commander of the 4th Air Fleet, and would command this unit in Poland in September 1939. (Author's collection)

The former Commander-in-Chief of the pre-war Austrian Air Force, and a general who wasn't promoted to *Generalfeldmarschall* because of Hitler's suspicions of the Austrian ruling class. Alexander Löhr was born in Turnu-Severin, Romania on 20th May 1885, the son a ship captain who had worked for a steam ship company along the Danube, his mother was an orthodox Russian from naval circles, whose father had served as a naval officer in the Black Sea Fleet. The young Alexander spent his youth in Turnu-Severin and went to school at a German evangelist school, it was more Prussian than anything and only German was spoken, so Löhr had to learn the language quickly. At home however his father spoke French mainly, but sometimes German and his mother only spoke Russian. In later life Löhr could speak fluently in German, French, Russian and Romanian and he could also speak well in Hungarian, Italian and even Serbian.

Löhr entered the Austrian army in August 1906 as a *Leutnant* and spent four years in the 85th Infantry Regiment as a Platoon Leader. In September 1910 he attended War School in Vienna before being appointed to a staff position with the

Army Observer unit. At the outbreak of World War I he was serving as a General Staff officer with 58th Infantry Troop Division and shortly afterwards was transferred to the Austro-Hungarian War Ministry where he remained until the end of the war. After the war he was responsible for the structure of the Austrian air defence with the rank of *Hauptmann* and by 1928 had been promoted to *Oberst* with the responsibility for the civil air protection of Austria. In 1934 after being promoted to *Generalmajor* he was appointed Air Protection Commander and in July 1935 was appointed commander of the Austrian Air-Force. After the Anschluss in 1938 he was appointed by Hitler as the Commanding General and Commander-in-Chief of the Luftwaffe in Austria with the rank of *Generalleutnant*.

In early 1939 Löhr was appointed Commanding General of the Luftwaffe Command "Ostmark" with its headquarters in Vienna. In March Löhr was promoted to *General der Flieger* and his command was upgraded to 4th Air Fleet and took a leading role in the Polish Campaign where it supported Army Group South in the main thrust of the German invasion. He was awarded the Knight's Cross on 30th September 1939 in recognition of the success of his command in supporting ground forces during the invasion. In March 1941 Löhr's Air Fleet had a supporting role again, this time during the invasion of Greece. Löhr was responsible for the support of the 12th Army during the invasion of Greece and the 2nd Army during the invasion of Yugoslavia, *Generalfeldmarschall* Sigmund Wilhelm List[34] commanded the ground forces. As a result of this massive support imitative Löhr's command was hurriedly reinforced with 576 aircraft deployed from Sicily, France and Germany, by April Löhr controlled just over 1000 aircraft.

On 6th and 7th April 1941 Löhr's command bombed Belgrade in an attempt to break all resistance, as a result more than 1,700 people were killed. Belgrade would get its revenge – eventually. On 15th April 1941 Löhr submitted a plan for the airborne attack on Crete; the plan appealed very much to Göring, and was approved by Hitler although minor changes were later made by Kurt Student. During the invasion the overall commander of air and ground forces was Löhr and Student was made his subordinate. In May 1941 Löhr was promoted to *Generaloberst* and became the Commander-in-Chief of the 12th Army in the Balkans.

On 1st January 1943 Löhr was appointed Commander-in-Chief "South-East" and became Air Commander in Italy, and

Generaloberst Löhr as Commander of the 4th Air Fleet, and at the same time commander-in-chief of the 12th Army, seen here in spring 1942. On his right is Admiral Karlgeorg Schuster, commander-in-chief of Naval Group Command "South", and to Löhr's left is Generalleutnant (later General der Luftnachrichtentruppe) Walter Surén, Signals Leader with 4th Air Fleet. (Author's collection)

Below: Löhr attends a meeting with the commander of the 5th Air Corps General der Flieger Robert Ritter von Greim in early 1942 on the Russian Front. (Author's collection)

at the same time was appointed Commander-in-Chief of Army Group "E" in the Balkans. He commanded over 300,000 men at this time and it seems inconceivable as to why he was never promoted to the rank of *Generalfeldmarschall*, but Hitler was suspicious of the Austrian officer class and Löhr was overlooked more than once. He was the only Luftwaffe general except for Kesselring, and the only Austrian general except for Lothar Rendulic[35] to become a theatre commander. He was an efficient air commander but had little knowledge of ground warfare. In September 1944 von Weichs started to counter attack against the increased strength and engagements of Tito's partisans and along with Löhr's support from his aircraft they managed over a period of four months to push Tito's men back across Greece, Albania and Yugoslavia and almost to the Alps. For achieving this outstanding act both Löhr and von Weichs were awarded the Oakleaves to their Knight's Cross, Löhr on 20th January and von Weichs the day before.

On 8th May 1945, the day of Germany's surrender there were still about 150,000 of Löhr's men in Yugoslavia and Löhr knew that Tito's partisans wouldn't take any notice of Germany's surrender and spare the lives of his men. He approached the British for help but this was rejected. There followed fierce fighting and finally on 15th May Löhr surrendered to save further blood shed, the Germans had lost over 95,000 men and 209,000 had surrendered including Löhr himself.

After his capture he faced trial as a war criminal, he was held responsible for the bombing of Belgrade and because he successfully recruited Croatian units to serve in the German army and together with his anti-guerrilla operations he was hated by Tito's Communists. At the end of the trial Löhr was found guilty of war crimes and sentenced to death by firing squad on 16th February 1947, the execution being carried out in the court yard of the main prison in Belgrade on 26th February.

General der Fallschirmtruppe Eugen Meindl with his adjutant during a meeting with his commanders during the Normandy Campaign. (Author's collection)

Eugen MEINDL
(1892-1951)
General der Fallschirmtruppe

Knight's Cross: Awarded on 14th June 1941 as *Generalmajor* and Commander of 1st Parachute Air Landing Assault Regiment for actions in Crete.

Oakleaves: Awarded as *General der Fallschirmtruppe* and Commanding General of 2nd Parachute Corps on 31st August 1944, as the 564th recipient.

Ranks:
Fahnenjunker – 27th July 1912
Fähnrich – 22nd March 1913
Leutnant – 17th February 1914
Oberleutnant – 18th April 1917
Hauptmann – 1st August 1924
Major – 1st April 1934
Oberstleutnant – 1st August 1936
Oberst – 1st April 1939
Generalmajor – 1st January 1941
Generalleutnant – 1st February 1943
General der Fallschirmtruppe – 1st April 1944

Awards:
Iron Cross 2nd Class – 18th July 1915
Iron Cross 1st Class – 17th January 1916
Imperial and Royal Austrian Order of the Iron Crown 3rd Class with War Decoration
Knight's Cross First Class of the Order of the Zähringen Lion with Oakleaves and Swords
Cross of Honour for Frontline Combatants
Turkish Iron Half-Moon Badge (The Gallipoli Star)
Armed Forces Long Service Award 1st Class
Bar to Iron Cross 2nd Class – 22nd October 1939
Bar to Iron Cross 1st Class – 10th June 1940
Narvik Shield – 10th November 1940
Wound Badge in Black – 25th October 1941

Medal for the Winter Campaign in Russia 1941/1942 – 9th August 1942
German Cross in Gold – 27th July 1942
Luftwaffe Parachutist Badge
KRETA Cufftitle – 25th May 1943
Wehrmacht Daily Report: 9 June 1941

Eugen Meindl was a talented commander and highly decorated officer who played a major role during the invasion of Poland, Denmark, Norway and Crete. He was born on 16th July 1892 in Donaueschingen and he joined the Artillery in July 1912 as a *Fahnenjunker.* He went on to serve with the 2nd Unter-Elsässisches Field Artillery Regiment No.67 where he served as battery officer. In February 1914 he was commissioned as a *Leutnant* and continued to serve with the same Regiment throughout the war. When the war ended Meindl remained in the 100,000 man army of the Reichswehr serving as a battery officer with the 13th Light Artillery and 5th Artillery Regiments.

In October 1924, now a *Hauptmann* Meindl was transferred to the staff of Wehrkreis Command V in Stuttgart where he was made responsible for training. A year later he was transferred to the 5th Division where he served as a staff officer. From October 1926 until September 1933 Meindl served in various staff positions within the Reichswehr. In October 1930 he served as adjutant of the 5th Artillery Regiment under its commander *Oberst* Ludwig Beck.[36]

On 15th October 1935 *Major* Meindl was appointed Commander of the 1st Battalion, 5th Artillery Regiment, and in August 1936 he was promoted to *Oberstleutnant.* Appointed commander of the 112th Mountain Artillery Regiment, part of *Generalmajor* Eduard Dietl's 3rd Mountain Division. He took part in the invasion of Poland and then served on the Western Front until he was transferred to play a major role in the invasion of Denmark and Norway. On 9th April 1940 men of Dietl's 3rd Mountain Division, about 2000 men were transported by destroyers to Narvik where they soon captured the town. The German destroyers were attacked by the British and sunk the survivors managed to get to Narvik in their life-boats and in doing so strengthened Dietl's defences. Narvik was vital in the Norwegian Campaign; an Anglo-French force had landed north of the town and along with Norwegian troops had started to attack Dietl's position. The fighting went on for weeks and the Allies recaptured Narvik on 28th May. Dietl's command was forced back against the Swedish border, low on supplies and ammunition, Dietl needed reinforcements quick. On 7th June Meindl volunteered to jump with the paratroopers, although he had no previous parachute training, with other reinforcements into Norway to help Dietl's beleaguered troops. However the

Meindl as a Generalmajor with Generalmajor Alfred Sturm, commander of the 2nd Fallschirmjäger Regiment. At right is the commander of the 3rd Fallschirmjäger Regiment Oberst Richard Heidrich. (Wehrkundearchiv)

British had evacuated their forces from Norway because of the collapse of France and on 8th June 1940 Dietl's troops re-entered the town of Narvik ending the Norwegian Campaign. Meindl had played his part of course; Dietl's troops were still desperate for food, and ammunition.

In August 1940 Meindl was rested and attached to the Commander of the Military District in Salzburg, and in September he was named as Commander of the 1st Parachute Air Landing Assault Regiment, known as Assault Regiment "Meindl". In January 1941 he was promoted to *Generalmajor* and in May was named as the Commander of Battle Group West during the airborne invasion of Crete. On 20th May he led his Assault Regiment and Battle Group into Crete, and landed in the area around Maleme airfield. Meindl parachuted in with his men and was wounded by machine-gun fire shortly after landing; his command was temporary handed over to *Oberst* Hermann-Bernhard Ramcke who along with 550 German reinforcements parachuted in the next day. Ramcke led the Battle Groups in the fierce fighting, and although it suffered heavy losses they captured their objective on 27th May. Although not able to lead his men, Meindl still took part in the assault and he was recognised for his bravery when he was awarded the Knight's Cross on 14th June 1941.

Generalleutnant Meindl in conversation with Generalfeldmarschall Erwin Rommel during Rommel's inspection of Normandy in early-1944. (Author's collection)

On 26th February 1942 Meindl's command was upgraded to divisional strength and Meindl was transferred to the Eastern Front. He now found himself under the command of the German Army once again, along with several other Luftwaffe commands. His division which had been formed from 1st Fallschirmjäger Air Landing Assault Regiment had been established in Northern Russia to control five Luftwaffe field regiments and a signals battalion. The main bulk of his command fought on the right flank of the Demjansk salient while the other part fought in the south in relief of the Cholm Pocket. In May the German forces finally broke the encirclement and the Luftwaffe ground troops played a major role in breaking through the Russian perimeter and taking the town. It was a great success and the Germans kept hold of the town until 1944; every soldier that took part in the 105 days of encirclement was awarded the Cholm Shield, including Meindl. In October Meindl returned to Germany as the Commanding General of the 13th Air Corps and here Meindl supervised the formation of twenty-two new Luftwaffe Field Divisions. In July 1943 he was appointed Inspector of the Luftwaffe Field Formations and was promoted to *Generalleutnant*.

On 5th November 1943 Meindl was made Commanding General of the 2nd Fallschirmjäger Corps, which had been formed from the 13th Air Corps, and by February 1944 came under the control of the Commander-in-Chief West in Paris. Meindl was promoted to *General der Fallschirmtruppe* on 1st April 1944 and his command was placed at the disposal of *Generaloberst* Friedrich Dollmann's 7th Army, and Meindl now oversaw the formation and training of the 3rd and 5th Parachute Divisions. Following the Allied landings in Normandy on 6th June 1944, the 2nd Parachute Corps along with the 3rd Parachute Division and the 17th SS-Panzer Grenadier Division "Götz von Berlichlingen" was deployed to counter attack the U.S. forces in the area around St. Lô. Following an unsuccessful bid to recapture Carentan in mid-June, Meindl's corps remained heavily engaged with U.S. forces in the St. Lô area until mid August. On the evening of 6th August 1944, *Oberstleutnant* von Kluge, the son of *Generalfeldmarschall* Günther von Kluge, the Commander-in-Chief of Army Group B and Commander-in-Chief West, visited Meindl's command post. He passed on his father's order for the 2nd Parachute Corps "to hold its position" so a major German panzer force could counter attack against the U.S. forces the following morning. Meindl was astonished by the order and told the young *Oberstleutnant* that he felt Normandy could no longer be held because his troops were exhausted and if *Generalfeldmarschall* von Kluge knew the true situation which included the allied superiority in the air he wouldn't issue such an order. Meindl went on to say that the attack by the panzers would fail unless it was done at night. The next morning the attack went ahead and Meindl's prediction was accurate. The panzer force was held by stubborn U.S. resistance and by the weight of the overwhelming Allied air superiority. After about five miles, the mauled panzer divisions ran out of fuel. Hitler would not allow a retreat and that order led to the encirclement and virtual destruction of two German armies in the Falaise Pocket. Meindl said later, "It was heart breaking to stand and watch!"

Right: Meindl, wearing the Knight's Cross and German Cross in Gold, with his immediate superior General der Fallschirmjäger Kurt Student, 1943. (Author's collection)

Below: Official photo of General der Fallschirmtruppe Meindl while in U.S. captivity in May 1945. He spent several months in various different prison camps before being released in September 1947. (Roger James Bender)

The 5th Panzer Army and the 7th Army had almost been encircled between the advancing American and Anglo-Canadian forces, the remnants of Meindl's corps now held a narrow corridor that allowed thousands of German troops to escape. On the night of 19th-20th August, Meindl and his chief of staff, *Oberst* Ernst Blauensteiner,[37] each led an assault group in a last chance bid to escape from the Falaise Pocket. After a desperate march through enemy territory they finally broke free of the encirclement. For his bravery and leadership during this breakout Meindl was awarded the Oakleaves on 31st August 1944 becoming the 564th recipient.

After the near disaster of the Falaise Pocket Meindl and what was left of his corps was refitted in Germany and then sent out to the Netherlands, to the Nijmegan area in September 1944 to counter the Allied airborne and ground offensive. He was assigned to *Generaloberst* Kurt Student's 1st Parachute Army, and Meindl's corps engaged the Allies on the Groesbeek Heights southeast of Nijmegan during the battle. The counter-attack against the Allies was a success and many prisoners were taken and the rest of the Allied forces were pushed back across the border. Later Meindl's corps saw action in Germany itself against a far superior Anglo-American force around the Siegfried Line, or "West Wall"[38] and suffered a heavy defeat.

Meindl finally surrendered to U.S. forces on 25th May 1945, and spent time in several different prison camps not being released until 30th September 1947. He spent the remaining years of his life an active member of the "Knight's Cross Association" and during this time he convinced the association that he had been awarded the Swords to his Knight's Cross and produced documents to prove the fact and his name was added to the recipient listings. However a recent investigation by a leading German historian has found that the award was never approved, and no award document was ever issued and subsequently no award was ever rendered. Eugen Meindl died in Munich on 24th January 1951.

Kurt Leopold PFLUGBEIL
(1890-1955)
General der Flieger

Knight's Cross: Awarded on 5th October 1941 as *Generalleutnant* and Commanding General of 4th Air Corps for actions on the Eastern Front.

Oakleaves: He became the 562nd recipient on 27th August 1944 as *General der Flieger* and Commander-in-Chief of 1st Air Fleet for actions near Kharkov.

Ranks:
Fahnenjunker-Unteroffizier – 13th August 1910
Fähnrich – 7th November 1910
Leutnant – 23rd November 1911
Oberleutnant – 21st October 1915
Hauptmann – 1st April 1921
Rittmeister – 1st October 1926
Major – 1st November 1931
Oberstleutnant – 1st August 1934

Oberst – 1st April 1936
Generalmajor – 1st January 1939
Generalleutnant – 1st September 1940
General der Flieger – 1st February 1942

Awards:
Iron Cross 2nd Class – 14th September 1914
Iron Cross 1st Class – 7th October 1916
Knight's Cross of the Royal Prussian Hohenzollern House Order with Swords – 17th April 1918
Knight's Cross of the Royal Saxony Military Order of St. Heinrich – 27th July 1915
Royal Prussian Pilot's Badge
Cross of Honour for Frontline Combatants
Armed Forces Long Service Award 1st Class
Commemorative Medal for 1st October 1938
Bar to Iron Cross 2nd Class – 7th October 1939
Bar to Iron Cross 1st Class – 15th June 1940
Observer's Badge
Medal for the Winter Campaign in Russia 1941/1942
Kurland Cuff-title
Wehrmacht Daily Report: 31 October 1941; 30 May 1942; 11 April 1944; 1 January 1945

General der Flieger Kurt Pflugbeil wearing the Knight's Cross, shown here as Commanding General of the 1st Air Fleet. (Wehrkundearchiv)

Kurt Leopold Pflugbeil was born in Hütten near Königstein, Elbe on 9th May 1890, he joined the infantry as a *Fahnenjunker* with 10th Royal Saxony Infantry Regiment in April 1910. When World War I broke out he was serving as a company officer with the same regiment and was promoted to *Oberleutnant* in October 1915. In December he volunteered as a trainee pilot with the 10th Flying Replacement Battalion, within a month he was flying combat missions with the 24th Squadron on the Western Front. In December 1916 he was appointed Squadron Leader of the 27th Squadron and on 23rd April 1918 he was shot down, finally returning to active duty in July.

After the war he joined the Border Police until September 1920 when he joined the 37th Reichswehr Infantry Regiment, he was promoted to *Hauptmann* in April 1921 when he was made Company Commander with the 11th Infantry Regiment. He transferred to the Calvary in October 1926 and joined the staff of the 11th Mounted Regiment, part of the 4th Division. In August 1927 he underwent secret aerial bombing training in Russia, Sweden and Italy before returning to Germany with the staff of the 3rd Division. In November 1931 he was promoted to *Major* and appointed Commander of the 2nd Transport Battalion where he served until June 1933 when he retired from active service.

In July 1933 he took part in secret training activities with Germany's new air force where he helped to train new pilots. In October 1933 he joined the Luftwaffe and was immediately assigned as a trainer at the new Luftwaffe pilot school at Lechfeld. In March 1934 he was made director of the High-Altitude Centre of the German Flight Weather Service, in fact this was a cover name for the Secret Bomber Flying School and here pilots were trained on high altitude bombing. In August 1934 he was promoted to *Oberstleutnant*, and in March 1935 he returned to Lechfeld when he was appointed commander of the Greater Bomber Flying School. In October he was made Inspector of Bomber Flying and in April 1936 was promoted to *Oberst*.

On 4th July 1938 he was appointed Deputy Commander of the 4th Air Division, under *Generalmajor* Hellmuth Bieneck[39] and later under *General der Flieger* Alfred Keller with its headquarters in Munich. Promoted to *Generalmajor* in January 1939, Pflugbeil took over as Commander of Air Region Command Belgium and Northern France when its formed commander *Generalmajor* Fritz Löb[40] was killed in an air crash near Brussels. On 20th August 1940 he was named as Commanding General of the 4th Air Corps, he led this command with great skill and his superior's soon noticed that he was a very capable commander. Promoted to *Generalleutnant* in September 1940 he led his troops with great success during the Russian Campaign. For his outstanding command in the southern sector of the Russian Front he was awarded the Knight's Cross on 5th October 1941, his unit had successfully supported the infantry divisions under the command of *General der Infanterie* Erich von Manstein.[41]

On 2nd February 1942 Pflugbeil was promoted to *General der Flieger* and in September 1943 he was appointed Com-

mander-in-Chief of the 1st Air Fleet and continued to lead his troops with skill. In May 1942 Pflugbeil and his troops had been given a special notice of appreciation by the High Command of the Wehrmacht for his outstanding support during the armies attack near Charkov. His name was mentioned again during another Wehrmacht Report in April 1944, when he was praised for his command and support of the ground forces near Ostrow. On 27th August 1944 Pflugbeil was named as the 562nd recipient of the Oakleaves in recognition of his outstanding leadership and of his defence against superior Soviet forces. In January 1945 his command was retreating across the southern part of the eastern front picking up remnants of other commands on the way and in February he was almost surrounded by the Soviets near Haserpoth in the Kurland. In April his command was re-designated Luftwaffe Command "Kurland" and along with his chief of staff *Oberstleutnant* Paul-Werner Hozzel[42] he defended this area until May 1945 when he finally surrendered to Soviet troops.

He was sentenced to twenty-five years hard labour in a Soviet prison camp and wasn't released until January 1954. The years inside a Soviet prison had taken its toll on Pflugbeil; a good percentage of his men never returned home, his chief of staff Hozzel however survived. Kurt Pflugbeil died on 31st May 1955 in Weende, Göttingen.

Generalmajor Pflugbeil as acting commander of the 4th Air Division and Inspector of Bomber Flying during a pre-war inspection tour in February 1939. Left to right back row: Oberleutnant Böhm; Hauptmann Aveves; Hauptmann Haubereit; Major Ulbricht and Hauptmann Weber. Front row: Hauptmann Fick; Major Köhler adjutant of the 3rd Air Division (later Generalmajor), Generalmajor Pflugbeil; Major Hentschel (later Generalmajor) Chief of Operations of the 3rd Air Division and Kapitänleutnant Bremicken. (Author's collection)

Wolfgang Friedrich Wilhelm Siegfried PICKERT (1897-1984)
General der Flakartillerie

Knight's Cross: Awarded the Knight's Cross on 11th January 1943 as *Generalmajor* and Commander 9th Flak Division for his courage and daring on the Eastern Front.

Oakleaves: He became the 489th recipient of the Oakleaves on 5th June 1944 as *Generalleutnant* and Commanding General of the 3rd Flak Corps, for his success during the defence of the Kuban Bridgehead.

Ranks:
Gefreiter – 27th January 1915
Unteroffizier – 22nd March 1915
Vizewachtmeister – 12th May 1916
Leutnant der Reserve – 7th October 1916
Leutnant – 3rd April 1918
Oberleutnant – 31st July 1925
Hauptmann – 1st February 1931

Major – 1st January 1936
Oberstleutnant – 1st December 1938
Oberst – 1st June 1940
Generalmajor – 1st October 1942
Generalleutnant – 1st November 1943
General der Flakartillerie – 1st March 1945

Awards:
Iron Cross 2nd Class – 2nd November 1916
Iron Cross 1st Class – 13th April 1918
Wound Badge in Black – World War I
Baltic Cross 1st & 2nd Classes
Cross of Honour for Frontline Combatants
Armed Forces Long Service Award 1st Class
Combined Pilot's and Observer's Badge
Bar to Iron Cross 2nd Class - 1940
Bar to Iron Cross 1st Class – 1940
German Cross in Gold – 7th December 1942
Anti-Aircraft Badge of the Luftwaffe
Wehrmacht Daily Report: 24 April 1944; 8 May 1944

Wolfgang Pickert as a Generalleutnant wearing the Knight's Cross with Oakleaves. (Author's collection)

Wolfgang Friedrich Wilhelm Siegfried Pickert was born on 3rd February 1897 in Posen and volunteered for service with the 73rd Field Artillery Regiment at the outbreak of war in August 1914. He served on both the Western and Eastern Fronts being commissioned as a *Leutnant* in the Reserves and he went onto win both the Iron Cross 1st and 2nd Classes. In March 1916 he was attached to the Field Artillery Flying School at Jüterbog and in December he served as an observation officer with the 2nd Battalion of the 93rd Field Artillery Regiment. In September 1917 he was appointed Regimental Adjutant and later served as battery officer with the 73rd Regiment. He remained in the Reichswehr after the war serving in various artillery posts and being promoted to *Oberleutnant* in July 1925.

In October 1934 he served as an instructor at the Flak Artillery School in Döberitz and Wustrow and in April 1935 he transferred to the Luftwaffe with the rank of *Hauptmann*. He spent the next two years as advisor in the office of the Inspector of Flak Artillery within the Air Ministry before being appointed Commander of a battalion in the 49th Flak Regiment. Promoted to *Major* in January 1936 he was made Chief of Staff of the Air Region Command XIII in July 1938 and before the end of the year he was promoted to *Oberstleutnant*.

In September 1940 Pickert was appointed Chief of Staff to *Generaloberst* Hubert Wiese the commander of the 1st Flak Corps in Neuwied. By October the 1st Flak Corps was re-designated Luftwaffe Command "Centre" with its headquarters in Berin-Wannsee and here it prepared for the planned attack on Russia. On 25th June 1942 Pickert succeeded *Generalleutnant* Otto Wilhelm von Renz[43] as commander of the 9th Flak Division. In January 1942 the division had been moved to Southern Russia and was responsible for supporting Army Group South until May when it was attached to the 6th Army. When Pickert arrived in Russia in June he immediately re-organised his forces and made ready for the attack on Stalingrad. Promoted to *Generalmajor* in October, by December his headquarters had moved nearer the front and was located in Stalingrad itself, his men supported the ground troops the best they could but the Russians dominated the skies. By February 1943 most of the 9th Flak Division had been destroyed, but most of the headquarters staff, which included Pickert, had been flown out of the beleaguered city before it fell. It was later reformed in the Crimea and Pickert remained as its commander until April 1944 when most of the division was destroyed, and again Pickert was one of the very few survivors. He was awarded the Knight's Cross on 11th January 1943 for his support of the 6th Army at Stalingrad and for his leadership during the Russian Campaign, and this was followed by his promotion to *Generalleutnant* in November 1943.

Pickert took over as Commander of the 3rd Flak Corps from *Generalleutnant* Johannes Hintz on 28th May 1944 shortly after Hintz had been killed in a road accident. His headquarters were in Paris but from D-Day they were moved to Normandy. On 5th June Pickert was awarded the Oakleaves for his leadership and aerial cover during the fighting around the Kuban Bridgehead in the Caucasus which resulted in high losses on both sides. In August he took part in the battle of the

Falaise Pocket when the Allies tried and almost encircled the 7th Army under *General der Panzertruppe* Heinrich Eberbach[44] and the 5th Panzer Army under *SS-Oberstgruppenführer* Paul Hausser,[45] part of Army Group B under *Generalfeldmarschall* von Kluge. Pickerts command supported the ground troops the best they could but within a days the Pocket had almost completely been encircled by British, Canadian and American troops. The losses were again heavy and about 100,000 German troops managed to escape including Pickert who seemed to have a charmed life, around 50,000 German troops were taken prisoner and 10,000 had been killed. The remnants of the 3rd Flak Corps withdrew to Germany and by September 1944 they were back in action at Cochem, near Koblenz supporting Army Group B once again.

In December 1944 the 3rd Flak Corps took part in the Battle of the Bulge in the Ardennes Forest in Belgium before being moved in early February 1945 to Bonn where they supported the 5th Panzer Army. In March Pickert was promoted to *General der Flakartillerie* and was transferred to the Office of the Commander-in-Chief of the Luftwaffe just before his corps was destroyed in the Ruhr-Pocket. He surrendered to U.S. forces on 8th May 1945 and was handed over to the British where he remained in captivity until his release on 5th January 1948. He died on 19th July 1984 in Weinheim near Mannheim, Germany.

Wolfram *Freiherr* von RICHTHOFEN (1895-1945) *Generalfeldmarschall*

Knight's Cross: Awarded on 17th May 1940 as Commanding General of the 8th Air Corps for actions during the Western Campaign.

Knight's Cross with Oakleaves: On 17th July 1941 von Richthofen became the 26th recipient of the award while serving as commander of the same unit for actions in the Balkans.

Ranks:
Fähnrich – 22nd March 1913
Leutnant – 19th June 1914
Charakter als Oberleutnant – 29th February 1920
Leutnant – 1st November 1923
Oberleutnant – 31st July 1925
Hauptmann – 1st February 1929
Major – 1st June 1934
Oberstleutnant – 20th April 1936
Oberst – 23rd January 1938
Generalmajor – 1st November 1938
Generalleutnant – skipped
General der Flieger – 19th July 1940
Generaloberst – 1st February 1942
Generalfeldmarschall – 16th February 1943

General der Flieger Wolfram Freiherr von Richthofen in full dress uniform wearing the Knight's Cross. He is shown shortly after the defeat of France in July 1940. (Author's collection)

Awards:
Iron Cross 2nd Class – World War I
Iron Cross 1st Class – World War I
Spanish Cross with Swords in Gold with Diamonds – 6th June 1939
Bar to the Iron Cross 2nd Class – 12th September 1939
Bar to the Iron Cross 1st Class – 25th September 1939
Pilot's Badge
Cross of Honour for Frontline Combatants
Armed Forces Long Service Award 4th Class
Combined Pilot's and Observers Badge in Gold with Diamonds
Spanish Pilot's Badge
Luftwaffe Cuff-title "Jagdgeschwader Frhr. v. Richthofen Nr.1 1917/1918"
Krim Shield
KRETA Commemorative Shield
Medal for the Winter Campaign in Russia 1941/1942
Wehrmacht Daily Report: 20 June 1940; 21 October 1941; 19 May 1942; 20 May 1942; 2 July 1942; 12 August 1942; 20 March 1943

Born on 10th October 1895 on the estate of Gut Barzdorf, near Striegau in Lower Silesia, Wolfram *Freiherr* von Richthofen was probably the most able Luftwaffe commander next to Kesselring. He was an aggressive man, very flamboyant and just like Kesselring an optimist. He was the young cousin of the famous World War I fighter ace, Manfred von Richthofen, the Red Baron. After attending cadet school in Berlin he became an officer candidate with 4th Hussar Regiment and in March 1913 he was commissioned as a *Leutnant*. He went on to see action on both fronts and remained with the same regiment until he decided to train to be a pilot. On 2nd March 1918 he qualified and was assigned to squadron of his famous cousin, the 1st Fighter Wing "Richthofen", where he remained until the end of the war. He served under Hermann Göring in the last few months of the war, shooting down eight enemy aircraft and becoming an ace.

Richthofen studied engineering after the war at a technical school in Hannover before joining the Reichswehr in November 1923, receiving his diploma in engineering the following year. From 1929 until 1932 he served as military attaché in Rome and helped to develop the training of future pilots of Germany by organizing their training with the Italian air force. When the Luftwaffe was officially created he became a member and took a position in the Air Ministry where in June 1934 became subordinate to the head of the Technical Department *Oberst* Wilhelm Wimmer.[46]

In January 1937 he was appointed as Chief of Staff to Hugo Sperrle in the Condor Legion in Spain. He was a close-combat specialist and made careful study of close support with the army, this worked well in Spain and it was in this role that he would later make a name for himself. In November 1938 Richthofen was promoted to *Generalmajor* and appointed commander of the Condor Legion succeeding Sperrle, he stayed on in Spain serving as an advisor to General Franco, returning to Germany in May 1939 to assume the command of the Condor Legion.

At the outbreak of World War II while commanding the 8th Air Corps he directed the attempt to destroy Warsaw from the air. During the invasion of France while commanding the same Corps, while under the command of Sperrle once again, he made easy work of the French armies after he perfected the use of dive-bombers on ground troops to terrifying effect. It was for actions in France and his leadership that he was awarded the Knight's Cross on 17th May 1940, followed shortly by his promotion to *General der Flieger* in July. If the invasion of England had succeeded Richthofen would have been responsible for the Folkestone area, where he would have had to support the landings made by *Generaloberst* Ernst Busch's army. Richthofen himself had doubts about the success of an invasion of England and was later proved correct.

Top: Studio portrait photograph of von Richthofen clearly wearing his Luftwaffe cufftitle "Jagdgeschwader Frhr. v. Richthofen Nr.1 1917/1918." (Wehrkundearchiv)

Bottom: Von Richthofen and his adjutant standing with members of the Bulgarian armed forces, circa 1941. (Author's collection)

In May 1941 von Richthofen's command was transferred to Greece under the command of *Generaloberst* Alexander Löhr. During the German attack von Richthofen commanded 500 aircraft against the RAF's seven squadrons with some eighty aircraft. It was for his outstanding leadership while in Greece that von Richthofen became the 26th recipient of the Oakleaves. In September while still commanding 8th Air Corps he was transferred to Russia along with Bruno Loerzer's 2nd Air Corps and *Generalleutnant* Walther Axthelm's 1st Flak Corps to make up Kesselring's 2nd Air Fleet in support of von Bock's Army Group Centre. During October 1941 Richthofen saved the day several times with fierce attacks by his Stuka dive-bombers on the Russian amour and mortar batteries when XLI Panzer Corps was in serious trouble. It was thanks to von Richthofen that the corps was saved and would fight another day.

In February 1942 von Richthofen was promoted to *Generaloberst* and made commander of 4th Air Fleet when he took an active part in trying to keep the encircled 6th Army at Stalingrad supplied from the air. Although he never really believed the 6th Army could be kept well supplied he tried his best. For seventy-two days and nights, until 2nd February 1943 when all ground resistance ended, his command had delivered 8,350 tons of supplies, at a cost of 488 aircraft and just over 1000 aircrew. Despite this failure von Richthofen was promoted on 17th February 1943, becoming the youngest *Generalfeldmarschall* at the age of forty-seven to serve in Hitler's Wehrmacht. His last command was that of Commander-in-Chief of the 2nd Air Fleet. On 27th October 1944 von Richthofen became ill and was granted extended leave, he was later diagnosed with a brain tumor and retired from active duty on 28th November, and put on the Führer Reserve. He died whilst being held in American captivity at Bad Ischl on 12th July 1945; he was forty-nine years old.

A very nice portrait photograph of Oberst Wilhelm Schmalz wearing the Knight's Cross with Oakleaves, and on his right breast pocket he displays the German Cross in Gold. (Author's collection)

Wilhelm SCHMALZ
(1901-1983)
Generalleutnant

Knight's Cross: Awarded on 28th November 1940, as a *Major* while commanding the 1st Battalion, 11th Infantry Regiment for actions during the French Campaign.

Oakleaves: He became the 358th recipient on 23rd December 1943 as commander of a Special Purpose Grenadier Brigade attached to the Panzer Division "Hermann Göring" as *Oberst* for action in Sicily.

Ranks:
Fahnenjunker-Unteroffizier – 1st April 1919
Fähnrich – 1st October 1921
Oberfähnrich – 1st October 1922
Leutnant – 1st February 1923
Oberleutnant – 1st February 1928
Rittmeister – 1st April 1934
Major – 1st April 1939
Oberstleutnant – 1st February 1942
Oberst – 1st October 1942
Generalmajor – 1st May 1944
Generalleutnant – 30th January 1945

Awards:
Armed Forces Long Service Award 1st Class
Iron Cross 2nd Class – 14th September 1939
Iron Cross 1st Class – 16th October 1939
Medal for the Winter Campaign in Russia 1941/1942
Hermann Göring cufftitle
German Cross in Gold – 8th February 1942
Luftwaffe Ground Assault Badge

Wilhelm Schmalz spent most of his career serving in the army where he was highly decorated and continued to be decorated when he transferred to the Luftwaffe towards the end of World War II. He was born on 1st March 1901 in Reußen, Weißenfels, and on completing his schooling and joined the Reichswehr at the age of eighteen. In January 1920 he joined the 15th Mounted Regiment and in October 1921 he was made an officer cadet. He later served as a platoon commander and by February 1928 he had reached the rank of *Oberleutnant*. He was a member of the Olympic Selection Team of the Cavalry School at Hannover and a member of the German Military Riding School.

In April 1934 Schmalz was promoted to *Rittmeister* and a few months later he joined the 16th Mounted Regiment, and in October 1935 he was appointed company commander with the 2nd Motorcycle Rifle Battalion. After a two year period working in the War Ministry Schmalz returned to active duty with the 11th Cavalry Rifle Regiment in October 1938. On 1st April 1939 he was promoted to the rank of *Major* and appointed Battalion Commander with the same Regiment and was involved in the first attack on Poland in September 1939. Schmalz led his unit during the French campaign in May 1940 and on 28th November he was awarded the Knight's Cross for actions in France while attached to the 9th Panzer Division.

In November he took over command of the 59th Motorcycle Rifle Battalion and saw action in the Balkans, and in February 1942 he was promoted to *Oberstleutnant* and appointed commander of the 11th Panzer Grenadier Regiment. After being promoted to *Oberst* in October 1942 he was transferred to Mont-de-Marsan in southern France, where in January 1943, he was appointed commander of a group that was part of the new Hermann Göring Division, an elite unit that took the name of the *Reichsmarschall* and became almost as fanatical as the Waffen-SS. In May 1943 Schmalz transferred to the Luftwaffe and took command of a Special Purpose Grenadier Brigade of the Panzer Division "Hermann Göring". His brigade fought a stubborn resistance in Sicily during the Allied invasion of Italy, and for his leadership and personal bravery during the defensive battles against Allied forces Schmalz was awarded the Oakleaves on 23rd December 1943.

Above: Generalmajor Wilhelm Schmalz as Commander of the Fallschirm-Panzer Division "Hermann Göring". (Wehrkundearchiv) Right: A studio portrait of Generalmajor Wilhelm Schmalz clearly wearing the Knight's Cross with Oakleaves, and German Cross. Also note the "Hermann Göring" cufftitle on his right sleeve. (Wehrkundearchiv)

In April 1944 Schmalz took over as commander of the Fallschirm-Panzer Division "HG", and soon after the Hermann Göring Division withdrew from Italy and was placed on the Reserve List. It made ready to refit in France but the allies launched their Gustav Line offensive against Cassino and broke out of the Anzio Beachhead and the HG Division was rushed in to counterattack. It managed to slow down the allied advance if only temporarily but enough to enable a large part of the 14th Army to escape. After the fall of Rome the division was sent to Poland with orders to counter the advancing Soviet Army. It was here that the HG Luftwaffe Division received a commendation from *Generalfeldmarschall* Walther Model[47] for its gallant defensive actions near Warsaw in August 1944. Why Schmalz wasn't recommended for the Swords is a surprise since the division he was commanding was given such high praise. Göring was informed and sent his own message of congratulations, but it wasn't all good news for the *Reichsmarschall*, during the heavy fighting in Russia, Heinrich Göring, his nephew was killed in action.

In October 1944 the division was expanded and made into a Panzer Corps and Schmalz remained as the commander now with the rank of *Generalmajor*. The corps was made up from a new panzer grenadier division and personnel from the Luftwaffe which included two signal battalions and a medium artillery battalion. However the mounting casualties were now outnumbering the replacements and Schmalz was forced to take infantry personnel with little or no combat experience. With the heavy fighting and the lack of experienced troops the new replacements did nothing to help stem the tide of the Allied advance.

In January 1945 Schmalz was promoted to *Generalleutnant* and his Fallschirm Panzer Division was transferred from East Prussia to Litzmannstadt where it fought along side the Großdeutschland Panzer Corps. The Panzer Division was assigned to the Großdeutschland Panzer Corps under direct leadership of *General der Panzertruppe* Georg Jauer,[48] and in March near Konigsberg, Saxony where it achieved its last victory of the war by destroying the 1st Polish Division. On 8th May Schmalz surrendered to the U.S. forces and went into captivity, he was accused of war crimes by an Allied War Court in Italy but charges were later dropped and he was acquitted. He was finally released in 1950, and lived out his retirement until his death in Braufels, Hesse on 15th March 1983.

Ludwig Schulz as an Oberstleutnant wearing the Knight's Cross. (Wehrkundearchiv)

Ludwig SCHULZ
(1896-1966)
Generalmajor

Knight's Cross: Awarded as *Major* and commander of 1st Group, 76th Bomber Wing on 16th August 1940 for bravery during the French Campaign.

Oakleaves: He became the 747th recipient on 19th February 1945 as *Generalmajor* and commander of the Air War School 5 in Breslau and Battle Group Commander in Fortress Breslau, awarded for his leadership and prevention of a Soviet breakthrough near the Oder River.

Ranks:
Gefreiter – 17th June 1915
Unteroffizier der Reserve – 27th August 1915
Vizefeldwebel der Reserve – 21st December 1915
Leutnant der Reserve – 31st August 1916
Leutnant – 30th September 1920
Hauptmann – 1st February 1935
Major – 1st August 1937
Oberstleutnant – 19th July 1940
Oberst – 1st April 1942
Generalmajor – 1st October 1944

Awards:
Iron Cross 2nd Class – World War I
Iron Cross 1st Class – World War I
Cross of Honour for Frontline Combatants

Armed Forces Long Service Award 4th Class
Bar to Iron Cross 2nd Class – 14th May 1940
Bar to Iron Cross 1st Class – 23rd May 1940
Commemorative Medal of 1st October 1938
Luftwaffe Honour Goblet – 8th July 1940

Ludwig Schulz was born on 4th August 1896 in Lissa, Posen and entered the German army as a reservist with the 227th Reserve Infantry Regiment in September 1914. He served with the 72nd Infantry Regiment almost the entire war and was commissioned as a *Leutnant* in August 1916. In February 1918 he transferred to the Flying Corps and after the surrender he joined the Freikorps "Neufville" in December and remained a member until he retired in September 1920.

After being in and out of work during his civilian life he joined the Luftwaffe in February 1935 as a *Hauptmann* and served for a time in the Air Ministry. In May he was transferred to Münster where he joined an Air Group and took the chance to familiarize himself with the new aircraft of the Luftwaffe. He was appointed a Squadron Commander with the 153rd Bomber Wing in February 1936, and a year later he became a tactics instructor at the 5th Air War School. Promoted to *Major* in August 1937 Schulz was transferred to the General Staff of the 2nd Air Corps in September 1938. In November 1939 he transferred to Crailsheim where he was appointed a Group Commander with the 76th Bomber Wing, under *Oberst* Stefan Fröhlich. He was wounded in June 1940 and while recovering he was promoted to *Oberstleutnant* and appointed commander of the 5th Air War School in Rogensberg-Obertraubling. On 16th August 1940 he was awarded the Knight's Cross for his bravery and leadership during the French Campaign. His command had successfully attacked the French near the Maginot Line and supported the ground troops during the attack in Dunkirk as well as the airfields in the area around Paris. Schulz remained the commander of the 5th Air School until early 1945, but was also appointed Air Base Commander at Breslau-Schöngarten and was made a Battle Group Commander when he served in Russia. In April 1942 Schulz was promoted to *Oberst* and in October 1944 he was promoted to the rank of *Generalmajor*. On 19th February 1945 Schulz became the 747th recipient of the Oakleaves, while serving as Battle Group Commander in Fortress Breslau, awarded for his leadership and for the prevention of a Soviet breakthrough near the Oder River.

In February 1945 Schulz was made High Commander of all Air War Schools with his headquarters in Dresden he now controlled over eight schools in the areas of Dresden, Gatow, Oschatz, Fürstenfeldbruck, Tulln, Straubing and Erfurt. However by late March the Luftwaffe had little aircraft and no fuel, and the trainee pilots from the air schools had nothing to fly. On 8th May 1945 Schulz was captured by U.S. forces and remained in captivity until May 1947. Ludwig Schulz died on 10th December 1966 in Mülheim in the Ruhr.

Hans Seidemann as Air Leader "Afrika" in August 1942, wearing the Knight's Cross. (Wehrkundearchiv)

Hans SEIDEMANN
(1902-1967)
General der Flieger

Knight's Cross: Awarded on 20th March 1942 as *Oberst* i.G. and Chief of the General Staff of the 2nd Air Fleet for actions in Russia.

Oakleaves: He became the 658th recipient on 18th November 1944 as *Generalleutnant* and Commanding General of the 8th Air Corps again for actions in Russia.

Ranks:
Fähnrich – 1st November 1921
Oberfähnrich – 1st November 1922
Leutnant – 20th December 1922
Oberleutnant – 1st August 1927
Hauptmann – 1st April 1934
Major i.G. – 1st August 1936
Oberstleutnant i.G. – 1st June 1939
Oberst i.G. – 1st October 1940

Generalmajor – 24th August 1942
Generalleutnant – 1st January 1944
General der Flieger – 1st March 1945

Awards:
Iron Cross 2nd Class – 25th September 1939
Iron Cross 1st Class – 20th May 1940
German-Spanish Cross with Swords
Armed Forces Long Service Award 2nd Class
AFRIKA Cuff-title
Wehrmacht Daily Report: 20 February 1944

Hans Seidemann was born on 18th January 1902 in Garlin, Westpriegnitz and was educated at the Royal Cadet School at Potsdam and later Lichterfelde. In January 1919 he joined the Freikorps and spent most of the year fighting against the Communists in the many street fights. In September he joined the elite Prussian 9th Infantry Regiment at Potsdam where he won his commission in December 1922. He later served as a platoon leader and was promoted to *Oberleutnant* in August 1927, within six months he had left the army. In April 1929 Seidemann took part in the secret flying training in Russia and when he returned to Germany in October he rejoined the 9th Infantry regiment. In October 1933 he underwent training as a staff officer and the following year he transferred to the Luftwaffe with the rank of *Hauptmann*. In July 1936 he was appointed to the Luftwaffe General Staff and the following month he was promoted to *Major*. Appointed Group Commander with the Instruction Wing "Greifswald", he was appointed Chief of Staff to the Condor Legion in December 1938 under the command of *Generalmajor* Wolfram von Richthofen, and saw action during the Spanish Civil War. Seidemann returned to Germany with the rank of *Oberstleutnant* and was appointed Chief of Operations of a Special Purpose Air Group attached to Army Group South.

In December 1939 this unit became the 8th Air Corps and Seidemann was appointed its Chief of Staff under his old commander from Spain von Richthofen. He went onto see action during the French Campaign and in August 1940 he was transferred to the 2nd Air Fleet in Brussels where he took over as Chief of Staff. He served under *Generalfeldmarschall* Kesselring in Warsaw before the 2nd Air Fleet moved to Smolensk on the Eastern Front in October 1941.

On 20th March 1942 Seidemann was awarded the Knight's Cross for his part in the successful support of Army Group centre during the campaign in Russia. Seidemann was promoted in August 1942 to *Generalmajor* and appointed Air Leader "Afrika" when he succeeded General Otto Hoffmann von Waldau. When Rommel's army reached Tunisia in February 1943 Seidemann's command was renamed Air Leader "Tunis". Although eventually defeated by the overwhelming superiority of the Allied forces Air Command "Tunis" was still resisting when the German front collapsed in May 1943. Seidemann flew out to Sicily with his pilots, his aircraft and ground crew just before the front fell. As soon as he arrived back in Europe his command was dissolved and he was sent back to Russia to take command of his old unit, the 8th Air Corps. In July 1943 Seidemann was made responsible for supporting the 4th Panzer Army during the battle of Kursk. He established his headquarters near Mikojanowka, southwest of Bjelgorod, and was responsible for 1,180 aircraft, and his actions reduced the advance of the Soviets in North Ukraine. He was promoted to *Generalleutnant* in January 1944, and the following month he saw action in Winniza and in May his forces saw action over Stanislau, Lemberg and Lublin and in July over Gorno. On 18th November Seidemann became the 658th recipient of the Oakleaves in recognition of his support of ground troops during the Russian Campaign.

Generalmajor Hans Seidemann as Air Leader "Afrika", talking to members of his staff at his headquarters, late 1942. (Author's collection)

In January 1945 Seidemann's command moved to Schweidnitz, Poland and became known as Luftwaffe Command Silesia. In February his headquarters moved again to Hermannstädtel, near Pardubitz in Czechoslovakia, and the following month Seidemann was promoted to *General der Flieger*. In April his command changed again and became known as Luftwaffe Command VIII with it's headquarters in Senftenberg on the Czech-German border, now under the command of the 6th Air Fleet. On 9th May 1945 Seidemann surrendered to the

Generalleutnant Seidemann as Commanding General of the 8th Air Corps during a tour of inspection where Seidemann gave out medals and took time to speak to the ordinary soldier. Seidemann was well respected among his men and officers alike and would often spend longer than usual speaking to them, building up moral and boasting their confidence. (Author's collection)

allies and spent the next two years in a prison camp. When he returned to his family in Braunschweig in 1947 he began to look for work, as he wasn't granted a pension. He soon found employment with a local metal sheet factory and rose to become a sales manager, apparently a very good one. He still loved flying and flew with a local flying club at the weekend, and helped to train young pilots. On 21st December 1967 while out Christmas shopping with his family he collapsed after a heart attack and was rushed to hospital where he died the same day. He was buried with military honours on 28th December and his funeral was full of ex-servicemen many of whom had served under him.

Major Walter Storp wearing the Knight's Cross with Oakleaves shortly after the award ceremony. He was awarded as Wing Commander of 210th Ground Attack Wing in July 1941. (Author's collection)

August Franz Walter STORP
(1910-1981)
Generalmajor

Knight's Cross: Awarded as *Hauptmann* and Commander of the 2nd Group, 76th Bomber Wing on 21st October 1940 for low-level attacks against targets in the English Channel.

Oakleaves: He became the 22nd recipient on 14th July 1941 as *Major* and Wing Commander of 210th Ground Attack Wing for actions on the Eastern Front.

Ranks:
Fähnrich zur See – 1st January 1930
Oberfähnrich zur See – 1st April 1931
Leutnant zur See – 1st October 1932
Oberleutnant – 1st October 1934
Hauptmann – 1st October 1938
Major – 1st November 1940
Oberstleutnant – 1st February 1943
Oberst – 1st August 1943
Generalmajor – 1st November 1944

Awards:
Armed Forces Long Service Award 4th Class
Pilot's Badge
Iron Cross 2nd Class – 2nd October 1939
Iron Cross 1st Class – 26th April 1940
Honour Goblet of the Luftwaffe – 20th October 1940
Wound Badge in Black – World War II
Combat Clasp for Bombers in Gold
Wehrmacht Daily Report: 27 September 1940; 4 November 1940

Walter Storp was born on 2nd February 1910 in Schnecken-Elchniederung, East Prussia and he joined the Navy in April 1928. After attending training school at Mürwik he served on board the cruisers "*Emden*" and "*Köln*", and was commissioned as *Leutnant* in October 1932. Storp transferred to the Luftwaffe exactly two years later with the rank of *Oberleutnant* serving with 1st Air Squadron. In May 1936 he served on board the armoured ship "*Admiral Scheer*" and five months later he was transferred to the Luftwaffe test stations at Travenmünde, Tarnewitz and in early 1938 to Rechlin where he served as a test pilot.

In October 1938 Storp was promoted to *Hauptmann* and transferred to the Luftwaffe Operations Staff as an advisor on tactics, and at the same time he was made chief pilot to *Generalmajor* Hans Jeschonnek, the Luftwaffe's Chief of Staff. He took part in the Polish Campaign and in January 1940 he flew with the 4th Bomber Wing "General Wever" and from August 1940 he served as commander of the 2nd Group, 76th Bomber Wing. He flew Ju 88A aircraft from the airbase in Creil, France and then from Ansbach in Germany and returning to France in 1941. In April 1940 he sank the Norwegian destroyer *"Aegir"* and the night before Dunkirk he sunk a troop transporter. On 27th September his bomber group was mentioned in the official Wehrmacht Report it stated, "... the crew of the aircraft under the command of Hauptmann Storp took part in daring low-level raids over England with great skill and courage ... their commander will be rewarded..."[49] His group managed to sink 12,000 tonnes of shipping in the English Channel and made successful attacks against military positions which included railway junctions in northern France and they were successful in night operations in France and Belgium. On 21st October 1940 Storp was awarded the Knight's Cross for his command and courage during the low-level bombing of enemy targets during the Western Campaign, and shortly after he was promoted to *Major*.

In April 1941 Storp formed a low-level ground attack bomber wing of Bf 110 fighter-bombers, and first saw action on the Eastern Front in May 1941 as the 210th Ground-Attack Bomber Wing. He led this wing again with great success while supporting the ground troops of General Guderian's 2nd Panzer Group. He organised and led low-level ground attacks against airfields, anti-aircraft emplacements, tanks, railway lines and bridges in the areas around Minsk, Orscha, Schatalowka, Witebsk and Seschtschinskaja. For this Storp was awarded the Oakleaves on 14th July 1941, becoming the 22nd recipient. In October Storp was transferred to the Luftwaffe Operations Staff in Berlin where he remained until August 1942 when he jumped at the chance of commanding a bomber wing once again. He took over the 6th Bomber Wing from *Oberstleutnant* Walter Bühring in September and saw action over France and in June 1943 over Italy and the Mediterranean area. He had been promoted to *Oberstleutnant* in February 1943 and by August he had risen to the rank of *Oberst*, and shortly afterwards he was appointed Bomber Leader of the Mediterranean.

Storp was appointed Chief of Staff of the 4th Air Corps in December 1943, where he remained for six months under the command of *General* Rudolf Meister, with its headquarters in

Walter Storp with Hauptmann Hermann Hogeback, both wearing the Knight's Cross with Oakleaves – Hogeback was later awarded the Swords in January 1945. Next to him on the right is Oberleutnant Rudolf Puchinger, Squadron Leader of the 8th Squadron, 76th Bomber Wing. (Wehrkundearchiv)

Below: Another photograph of Storp (centre) with Rudolf Puchinger, and Hermann Hogeback. (Wehrkundearchiv)

the Ukraine and later Brest-Litovsk in Poland. In June 1944 he took command of the 76th Bomber Wing where he saw action over Italy and later from its headquarters in Alt-Lönnewitz, Germany. In October Storp was made General of Bomber Flying, an important sounding title but the majority of Germany's bombers were out of action, nevertheless he reorganised flying groups and used his great experience and skill to do the best job he could, the following month he was promoted to *Generalmajor*. His last command of the war came in February 1945 when he took over command of the 5th Air Division under the control of the Commanding General of the Luftwaffe in Norway, *Generalleutnant* Ernst-August Roth.

Storp surrendered to British troops on 8th May 1945, and spent almost three years in captivity, being released in February 1948. Walter Strop one of the most able bomber commanders of the war died on 9th August 1981 in Goslar.

Kurt Arthur Benno STUDENT
(1890-1978)
Generaloberst

Knight's Cross: Awarded on 12th May 1940 as Commanding General of the 7th Air Division for the successful air and land operations at Eben-Emael on the Belgium border.

Knights Cross with Oakleaves: Student became the 305th recipient of the Oakleaves on 27th September 1943 for actions in and around Sicily and for the rescue of Mussolini from Italian partisans.

Ranks:
Fähnrich – 3rd March 1910
Leutnant – 20th March 1911
Oberleutnant – 18th June 1915
Hauptmann – 20th June 1918
Major – 1st January 1930
Oberstleutnant – 1st January 1934
Oberst – 1st October 1935
Generalmajor – 1st April 1938
Generalleutnant – 1st January 1940
General der Flieger – 29th May 1940
General der Fallschirmtruppe – 1st August 1940
Generaloberst – 13th July 1944

Awards:
Knight's Cross of the Royal Prussian Hohenzollern House Order with Swords – 5th June 1917
Iron Cross 2nd Class – 26th September 1914
Iron Cross 1st Class – 29th August 1915
Royal Prussian Pilots Badge – 27th February 1914
Knight's Cross of the Saxony Order of Albert with Swords – 21st June 1915

Generaloberst Kurt Student wearing the Knight's Cross with Oakleaves, September 1943. (Author's collection)

Wound Badge in Black – World War I
Honour Goblet for aerial combat
Flier's Commemorative Badge – 10th September 1919
Military Pilot's Badge – 21st May 1935
Armed Forces Long Service Award 1st Class
Bar to Iron Cross 2nd Class – 20th September 1939
Bar to Iron Cross 1st Class – 20th September 1939
Cross of Honour for Frontline Combatants
Commemorative Medal for 1st October 1938 with Bar "Prague Castle"
Wound Badge in Silver – World War II
Pilot's Badge with Diamonds
KRETA Commemorative Shield
Combined Pilot's and Observer's Badge in Gold with Diamonds

Born on 12th May 1890 in Birkholz, a village in the area of Züllichau-Schwiebus now a region of Poland, Kurt Student was the son of the owner of a large estate. In March 1910 he and his four brothers entered cadet school and the young Kurt was assigned to 1st Jäger Battalion, part of the Graf York von Wartenburg Regiment. In March 1911 he was commissioned as a *Leutnant* and two months later he underwent pilot training at the Military Flying School in Berlin, and gained his licence in August 1913. In February 1914 he was attached to Flying Station Posen where he became a reconnaissance pilot, then a bomber pilot, and finally as a fighter pilot with 9th Fighter Squadron. In June 1915 he was promoted to *Oberleutnant* and in October of the same year he was appointed commander of 9th Squadron. He went onto score a total of six confirmed aerial victories and was awarded the Knight's Cross of the Royal Prussian Hohenzollern House Order with Swords in June 1915 in recognition of his skill as a fighter pilot. In May 1917 he was wounded in aerial combat and after spending time in hospital, was appointed commander of 3rd Fighter Group operating on the western front, he failed to improve on his tally of six air victories and ended the war with the rank of *Hauptmann*.

In October 1919 he joined the Reichswehr and was attached to the Reich War Ministry in the Inspectorate of Weapons and Equipment. For the next few years he had various different assignments, he was for a time attached to the Army Peace Commission, he became a consultant in what was called "Flight Technology" and in October 1921 following a crash in a sports glider he was assigned to the staff of the Replacement Battalion of 2nd Infantry Regiment. In January 1929 he appointed commander of 1st Battalion of the same Infantry Regiment, and a year later he was promoted to the rank of *Major*.

He transferred to the Luftwaffe in September 1933 and was assigned to the Reich Air Ministry and was soon promoted to *Oberstleutnant*. Appointed commander of the test centre for flying equipment and at the same time was appointed as airfield commandant in Rechlin. In September 1935 he commanded 3rd Air Regiment which took part in the Reich Party Day at Nuremberg. In March 1937 he was appointed commander of the Aviation Weapons School and became Chief of Staff to the commander of Flying Schools in the Reich. He was promoted to *Generalmajor* in April 1938 and appointed commander of the 7th Air Division; it was from this time that he became

Student as General der Fallschirmtruppe wearing the Knight's Cross. He is seen here in both photographs as the Commander of the 11th Air Corps, 1941. (Author's collection and Wehrkundearchiv)

totally devoted to the concept of airborne warfare. On 1st July 1938 Student was appointed as the commander of all German parachute troops, he now oversaw its creation and in September the first parachute division was formed – Student made sure his new division was well equipped with air-landed artillery, flak and anti-tank guns.

When World War II began with the invasion of Poland, Student's troops were not used because Hitler didn't want to comprise the existence of his new weapon. In October 1939 Hitler met with Student and told him of his ideas and what he had in mind for his new airborne troops. Hitler told him that their first mission was to take the Belgian fortress of Eben Emael then to seize the bridges across the Albert Canal and hold them until army units arrived. So Student formulated a plan of which Hitler agreed. Together with *Oberst* Bruno Bräuer of the 1st Parachute Regiment, Students troops landed near the fortress of Eben Emael in gliders. Student used 500 glider troops and on 10th May 1940, four thousand parachutists dropped around The Hague and Rotterdam and Student personally directed his troops with great success. Hitler was overjoyed with the success and awarded Student, now a *Generalleutnant*, with the Knight's Cross on 12th May. Two days later Student was seriously wounded when a stray bullet struck him in the head while he was in Rotterdam negotiating the Dutch surrender. It was thought that the bullet was fired by troops of the 1st SS Panzer Regiment. Student spent months in hospital and didn't return to active duty until January 1941.

Student returned to active duty in January 1941 as the Commanding General of 11th Air Corps with the rank of *General der Fallschirmtruppe*. On 20th April 1941, Hitler's 52nd birthday, Student was summoned to Hitler's headquarters at Semmering, after wishing his Führer a happy birthday the two men sat down and discussed the plan for the invasion of Crete by air. Hitler was impressed by Student's plan and agreed to the operation. On 23rd May Student flew with his staff to Crete to personally supervise the battle. Within seven days Crete was overrun but Students parachute troops who had suffered heavy losses, of the 6500 German airborne troops that fought in Crete almost 4000 were killed. These huge losses caused Hitler to drop any idea of further action using paratroopers, and when Student proposed an air attack on Malta Hitler quickly rejected it.

Student continued to direct all airborne forces of the Reich and was greatly involved in the plan to rescue Mussolini in September 1943 from the Campo Imperatore mountain hotel on the Gran Sasso in Italy. It was his idea to land forces by gliders under the command of one of Hitler's favourite soldiers *SS-Sturmbannführer* Otto Skorzeny.[50] On 27th September Student was awarded the Oakleaves to his Knight's Cross for his continued leadership and co-ordination of airborne troops and for his part in the rescue of Il Duce.

Oberst Richard Heidrich, Commander of the 3rd Fallschirmjäger Regiment; General der Fallschirmtruppe Kurt Student; Major Ludwig Heilmann, Commander of the 3rd Battalion, 3rd Fallschirmjäger Regiment and Hauptmann Gerhart Schirmer, Commander of the 6th Company, 2nd Fallschirmjäger Regiment, seen here shortly after being presented the Knight's Cross by Student on 14th June 1941. (Wehrkundearchiv)

Student seen talking tactics with Generalfeldmarschall Wilhelm List in late 1941. (Wehrkundearchiv)

In March 1944 Student was appointed Commander-in-Chief of 1st Fallschirm Army, and his troops fought against all the odds to free themselves from encirclement and occupied Rome. Student's troops now took part in the Battle of Monte Cassino and the attempted defence against the allied landings at Anzio, taking a defensive role. In August 1944 Student was promoted to *Generaloberst* and was at his command post near Vught when the allies launched Operation "Market Garden", the airborne invasion of Europe, on 17th September. It was Student who personally led his troops against the American 101st Airborne Division, because of his skill and because his troops were so near to all the Allied drop zones, was the main reason why the American objective failed.

On 29th April 1945, the day before Hitler committed suicide, *Generalfeldmarschall* Wilhelm Keitel dismissed *Generaloberst* Gotthard Heinrici[51] as commander of Army Group Weichsel and named Student as his successor. However, Student did not arrive from Holland until 1st May to assume actual command. The day after Student took command the end was clearly insight for Germany, as American tanks overran his command Student narrowly escaped capture.

On 28th May 1945 Student surrendered to British troops and became a prisoner of war, transferred to the London District Cage, a prison camp for high ranking Nazis. He was then sent to the Island Farm Special Camp, near Bridgend, South Wales. Later charged with war crimes that had allegedly taken place in Crete, he was sentenced to five years imprisonment. He was found guilty on three of the eight charges and later the Greek authorities asked for his extradition. He was released after just two years on medical grounds, his old brain injury sustained during the invasion of Holland in 1940 was making him seriously ill. He returned to Germany and became president of the Association of German Parachute troops in 1949 and he held this position until his death on 1st July 1978.

Student seen with an unknown Major, probably his adjutant, on an inspection tour. You can clearly see both officers are wearing the KRETA cufftitle. (Author's collection)

Heinrich (Heinz) TRETTNER
(1907-2006)
Generalleutnant

Knight's Cross: Awarded on 24th May 1940 as *Major* i.G. and Chief of Operations of 7th Air Division for the planning of the invasion of Holland.

Oakleaves: He became the 586th recipient on 17th September 1944 as *Generalmajor* and commander 4th Fallschirmjäger Division for his outstanding leadership during the fighting in Anzio.

Ranks:
Fahnenjunker-Unteroffizier – 1st November 1926
Fähnrich – 1st August 1927
Oberfähnrich – 1st August 1928
Leutnant – 1st February 1929
Oberleutnant – 1st June 1933
Hauptmann – 1st June 1935
Major – 1st August 1939
Oberstleutnant – 1st October 1941
Oberst – 1st March 1943
Generalmajor – 1st July 1944
Generalleutnant – 1st April 1945

Awards:
Armed Forces Long Service Award 4th Class
Spanish Campaign Medal – 1st December 1938
Spanish Brest Star to the War Cross – 30th September 1938
Spanish Cross in Gold with Swords – 6th June 1939
Iron Cross 2nd Class – 12th May 1940
Iron Cross 1st Class - 12th May 1940
Pilot's Badge with Diamonds
Combined Pilot's and Observer's Badge in Gold with Diamonds
KRETA Cufftitle
Wound Badge in Black – 3rd March 1944
Wehrmacht Daily Report: 28 June 1944

Heinrich "Heinz" Trettner was one of the most successful generals of the Luftwaffe, he was an excellent divisional commander and an outstanding staff officer. Born on 19th September 1907 in Minden, he was the son of a Prussian officer and he graduated from the Hohenzollern Gymnasium in Düsseldorf and in April 1925 entered the army.

Trettner was attached to the 18th Mounted Regiment as an officer cadet and in November 1926 he was assigned to the Infantry School at Dresden and from November 1927 he spent six months in Hannover at the Cavalry School. In February 1929 he was commissioned as a *Leutnant* and in November 1932 he took flying lessons at Braunschweig. He then flew with Lufthansa and the Royal Italian Air Force before joining the Luftwaffe in May 1933, and was shortly afterwards promoted to *Oberleutnant*. He served in various Luftwaffe schools as an adjutant and in June 1935 was promoted to Hauptman and went on to serve as a Personnel Officer on the staff of the Air Commander of Dresden. After completing his third training course at the 2nd Air War School in Berlin, Trettner joined the Condor Legion as Chief Personnel Officer, and was adjutant to its commander *Oberst* Wolfram von Richthofen. In September 1937 Trettner was made Squadron Leader of the 1st Squadron of K88, the Bomber Wing of the Condor Legion, and saw action during the Spanish Civil War. He returned to Germany in January 1938 and started training as a staff officer at the Berlin War Academy.

In July 1938 he was appointed Operations Officer on the staff of the 7th Air Division, under the command of *Generalleutnant* Kurt Student, and was promoted to *Major* in August 1939. He took part in the invasion of Belgium and Holland in 1940, and was with Student during the negotiations for surrender in Rotterdam when Student was struck in the head by a stray bullet from which he later recovered. For his part in the planning of the invasion of Holland Trettner was awarded the Knight's Cross on 24th May 1940, he was responsible for organising the troops, equipment and training. In fact he was so busy during this time that he failed to take parachute training and had to jump during the invasion of Holland without having made any practice jumps and subsequently was never awarded the Parachutist Badge.

Trettner took over as Operations Officer with the 11th Air Corps in December 1940 which had been formed in Berlin under the command of General Student. In October 1941 he was promoted to *Oberstleutnant* and in September the following year he was appointed its Chief of Staff at its headquarters at Berlin-Tempelhof. He was later involved in the preparation and planning of the invasion of Crete and saw action in Russia. In early 1943 now with the rank of *Oberst* Trettner's headquarters was moved to Nimes in Southern France. On 4th October 1943, at his own request Trettner was given his own command, he was told to form the 4th Fallschirmjäger Division. His new

Top: Trettner as a Generalmajor wearing the Knight's Cross with Oakleaves. (Wehrkundearchiv)

Bottom: Generalmajor Trettner at his desk as Commander 4th Fallschirmjäger Division. (Wehrkundearchiv)

command was formed in Italy from the 2nd Fallschirmjäger Division and two Italian parachute divisions. It first saw action in January 1944 when it was part of the battle containing the Allied beachhead at Anzio-Nettuno as part of General Alfred Schlemm's 1st Fallschirm Corps. For the next sixteen months the 4th Fallschirmjäger Division saw action in Italy during the battles of Rome, north of Florence, Rimini, Bologna and in the struggle for the Gothic Line. In July 1944 Trettner was promoted to *Generalmajor* and on 17th September he became the 586th recipient of the Oakleaves awarded for his outstanding leadership as a divisional commander and in recognition of his qualities as a staff officer.

In April 1945 Trettner was promoted to *Generalleutnant*, and by this time his command had suffered many casualties and was fighting for survival at Verona where on 3rd May it finally surrendered to American troops. Trettner was made a prisoner of war and was later handed over to the British who kept him in captivity until April 1948 when he returned home. In May 1949 Trettner completed an apprenticeship at Vaupal and Son glass wholesalers in Düsseldorf. In November 1953 he studied economics and law at the Rheinischen Friedrich-Wilhelm University in Bonn, and he received his diploma in 1956. That same year he joined the Bundeswehr (West German armed forces) with the rank of *Generalmajor* and was until 1959 head of logistics at NATO headquarters in Paris. In February 1960 he commanded the 1st Corps in the Bundeswehr and was later appointed Inspector General of the Bundeswehr in January 1964. He retired from active service in August 1966 as a full general. Heinrich "Heinz" Trettner died on 18th September 2006 in Munchen-Gladbach, he was the last general of the Luftwaffe to die.

Heinz Trettner as a Generalmajor after the war during his time as head of logistics at NATO in 1959. (Author's collection)

KNIGHT'S CROSS

Kurt Georg Heinrich ANDERSEN
(1898-2003)
Generalmajor

Knight's Cross: Awarded on 21st December 1942 as *Oberst* and Commander of 153rd Flak Regiment for actions on the Eastern Front.

Ranks:
Gefreiter – 19th January 1915
Polizei-Leutnant – 15th December 1925
Polizei-Oberleutnant – 11th August 1928
Polizei-Hauptmann – 1st January 1934
Hauptmann – 1st August 1935
Major – 1st October 1938
Oberstleutnant – 1st January 1941
Oberst – 1st July 1942
Generalmajor – 17th February 1945

Awards:
Iron Cross 2nd Class – World War I
Wound Badge in Silver – World War I
Baltic Cross 1st & 2nd Classes
Cross of Honour for Frontline Combatants
Armed Forces Long Service Award 2nd Class
Iron Cross 1st Class – 3rd May 1940
Bar to Iron Cross 2nd Class – 22nd September 1940
Luftwaffe Ground Assault Badge – 24th December 1942

Kurt Georg Heinrich Andersen was born on 2nd October 1898 in Hohenrade, Königsberg, East Prussia and entered the army as a war volunteer with 3rd Replacement Machine-Gun Company in January 1915. In October 1916 he was transferred to the 1st Telegraph Battalion in Tereptow, and ended the war in Königsberg with 1st Signals Battalion. He remained in the army after the war with the 15th Volunteer Company in the "Iron Division" under *Major* Josef Bischoff a *Pour le Mérite* recipient, taking part in the Baltic campaign. On 16th September 1919 Andersen joined the Protection Police in Elbing-Marienburg, Dortmund and Düsseldorf.

By January 1934 he had risen to the rank of *Hauptmann*, and in August of the following year he was attached to the Air Ministry. He was transferred to the 23rd Flak Regiment in Düsseldorf as a Battery officer in October 1935 where he remained

Kurt Andersen as Oberst and Commander of 153rd Flak Regiment. (Wehrkundearchiv)

Captured by British forces near Tangemünde, Andersen was transferred to the Island Farm Special Camp in January 1946. In this photograph of Anderson at the time of his capture in May 1945, he looks almost cheerful. (Roger James Bender)

until June 1938 and was promoted to *Major* in October and appointed Commander of 2nd Battalion of the Flak Demonstration Regiment and saw action in Poland and France in May 1940. In June he was appointed Commander of the Flak School at Stolpmünde, and was promoted to *Oberstleutnant* in January 1941 and to *Oberst* in July 1942. Then appointed Commander of the 153rd Flak Regiment on the Eastern Front in November 1942, and as part of the 10th Flak Division he saw heavy action at Kursk. His command went on to destroy forty-three Russian tanks near the Don River area and for this he was awarded the Knight's Cross on 21st December 1942.

Andersen was transferred to the staff of the Commander of the Flak Artillery School where he was appointed Commander of Air War School VI in June 1943. From April 1944 until January 1945 he was made Flak Inspector "East". On 30th January he succeeded *Oberst* Oskar Vorbrugg as Commander of 23rd Flak Division operating on the Eastern Front in the Baranovitschi-Minsk area while supporting the 9th Army, and shortly afterwards was promoted to *Generalmajor*. His command took part in heavy ground combat and went on to see action in Frankfurt am Oder, Küstrin and Eberswalde, his division then moved to Döberitz where it surrendered after heavy losses on 8th May 1945. Andersen himself was captured near Tangemünde by British forces; he was transferred to the Island Farm Special Camp in January 1946, and was repatriated to Germany two years later.

In August 1951 Andersen entered the Bundesgrenzschutz (Federal Border Guards) as a Brigadegeneral, and was appointed, the following year, commander of the Bundesgrenzschutz School at Lübeck. In July 1956 he became the Inspector of the Bundesgrenzschutz in the Federal Ministry of the Interior in Bonn, serving there until March 1961 when he retired. He died on 9th January 2003 in Bonn, at the age of 104.

Karl ANGERSTEIN
(1890-1985)
Generalleutnant

Generalmajor Kurt Angerstein wearing the Knight's Cross. (Wehrkundearchiv)

Knight's Cross: Awarded as *Oberst* and Commander 1st Bomber Wing "Hindenburg" on 2nd November 1940 for actions on the Western Front.

Ranks:
Fahnenjunker – 25th September 1911
Fähnrich – 22nd May 1912
Leutnant – 18th February 1913
Oberleutnant – 6th June 1916
*Polizei-Oberl*eutnant – 1st October 1919
Polizei-Hauptmann – 13th July 1921
Polizei-Major – 18th December 1929
Major – 1st July 1935
Oberstleutnant – 1st August 1937
Oberst – 1st February 1940
Generalmajor – 1st April 1941
Generalleutnant – 1st April 1943

Awards:
Knight's Cross of the Royal Prussian Hohenzollern House Order with Swords – 17th April 1918
Iron Cross 2nd Class – World War I
Iron Cross 1st Class – World War I
Royal Prussian Pilot's Badge
Wound Badge in Black – World War I
Cross of Honour for Frontline Combatants
Armed Forces Long Service Award 1st Class
Bar to Iron Cross 2nd Class
Bar to Iron Cross 1st Class
German Cross in Gold – 16th July 1942
Pilot's Badge with Diamonds
Combined Pilot's and Observer's Badge in Gold and Diamonds
Combat Clasp for Bombers in Gold
Wehrmacht Daily Report: 19 August 1943; 9 October 1943

Karl Angerstein was born on 4th December 1890 in Mühlhausen, Thüringen, after finishing his schooling he joined the Imperial Army as a *Fahnenjunker* with the 87th Infantry Regiment. In February 1913 he was commissioned as a *Leutnant* and in June 1914 he joined the 3rd Air Battalion where he learnt to fly. In August he served with 4th Flying Replacement Battalion as a pilot and saw action on the Western Front. He was wounded in November 1914 and spent time in Posen and Erfurt hospitals before returning as a pilot with the 52nd Field Flying Battalion in January 1915. He spent the rest of the war flying as a pilot in various flying battalions and in June 1916 was promoted to *Oberleutnant*. Shortly after his promotion he was wounded again and spent six months recovering first in a hospital in Eberswalde and then in Wiesbaden. He returned to duty on 22nd December 1916 and was posted to the Flying Observation School, and then in August 1917 he was assigned to 17th Squadron, 3rd Bomber Wing and was later appointed Squadron Commander of the 18th Bomber Squadron operating on the Western Front.

When the war ended Angerstein served briefly with the Border Police as a pilot in a squadron attached to Command North between March and September 1919. In October he transferred to the Protection Police and served in the Air Department in Königsberg until May 1920. In June he was appointed leader of the technical unit of the Protection Police in Elbing and in July 1921 he was promoted to *Polizei-Hauptmann*, and went on to serve in similar positions in Deutsch-Eylau and in Stuhm. In May 1924 he served as an air transport expert in the President of Magdeburg's Office and in October he was appointed director of the Air Police Surveillance Unit while still attached to the Magdeburg office. He was promoted to *Polizei-Major* in December 1929 and was appointed Inspector of the Prussian Air Police in the Office of the Prussian Prime Minister Hermann Göring in May 1933. In October 1934 he served as Director of the Air Office in Munich and in July 1935 he was finally transferred to the Luftwaffe with the rank of *Major*. He spent the next few years attached to the Air Ministry in Berlin without many duties, and in July 1937 he was transferred to 155th Bomber Wing and at the same time was appointed Air Base Commander at Brünn, now with the rank of *Oberstleutnant*.

At the beginning of World War II Angerstein's Bomber Wing 155 became the 2nd Group of 77th Bomber Wing under the command of *Generalmajor* Wolf von Stutterheim in November 1939. Its headquarters was located in Düsseldorf and it operated with Dornier Do 17Z, but saw little action to begin with. In January 1940 Angerstein was appointed Commander of 28th Bomber Wing and shortly after he was promoted to *Oberst*, where he saw action during the French Campaign. In July 1940 he succeeded *Oberst* Josef Kammhuber as Commander of 1st Bomber Wing "Hindenburg", here his aircraft consisted of Heinkel He 111H operating from Rosieres-en-Santerre and Amiens-Glizy in France and then he saw action during Operation Barbarossa. Angerstein was awarded the Knight's Cross on 2nd November 1940 for his success and leadership as Commander of 1st Bomber Wing "Hindenburg" and for actions on the Western Front. In April 1941 he was promoted to *Generalmajor* and in July 1942 was appointed Commander of the Bomber and Stuka Dive Bomber Schools where he remained until June 1943.

On 15th June 1943, now *Generalleutnant*, Angerstein was appointed Commander of 1st Air Corps seeing action in Russia near Simferopol and Nikolayer, while subordinated to 4th Air Fleet under the command of *Generalfeldmarschall* von Richthofen and from September 1943 under *Generaloberst* Otto Deßloch. In November 1943 he was put on the Reserve List, and then in February 1944 he was transferred to the staff of *General* Walter von Unruh where he was assigned to special duties within the Oberkommando der Wehrmacht (High Command of the Armed Forces). In September he became the liaison officer between Air Fleet Reich, under *Generalmajor* Andreas Nielsen[52] and the OKW and then served as a staff officer with 10th Army Corps in Hamburg. In October he was assigned to the Reichs War Courts where he presided over various court-martials and other such military matters.

He was taken into Allied captivity on 8th May 1945 and was eventually released on 30th June 1947. He lived in quiet retirement until his death at the age of ninety-four on 20th September 1985 in Feldkirchen, Straubing-Bogen in Bavaria.

Werner Rudolph ANTON
(1895-1948)
Generalleutnant

Knight's Cross: Awarded on 9th June 1944 as *Generalmajor* and Commander of 6th Flak Division for actions on the Eastern Front.

Generalmajor Werner Anton shortly after being awarded the Knight's Cross on 9th June 1944. (Wehrkundearchiv)

Ranks:
Fähnrich – 1st December 1914
Leutnant – 5th March 1915
Polizei Leutnant – 3rd May 1920
Polizei-Oberleutnant – 2nd September 1921
Polizei-Hauptmann – 1st September 1929
Polizei-Major – 9th November 1933
Major – 1st August 1935
Oberstleutnant – 1st October 1937
Oberst – 1st August 1939
Generalmajor – 1st February 1943
Generalleutnant – 1st July 1944

Awards:
Knight's Cross of the Royal Saxony Military Order of St. Heinrich – 20th November 1916
Iron Cross 2nd Class – 4th February 1915
Iron Cross 1st Class – 22nd August 1918
Knight's Cross of the Order of Albert the Bear 2nd Class with Swords – 19th February 1916

Royal Prussian Observer's Badge – 8th August 1917
Honour Goblet for aerial combat – 3rd July 1918
Cross of Honour for Frontline Combatants
Armed Forces Long Service Award 1st Class
Bar to Iron Cross 2nd Class
Bar to Iron Cross 1st Class
Commemorative Medal for 1st October 1938 with Bar "Prague Castle"
Luftwaffe Ground Combat Badge – 12th September 1942
German Cross in Gold – 29th April 1943
Kurland Campaign Cuff-title
Wehrmacht Daily Report: 30 October 1944

Werner Anton was born 3rd April 1895 in Dresden and entered the Imperial Army on 22nd August 1914 as a *Fähnrich* with 103rd Infantry Regiment. In March 1915 Anton was commissioned as a *Leutnant* and became a Platoon Leader with the same regiment, seeing action on the Western Front. In May 1915 he was appointed Battalion Adjutant and two years later he became Ordnance Officer and a staff officer. In September 1916 he was wounded and spent almost eight months recovering, and on 11th August 1917 he was appointed Company Commander with the same regiment and in October he transferred to an air battalion where he trained as an observer. He ended the war as a pilot attached to the air base at Großenheim.

In February 1919 he joined the 2nd Border Jäger Battalion and in April 1920 he retired from the army. In May after a friend told him to apply he was accepted into the State Police in Zittau, Saxony, and in September 1921 he was promoted to *Oberleutnant* and appointed leader of the 4th Motorised Platoon. In October 1922 he was appointed leader of the Motorised Emergency Unit "Zittau", and spent the next seven years as a front-line police officer. In September 1929 he was promoted to *Polizei-Hauptmann* and transferred to the office of the Director of Motorised Units attached to the Police President's Office in Dresden. Promoted to *Polizei-Major* in November 1933, he was made Director of the Police Motor Transport School and advisor in all police motor affairs within the Ministry of the Interior for Saxony.

Anton was transferred to the Luftwaffe in August 1935 with the rank of *Major* and was immediately attached to the Motor Transport Command of Air District III in Dresden. On 1st May 1937 he was transferred to the 10th Flak Regiment for training as a Battery Commander. In October he was promoted to *Oberstleutnant* and assigned to the 43rd Flak Regiment as a Battery Commander. In August 1938 he was appointed commander of 94th Light Flak Battalion in Krems, Austria, and in May 1939 was made Commander of 1st Battalion, 7th Flak Regiment.

Appointed Commander of the 13th Flak Regiment on 30th September 1939, *Oberst* Anton stayed with this command in Leipzig for eighteen months. In April 1941 he succeeded *Generalmajor* Johann Seifert[53] as Commander of 3rd Flak Brigade in Ploesti. In February 1943 Anton was promoted to *Generalmajor* and took over as Commander of the 6th Flak Division from General Job Odebrecht in Ostrow, Poland. Responsible for anti-aircraft support for Army Group North, his command celebrated in June 1944 when they shot down their 1000th enemy aircraft. Anton himself was awarded the Knight's Cross on 11th June 1944, and a month later he was promoted to *Generalleutnant*.

Anton's war ended on 8th May 1945, when he surrendered in the Libau area and after his command had seen action in the Kurland. He died while in Allied captivity after an accident near Wolfsburg on 12th September 1948.

Walther von Axthelm as a Generalmajor. (Wehrkundearchiv)

Walther Moritz Heinrich Wolfgang von AXTHELM (1893-1972)
General der Flakartillerie

Knight's Cross: Awarded on 4th September 1941 as *Generalmajor* and Commander of 1st Flak Corps for support of Guderian's 2nd Panzer Group on Eastern Front.

Ranks:
Fahnenjunker – 15th September 1913
Fähnrich – 8th July 1914

Leutnant – 24th September 1914
Oberleutnant – 6th April 1918
Hauptmann – 1st October 1926
Major – 1st August 1934
Oberstleutnant – 1st January 1937
Oberst – 1st February 1939
Generalmajor – 19th September 1940
Generalleutnant – 1st October 1942
General der Flakartillerie – 1st April 1944

Awards:
Iron Cross 2nd Class – 5th October 1914
Iron Cross 1st Class – 25th August 1915
Wound Badge in Black – 10th June 1918
Cross of Honour for Frontline Combatants – 21st December 1934
Royal Bavarian Service Award 4th Class with Swords – 22nd February 1915
Royal Bavarian Service Award 4th Class with Swords and with Crown – 2nd May 1918
Armed Forces Long Service Award 1st Class – 1st October 1938
Commemorative Medal for 13th March 1938 – 16th December 1938
Commemorative Medal for 1st October 1938 with Bar "Prague Castle"
Bar to Iron Cross 2nd Class – 29th May 1940
Bar to Iron Cross 1st Class – 27th June 1940
Luftwaffe Anti Aircraft Badge – 3rd October 1941

Friedrich-Wilhelm Jakoby as an Oberst and commander of the 11th Air Signals Regiment. Jakoby went on to be promoted to Generalleutnant in January 1945, and was appointed Higher Signals Leader with the Luftwaffe High Command. He spent the last days of the war in hospital recovering from a head injury. He died on 19th January 1967 in Düsseldorf.

Walter von Axthelm was born on 23rd December 1893 in Hersbruck, near Nuremberg. He joined the Imperial Army in September 1913 as a *Fahnenjunker*, a year later he was commissioned as a *Leutnant* where he saw action during World War I with 8th Bavarian Field Artillery Regiment. In December 1916 after winning the Iron Cross 1st and 2nd Classes he was appointed commander of 2nd Battalion of the same regiment. Appointed adjutant of the 8th Field Artillery Regiment in January 1917 he became a Battery commander nine months later, and this was to be his last command before the end of the war.

He stayed in the Reichswehr after the war and in February 1919 he was appointed Regimental Adjutant to his old regiment with the rank of *Oberleutnant*. Between March 1919 and September 1931 he served in various positions within the artillery, being promoted to *Hauptmann* in October 1926. In September 1929 he briefly commanded a Flak training unit in Königsberg where he performed well, his official report stating that he was "outstanding in his skill and understanding of Flak tactics." He went on to serve in the Reich War Ministry in October 1931, working in the department of the Inspector of Artillery.

In August 1934 Axthelm joined the Luftwaffe with the rank of *Major*, and in April 1935 was appointed section head of the Inspector of Artillery department within the Air Ministry. In August 1936 he succeeded *Oberstleutnant* Friedrich-Wilhelm Jakoby as commander of the Luftwaffe Regiment "General Göring", later called the 103rd Flak Regiment. He became responsible for the training of this regiment and at it was at this time that the Army High Command began to recognize the full potential and importance of parachute units as an offensive weapon. In September 1937 von Axthelm took part in the important military exercises at Mecklenburg and in March 1938 he led his regiment into Austria and was one of the first units to march past Hitler in Vienna. He later went on to participate in the occupation of the Sudetenland in October and also took part in the march into Prague in March 1939. In September at the time of the Polish Campaign von Axthelm and his men remained in Germany, von Axthelm now an *Oberst* was responsible for Flak defence training in Berlin and his men were also responsible for the guarding of Göring's headquarters at the Air Ministry. After the fall of Poland three units from his command were transferred to the Western Front.

On 1st June 1940 von Axthelm was appointed commander of 1st Flak Brigade, where he was made responsible for the

Generalmajor Axthelm as commander of the 1st Flak Corps, is seen here relaxing with his staff which include his adjutant and chief of staff Major Kurt Hein. Axthelm was well respected by his men and the photographs show this, and also how relaxed he and his staff were off duty. (Author's collection)

air defence of Paris. Promoted to *Generalmajor* in September 1940 his command was transferred in December to Dessau in Germany. In March 1941 his command was upgraded to Corps level and he became the Commanding General of 1st Flak Corps when he succeeded *Generaloberst* Hubert Wiese. His headquarters was in Warsaw and then in June 1941 at the start of Operation Barbarossa, it was later moved to Brest-Litovsk where von Axthelm was made responsible for the support of Panzergruppe 2 under *Generaloberst* Heinz Guderian. Later along with 2nd and 8th Flak Corps his command helped to make up Kesselring's 2nd Air Fleet supporting von Bock's Army Group Centre. On 4th September von Axthelm was awarded the Knight's Cross in recognition of his distinguished service, especially his command of 101st and 104th Motorized Flak Regiment who had distinguished themselves in support of 2nd Panzer Army.

In January 1942 he was appointed Inspector of Flak Artillery within the Air Ministry and in October he was promoted to the rank of *Generalleutnant*, this was followed by his promotion to *General der Flakartillerie* in April 1944. He became responsible for all anti-aircraft troops in the Reich, and during the last month of the war he was also responsible for the training of the reserves, which consisted mainly of Hitler Youth and old men of the Volkssturm.

Von Axthelm was very briefly the last commander of 1st Flak Corps in May 1945, his orders were to support 4th Panzer Army but after just six days his command was overrun and he surrendered to American troops on 8th May 1945, while trying to make his way from Berlin to the Western lines, he remained in captivity until his release in July 1947. He died at his home in Traunstein, Bavaria on 6th January 1972, at the age of seventy-eight.

Walter Boenicke as General der Flieger wearing the Knight's Cross as the Commander of 3rd Air Division, 1944. (Wehrkundearchiv)

Walter BOENICKE
(1895-1947)
General der Flieger

Knight's Cross: Awarded on 14th May 1944 as *Generalleutnant* and Commander of 3rd Air Division while operating on the Russian Front.

Ranks:
Fahnenjunker-Gefreiter – 7th October 1914
Fahnenjunker-Unteroffizier – 10th November 1914
Fähnrich – 24th November 1914
Leutnant – 14th January 1915
Oberleutnant – 1st July 1925
Hauptmann – 1st July 1933
Major – 1st December 1934
Oberstleutnant – 1st January 1937
Oberst – 1st April 1939
Generalmajor – 1st September 1941
Generalleutnant – 1st September 1943
General der Flieger – 1st March 1945

Awards:
Iron Cross 2nd Class – World War I
Iron Cross 1st Class – World War I
Knight's Cross of the Royal Prussian Hohenzollern House Order with Swords
Grand Duchy of Mecklenburg-Schwerin War Service Cross 2nd Class
The Anhalt Friedrich Cross, 1914
Luftwaffe Observers Badge
Cross of Honour for Frontline Combatants
Bar to Iron Cross 2nd Class
Bar to Iron Cross 1st Class
Armed Forces Long Service Award 3rd Class
Combined Pilot's and Observer's Badge
German Cross in Gold – 20th March 1944

Walter Boenicke was born in Radisleben near Magdeburg on 15th December 1895, the son of a local businessman. He attended the local school before joining the army in August 1914 as a young recruit and officer cadet. In December he was transferred to a training battalion attached to 9th Army Corps but was yet to see any action. On 14th January 1915 he was commissioned as a *Leutnant* at the age of nineteen. He went on to serve in several different posts within the 9th Army Corps before training as an observer with 1st Flying Unit at Altenburg, then as an artillery observer in Jüterbog. In January 1917 he became a fully trained observer and saw action in a front-line flying unit where he remained until the end of the war.

He left the army in 1919 and tried to settle down to civilian life but hated it, he then joined a training camp in Göttingen as a company commander where he trained soldiers illegally against the terms of the Versailles Treaty. In 1924 he rejoined the army and was even promoted to *Oberleutnant* in July 1925 after being appointed a platoon commander. In November 1928 he went to Russia and took part in secret training as a pilot, returning in early 1931 where he was appointed to the staff of 2nd Motorized Battalion. In October he was assigned to the Chief of Staff of the Army Command on behalf of the 1st Division.

In April 1934 now a *Hauptmann* he was assigned to the Luftwaffe Personnel Department, and was part of the General Staff of the Luftwaffe. Promoted to *Major* in December 1934 and to *Oberstleutnant* in January 1937, he was later attached to the Reich Air Ministry as a staff officer. In April 1938 he was appointed commander of the 12th Reconnaissance Group while attached to the Military Airfield at Stargard. He became a department head in the Air Ministry in February 1939, and two months later was promoted to *Oberst*.

When World War II broke out he didn't see action until the Western Campaign when he was appointed Chief of the General Staff of 1st Air Corps in June 1940. In September 1941 he was promoted to *Generalmajor*, and in November he was appointed Chief of Staff of Fortress Crete under the command of *General der Flieger* Alexander Andrae, where he saw heavy fighting. In June 1942 he was appointed Chief of the General Staff of the Luftwaffe Commander-in-Chief "Centre" *Generaloberst* Hubert Weise where he remained until January 1944. On 6th January he succeeded *Generalmajor* Werner Zech as Commander of 3rd Air Division with his headquarters in Pechory in Estonia, while attached to 1st Air Fleet under the command of *General der Flieger* Kurt Pflugbeil. Wounded in February 1944, he remained absent from frontline duty for many months. However in recognition of his leadership as commander of 3rd Air Division he was awarded the German Cross in Gold in March 1944, and in May was awarded the Knight's Cross.

On 20th February 1945 he was recalled to active duty and in March was promoted to *General der Flieger* and appointed Commander-in-Chief of Air District III in Berlin-Wannsee, under the overall command of *Generaloberst* Hans-Jurgen Stumpff's Air Fleet "Reich". Boenicke was now responsible for the air defence of the entire capital of the Reich, but had little aircraft and troops in which to defend such a huge area. By April 1945 he knew all was lost and began his withdrawal with his staff towards the Western Allies. At the end of May 1945 he surrendered to British troops and was held in a prisoner of war camp in Munster. With rumours of possible war crime trials for crimes committed in Crete under both Generals Andrae and Bruno Bräuer, and suffering pain from the wounds he received earlier in the war Boenicke committed suicide while in his cell on 21st April 1947.

General der Flieger Rudolf Bogatsch in a studio portrait photograph taken shortly after being awarded the Knight's Cross in March 1942. (Author's collection)

Rudolf BOGATSCH
(1891-1970)
General der Flieger

Knight's Cross: Awarded on 20th March 1942 as *General der Flieger* and Commander of army flying units and liaison officer with the High Command and Inspector of Reconnaissance.

Ranks:
Fahnenjunker – 19th March 1910
Fähnrich – 18th October 1910
Leutnant – 18th August 1911
Oberleutnant – 18th August 1915
Hauptmann – 1st February 1922

Major – 1st February 1930
Oberstleutnant – 1st April 1933
Oberst – 1st April 1935
Generalmajor – 1st January 1938
Generalleutnant – 1st January 1940
General der Flieger – 1st July 1941

Awards:
Iron Cross 2nd Class – World War I
Iron Cross 1st Class – World War I
Wound Badge in Black - World War I
Bar to Iron Cross 2nd Class
Bar to Iron Cross 1st Class
Armed Forces Long Service Award 1st Class
Cross of Honour for Frontline Combatants
Royal Saxony War Service Cross of Honour

Rudolf Bogatsch, commander of the 4th Anti-aircraft Corps. (Wehrkundearchiv)

A gifted anti-aircraft commander, Rudolf Bogatsch was born in Breslau on 14th September 1891. He left school with enough qualifications to enable him to join the army as an officer cadet and upon receiving his commission in August 1911 he was appointed Battery officer with 6th Field Artillery Regiment. When war was declared he went with his regiment to the Western Front and in January 1915 was appointed adjutant to 1st Battalion, taking over as battery commander in March 1915. On 20th May he was wounded and spent almost a month in hospital before returning to his unit as adjutant. In August he was promoted to *Oberleutnant* and was transferred to the 2nd Battalion, 6th Field Artillery Regiment. In October he was appointed as regimental adjutant and went on to win the Iron Cross 2nd and 1st Classes. On 19th October 1917 he was made deputy commander of his battalion while serving on the western front with 7th Army. In December he was transferred to the 235th Infantry Division as deputy staff officer. He went onto serve in a number of staff positions within the General Staff before the armistice in 1918. He remained in the Reichswehr after the war and continued to serve as a General Staff officer in various different units, including the 2nd and 7th Cavalry Regiment and the 4th Division. He was promoted to *Hauptmann* in February 1922; in October 1926 he was transferred to the 1st Artillery Regiment as a battery commander. In September 1929 he went on an anti-aircraft course in Königsberg and in February 1930 was assigned to the Organizational Department in the War Ministry.

In January 1933 shortly after the Nazis came to power Bogatsch was appointed Inspector of the Armaments School while still attached to the War Ministry. Promoted to *Oberstleutnant* in April 1933 he joined the Luftwaffe in April 1935 with the rank of *Oberst*. His first appointment in the Luftwaffe was as commander of the anti-aircraft battalion in Lankwitz, and on 12th October 1937 he was also named as the new commander of Luftgau VII, responsible for the area around Dresden.

In February 1939, now with the rank of *Generalmajor* he became commander of army flying units that were attached to the Luftwaffe and was liaison officer with the army high command and inspector of all reconnaissance aircraft. In January 1940 he was promoted to *Generalleutnant* and in July 1941 he was promoted to *General der Flieger*. He was now the Reichs expert on anti-aircraft techniques and for recognition of his efforts and expertise he was awarded the Knight's Cross on 20th March 1942. In August 1942 he was appointed Commanding General of Luftgau XVII, when he succeeded *General der Flakartillerie* Friedrich Hirschauer,[54] with his headquarters in Vienna.

He was responsible for the area around the Protector in Czechoslovakia. His last command of the war came in September 1944 when he succeeded *General der Flakartillerie* Otto Wilhelm von Renz as Commander of 4th Flak Corps. This unit had been hastily reformed in Edenkoben under Luftwaffe Kommando West and saw action in the area around Army Group C, from Mosel to the Swiss border. On 4th May 1945 Bogatsch surrendered to U.S. forces, he remained in Allied captivity until 30th May 1945. Rudolf Bogatsch died in Munich twenty-five years later, on 5th June 1970, at the age of seventy-eight.

Rudolf Bogatsch during an inspection tour when he held the position of the Reichs expert of anti-aircraft techniques. (Author's collection)

Bruno Oswald BRÄUER
(1893-1947)
General der Fallschirmtruppe

Knight's Cross: Awarded for his leadership during the air assault on Holland as *Oberst* and Commander of 1st Parachute Regiment on 24th May 1940.

Ranks:
Gefreiter – 1st December 1911
Unteroffizier – 1st July 1912
Sergeant – 1st October 1915
Vizefeldwebel – 1st December 1916
Offiziers-Stellvertreter – 1st October 1917
Leutnant – 7th August 1919
Polizei-Leutnant – 1st January 1920
Polizei-Oberleutnant – 29th September 1923
Polizei-Hauptmann – 4th April 1928
Polizei-Major – 1st June 1935
Major – 15th October 1935
Oberstleutnant – 1st January 1938
Oberst – 1st January 1939
Generalmajor – 1st September 1941
Generalleutnant – 6th September 1942
General der Fallschirmtruppe – 1st June 1944

Awards:
German Cross in Gold – 31st March 1942
Iron Cross 2nd Class – 14th October 1914
Iron Cross 1st Class – 1st April 1917
Armed Forces Long Service Award 1st Class
Cross of Honour for Frontline Combatants
Bar to Iron Cross 2nd Class – 20th October 1939
Bar to Iron Cross 1st Class – 23rd May 1940
Commemorative Medal for 13th March 1938
Commemorative Medal for 1st October 1938
KRETA Commemorative Shield
Luftwaffe Parachutist Badge
Ground Assault Badge of the Luftwaffe
Wehrmacht Daily Report: 9 June 1941

Willrich postcard showing Oberst Bruno Bräuer wearing the Knight's Cross and in the uniform of a parachutist, commissioned especially to celebrate the success of Bräuer's command during the invasion of Crete. (Author's collection)

One of the most unfortunate men of the Luftwaffe, executed at the end of the war for crimes committed in Crete which had nothing to do with him. Bruno Bräuer was born on 4th February 1893 in Willmannsdorf, Silesia and his military career began as a cadet in April 1905 when he joined the Military School in Anstalt Annaburg. In April 1908 he attended the officer training school at Greifenberg, two years later he attended the military school at Treptow. In 1912 Bräuer was transferred to 155th Infantry Regiment as an *Unteroffizier* and it was with this unit that he served throughout the First World War. In December 1916 he was promoted to *Vizefeldwebel* and soon afterwards won both the Iron Cross 1st and 2nd Classes.

At the end of the war Bräuer was accepted into the Reichswehr and in August 1919 he was commissioned as a *Leutnant*. In January 1920 he joined the State Police (*Schutzpolizei*), serving in Unruhstadt and Berlin. When the Wecke State Police was formed in February 1933 he joined and commanded the units 1st Company as a *Polizei-Hauptmann*. In June 1935 he led the *Landespolizeigruppe* "General Göring", and in October was transferred to the Luftwaffe as part of the new "Hermann Göring" Regiment with the rank of *Major*. Bräuer's command was selected to begin the first parachute training course in March 1936, and on 11th May Bräuer made the first parachute jump from the wing of an aircraft and became the first German to be awarded with a parachute license.

On 23rd November 1938 Bräuer was appointed Battalion Commander of the 1st Parachute Regiment and in January 1939 was promoted to *Oberst*. In September he led this unit during the attack on Poland and it was here that the parachute troops suffered their first casualties; in fact it was to be the first of thousands! In May 1940 he led his troops during the airborne invasion of Holland. His objective was to take two bridges – the first at Moerdijk was captured by the 2nd Battalion, the second bridge was attacked by the 1st Regiment and ran into heavy resistance and as a result the bridge remained in Dutch hands. An airfield nearby was taken by Bräuer's troops by luring the defenders away from the airfield so aircraft could be landed. The Dutch resistance at the bridge increased and Bräuer had to take drastic action, he commandeered Dutch vehicles and after fierce fighting on both sides and incredible bravery especially by Bräuer himself the bridge was taken intact. For this act Bräuer was awarded the Knight's Cross on 24th May, a few days later the award was presented to Bräuer personally by Hitler.

When Crete was finally occupied by German forces, orders were issued on 31st May 1940 which stated: "... the civilian population including women and children who have taken part in the fighting and have committed sabotage and killed wounded German soldiers will be punished ... the harshest measures must be taken ... anyone guilty will be shot."[55]

When this order was issued a number of officers protested against the indiscriminate executions of civilians. *Major* von Uxkull, the parachute division's chief of staff denounced the plan fearlessly and even Bräuer himself disagreed with the order and laughed off the stories of torture as fabrication. Nevertheless

Generalleutnant Bruno Bräuer wearing the Knight's Cross as Commander of Fortress Crete. (Author's collection)

there were more than 1,130 Cretans executed by the Germans from the start of the invasion until September 1941.

In November 1942 Bräuer succeeded *General der Flieger* Alexander Andrae as the Commander of Fortress Crete. Bräuer proved to be a more humane commander, and he tried to make his officers understand the Cretan attitude towards the occupying power; he tried to explain why they fought so bravely and fiercely during the fight for occupation. On 25th March 1943, Greek National Day, Bräuer ordered the release from prison of one hundred Cretan nationals. They included Constantinos Mitsotakis, later to become the Prime Minister of Greece, who was then a lieutenant in the army, and a member of the resistance. Not long after he had been released he spotted Bräuer in the suburb of Halepa and went up to him, he thanked the general for releasing him. Bräuer then invited Mitsotakis to his official residence for a coffee. He told Mitsotakis that he had released him because, he had good things about him and had a feeling

Right and below: Oberst Bruno Bräuer in typical poses holding his cigarette during the invasion of Crete. (Private source)

Bottom right: General der Flieger Alexander Andrae, the first commander of Fortress Crete, was given six life sentences for his part in the occupation of Crete. He was released just four years later and returned to Germany where he died in Wiesbaden on 3rd April 1979. (Wehrkundearchiv)

that one day he may play an important part in his countries affairs. He ended the conversation by saying that Mitsotakis should, "keep out of trouble."[55a]

Bräuer was himself relieved of command in May 1944, and placed on the Reserve list where he remained until being recalled in March 1945 as the Commander of 9th Fallschirmjager Division. He now led his troops into battle on the Eastern Front and two of his battalions were encircled by the Russians near Breslau and destroyed. The rest of his division retreated all the way back to the Seelow Heights where they dug in and prepared to defend against a Russian offensive. However because his troops were either too old or members of the Hitler Youth who had seen little or no action before, they fled the moment the Russian attacked. It didn't take long before Bräuer's defence collapsed and Bräuer himself suffered a break-down and was again relieved of his command in April.

In May 1945 Bräuer was captured by British forces, held in a prison camp until early 1946 when the Greek authorities demanded his extradition to face trial for war crimes committed in Crete. On 9th February Bräuer was handed over to the Greeks for trial, there was little evidence against him and many thought that he was the most humane of all the commanders during the German occupation.

The first commander General Andrae was given six life sentences for his part in the occupation, General Kreipe who was kidnapped by the British was released in 1947. *Generaloberst* Kurt Student the most senior commander responsible for all parachute troops was never tried; *General* Ringel whose troops had taken part in reprisal killings was never tried either. The only general to stand trial with Bräuer was *General* Friedrich-Wilhelm Müller, who was generally thought to have been the most brutal of all commanders in Crete. It was no surprise when Müller was found guilty and sentenced to death; however the surprise came when the Greek authorities sentenced Bräuer to death. The execution was delayed so it could be carried out on the 6th Anniversary of the invasion of Crete, 20th May 1947. After the execution the bodies of Müller and Bräuer were buried at the Chaidari Barracks in Athens. Many years later, at the request of the Association of German Airborne Troops, Bräuer's body was brought to Athens to the cemetery overlooking Maleme where he was reburied with full honors.

Generalmajor Alfred Bülowius in conversation with an unknown Hauptmann in late 1941. (Wehrkundearchiv)

Alfred BÜLOWIUS
(1892-1968)
General der Flieger

Knight's Cross: Awarded on 4th July 1940 as *Oberst* and Commander of 1st Training Wing, for actions during the French Campaign.

Ranks:
Fahnenjunker – 23rd January 1911
Fähnrich – 18th August 1911
Leutnant – 18th June 1912
Oberleutnant – 18th August 1917
Hauptmann – 1st May 1934
Major – 1st September 1934
Oberstleutnant – 1st October 1936
Oberst – 1st January 1939
Generalmajor – 1st June 1941
Generalleutnant – 1st June 1943
General der Flieger – 1st December 1944

Awards:
German Cross in Gold – 9th December 1942
Iron Cross 2nd Class – World War I
Iron Cross 1st Class – World War I
Royal Prussian Pilot's Badge
Armed Forces Long Service Award 1st Class
Cross of Honour for Frontline Combatants
Wound Badge in Black - 1940
Bar to Iron Cross 2nd Class
Bar to Iron Cross 1st Class
Wehrmacht Daily Report: 5 October 1944

Alfred Bülowius was born in Königsberg, Prussia on 14th January 1892, after his schooling he entered the Imperial army as an officer cadet joining the 41st Infantry Regiment. Commissioned in June 1912 he was appointed a Company Commander with 41st Infantry Regiment and was serving in this capacity when World War I started. In 1915 he was appointed Regimental Adjutant and a few months later joined the Air Corps where he served as a Squadron Leader with Bomber Wing 3 until Germany's surrender. In October 1919 he joined the Police Aerial Squadron in East Prussia, he must have found it affable, either that or the fact it was steady money, because he remained in this position until August 1922. There was a short period of time when he left the military services but in April 1925 he re-entered the military and was appointed air defence representative on the staff of Wehrkreis Kommando I in Königsberg.

On 1st May 1934 he transferred to the Luftwaffe with the rank of *Hauptmann* and immediately joined the Air Ministry as a consultant. In early 1936 he was appointed Squadron Commander at Merseburg, later being appointed Group Commander of the Bomber Wing "General Wever". Now with the rank of *Oberstleutnant* he was appointed commander of the Bomber School at Tutow and went on to command the 1st Training Wing at Greifswald and while flying over the skies of France in June 1940 he was shot down by aircraft of the RAF. He crash landed in France and after receiving medical attention was sent to a prisoner of war camp. On 21st June he returned from captivity after the fall of France and was awarded the Knight's Cross on 4th July 1940 in recognition of the success his Bomber Wing had in the defeat of France.

In October 1940 Bülowius was appointed Commander of the 7th Training Battalion, and in January 1941 was named as the new commander of the Bomber and Dive-Bomber Flying School in Prague, shortly afterwards being promoted to *Generalmajor*. He was briefly named as commander of the Battle Unit North, part of the Luftwaffe Tactical Air Command Don and part of von Richthofen's command. Bülowius arrived at von Richthofen's headquarters east of Kursk on 10th July 1942; his small command was to operate alone in the Voronezh Sector after the 8th Air Corps had flown out the following day. His command consisted of 76th Bomber Wing, the 10th Reconnaissance Group and an ever changing collection of fighter and dive-bomber aircraft. His mission was to support the 2nd Army which he did very successfully even after the fighting intensified during the following weeks he managed to support the ground troops with whatever aircraft he had left.

In November 1942 he succeeded *Generalleutnant* Hermann Plocher as Commander of 1st Air Division with its headquarters in Dugino, Russia while attached to Luftwaffen Kommando Ost, under *General der Flieger* Ritter von Greim. On 1st June 1943 he was promoted to *Generalleutnant* and in June was appointed Commanding General of 2nd Air Corps

Oberst Bülowius with General der Flieger Alfred Keller who has just presented Bülowius with the Knight's Cross, 4th July 1940. (Author's collection)

with it headquarters in Sala Consilina, Merate and later in 1944 in Verona, under the overall command of *Generalfeldmarschall* Kesselring's 2nd Air Fleet. In December the 2nd Air Corps was transferred to France and Bülowius became responsible for all fighter aircraft used in the support of the Army. On 6th June 1944, D-Day, the Allied invasion of Europe, the 2nd Air Corps had a headquarters but no aircraft, apparently most were being refitted in Germany. The ground troops had little or no battle experience and didn't know how to read maps. Bülowius aware of their inexperience proposed that aircraft be sent out to guide the troops and any reinforcements to where they were needed, however the responsibility for the movement of aircraft in that area fell to the commander of Air Fleet Reich and Bülowius was not consulted. The result was that on D-Day the German units were scattered and the aircraft got lost on their flights from Germany and had to make emergency landings, very few arrived at the assigned air bases.

On 16th October 1944 Bülowius was recalled to Germany and appointed Commanding General of Luftgau XVI in Dresden, here he had to co-ordinate the air defence of the area, but with very few aircraft and almost no fuel it was an impossible task. Promoted to *General der Flieger* in December, perhaps to urge his important defensive role and he briefly took command of Luftgau XV, in Prague, before being assigned to the staff of Luftgau Command III back in Dresden. His last command was that of Commander of all Wehrmacht troops in the Tirol area and it was while in this command that he was captured by U.S. troops in May 1945.

Bülowius wasn't accused of any war crimes but remained in U.S. captivity until June 1947 when he was released and returned home, where he died on 9th August 1968, in Detmold, Germany.

Ernst Joachim Valentin Gustav BUFFA
(1893-1971)
Generalleutnant

Knight's Cross: Awarded on 5th September 1944 as *Generalleutnant* and Commander 12th Flak Division (mot.), for actions on the Russian Front.

Ranks:
Fahnenjunker-Gefreiter – 21st March 1912
Fahnenjunker-Unteroffizier – 24th August 1912
Fähnrich – 19th November 1912
Leutnant – 18th August 1913
Oberleutnant – 5th October 1916
Hauptmann – 1st December 1923
Major – 1st October 1933
Oberstleutnant – 1st April 1936
Oberst – 1st August 1938
Generalmajor – 1st August 1940
Generalleutnant – 1st February 1943

Awards:
Iron Cross 2nd Class – 27th January 1915
Iron Cross 1st Class – 18th January 1917
Turkish Iron Half-Moon Badge (The Gallipoli Star)
Cross of Honour for Frontline Combatants
Armed Forces Long Service Award 1st Class
Commemorative Medal for 1st October 1938 with Bar – 9th July 1940
Commemorative Medal of 13th March 1938 – 1st September 1939
Bar to Iron Cross 2nd Class – 19th May 1940
Bar to Iron Cross 1st Class – 3rd June 1940
Luftwaffe Anti Aircraft Badge
German Cross in Gold – 9th November 1943

Generalleutnant Ernst Buffa as Commander of the 12th Anti-Aircraft Division wearing the Knight's Cross. (Wehrkundearchiv)

Ernst Buffa was born on 14th February 1893 in Oppeln, Silesia, on completion of his schooling he joined the Imperial Army as a *Fahnenjunker-Gefreiter* on 21st March 1912, with the 5th Foot Artillery Regiment in Niederschlesiche. In August 1913 he was commissioned as a *Leutnant* and attended Artillery School in August 1915 before being assigned as a Company Commander with the same unit in May 1916. He was promoted to *Oberleutnant* in October and remained with this command until Germany's surrender in November 1918.

Buffa remained in the army after the war and was assigned to the Hanover Riding School in June 1919. In January 1921 he was appointed Battery Officer with the 3rd Instructional Battalion, part of the 3rd Artillery Regiment. In May 1923 he attended an anti-aircraft course in Juterbog and in December was promoted to *Hauptmann*. In October 1924 he was assigned to the staff of the Commander of Wilhelmshaven where he took a leading role in an anti-aircraft training course, working as a senior instructor. In September 1925 he was appointed Battery Officer with the 3rd Battalion of the 4th Artillery Regiment in Dresden and a year later Buffa served as an instructor at the Anti-Aircraft School at Königsberg. He returned to the 4th Artillery Regiment in November 1926 and was appointed Regimental Battery Commander in February 1927. Now employed as an anti-aircraft expert and became Squadron Commander with the 4th Transport Battalion in October 1929 – this would be his final army command.

Promoted to *Major* in October 1933, Buffa was transferred to the Luftwaffe in April 1935 where he was assigned as Commander of the 1st Battalion, 13th Flak Regiment in Leipzig. On 1st April 1936 he was transferred to the 3rd Flak Regiment in Weimar, now with the rank of *Oberstleutnant* and took over as commander in October 1937. In August 1938 he was promoted to *Oberst* and in June 1939 was appointed Commander of the 11th Flak Regiment in Königsberg, later re-designated as 104th Flak Regiment seeing action during the Polish and French campaigns. In August 1940 he was appointed Anti-Aircraft Artillery Inspector in Holland with the rank of *Generalmajor* and in March 1942 was appointed to the same position in Norway.

In June 1942 he helped to create the 13th Flak Brigade in Rovaniemi, Finland, with orders to protect the area around Rovaniemi, and also Alakurtti, Nautsi, Lirkenes and Litza. His command was subordinated to *Generaloberst* Hans-Jurgen Stumpff's 5th Air Fleet. In December 1942 he succeeded *Generalleutnant* Gotthard Frantz as the commander of 12th Flak Division where he saw action near Orel and later at Kursk. In January 1943 Buffa was promoted to *Generalleutnant* and on 5th February 1944 he was awarded the Knight's Cross for actions near Bobruisk on the Eastern Front. In June he was appointed Commander of 21st Flak Division in Darmstadt where he came under the control of Air Region Commando VII and his command now helped with the defence of the Reich.

From 1st December 1944 to early January 1945 he spent on the Reserve List until he was recalled and assigned to the Reich War Court where he presided over the many court martials heard during the closing stages of the war. He surrendered to U.S. forces in May 1945 and remained in captivity until his release on 5th June 1947. Ernst Buffa died on 19th September 1971 in Traben-Trarback, Bernkastel-Wittlich, Germany.

Wolfgang von CHAMIER-GLISCZINSKI
(1894-1943)
Generalleutnant

Knight's Cross: Awarded on 6th October 1940 as *Oberst* and Commander of 3rd Bomber Wing for actions over England.

Ranks:
Fahnenjunker-Unteroffizier – 18th March 1913
Fähnrich – 20th November 1913
Leutnant – 19th April 1914
Oberleutnant – 1st February 1924
Hauptmann – 1st January 1929
Major – 1st October 1934
Oberstleutnant – 1st October 1936
Oberst – 1st October 1939
Generalmajor – 1st November 1941
Generalleutnant – 25th October 1943

Awards:
Iron Cross 2nd Class – World War I
Iron Cross 1st Class – World War I
Royal Prussian Observer's Badge – World War I
Wound Badge in Black – World War I
Royal Prussian Pilot's Badge – World War I
The Hanseatic Cross
The Lübeck Service Cross
Cross of Honour for Frontline Combatants
Armed Forces Long Service Award 2nd Class
Bar to Iron Cross 2nd Class
Bar to Iron Cross 1st Class

Oberst Wolfgang von Chaimer-Glisczinski wearing the Knight's Cross. (Wehrkundearchiv)

Born on 16th April 1894 in Hagen, Westphalia, Wolfgang von Chamier-Glisczinski joined the 143rd Infantry Regiment as a *Fahnenjunker* in March 1913, and was commissioned as a *Leutnant* in April 1914. He served for almost eighteen months as a Company Commander before training as an aircraft observer in October 1915 with the Army Air Park in Falkenhausen. He soon qualified and was posted to the Western Front as an observer with the 12th Air Battalion and was shot down in March 1918 and crash-landed in France where he was taken prisoner, and where he remained until February 1920. On his return to Germany he decided to remain in the army and served as a company officer with the 16th Infantry Regiment. Promoted to *Oberleutnant* in February 1924 he went on a leadership-training course as part of the Military District Command before being assigned as a photographic officer with the 3rd Division. In October 1930 he was transferred as a staff officer with the 16th Mounted Regiment and in April 1933 was assigned to the 15th Infantry Regiment.

He transferred to the Luftwaffe as a Squadron Captain in Gotha in June 1934 with the rank of *Major*. In March 1935 he was appointed Commander and Airport Commandant at Cottbus airbase before being assigned as the Commander of the Long Distance Flying School and Commander of Flight Command in Berlin in February 1936. Promoted to *Oberstleutnant* in October 1936, he was appointed Wing Commander of the 3rd Bomber Wing "Blitz" on 1st April 1939, formed in Heilgenbeil. His command consisted of Dorniers and Junkers 88s with his headquarters first in Elbing then in Würzburg, Le Culot and Wunstorf. Awarded the Knight's Cross on 6th October 1940 for his leadership while commanding the same Bomber Wing; he was later appointed Commander of the Greater Bomber Flying School in Tutow in December 1941 shortly after being promoted to *Generalmajor*.

In April 1943 he was appointed Air Leader of South East Croatia a unit formed in Agram, he led this unit with great skill and was beginning to make an impression with his superiors when he was killed near Zabreb, Croatia when his aircraft carshed duirng terrible storms on 22nd August 1943, he was posthumously promoted to *Generalleutnant*.

Generalleutnant Joachim Coeler. (Wehrkundearchiv)

Joachim COELER
(1891-1955)
General der Flieger

Knight's Cross: Awarded on 12th July 1940 as *Generalmajor* and Commander 9th Air Division for his part in the defeat of France.

Ranks:
Fähnrich zur See – 12th April 1913
Leutnant zur See – 22nd March 1915
Oberleutnant zur See – 25th December 1917
Kapitänleutnant – 1st January 1924
Korvettenkapitan – 1st October 1931
Oberstleutnant – 1st August 1934
Oberst – 1st April 1936
Generalmajor – 1st January 1939
Generalleutnant – 19th July 1940
General der Flieger – 1st January 1942

Awards:
Iron Cross 2nd Class – World War I
Iron Cross 1st Class – World War I
Royal Prussian Pilot's Badge - World War I
Imperial Navy Land Plane Pilot's Badge - World War I
Armed Forces Long Service Award 1st Class
Cross of Honour for Frontline Combatants
Bar to Iron Cross 2nd Class
Bar to Iron Cross 1st Class
Wehrmacht Daily Report: 19 June 1940; 15 February 1942

Born in Posen, Poland on 1st June 1891, Joachim Coeler started his career in the Navy, his father had been a naval officer, and pushed his son into a naval career. Coeler joined the German Imperial Navy as an officer cadet in April 1912, after being assigned to various naval schools and served on the officers training ship "Vineta", and finally the Torpedo training ship "Blücher" in June 1914. In March 1915 he was commissioned as a *Leutnant* and appointed as a flying instructor with the 1st Naval Bomber Battalion at Putzig, Holtenau and finally ending the war in Flensburg.

Coeler stayed in aviation during the Reichswehr years and in March 1922 was appointed Watch Officer, with the rank of *Oberleutnant zur See,* on the cruiser "Brunswick". In January 1924 he was promoted to *Kapitänleutnant* and was appointed company commander of the Naval Coastal Defence Department. Over the next few years he served in a number of various positions, including adjutant on board the "Schleswig-Holstein", Naval Navigation Officer in Wilhelmshaven, and finally as Navigation Officer on the "Hessen" with the rank of *Korvettenkapitän.*

In August 1934 Coeler transferred to the Luftwaffe with the rank of *Oberstleutnant* and was assigned to various staff positions which included a tour of duty with the German mission in Tokyo. In 1935 he was assigned to Luftkreis VI, and in April 1936 was promoted to *Oberst* and appointed Inspector of Naval Aircraft with Luftkreis VI and held a similar position with Luftwaffe Command in Kiel two years later. In January 1939 he was promoted to *Generalmajor* and when World War II started he was still in Kiel serving as the Commander of Naval Air Group West, and would spend the next six months under the command of the Navy. He now had 228 aircraft, mostly seaplanes and a few Stukas and Me 109s that had been specially adapted for naval support operations. He made the most of the resources at his disposal and conducted an aggressive mine-laying campaign against the British Royal Navy. He had been so successful that his aircraft had been responsible for sinking over 1,000 tonnes of British shipping and as a direct result his command was upgraded and became the 9th Air Division in February 1940.

After the fall of France, Coeler was recognised for his part in his mine-laying campaign when on 12th July 1940 he was awarded the Knight's Cross and five days later he was promoted to *Generalleutnant*. He took part in the Battle of Britain in August 1940 as part of Kesselring's 2nd Air Fleet and in October 1940 his command was again upgraded to Corps level, with its operational headquarters in Soesterberg and later Franc Port, near Soissons. He continued with his mine-laying operations and continued to inflict heavy losses in both shipping and men, his efforts were recognised further when he was promoted to *General der Flieger* in January 1942.

In December 1942 Coeler was put on the Reserve List where he remained until September 1943 when he was recalled to command the 14th Air Corps in Tutow. In August 1944 his command was renamed General of Transport Aircraft and its headquarters moved near Schloß Putbus, Rügen. This was Coeler's last command and in February 1945 he found himself on the Reserve List again. He ended the war at home with his family and after being interned briefly by the Allies, mainly because of his high rank he was soon released. He died in Garmisch-Partenkirchen, Bavaria on 14th May 1955 at the age of sixty-three.

Dipl.Ing. Gerhard CONRAD
(1895-1982)
Generalleutnant

Knight's Cross: Awarded the Knight's Cross on 24th May 1940 as *Oberst* and as Wing Commander of the Special Purpose Air Landing Wing 2.

Generalleutnant Gerhard Conrad wearing the Knight's Cross. (Wehrkundearchiv)

Ranks:
Unteroffizier – 3rd November 1914
Fähnrich – 7th December 1914
Leutnant – 29th January 1915
Oberleutnant – 1st April 1925
Hauptmann – 1st February 1930
Major – 1st January 1935
Oberstleutnant – 1st March 1937
Oberst – 1st June 1939
Generalmajor – 1st April 1941
Generalleutnant – 1st April 1943

Awards:
Knight's Cross of the Royal Prussian Hohenzollern House Order with Swords – 1917
Knight's Cross of the Saxony Order of Albert with Swords, 2nd Class
Iron Cross 2nd Class – World War I
Iron Cross 1st Class – World War I
Wound Badge in Silver – World War I
Cross of Honour for Frontline Combatants
Armed Forces Long Service Award 1st Class
Bar to Iron Cross 2nd Class – September 1939
Bar to Iron Cross 1st Class – September 1939
Combat Clasp for Bombers
KRETA Cufftitle

Gerhard Conrad was born in Pregelmühle near Alsleben, Saale on 21st April 1895, he entered the Imperial German Army in August 1914 as an officer candidate. In January 1915 he was commissioned as a *Leutnant* and became Platoon Leader with the 93rd Infantry Regiment before being appointed as battalion adjutant in September 1916. In March 1918 he spent almost a week in hospital after being wounded, he returned to the 93rd Infantry Regiment as adjutant and from late June until the end of the war he served as a company commander.

He joined the Border Protection Police in Silesia before serving as a Platoon Leader with various Infantry Regiments in the Reichswehr. In April 1925 he was promoted to *Oberleutnant* and continued to serve with the infantry until September 1926 when he was transferred to the War Ministry where he served in an administrative role. In February 1930 he was promoted to *Hauptmann* and appointed Director within the Army Weapons Office being responsible for weapons testing. In April 1933 he was transferred to the 11th Infantry Regiment as Company Commander where he remained for nearly two years.

On 1st January 1935 Conrad was promoted to *Major* and transferred to the Luftwaffe where he attended a flying course in Faßberg. In April 1936 he was appointed Squadron Commander of the 1st Bomber Wing "Hindenburg", less than a year later he was made Group Commander. He was briefly made Commander of Air Command Berlin before being promoted to *Oberst* in June 1939. He took over as Commander of the 2nd "Special Purpose" Glider Wing in August 1939 and led this command during the Battle of France. On 24th May 1940 Conrad was awarded the Knight's Cross for his leadership and success in the victory over France

In June 1940 he took over from *Oberstleutnant* Bernhard Georgi as the Commander of 27th Bomber Wing "Boelcke". From his headquarters in Tours, France his aircraft, mainly Heinkels took part in the aerial assault on Holland. From October to December 1940 he was the head of the Luftwaffe Control Commission III, which looked at the Luftwaffe's strength and resources during the Western Campaign. On 21st December he was appointed Air Commander of 11th Air Corps under the command of *General der Fallschirmtruppe* Kurt Student. His command was formed in Berlin-Templehof as a replacement and training unit for paratroopers, it remained in Berlin until early 1943 when it was moved to Nimes, France.

Conrad was promoted to *Generalmajor* in April 1941 and the following month he took part in the invasion of Crete where his unit saw heavy action. Although he took part in the action himself he didn't distinguish himself and took the role of staff officer. However in February 1943 he was promoted to *Generalleutnant* and took over as the commander of air troops attached to the 4th Air Fleet. He remained with this command until the end of the war and saw action on the Eastern Front in Dnjepropetrovsk and Uman in the Ukraine and then in Proskurov and Morczyn in Russia. He went on to see further action in Hungary during the attack on Budapest in 1944. In March 1945 he was appointed Military Replacement Inspector in Leipzig responsible for securing recruits and sending them to the frontline, it wasn't very successful and eventually Conrad knew that all was lost. On 20th April 1945, Hitler's last birthday, Conrad surrendered to U.S. forces; he remained in captivity until July 1947 when he returned to Germany. He died on 28th May 1982 in Ruhpolding, Upper Bavaria at the age of eighty-five.

Paul Deichmann as Generalleutnant, 1944. (Wehrkundearchiv)

Paul DEICHMANN
(1898-1981)
General der Flieger

Knight's Cross: Awarded on 26th March 1944 as Commanding General of the 1st Air Corps for his leadership skills on the Eastern Front.

Ranks:
Fähnrich – 29th March 1916
Leutnant – 20th August 1916
Oberleutnant – 1st August 1925

Hauptmann – 1st April 1933
Major – 1st August 1935
Oberstleutnant – 1st January 1938
Oberst – 1st August 1940
Generalmajor – 1st August 1942
Generalleutnant – 20th May 1944
General der Flieger – 20th April 1945

Awards:
Iron Cross 2nd Class – World War I
Iron Cross 1st Class – World War I
Wound Badge in Black – World War I
The Hanseatic Cross, 1914
Royal Prussian Observer's Badge
Cross of Honour for Frontline Combatants
Armed Forces Long Service Award 2nd Class
Bar to Iron Cross 2nd Class
Bar to Iron Cross 1st Class
German Cross in Gold – 20th April 1942

Born in the province of Hesse in the town of Fulda on 27th August 1898, Paul Deichmann was educated at the prestigious Gross-Lichtefelde Cadet Academy. He joined the Imperial German Army in March 1916 as a Platoon Leader with 86th Fusilier Regiment seeing action on the Western Front. In August he was commissioned as a *Leutnant* and saw action with 3rd Replacement Company in France before being assigned as an observer with the 8th Air Battalion. When the war ended he joined the Reichswehr and served in the Baltic States with various flying units. Promoted to *Oberleutnant* in August 1925 he served as a battalion adjutant with the 3rd Infantry Regiment and then as Company Commander before being attached to the Technical College in Charlottenberg training as a photographic officer. In November 1928 he went on a pilots course first in Berlin and then in Lipezk in Russia and was assigned as an advisor to the War Ministry.

He transferred to the Luftwaffe as a *Hauptmann* in 1934 and in August a year later he was promoted to *Major* and appointed Director of the Luftwaffe General Staff and at the same time was Chief of the Command Office with the Air Ministry. He remained on the General Staff until June 1940 when he was appointed Chief of Staff of the 2nd Air Corps serving under *Generalleutnant* Bruno Loerzer, seeing action on the Western Front. In 1940, shortly after the Norwegian campaign Deichmann had an idea of using old Ju 86s as training aircraft. This aircraft was obsolete and had been used as a bomber in Poland but was dropped from the armament program without giving advanced warning to the aircraft industry so new aircraft no longer needed were still being produced. All it needed was a small factory to assemble them. The Air Minister Erhard Milch approved the plan but Göring decided against it and all of Deichmann's arguments were brushed aside and the idea was forgotten.

In August 1942 Deichmann was promoted to *Generalmajor* and succeeded Hans Seidemann as Chief of Staff to the Commander-in-Chief South and Chief of Staff to the 2nd Air Fleet both under the command of *Generalfeldmarschall* Albert Kesselring. Kesselring thought highly of Deichmann, they had served together before in 1937 when Deichmann was Chief of the Operations section in the General Staff. In June 1943 he was given his own command on the Eastern Front in Orel when he was appointed commander of the 1st Air Division and in November it was upgraded to the 1st Air Corps. Here he commanded over 700 aircraft, part of 4th Air Fleet under the command of *Generaloberst* Otto Deßloch in Russia, Hungary and Austria. On 26th March he was awarded the Knight's Cross for his leadership skills and in his efforts in directing aircraft in support of ground troops. In May 1944 he supported the 17th Army in the Black Sea area and in the Simferopol area where his aircraft destroyed over fifty Soviet tanks.

He was briefly named as the commander of the 18th Air Division in April 1945 and at the same time was promoted to *General der Flieger*. His last command was as Commander-in-Chief of Luftwaffe Command 4, which had previously been known as 4th Air Fleet, then for the last twelve days of the war he spent commanding troops in the Balkans, Hungary and Slovakia. He surrendered to U.S. troops on 15th June 1945 and spent over two years in Allied captivity before being released on 22nd December 1947. Deichmann died on 10th January 1981 at the age of eighty-two in Hamburg.

Ullrich DIESING
(1911-1945)
Generalmajor

Knight's Cross: Awarded on 6th September 1942 as *Major* and Commander of 1st Destroyer Wing for actions in Russia.

Ranks:
Polizei-Unterwachtmeister – 1st July 1933
Polizei-Wachtmeister – 15th October 1933
Polizei-Oberwachtmeister – 1st January 1934
Polizei-Leutnant – 1st December 1934
Leutnant – 1st February 1935
Oberleutnant – 1st October 1936
Hauptmann – 1st June 1939
Major – 1st April 1942
Oberstleutnant – 1st March 1943
Oberst – 1st March 1944
Generalmajor – 1st November 1944

Awards:
Armed Forces Long Service Award 4th Class
Luftwaffe Pilot's Badge
Spanish Cross in Gold
Iron Cross 2nd Class – World War II

Ulrich Diesing as a Major wearing the Knight's Cross. Also visible are the Pilot's Badge, Iron Cross, and Spanish Cross. (Author's collection)

Leutnant Diesing shortly after being transferred to the Luftwaffe in February 1935. (Private source)

Iron Cross 1st Class – World War II
Combat Clasp for Bombers in Gold

Ullrich Diesing was born in Trebschen, Silesia on 12th March 1911, on completion of his schooling he decided to learn to fly. In April 1931 he joined the German Commercial Flying School as a flight student where he earned his pilots licence. In October 1932 he joined the Mecklenburg State Police, serving for three years and rising to the rank of *Leutnant*. In February 1935 he transferred to the Luftwaffe where he was immediately assigned to the Flying-School in Cottbus and in July he became a pilot on the staff of Command Berlin and was attached to Bomber Wing 152. In October 1936 he was promoted to *Oberleutnant* and in January the following year he was transferred to Greifswald as a pilot instructor. In April 1938 he was attached to the Reich Air Ministry where he became an advisor, and by June 1939 had been promoted to *Hauptmann*.

In August 1939 Diesing was appointed to the staff of the Chief of Operations of the Luftwaffe and in April 1940 he served on the staff of the General Quartermaster of the Luftwaffe. It was a great responsibility and high position for an officer of junior rank, but nevertheless Diesing had impressed his superiors and was soon given a field command. In January 1941 he succeeded *Hauptmann* Wolfgang Falck[56] as Commander of the 1st Group of the 1st Destroyer Wing, with its headquarters in Lechfeld. On 3rd March 1942 he was appointed Wing Commander of 1st Destroyer Wing operating from Smolensk, Russia under the command of 8th Air Corps. Diesing was promoted to *Major* in April 1942 and remained in Russia for the next five months. On 6th September 1942 Diesing was awarded the Knight's Cross for his successful leadership as Wing Commander of 1st Destroyer Wing on the Eastern Front.

On 22nd September 1942 Diesing was once again transferred to the Air Ministry where he was appointed Operations Officer to Hans Jeschonnek, the Chief of Operations of the Luftwaffe. He was now rapidly promoted and by March 1943 had been promoted to *Oberstleutnant*, twelve months later he was promoted to *Oberst* and by November 1944 at the age of just thirty-three he was promoted to *Generalmajor*. He worked closely with Bernd von Brauchitsch, Göring's chief adjutant and never really got on with his immediate superior Jeschonnek, by 1943 Göring was issuing orders direct to both Diesing and von Brauchitsch and completely bypassing Jeschonnek who had fallen out of favour.

In March 1944 Diesing was appointed Chief of the Planning Office with the Air Ministry, however by June the whole department had been transferred to the Office of the Armaments Minister Albert Speer. Diesing took over as Chief of the Technical Office of the Luftwaffe in August 1944, and later under its new head it was renamed the "Technical Air Armament Office". Göring's small inner circle now controlled the Air Ministry; this became more apparent when Milch lost his title of Air Minister, thanks to Göring. However Göring would not replace Milch, instead he put the office under the control of his two trusty cohorts, Diesing and von Brauchitsch.

On 17th April Diesing was killed in an accident near Boizenburg and is buried in the German War Grave Cemetery in Boizenburg approx. thirty-five miles from Hamburg, his grave is located on Block 2, Row 2, Grave 3.

Hans-Wilhelm Doering-Manteuffel as an Oberst on the staff of the Higher Command of Flak Artillery Schools. (Wehrkundearchiv)

Hans-Wilhelm DOERING-MANTEUFFEL
(1898-1963)
Generalmajor

Knight's Cross: Awarded on 10th September 1944 as *Oberst* and Commander of 10th Flak Regiment for actions on the Eastern Front.

Ranks:
Fahnenjunker-Gefreiter – May 1917
Fähnrich – 4th January 1918
Leutnant – 13th February 1918
Oberleutnant – 1st April 1925
Rittmeister – 1st April 1933
Hauptmann – 1st April 1935
Major – 1st January 1937
Oberstleutnant – 1st June 1939
Oberst – 1st January 1942
Generalmajor – 20th April 1945

Awards:
Iron Cross 2nd Class – World War I
Knight's Cross 2nd Class of the Royal Sachsburg Albrecht Order with Swords
Cross of Honour for Frontline Combatants
Silesian Eagle Order 2nd Class
Commemorative Medal for 1st October 1938
Armed Forces Long Service Award 2nd Class
Bar to the Iron Cross 2nd Class – 17th July 1941
Iron Cross 1st Class – 19th December 1941
Luftwaffe Flak Badge
German Cross in Gold – 14th April 1942

Hans-Wilhelm Doering-Manteuffel was born on 17th July 1898 in Heidersdorf, Silesia and entered the Imperial Army as a recruit seeing action on the Western Front. He later served as an observer and Battery Officer in the 64th Field Artillery Regiment and was commissioned in February 1918 and made Platoon Leader with the same regiment. When the war ended he joined the Freikorps serving as an Ordnance Officer in the 2nd Naval Brigade in February 1919. In October he joined the 39th Infantry Battery and a year later was appointed battery officer in the 4th Artillery Regiment, being promoted to *Oberleutnant* in October 1923.

Transferred to the Luftwaffe in April 1935 with the rank of *Hauptmann* he was assigned as battery commander in a Flak Battalion in Ludwigsburg. In October 1936 he was appointed Battalion Commander in the 24th Flak Regiment serving under *Oberst* Georg von Kutzleben[57] before being assigned to the Flak Artillery School in Rerik. He was promoted to *Major* in January 1937 and in October 1938 he was appointed commander of the training staff at the Flak Artillery School, where he remained until July 1940.

He had been promoted to *Oberstleutnant* in June 1939 and was now appointed commander of the 101st Flak Regiment where he saw little action until he was posted to the Eastern Front in June 1941. Now in Warsaw he made sure his command was ready for the invasion of Russia and was soon in action in the Orel area of central Russia supporting *Generaloberst* Heinz Guderian's 2nd Panzer Group. In January 1942 he was promoted to *Oberst* and in April was transferred to the staff of the Higher Command of Flak Artillery Schools under *Generalleutnant* Werner Prellberg.[58] This was a brief posting, by the end of the month he was transferred to the staff of the General of Flak Weapons *Generalmajor* Walther von Axthelm.

Towards the end of 1943 Doering-Manteuffel was serving as an officer on the staff of the German Military Mission in Rumania and from there was transferred to 10th Flak Regiment where he took over as Commander in March 1944. In July 1944 he was wounded and spent several months resting and returned to active duty in October as Commander of the 20th Flak Division. Here he was responsible for its withdrawal from the Balkans while under the command of the 5th Flak Corps led by General Otto-Wilhelm von Renz. In January 1945 he took up his last command of the war when he was appointed Commander of the 15th Flak Division in Hungary. His command had absorbed the remnants of the 5th Flak Division and was finding it difficult holding out in the area near Stuhlweissenburg, against strong U.S. forces. Doering-Manteuffel was promoted to *Generalmajor* on 20th April 1945, however just over two weeks later the war ended for him when he surrendered to the Americans. He was soon released from Allied captivity and returned home in September 1945. Doering-Manteuffel died at the age of sixty-four on 21st January 1963 in Stuttgart.

Generalleutnant Wolfgang Erdmann. (Wehrkundearchiv)

Wolfgang ERDMANN
(1898-1946)
Generalleutnant

Knight's Cross: Awarded on 8th February 1945 as *Generalleutnant* and Commander of 153rd Flak Regiment for actions in Arnhem.

Ranks:
Fahnenjunker – 10th January 1916
Fähnrich – 8th November 1916
Leutnant – 27th January 1917
Oberleutnant – 1st April 1925
Hauptmann – 1st April 1933
Major – 1st August 1936
Oberstleutnant – 1st January 1939
Oberst – 1st November 1940
Generalmajor – 1st March 1943
Generalleutnant – 1st July 1944

Awards:
Iron Cross 2nd Class – World War I
Iron Cross 1st Class – World War I
Wound Badge in Black – World War I
Cross of Honour for Frontline Combatants
Armed Forces Long Service Award 2nd Class
Bar to Iron Cross 2nd Class – 16th September 1939
Bar to Iron Cross 1st Class – 14th June 1940
War Service Cross 2nd Class with Swords – 30th January 1943
German Cross in Gold – 28th December 1943
Tank Destruction Badge

Born in Königsberg, Prussia on 13th November 1898, Wolfgang Erdmann joined the army as an officer cadet in January 1916, serving with the 3rd Foot Artillery Regiment. In July 1916 he was assigned to the 26th Foot Artillery Regiment and was commissioned in January 1917 as a *Leutnant*. His last assignment of the war was that of adjutant to the 156th Foot Artillery Regiment in August 1918. Erdmann saw action on the Western Front being awarded the Iron Cross 1st and 2nd Classes for bravery. He remained in the army after the war serving in the Reichswehr as an adjutant and ordnance officer. He was later allowed leave to study at the Berlin Technical College where he completed his studies and graduated with an engineering degree in 1924. In April 1925 he was promoted to *Oberleutnant* and served for the next ten years as a battery officer in the 2nd Artillery Regiment He was promoted to *Hauptmann* in April 1933, and three years later this was followed by his promotion to *Major*.

Transferred to the Luftwaffe in July 1937, Erdmann served as a General Staff Officer in the Organisation Department. A year later he was appointed Chief of Operations on the staff of Air Region Command XVII in Vienna, and in January 1939 was promoted to *Oberstleutnant*. In March he was appointed commander of the newly formed 2nd Group of the 4th Bomber Wing "General Wever" with its headquarters in Erfurt-Bindersleben. Named as Chief of 2nd Department in the Luftwaffe General Staff in January 1940, he was promoted to *Oberst* in November.

In March 1943 Erdmann was promoted to *Generalmajor* and the following month he was appointed commander of the 18th Luftwaffe Division covering the areas around Dunkirk and Calais, as part of the 82nd Army Corps. Appointed Air Leader in Croatia in August when he succeeded *Generalleutnant* Wolfgang von Chamier-Glisczinski. In May 1944 he was transferred to France where he joined the 1st Parachute Army as its new Chief of Staff, under *Generaloberst* Kurt Student. He served throughout its time in France where he was attached to Army Group D while it underwent training duties.

On 1st July 1944 Erdmann was promoted to *Generalleutnant* and by August he was transferred from the 1st Parachute Army just before they were sent into action. He was now appointed commander of the Parachute Training Division "Erdmann", an emergency unit formed in Bitsch to help reinforce the army at Arnhem. It had been formed from the remnants of other units and from units attached to the parachute training schools in Germany. In October 1944 it was renamed the 7th Parachute Division and operated under the control of the 86th Army Corps in Hechtel, Arnhem and in the Venlo areas. He was awarded the Knight's Cross on 8th February 1945 for his leadership and bravery during the heavy fighting in the Arnhem area. A few weeks later his command was caught in heavy fighting with British troops in the Oldenburg area of Germany and after fierce fighting on both sides he finally ordered his troops to surrender on 8th May 1945.

Wolfgang Erdmann committed suicide while in British captivity at the Munsterlager Prison Camp on 5th September 1946.

Johannes FINK
(1895-1981)
General der Flieger

Knight's Cross: Awarded on 20th June 1940 as Commander of 2nd Bomber Wing for his part in the defeat of France and the Low Countries.

General der Flieger Johannes Fink as commander of the 2nd Air Corps, 1944. (Author's collection)

Ranks:
Gefreiter – 30th June 1914
Fahnenjunker-Gefreiter – 15th August 1914
Fahnenjunker Unteroffizier – 15th October 1914
Fähnrich – 30th October 1914
Leutnant – 24th December 1914
Oberleutnant – 18th October 1918
Hauptmann – 1st February 1928
Major – 1st July 1934
Oberstleutnant – 1st March 1936
Oberst – 1st June 1938
Generalmajor – 1st October 1940
Generalleutnant – 1st October 1942
General der Flieger – 1st April 1944

Awards:
Iron Cross 2nd Class – World War I
Iron Cross 1st Class – World War I
Knight's Cross of the Royal Württemberg Military Service Order
Wound Badge in Black – World War I
Cross of Honour for Frontline Combatants
Armed Forces Long Service Award 1st Class

Bar to Iron Cross 2nd Class
Bar to Iron Cross 1st Class
German Cross in Gold – 1st October 1944

Johannes Fink was born in Pfullingen, Württemberg on 28th March 1895, he left school at the age of nineteen and volunteered for active service in 1914 joining the 9th Württemberg Infantry Regiment. He would remain with this regiment throughout the entire war; he was wounded in April 1915 and spent almost three months recovering. He returned to active duty as a *Leutnant*, serving as a Platoon Commander and went on to serve as Battalion adjutant and finally ended the war as the Regimental adjutant with the rank of *Oberleutnant*.

He stayed in the Reichswehr after the war and served as a Platoon Commander in 25th Regiment and then for almost three years he served as a staff officer. In September 1922 he was transferred to the Infantry School in Munich where he stayed for almost twelve months. He then spent the next few years as a staff officer and attended a weapons training course, a pilot's course in Berlin in April 1926. In April 1931, now promoted to *Hauptmann*, he became a consultant for the Army Weapons Department while attached to the Reich War Ministry, and went on to be liaison officer between the army and the Reich Commissioner of Aviation.

On 1st September 1933 he transferred to the Luftwaffe and the following year was promoted to *Major* and transferred as Squadron Leader of the Hanseatic Flying School in Faßberg as part of Fighter Wing "Boelcke". He became the Commander of the Bomber Wing "Boelcke in April 1935 and a year later was appointed as Inspector of Flight Security and Equipment, being promoted to *Oberstleutnant* in March 1936. Two years later he was promoted to *Oberst* and appointed Commander of the 2nd Bomber Wing taking part in the Battle of Britain, being appointed "Kanalkampfführer" or Channel Battle Leader in 1940. His force consisted of Do 17Z bombers and Ju 87 and fighters of the 26th and 53rd Fighter Wings. His mission was to patrol the straits of Dover and attack all British shipping in the Channel, he stationed himself in a bus near Bleriot's statute at Cap Gris Nez, it was in sight of the white cliffs. This made Fink one of the very few aerial commanders to be able to personally view battles from a command post. For his leadership skills in his part in the defeat of France and the Low Countries Fink was awarded the Knight's Cross on 20th June 1940.

On 13th August 1940 a Fink was ordered to lead his bombers across the Channel and bomb the RAF field at Eastchurch on the south bank of the Thames estuary. He led seventy-three Dornier bombers and was to be escorted by thirty Bf 110s led by *Oberstleutnant* Joachim Huth. Not long after the takeoff, Huth and the other Bf 110 pilots received a recall order. However the order did not reach Fink, whose bombers continued to fly towards England. Huth tried to contact Fink on the radio but couldn't reach him; the Luftwaffe Signals Service had failed to provide the Dorniers with the right crystals for their radio wavelengths. Huth sped across the flight path of Fink's formation flying up and down and sideways trying to signal Fink and the others to turn back. Fink was puzzled at Huth's antics but kept on course. Clouds then hid the fighters and bombers from each other and Huth had to give up. Fink's bombers continued towards England at 1500 feet and dropped their bombs, destroying hangars aircraft. However the aircraft destroyed were not the RAF fighters they thought instead they were Blenheim bombers. On the way back to Germany more bad luck followed Fink's formation were attacked by British fighters and five bombers were destroyed and five more landed in France too damaged to take off again. When he landed Fink climbed out of his seat in fury and called *Generalfeldmarschall* Kesselring to complain about the incredible confusion. Kesselring left his underground headquarters at Cap Blanc-Nez, near Calais, and travelled to Arras to offer his personal apologies for the mix-up.

On the 1st October 1940 Fink was promoted to *Generalmajor* and on the 21st October he was appointed Inspector of Bombers and Dive Bombers. He was further promoted to *Generalleutnant* two years later and in November 1942 was appointed Commander of 2nd Air Division in Southern France under the command of *Generalfeldmarschall* Kesselring's 2nd Air Fleet. In February 1944 he was appointed Commanding General of the Luftwaffe in Greece, with his headquarters in Athens and in April he was promoted to the rank of *General der Flieger*. In October he was awarded the German Cross in Gold and was shortly afterwards relieved of command and replaced by *Generalmajor* Hans Korte.

Fink returned to active service in December 1944 when he took over the command of the 2nd Air Corps with his headquarters in Fünfkirchen, Hungary, under the command of *Generaloberst* Otto Deßloch. For two days in February 1945 he was Deputy Commander of the 1st Air Fleet. He saw little action in the last months of the war and was on the Reserve List but remained at the disposal of Air Region V. He was captured by British troops in Kloster Heggbach, near Stuttgart in April 1945. He was transferred to various prison camps and in July 1946 was sent to the Island Farm Special Camp where in May 1948 he returned to Germany. Johannes Fink died on 1st June 1981, at his home in Pfullingen.

Helmuth FÖRSTER
(1889-1965)
General der Flieger

Knight's Cross: Awarded on 22nd February 1942 as Commanding General of 1st Air Corps in recognition of his personal bravery in Russia.

Ranks:
Gefreiter – 23rd September 1907
Fähnrich – 18th May 1908
Leutnant – 27th January 1909
Oberleutnant – 27th January 1914

Hauptmann – 8th June 1915
Major – 31st March 1919
Oberstleutnant – 1st April 1934
Oberst – 1st August 1935
Generalmajor – 1st February 1938
Generalleutnant – 1st January 1940
General der Flieger – 19th April 1941

Awards:
Knight's Cross of the Royal Prussian Hohenzollern House Order with Swords
Iron Cross 2nd Class – World War I
Iron Cross 1st Class – World War I
Cross of Honour for Frontline Combatants
Armed Forces Long Service Award 3rd Class
Bar to Iron Cross 2nd Class
Bar to Iron Cross 1st Class
Wehrmacht Daily Report: 21 October 1941

Born on 19th April 1889 in Groß-Strehlitz, Upper Silesia, Helmuth Förster joined the Imperial Army on 23rd September 1907 with the 1st Railway Regiment. Commissioned as a *Leutnant* in January 1909 he transferred to a flying test unit in Döberitz before being assigned as adjutant to the Inspector of Flying Troops in October 1913. In January 1914 he was promoted to *Oberleutnant* and shortly after the start of the First World War he served as a pilot with the 31st Flying Battalion on the Western Front. From January 1915 until the end of the war he was a staff officer on the General Staff of the Commanding General of the German air force. He retired from active service on 31st March 1919.

Förster returned to active service on 1st March 1934 when he joined the Luftwaffe with the rank of *Oberstleutnant*. In April he was appointed Chief of Staff of the Air Office in Königsberg, under *General der Flieger* Edmund Wachenfeld.[59] In August 1935 he was promoted to *Oberst* and appointed Commander of the 253rd Bomber Wing "General Wever", a flying unit formed

Helmuth Förster as a Generalleutnant as chief-of-staff of the 5th Air Fleet. (Wehrkundearchiv)

General der Flieger Förster wearing the Knight's Cross as Commanding General of 1st Air Corps. (Author's collection)

in Gotha. Appointed Commander of a training unit in October 1937, he was promoted to *Generalmajor* in February 1938 and appointed commander of a Luftwaffe Training Division in Greifswald. His division was responsible for the support of the 3rd Army in East Prussia and went onto support the 4th Army in Poland.

In October 1939 Förster was transferred to the Office of the State-Secretary of Aviation, *Generaloberst* Erhard Milch. In January 1940 he was promoted to *Generalleutnant* and was appointed Chief of Staff to the 5th Air Fleet under his old boss Milch. In April 1940 the 5th Air Fleet was transferred from Hamburg to Oslo where it took part in the invasion of Norway and in July after the defeat of France he became a leading member of the German-French Armistice Committee. From April to May 1941 he took over as the Military Commander of Serbia, with the rank of *General der Flieger*.

In June 1941 he was appointed Commanding General of 1st Air Corps when he succeeded *Generaloberst* Ulrich Grauert who had been shot down and killed over France. He led this new unit during the heavy fighting in the area around Leningrad as part of the 1st Air Fleet under the over-all command of *Generaloberst* Alfred Keller. He was awarded the Knight's Cross on 22nd February 1942, in recognition of his efforts on the Eastern Front in support of ground troops. In August he succeeded *General der Flakartillerie* Günther Rudel[60] as Chief of the Air Defence and at the same time was appointed Commander of 1st Special Bomber Wing stationed near Tatsinskaya and was given command of all Ju 52 aircraft in the area with responsibility for the airlift out of Stalingrad.

He surrendered to Allied troops on 9th May 1945 and spent time at Nuremberg as a witness and wasn't released from captivity until 30th June 1947. He returned home and died on 7th April 1965 in Lenggries near Bad Tolz.

Helmuth Förster at Nuremberg where he was a witness, and where he remained until 1947. (Ian Sayer)

Awards:
Iron Cross 2nd Class – 15th September 1914
Iron Cross 1st Class – 17th June 1915
Wound Badge in Black – 14th April 1918
Cross of Honour for Frontline Combatants – 21st January 1935
Armed Forces Long Service Award 1st Class
The Hanseatic Cross – 21st January 1918
Bar to Iron Cross 2nd Class – 13th April 1940
Bar to Iron Cross 1st Class – 7th July 1940
Wound Badge in Silver
AFRIKA Cufftitle
Luftwaffe Anti Aircraft Badge
Commemorative Medal for 1st October 1938
German Horseman's Badge in Silver
German Cross in Gold – 1st September 1942

Gotthard Anton Bernhard Albert FRANTZ (1888-1973) *Generalleutnant*

Knight's Cross: Awarded on 18th May 1943 while Commanding Officer of the 19th Flak Division for action in North Africa.

Ranks:
Fahnenjunker – 4th March 1907
Fähnrich – 18th November 1907
Leutnant – 18th August 1908
Oberleutnant – 28th November 1914
Hauptmann – 18th April 1916
Major – 3rd August 1921
Oberstleutnant – 1st November 1937
Oberst – 1st January 1939
Generalmajor – 1st September 1941
Generalleutnant – 1st April 1943

A perfect caricature of the Prussian general he was of medium height, slim, beak nosed with a wrinkled face and wore a monocle. Gotthard Frantz was born on 5th May 1888 in Berlin, and joined the Imperial Army at the age of seventeen shortly after completing his final examinations. He joined the Neumark Artillery Regiment in March 1907 as an officer candidate. He attended training a course in Glougau in October 1907 before being commissioned as a *Leutnant* in August 1908 and attended the Technical Institute at Spandau from March 1913 for three months and went on to see action at the front as a Battalion Adjutant with the 54th Field Artillery Regiment where he won the Iron Cross 1st and 2nd Classes. Promoted to *Hauptmann* in April 1916 he went on to serve as a Battery Commander and later as an artillery adjutant. He remained in the artillery after the war serving in the peace time army until August 1921 when he went to university to study philosophy until January 1922. Exactly a year later he was employed with the Dresdner Bank in Potsdam and later worked in Berlin for the next ten years.

In October 1933 he served as commander of a Border Police Regiment with the rank of *Major* and towards the end of 1936 he joined the Luftwaffe. He first served as an officer with special duties while assigned to the Reich Air Ministry, later serving in the 1st Battalion of the 2nd Flak Regiment in Stettin. In February 1937 he was appointed Battery Leader with 2nd Flak Regiment and shortly afterwards was accepted as an instructor with a training regiment, and was promoted to *Oberstleutnant* in November. In February 1938 he was named as the new Commander of the 1st Battalion of the 20th Flak Regiment and just over ten months later was appointed Commander of 1st Battalion of the 7th Flak Regiment.

In January 1939 Frantz was promoted to *Oberst* and became the first Commander of the 7th Flak Regiment in Breslau. Frantz saw his first action of World War II in Poland when he was appointed Commander of all anti-aircraft units within 8th Air Region. In the Western Campaign following the occupation of Luxembourg, he led the 7th Flak Brigade, part of Guderian's Panzer Group, from the Aisne to the Swiss border. He was later responsible for the defence of the Channel sector between Le Harve and Cherbourg under the control of von Richthofen's 8th Air Corps. In November 1940 he was appointed commander of the Berlin-Bernau School of Air Warfare.

Following his promotion to *Generalmajor* in September 1941 Frantz was appointed Commander of the 12th Flak Division, when he succeeded *Generalmajor* Rudolf Eibenstein. He led this unit in Russia at Ripshero and in May 1942 he saw action in the southern sector as part of Army Group Centre. Frantz was wounded three times in Russia and was awarded the German Cross in Gold on 21st September 1942. In December he was made Commander of the 19th Flak Division and went on to serve in Tunisia. In April 1943 he was promoted to *Generalleutnant* and fought with great leadership and bravery often directing his guns from exposed positions as they engaged enemy air and ground targets. In May his troops came under strong attack from the Allies and on 13th May 1943 along with his command Frantz surrendered to U.S. forces and went into captivity. While in a prison camp he was informed that he had been awarded the Knight's Cross for his actions in Tunisia against overwhelming Allied superiority.

On 1st February 1945 Frantz was released from captivity due to ill health and once back in Germany he was placed at the disposal of an Flak Division in Leipzig but saw no action. He was captured in April 1945 by Soviet forces and remained in a prison camp for the second time until his release in November 1949. He died in Bad Homburg on 21st January 1973 at the age of eighty-four.

Stefan FRÖHLICH
(1889-1978)
General der Flieger

Knight's Cross: Awarded on 4th July 1940 as *Generalmajor* and Commander of the 76th Bomber Wing for actions during the French Campaign.

Ranks:
Kadett-Offizier – 18th August 1908
Leutnant – 1st May 1911
Oberleutnant – 1st August 1914
Hauptmann – 1st August 1917
Major – 19th January 1928
Oberstleutnant – 28th December 1935
Oberst – 1st April 1939
Generalmajor – 1st July 1940
Generalleutnant – 1st January 1942
General der Flieger – 1st July 1943

Awards:
Iron Cross 2nd Class – World War I
Royal Bavarian Prince Regent Leopold Jubilee Medal
Austro-Hungarian Military Service Medal 3rd Class with War Decoration and Swords
Austro-Hungarian Military Service Medal in Bronze with Swords
Austro-Hungarian Military Service Medal in Silver with Swords
Austrian War Commemorative Medal with Swords
Austrian Golden Service Badge
Cross of Honour for Frontline Combatants
Armed Forces Long Service Award 3rd Class
Commemorative Medal of 1st October 1938
Luftwaffe Observer's Badge
Iron Cross 1st Class
Bar to Iron Cross 2nd Class
German Cross in Gold – 11th May 1942
AFRIKA cufftitle
Wehrmacht Daily Report: 10 November 1943; 19 October 1944

Stefan Fröhlich was born in Orsova, Hungary on 7th October 1889, after graduating from the Imperial Austrian Pioneer Cadet School at Hainburg he joined the Austro-Hungarian army as an officer cadet on 18th August 1908. Commissioned in May 1911 he served as Company Commander with 12th Pioneer Battalion and fought mainly on the Italian Front during the war and was highly decorated. During the last months of the war he served as an instructor at the Technical Academy at Hainburg, ending the war with the rank of *Hauptmann*. He remained in the army after the war and served in a technical battalion and in November 1923 he was appointed adjutant and Company Commander in the 2nd Pioneer Battalion. He was promoted to

Right: Generalleutnant Stefan Fröhlich wearing the Knight's Cross. (Wehrkundearchiv)

Far right: Stefan Fröhlich as Commanding General of 17th Air Region, September 1943. (Wehrkundearchiv)

Major in January 1928 and was transferred as an engineer with the Austrian Federal Ministry for Army Affairs.

In 1935 he completed his training as a pilot and became interested in aviation and looked for a suitable role within the armed forces. On 1st April 1937 he was appointed Commandant of the Air Base Zeltweg before being transferred to the German Luftwaffe in March 1938. At the beginning of 1939 he served with 76th Bomber Wing and at the same time was Air Base Commandant in Wiener-Neustadt, near Vienna. In April 1939 he was promoted to *Oberstleutnant* and commanded the 1st Bomber Group in Poland and in November he was appointed Commander of the 76th Bomber Wing and led this unit during the campaign in France and the Low Countries. In July 1940 he was promoted to *Generalmajor* and on 4th July was awarded the Knight's Cross for his achievements during the Western Campaign, he went on to command this Wing during the Battle of Britain.

In February 1941 he was appointed Air Leader in Africa, under the command of *General der Flieger* Hans Geisler's 10th Air Corps, working closely with General Rommel, although the two men were never friends. In January 1942 Fröhlich was promoted to *Generalleutnant* and in April he was transferred to Germany where he oversaw the formation of the 2nd Air Division. In December he was appointed Commanding General of 9th Air Corps, and in July 1943 he was promoted to *General der Flieger*. He now became responsible for supporting Rommel's ground forces in the area of Tunis, and it wasn't very successful. The friction between the two men increased and Rommel wouldn't complain about Fröhlich to Göring because the *Reichsmarschall* and Rommel didn't get on either. In fact Rommel once called Göring his "bitterest enemy". Göring wanted the Luftwaffe to be put in charge of the African area and so supported Frohlich. However this would mean getting rid of Rommel, one of Hitler's favourite generals and because of the hostility between Rommel and Göring, Hitler intervened and the unfortunate Fröhlich lost his command.

In September 1943 he succeeded General Friedrich Hirschauer as Commanding General of 17th Air Region in Vienna before being assigned to the staff of 3rd Air Fleet in Paris under the command of *Generalfeldmarschall* Hugo Sperrle. On 1st September 1944 he became the last commander of Luftwaffe Command South-East succeeding *General der Flieger* Martin Fiebig. From February 1945 he succeeded *General der Flieger* Hans-Georg von Seidel[61] as Commander-in-Chief of 10th Air Fleet a replacement unit set up to defend Berlin, a unit that had been formed in July 1944, but by the time Fröhlich had taken over command it had been almost stripped of all of its troops and aircraft. It had been left with reserve and replacement troops who badly needed training and equipment.

Fröhlich was arrested by American troops in May 1945 but released soon afterwards on parole in the British zone of Austria. He returned home and received a full West German pension from the government until his death in Duisburg on 2nd October 1978.

Robert FUCHS
(1895-1977)
Generalmajor

Knight's Cross: Awarded on 6th April 1940 as Commander of 26th Bomber Wing for actions on the Western front.

Ranks:
Vizewachtmeister – 28th February 1915
Leutnant der Reserve – 7th August 1915
Leutnant (active) – 6th October 1917
Oberleutnant – 1st April 1925
Hauptmann – 1st February 1930
Major – 1st November 1935
Oberstleutnant – 1st March 1937
Oberst – 1st November 1938
Generalmajor – 1st September 1943

Awards:
Iron Cross 2nd Class – World War I
Iron Cross 1st Class – World War I
Wound Badge in Black – World War I
Cross of Honour for Frontline Combatants
Armed Forces Long Service Award 1st Class
Bar to Iron Cross 2nd Class
Bar to Iron Cross 1st Class

Generalmajor Robert Fuchs as Commander of the 1st Air Division, succeeding Generalmajor Paul Deichmann in September 1943. (Wehrkundearchiv)

Robert Fuchs was born into a middle-class family on 11th May 1895 in Berlin-Reinickendorf, he entered the Imperial Army as a war volunteer with the 1st Guards Ulanen Regiment in August 1914. He was commissioned as a *Leutnant der Reserve* a year later and served as a Platoon Leader with 15th Reserve Jäger Battalion and with the 49th Reserve Infantry Regiment in September 1915. In December 1917 serving with the same regiment he was appointed company leader and went on to win the Iron Cross 1st and 2nd Classes ending the war as Company Commander with the 34th Fusilier Regiment on the Western Front.

Fuchs remained in the infantry after the war serving in the Reichswehr, but not being promoted until April 1925. Three years later he left the infantry to continue his education at the Technical College in Berlin-Charlottenburg, where he received his engineering doctorate in September 1932. He returned to the infantry a month later as Company Commander with the 17th Infantry Regiment as a *Hauptmann*. In October 1933 he transferred to the Luftwaffe and was attached to the Air Ministry as a technical advisor and a year later he served as an instructor at the Juterbog Flying School. In November 1935 he was promoted to *Major* and in March 1936 was appointed commander of the 153rd Bomber Wing and at the same time was named as Airbase Commander at Altenburg. Promoted to *Oberstleutnant* in March 1937 Fuchs was assigned to the Air Ministry and was attached to Göring's Office for a time and then as technical officer in the training department.

On 29th September 1939 Fuchs took over as Commander of the 26th Bomber Wing "Löwen", now with the rank of *Oberst*. He then saw action on the Western Front and on 6th April 1940 he was awarded the Knight's Cross for his outstanding leadership during the campaign in France. Placed on the Reserve List until December 1942 he assumed command of the 33rd Luftwaffe Jäger Regiment and was named as Commander of the 20th Luftwaffe Field Division in August 1943, with its headquarters in Aalborg, Denmark.

Fuchs was promoted to *Generalmajor* in September 1943, and two months later was appointed commander of the 1st Air Division, being the last commander when he succeeded *Gen-*

eralmajor Paul Deichmann. He remained with this command until the end of the war seeing action mostly on the Eastern Front with his last headquarters in Neubrandenburg, East Germany. He surrendered to Allied forces on 8th May 1945 and went into captivity. Robert Fuchs died in Göttingen, Germany on 15th January 1977.

Generalleutnant Hans Geisler in 1939. (Wehrkundearchiv)

Hans Ferdinand GEISLER
(1891-1966)
General der Flieger

Knight's Cross: Awarded on 4th May 1940 as *Generalleutnant* and Commanding General of 10th Air Corps in recognition of his efforts in sinking British shipping.

Ranks:
Fähnrich zur See – 12th April 1910
Leutnant zur See – 19th September 1912
Oberleutnant zur See – 2nd May 1915
Kapitänleutnant – 21st January 1920
Korvettenkapitän – 1st January 1928
Fregattenkapitän – 1st January 1933
Oberst – 1st September 1934
Generalmajor – 1st April 1937
Generalleutnant – 1st April 1939
General der Flieger – 19th July 1940

Awards:
Iron Cross 2nd Class – World War I
Iron Cross 1st Class – World War I
Cross of Honour for Frontline Combatants
Armed Forces Long Service Award 1st Class
Bar to Iron Cross 2nd Class
Bar to Iron Cross 1st Class
Commemorative Medal for 1st October 1938 with Bar "Prague Castle"
Commemorative Medal of the Return of the Memel District
German Cross in Gold – 9th November 1942
Wehrmacht Daily Report: 10 April 1940; 27 February 1941; 17 June 1941

Hans Ferdinand Geisler was born on 19th April 1891 in Hannover, and he entered the Naval Academy as a cadet in April 1909, soon after leaving school. He continued his training on board the heavy cruiser "Hertha" before being transferred on board the Liner "Nassau" in October 1911. He was promoted to *Leutnant zur See* in September 1912 and served as an aerial observer during the First World War, ending the war as a naval reconnaissance commander with the German Imperial Navy.

After the war he remained in the navy and was appointed a commander of a naval battalion and was promoted to *Kapitänleutnant* in January 1920. In June he was appointed acting commander of the Sea-Flying Battalion at Holtenau before becoming a Company Commander with a Naval Station in the Baltic Sea in September 1920, and spent the next few years assigned to various training staff positions in the Baltic Sea area. In January 1928 he was promoted to *Korvettenkapitän* and in October 1932 he was assigned as First Officer on the Liner "Schleswig-Holstein. In January 1933 he was promoted to *Fregattenkapitän* and appointed department head within the Naval Command, this would be his last naval command.

In September 1934 he was transferred to Luftwaffe where he headed the Naval Air Unit until April 1939 when he was assigned to the Reich Air Ministry. In June 1939 now with the rank of *Generalleutnant* he was assigned to the staff of 2nd Air Fleet responsible for Germany's Coastal Command and the Luftwaffe in Hamburg. In September he was appointed commander of 10th Air Division in charge of anti-seaborne forces, but he had virtually no bombers at his disposal. In October his command was upgraded to Corps level and he was allocated more aircraft, he was responsible for bombing British merchant shipping in the Channel but was still very short of aircraft. In early 1940 he made a suggestion to Hans Jeschonnek, the Chief of Staff of the Luftwaffe, that the Focke-Wulf 200, a four-engined civilian aircraft, be converted into a

Above: General der Flieger Geisler with his wife leaving church in 1940. (Author's collection)

Right: Hans Geisler in Sicily talking to an unknown officer. At right is Oberstleutnant Siegfried Westphal. (Author's collection)

military aircraft until the Heinkel 177 bomber was ready for production. Jeschonnek thought the idea was good and so did Göring, and within a few short months the converted Focke-Wulf's were delivered to Geisler's command where they were used as long-range reconnaissance bombers. Geisler could now focus on attacking the British convoys and merchant shipping in the Channel once more, and was very successful. On 4th May 1940 he was awarded the Knight's Cross for his efforts in sinking Allied shipping, and after the successful defeat of France was promoted to *General der Flieger*.

During the invasion of Denmark the 10th Air Corps were given 1000 aircraft, which included He 111s, almost forty Ju 87s, thirty Me 109s, seventy reconnaissance and coastal aircraft and 500 Junker 52 transport planes. Later in 1940 he was responsible for the planning of the aerial operations and objectives for the war against England. However his conclusions regarding the strength and capability of the Royal Air Force were ignored. He had always stated that an attack on England would mean the Luftwaffe successfully gaining complete air superiority, and he believed that with the forces Germany had at that time this could not be achieved. Geisler wasn't a very successful air corps commander and his early success against British shipping was never repeated, although it wasn't all his fault as most of his aircraft was taken away from him and redeployed to Russia in June 1941. In January 1941 his 10th Air Corps was transferred to Sicily where he setup his headquarters in Taormina and his forces were responsible for many attacks on Malta.

In August 1942 Geisler was transferred back to the Air Ministry where he remained until October when he was put on the reserve list and officially retired on 31st October 1942. He wasn't a very successful Air Corps commander and was perhaps too outspoken he was lucky to have escaped severe punishment in February 1940 when by mistake two of his aircraft sank two German destroyers in the Dogger Bank area of the North Sea. There was a painful court of enquiry about the disaster and Geisler was lucky not to have been court martialled. He spent the rest of the war at home in quiet retirement, he died on 25th June 1966 in Cologne.

Walter GRABMANN
(1905-1992)
Generalmajor

Knight's Cross: Awarded on 14th September 1940 as Oberst and Commander of 76th Destroyer Wing for actions over England.

Ranks:
Polizei-Leutnant – 1st November 1926
Polizei-Oberleutnant – 1st November 1930
Oberleutnant – 1st October 1934
Hauptmann – 1st April 1935
Major – 1st December 1938
Oberstleutnant – 19th July 1940
Oberst – 1st April 1942
Generalmajor – 1st August 1944

Awards:
Iron Cross 2nd Class – World War II
Iron Cross 1st Class – World War II
Armed Forces Long Service Award 3rd Class

Spanish Cross in Gold with Swords
Combined Pilot's and Observer's Badge
Operational Flying Clasp for Long-Range Day Fighters in Gold
Honour Goblet of the Luftwaffe – 8th July 1940

Walter Grabmann was born into a Catholic family in Bad Reichenhall on 20th September 1905. In May 1924 he joined the Bavarian Land Police in Nuremberg and served as a Company Commander and finally as a police recruit trainer with the rank of *Oberleutnant*. In April 1931 he took part in a pilot training course with the police and was assigned to the Flight Surveillance Department for the North Bavarian area. In October 1934 he transferred to the Luftwaffe and was assigned to the Lechfeld Combat Flying School. Promoted to *Hauptmann* in April 1935 he was assigned to a fighter course at Schleißheim, the following March he was appointed adjutant of the 134th Fighter Wing "Horst Wessel". A year later he took over command of the 234th Fighter Wing and at the same time was appointed airfield Commandant of Cologne-Ostheim.

In September 1938 he volunteered for service with the Condor Legion in Spain where he was attached to a fighter group where he flew He 51 biplanes and later the Messerschmitt Bf 109. He was credited with six aerial victories while in Spain and was awarded the Spanish Cross in Gold with Swords. He returned to Germany in April 1939 as a *Major* and was assigned as the Commander of the 1st Group, after a brief time as Commander of the 5th Group he took part in the invasion of Poland in September. He was injured on the first day of the war when his Bf 110 was attacked by a Polish fighter aircraft that was attacking a formation of German bombers that he was escorting, he managed to land safely.

Grabmann quickly recovered from his injuries and returned to active service soon afterwards and in April 1940 he was appointed Commander of the 76th Destroyer Wing and from June he simultaneously became the Fighter Leader for North Norway. In May Grabmann was shot down by an enemy fighter while he was attempting a low-level attack on Douai airfield in France, he parachuted to safety but was quickly captured by French troops and six days later he was rescued and by an advancing Panzer unit and returned to his command. He saw heavy action on the Western Front and was promoted to *Oberstleutnant* in July 1940 shortly after the fall of France, and in September he was awarded the Knight's Cross for his leadership skills.

In August 1941 Grabmann was made Commander of Destroyer School 2 in Memmingen, and in April 1942 he was promoted to *Oberst*. In August he was appointed Fighter Leader for the Holland and Ruhr area, a unit that had been formed in Amsterdam-Schiphol to co-ordinate fighter units in the area.

Oberst Walter Grabmann wearing the Knight's Cross. (Author's collection)

On 11th November 1943 he was made Commander of the 3rd Fighter Division, leading this unit until April 1945 and seeing action in Deelen, Duisburg and Weidenbrück, he was at this time subordinated to the 1st Fighter Corps under the command of *Generalleutnant* Josef Schmid and later *Generalmajor* Dietrich Peltz. His leadership skills were recognised when he was promoted to the rank of *Generalmajor* in August 1944.

He took over as Commander of the 1st Fighter Division in Ribbeck, a small unit pulled together by Grabmann in an attempt to support the remaining ground troops in that area. With the war almost over Grabmann took up his final command when he led the 15th Air Division on 30th April, part of Air Fleet "Reich", under the command of Generaloberst Stumpff. Here he bravely supported what was left of Army Group B in the Ruhr area.

Grabmann was taken prisoner on 30th April by British troops, he remained in captivity until his release on 12th May 1948. He died in Munich on 20th August 1992 at the age of eighty-six.

Ulrich GRAUERT
(1889-1941)
Generaloberst

Knight's Cross: Awarded on 29th May 1940 as *General der Flieger* and Commanding General of 1st Air Corps.

Ranks:
Fähnrich – 13th March 1909
Leutnant – 27th January 1910
Oberleutnant – 25th February 1915
Hauptmann – 18th August 1917
Major – 1st February 1929
Oberstleutnant – 1st October 1932
Oberst – 1st July 1934
Generalmajor – 1st October 1936
Generalleutnant – 20th April 1938
General der Flieger – 1st October 1939
Generaloberst – 19th July 1940

Awards:
Knight's Cross of the Royal Prussian Hohenzollern House Order with Swords
Iron Cross 2nd Class – World War I
Iron Cross 1st Class – World War I
Armed Forces Long Service Award 1st Class
Bar to Iron Cross 2nd Class – 12th September 1939
Bar to Iron Cross 1st Class – 25th September 1939
Pilot's Badge with Diamonds
Imperial and Royal Austrian Order of the Iron Crown 3rd Class with War Decoration
Cross of Honour for Frontline Combatants
Royal Prussian Flier's Commemorative Badge
Combined Pilot's and Observers Badge
Combined Pilot's and Observers Badge in Gold with Diamonds
Wehrmacht Daily Report: 30 May 1940; 24 May 1941

Born on 6th March 1889 in Berlin, Ulrich Grauert completed his education before joining the Imperial Army in March 1909 as an officer candidate with 2nd Field Artillery Regiment. He was commissioned as a *Leutnant* in January 1910 and attended Artillery School the following year. In October 1912 he briefly attended the Technical Institute of Artillery at Spandau before joining the 3rd Field Artillery Brigade as an Ordnance Officer in September 1914. In February 1915 he was promoted to *Oberleutnant* a month later he joined the 56th Field-Flying Battalion as an observer before spending a brief assignment with the 5th Battle Wing. In December 1916 he was appointed commander of the 9th Flying Squadron seeing action on the Western Front and was promoted to *Hauptmann* in August 1917. 18th April 1918 he was appointed company commander in the 30th Field Infantry Regiment and his last assignment of World War I was as an Observer with 103rd Balloon Platoon.

Ulrich Grauert as a Generalmajor shown wearing the Knight's Cross. The award looks larger than normal and has obviously been added afterward. (Author's collection)

He remained with the Reichswehr after the war and in January 1919 was appointed leader of the Flying Unit of the Guards Cavalry Rifle Division. In April 1920 he was appointed adjutant to the Inspector of Flying, and for the next few years served as a staff officer with various flying units. In January 1926 he was appointed Battery commander with 1st Artillery Regiment where he remained for the next two-and-a-half years. He was made advisor within the War Ministry in October 1928 where he remained until November 1931, having being promoted to *Major* in February 1929. In December 1931 Grauert was appointed as Commander of the 3rd Battalion of 6th Artillery Regiment, and was promoted to *Oberstleutnant* in October 1932. In January 1933 he was again attached to the War Ministry and assigned to the Air Protection Office before being transferred to the newly formed Luftwaffe in September 1933 with his first assignment as commander of the Weapons Schools. In November he was appointed a department head with the Reich Air Ministry and was promoted to *Oberst* in July 1934 and to *Generalmajor* in October 1936.

He began his training as a future Luftwaffe commander in April 1937 at a Commanders course in Brandis, then one in Greifswald followed by a reconnaissance training course in Jütterbog. On 20th April 1938 he was promoted to *Generalleutnant* and in July was appointed as commander of 1st Air Division. He was beginning to make a name for himself, and was highly thought of by Göring and other senior commanders; he was always very professional and highly competent and led the 1st Air Division with some distinction during the Polish campaign in 1939, being promoted to *General der Flieger* soon after the victory.

In 1940 his command was upgraded to 1st Air Corps and his headquarters was moved to Brussels where he directed his command successfully against the Allied troops in France and the Low Countries. He was awarded the Knight's Cross on 29th May 1940 in recognition of his highly successful command of his forces during the campaign in France. When France fell in June the same year Grauert was promoted to *Generaloberst* and became the 8th most senior Luftwaffe commander. After the victory parades which followed the fall of France Grauert returned to his headquarters in Brussels and waited for his orders which surely would have been a command in the Soviet Union, this time as commander of an Air Fleet.

On 15th May 1941 Grauert flew on an inspection tour to France, and while flying over St. Omar his Junkers 52 which was being escorted by Bf 109s was attacked by Allied aircraft. Grauert's aircraft was attacked by two Spitfires piloted by Flight Sergeant Waclaw Giermer and Flight Lieutenant Jerzy Jankiewicz, attached to 303rd Polish Squadron stationed at RAF Northolt. The aircraft was badly damaged and crashed near St. Omar and Grauert was killed immediately along with the crew, his body was later recovered and he was given a military funeral with all honors, attended by *Generalfeldmarschall*'s Erhard Milch, Hugo Sperrle and Albert Kesselring.

Generaloberst Ulrich Grauert is buried today, with the rest of the crew of the Junkers 52, at the German Military Cemetery in Nampcel, France: Block 6, Grave # 784.

Generaloberst Ulrich Grauert is seen talking to an unknown Flieger, 1940. (Author's collection)

Fritz GRIESHAMMER
(1899-1956)
Generalmajor

Knight's Cross: Awarded on 12th April 1945 as *Generalmajor* and Commander of 24th Flak Division for actions on the Eastern Front.

Ranks:
Gefreiter – 14th May 1915
Unteroffizier – 1st August 1915
Offiziers-Aspirant – 10th February 1916
Vizewachtmeister – 28th February 1916
Leutnant der Reserve – 6th March 1917
Polizei-Leutnant – 3rd October 1920
Polizei-Oberleutnant – 1st December 1923
Polizei-Hauptmann – 1st July 1932
Hauptmann – 1st August 1935
Major – 1st April 1936
Oberstleutnant – 1st February 1939
Oberst – 1st April 1941
Generalmajor – 1st April 1944

Awards:
Iron Cross 2nd Class – World War I
Iron Cross 1st Class – World War I
Wound Badge in Black - World War I
Cross of Honour for Frontline Combatants – 20th December 1934
Armed Forces Long Service Award 2nd Class
Bar to Iron Cross 2nd Class – 19th January 1940

Bar to Iron Cross 1st Class – 16th December 1940
Luftwaffe Flak Badge – 16th December 1941

Fritz Grieshammer was born in Rehau, Upper Franconia on 30th March 1899, and he entered the Imperial Army as a war volunteer on 25th January 1915 with the 3rd Bavarian Train Battalion. He went onto serve with the 6th Bavarian Transport Column on the Western front and won both the Iron Cross 2nd and 1st Classes. In January 1917 he was transferred to a Staff position as Liaison Officer with the Army High Command, in March of the same year he was commissioned as a *Leutnant*. In early 1918 he returned to active duty at the front with 7th and 8th Bavarian Field Artillery Regiments until he was wounded in November 1918. He remained in hospital in Nuremberg until after the surrender and was well enough to go home in January 1919.

He remained in the army after the war as a Battery Officer with the 2nd Battalion of the 8th Bavarian Artillery Regiment, and in July 1919 he was assigned to the 1st Munitions Column of the 24th Artillery Regiment. In April 1920 he joined the Freikorps movement and became the Horse Depot Leader of Brigade Epp, and returned to 24th Artillery Regiment in May. In October 1920 he transferred to the Bavarian State Police and was appointed Unit Officer and recruitment leader of the State Police in Eichstätt. In November 1924 he was appointed as advisor at the Gendarmerie and Police School in Fürstenfeldbruck, and in September 1928 he served as an officer with the State Police in Augsburg.

In August 1935 he transferred to the Luftwaffe and attended a Battery Chief Course at the Flak School in Wustrow, he then went on to serve as a Battery Commander with the 8th and 18th Flak Regiment. Grieshammer was appointed Commander of the 32nd Fortress Flak Battalion in St. Wendel, being promoted to *Oberstleutnant* in February 1939 he went onto serve as Commander of the Flak Group Kassel. In October 1940 he became Commander of the Motorised Flak Regiment "Grieshammer", attached to Panzer Group Guderian during the Western Campaign. In January 1941 he was appointed Commander of the 9th Flak Brigade and saw action in Western and Southern France and in April he was promoted to *Oberst*. In May he was made Commander of the 6th Flak Brigade when he succeeded *Oberst* Werner Prellberg, with its headquarters in Paris and then in Ploesti. In July 1942 Grieshammer was injured and spent almost two weeks recovering in hospital in Bucharest, returning to duty in October when he was assigned to the Air Ministry.

In January 1944 Grieshammer was appointed Commander of the 24th Flak Division which had been formed in Vienna from staff of various Flak commands. In April he was promoted to *Generalmajor* and although he was put on the Reserve List he remained as a leader with the Flak units that had managed to escape capture from the Viennese Pocket. On 12th April 1945 he was awarded the Knight's Cross for his leadership and resourcefulness in forming this unit. On 8th May he was captured by U.S. troops and went into captivity until his release in June 1947. Fritz Grieshammer died on 26th December 1956 in Munich.

Fritz Grieshammer in the uniform of a Hauptmann shortly before he was transferred to the Luftwaffe. (Wehrkundearchiv)

Johannes HINTZ
(1898-1944)
Generalleutnant

Knight's Cross: Awarded on 29th July 1940 as *Oberstleutnant* and Commander of 101st Flak Regiment, for actions during the French Campaign.

Ranks:
Gefreiter – 26th June 1915
Leutnant der Reserve – 16th January 1917
Polizei-Leutnant – 5th November 1919
Polizei-Oberleutnant – 7th April 1925
Polizei-Hauptmann – 1st October 1928
Hauptmann – 1st August 1935
Major – 20th April 1936

Oberstleutnant – 1st November 1938
Oberst – 19th July 1940
Generalmajor – 1st April 1943
Generalleutnant – 26th July 1944

Awards:
Iron Cross 2nd Class – World War I
Iron Cross 1st Class – World War I
Cross of Honour for Frontline Combatants – 21st January 1935
Armed Forces Long Service Award 2nd Class
Spanish Cross with Swords
Bar to Iron Cross 2nd Class – 11th May 1940
Bar to Iron Cross 1st Class – 26th May 1940

Born on 1st October 1898 in Metz, Johannes Hintz volunteered for war in June 1915 when he joined the 74th Infantry Regiment. By January 1917 he had been commissioned as a *Leutnant* and was appointed Company Commander, and later Ordnance Officer with the same Regiment. He was awarded the Iron Cross 1st and 2nd Classes for actions during the Western Campaign.

When the war was over Hintz joined the police in Kattowitz and later in Hannover. He became an instructor and was promoted to *Hauptmann* in October 1928. In August 1935 he returned to active service when he joined the Luftwaffe as a Battery Commander with the 12th Flak Regiment. In November 1936 with the rank of *Major* he served in the Condor Legion during the Spanish Civil War when he was assigned once again as a Battery Commander. He fought with distinction during the war and was awarded the Spanish Cross with Swords.

He returned to Germany in October 1937 and was appointed Commander of the 1st Battalion of the 12th Flak Regiment. He was promoted to the rank of *Oberstleutnant* the following month, and in August 1939 he was made Commander of the 32nd Flak Regiment in Berlin. In October his command was re-designated the 101st Motorised Flak Regiment and took an active part during the invasion of France where it supported the 12th Army Group. For his role in the successful invasion of France Hintz was promoted to *Oberst* and on 29th July 1940 he was awarded the Knight's Cross in recognition of his efforts in supporting the ground troops during the fierce fighting.

Hintz took command of the 1st Flak School at the end of July, and at the same time he was named as Commander of the flak range in Rerik. In March 1943 he was appointed Commander of the 4th Flak Division becoming responsible for all Flak units in Essen, Dorsten, Düsseldorf and Duisberg. Promoted to *Generalmajor* in April 1943 he was named acting Commanding General of the 3rd Flak Corps in March 1944 when he succeeded *Generalleutnant* Wolfgang Pickert. This command had been formed in Paris from the staff of the 11th Flak Division and came under the control of the 3rd Air Fleet.

On the morning of 14th May 1944 Hintz was involved in a serious car accident and was severely wounded, he died seven days later on 21st May. He was posthumously promoted to the rank of *Generalleutnant* on 26th July 1944.

Walter von Hippel as an Oberstleutnant is seen wearing the Knight's Cross. (Wehrkundearchiv)

Walter von HIPPEL
(1897-1972)
Generalleutnant

Knight's Cross: Awarded on 29th July 1940 as an *Oberstleutnant* and Commander of the 102nd Flak Regiment.

Ranks:
Fähnrich – 8th August 1914
Leutnant – 24th December 1914
Oberleutnant – 10th August 1925
Hauptmann/Rittmeister – 1st April 1931
Major – 1st January 1936
Oberstleutnant – 1st January 1939
Oberst – 29th July 1940
Generalmajor – 1st April 1943
Generalleutnant – 1st August 1944

Awards:
Iron Cross 2nd Class – 16th March 1915
Iron Cross 1st Class – 27th May 1917
Knight's Cross of Grand Duchy of Saxony-Weimar House Order of White Falcon 2nd Class with Swords – 22nd March 1915
Grand Duchy of Saxony-Weimar Wilhelm Ernst War Cross – 8th August 1917
Wound Badge in Silver – September 1918
Grand Duchy of Hessen Medal for Bravery – 1st October 1918
Cross of Honour for Frontline Combatants
Armed Forces Long Service Award 1st Class
Bar to Iron Cross 2nd Class – 15th May 1940
Bar to Iron Cross 1st Class – 1st June 1940
Luftwaffe Anti Aircraft Badge – 25th August 1941
Luftwaffe Ground Assault Badge – 13th October 1942

Born on 27th May 1897 in Friedrichsthal, Kreuzburgerhütte near Breslau Walter von Hippel joined the infantry as a war volunteer in August 1914. He was commissioned as a *Leutnant* in December and served as a Platoon Leader with the 94th Infantry Regiment. Wounded in March 1915 he spent time in hospital being before being assigned to the War School at Kassel, although not fully recovered he did attend a number of training courses and eventually returned to active duty in August 1916. However he hadn't been back at the front for long before he was readmitted to hospital, probably due to his previous injuries and eventually returning to his regiment as adjutant in November. In September 1918 he was appointed Battalion Commander with the 94th Infantry Regiment and was assigned to the Western Front where he was again injured and taken prisoner by the British.

In July 1919 he was released from prison and on his return to Germany made the decision to stay in the army and was appointed Ordnance Officer with the 59th Regiment in August and the following year he transferred to the 5th Infantry Regiment. He then spent the next seven years in the infantry; he served as an ordnance officer, platoon leader and company leader, being promoted to *Oberleutnant* in August 1925. In April 1928 he joined the staff of the 3rd Division and served as assistant Operations Officer being transferred a year later to the Baltic Coast. Von Hippel was transferred to the cavalry in October 1929 and joined the 11th Cavalry Regiment, being promoted to *Rittmeister* in April 1931.

He transferred to the Luftwaffe in April 1935 and was appointed Battery Commander with the Brandenburg Flak Battalion. Promoted to *Major* in January 1936 he served as Head Personnel Officer on the staff of the Flak Artillery Commander of Berlin, *Generalmajor* Hubert Weise. This unit was responsible for the defence of the areas around, Berlin-Lankwitz, Stettin, Doberitz, Brandenburg and Berlin-Heiligensee. He transferred to Dresden in April 1938 where he was appointed chief of staff to *Generalmajor* Wilhelm Mayer,[62] the commander of Air Region "Dresden". From October 1938 he took command of three battalions of the Luftwaffe Regiment "General Göring".

He took over command of the 102nd Flak Regiment on 1st October 1939, and was promoted to *Oberstleutnant* on New Years Day, and went on to lead his regiment during the invasion of France in May 1940. With the success of the French Campaign von Hippel was promoted to *Oberst* and on 29th July he was awarded the Knight's Cross for his part in the victory. In August he briefly commanded the 43rd Flak Regiment before being appointed tactics instructor at the Air War Academy in Berlin-Gatow the following month. He took over as Commander of the 1st Flak Brigade in February 1941 after succeeding *Generalmajor* Walther von Axthelm. In March a new brigade was formed, the 10th Flak Brigade which had been created to defend the skies of the Bochum-Münsterland Region and von Hippel took command.

In July 1942, Hippel was made Commander of the 3rd Flak Division in Hamburg, which was later transferred to Denmark. Promoted to *Generalmajor* in April 1943, a year later he took over as Commander of the 25th Flak Division formed in Milano and made responsible for the air defence of Northern Italy. In August 1944, Hippel was promoted to *Generalleutnant* and in February 1945 was named as the Flak Leader of the 10th Army in Italy where he served until his surrender in May to British troops. Released from allied captivity in May 1948 Walter von Hippel died at the age of seventy-five in Bandelstorf on 29th November 1972.

OTTO HÖHNE
(1895-1969)
Generalmajor

Knight's Cross: Awarded on 5th September 1940 as *Oberstleutnant* and Commander of 54th Bomber Wing "Totenkopf" for actions over England.

Ranks:
Unteroffizier – 14th March 1915
Vizefeldwebel – 2nd May 1915
Leutnant der Reserve – 14th May 1915
Oberleutnant – skipped
Hauptmann – 1st July 1934
Major – 1st December 1935
Oberstleutnant – 1st August 1938
Oberst – 1st January 1941
Generalmajor – 1st April 1944

Awards:
Knight's Cross of the Royal Prussian Hohenzollern House Order with Swords – 22nd August 1918
Iron Cross 2nd Class – World War I
Iron Cross 1st Class – World War I
Royal Prussian Pilot's Badge

Silesian Eagle Order 2nd Class
Cross of Honour for Frontline Combatants
Armed Forces Long Service Award 4th Class
Bar to Iron Cross 2nd Class
Bar to Iron Cross 1st Class
Luftwaffe Cuff-title "Jagdgeschwader Boelcke No.2 1916/1918"

Otto Höhne was born on 30th April 1895 in the small town of Woinowitz in Ratibor, Upper Silesia, he volunteered for war at the age of nineteen joining the 2nd Grenadier Regiment as a reservist. On 15th September 1914 he was sent to the front with 49th Infantry Regiment and two months later was injured. He remained in hospital until the beginning of 1915. On his return to active duty he went on an officer's training course and in May was commissioned as a *Leutnant*. On 31st July 1915 he trained as a pilot with the 7th Flying Replacement Battalion near Cologne and in March 1916 he flew as a pilot with the 4th Battle Wing, later taking part in the fighting in Verdun. His flying was observed by the famed fighter pilot and *Pour le Mérite* holder *Hauptmann* Oswald Boelcke, and Höhne was asked to join his squadron in August 1916. In January 1917 Höhne was wounded and once recovered was sent to a single-seater combat school in Großenheim and in July he joined the 2nd Flying Replacement Battalion. He became a flying instructor in October 1917 and three months later he was appointed Squadron Commander with the 52nd Squadron.

With the armistice signed and the war over Höhne decided to return home and continue with his studies in mechanical engineering at University. In 1921 he passed his exams and took a job with a large engineering works and worked his way up to plant manager and later as factory manager. In January 1930 he took a job training pilots for the secret German air force, and as a World War I fighter pilot he soon became known to Göring who needed good pilots, and as a result he joined the Luftwaffe in July 1934. He entered with the rank of *Hauptmann* and was assigned as an instructor at the Bomber School in Lechfeld. Already by December 1935 he had been promoted to the rank of *Major*, probably through the insistence of Göring, who knew Höhne was an ex-member of the famed Boelcke Squadron. Höhne wore the much coveted "Jagdgeschwader Boelcke" cufftitle and had been awarded the Knight's Cross of the Royal Prussian Hohenzollern House Order with Swords, one of the highest awards given during World War I. In December 1934 Höhne had been appointed instructor and adjutant of the Bomber Flying School at Faßberg and in March 1936 he had been made Squadron Commander in the Bomber Wing "Boelcke". A year later he was made Group Commander in 254th Bomber Wing, and by August 1938 he had been promoted to *Oberstleutnant*. By November the 254th Bomber Wing was equipped with the latest He 111 bombers, by May 1939 it was known as the 54th Bomber Wing "Totenkopf", and was the largest bomber wing in the Luftwaffe.

Generalmajor Otto Höhne shortly after he returned to duty and was assigned to 4th Air War School in Fürstenfeldbruck, where he stayed until the end of the war. (Wehrkundearchiv)

In May 1940 he took part in the bombing of Rotterdam, a tragic episode that could have been avoided had better communication been possible. On 13th May the situation in Rotterdam was one of a stalemate. The Dutch forces had prevented the Germans from crossing the main river of the city. On 14th May an assault on the city by SS Panzer forces supported by flame throwers and engineers was planned. The SS were planning to cross the river and make a flank attack through the Kralingen district. The attack was to be preceded by a massive bombardment from the air which included twenty-five bombers and Stukas. However the commander of the Luftwaffe in the area General Student had requested a carpet bombing of the city area and he replaced the Stukas with a massed attack of He 111 bombers. The German ground force commander *General* Schmidt used the pending attack of aircraft to force the Dutch commander to surrender the city, but he refused to surrender and negotiations dragged on. Finally the Dutch surrendered the city and as the Dutch negotiator was crossing over the Willemsburg to relay the information of the surrender the sound of approaching aircraft could be heard. A total of ninety bombers from the 54th Bomber Wing approached the city. Red flares were fired into the sky apparently to warn the bombers off, but it was later discovered that in fact the German troops had fired flares to let the bomber pilots know their position and so save them from being bombed by their own aircraft. The bombers approached in two columns and were equipped with 50 and 250 kilogram bombs. They had taken off from airfields in Quakenbrück, Delmenhorst and Hoya the right hand column under the command of *Oberst* Lackner and the left hand column under Höhne. The bombers went in wave after wave and almost destroyed Rotterdam, it was estimated that between 800 and 900 people were killed and about 80,000 people were made homeless. Almost one square mile of the city was completely flattened. 24,978 homes, twenty-four churches, 2,320 stores and sixty-two schools were destroyed.

In June 1940 Höhne was appointed as Wing Commander of the 54th Bomber Wing and took part in the fighting in the West, taking part in the battle for France, then at Antwerp, and during the tank battle of Namur and later at Dunkirk. On 5th September 1940 Höhne was awarded the Knight's Cross for his leadership skills and success in bombing targets during the Western Campaign against France and England. On 15th August 1941 Höhne was being flown in a He 111 transport plane when it got into difficulties and crashed near Ohlau in Poland, two passengers were killed and Höhne was severely wounded. He spent months in hospital and remained away from frontline action for the next two years. Finally in September 1943 he returned to duty but not at the front but instead was assigned to the 4th Air War School in Fürstenfeldbruck where he remained until the end of the war. In April 1944 he was promoted to *Generalmajor* and in September he even found time to visit his old squadron who had been equipped with Me 262 jet aircraft, but they were too little too late.

Höhne surrendered to the Allies on 8th May 1945 and after spending almost a year in captivity he returned to Germany. He died in Jachenau near Bad Tölz on 29th November 1969.

Otto HOFFMANN VON WALDAU (1898-1943) *General der Flieger*

Knight's Cross: Awarded on 28th June 1942 as *Generalleutnant* and Air Leader in Africa, for his leadership skills in supporting Rommel's ground troops.

Ranks:
Fähnrich – 27th January 1917
Leutnant – 22nd March 1917
Oberleutnant – 1st August 1925
Rittmeister – 1st March 1933
Hauptmann – 20th May 1933
Major – 1st August 1935
Oberstleutnant – 1st October 1937

Generalleutnant Otto Hoffmann von Waldau wearing the Knight's Cross as Air Leader in Africa. (Wehrkundearchiv)

Oberst – 22nd September 1939
Generalmajor – 19th July 1940
Generalleutnant – 1st March 1942
General der Flieger – 30th January 1943

Awards:
Iron Cross 2nd Class – World War I
Iron Cross 1st Class – World War I
Wound Badge in Black – World War I
Cross of Honour for Frontline Combatants
Armed Forces Long Service Award 2nd Class
Combined Pilot's and Observer's Badge
Bar to Iron Cross 2nd Class
Bar to Iron Cross 1st Class
AFRIKA Cufftitle
Wehrmacht Daily Report: 17 June 1942

Otto Hoffmann von Waldau was a very capable officer, he was forthright in his opinions and for a time was the third most senior man within the Luftwaffe. He was born on 7th July 1898 in

Right: Von Waldau shortly after being awarded the Knight's Cross on 28th June 1942, North Africa. (Roger James Bender)

Bottom right: Generalleutnant von Waldau walking with Generalfeldmarschall Rommel. Von Waldau was transferred to North Africa when he succeeded Stefan Fröhlich. Rommel preferred von Waldau to Fröhlich and the two men worked well together. (Wehrkundearchiv)

Bankau, Upper Silesia, and was the son of a Prussian General Staff officer, and he joined the 8th Dragoons in Oels in December 1915. During the First World War he proved himself a brave soldier and won both classes of the Iron Cross. He served in the Reichswehr after the war in Germany's 100,000-man army, first as an Ordnance officer on the staff of a Cavalry Division with the rank of *Leutnant* then in October 1919 as a Platoon Commander in the 8th Cavalry Regiment in Oels. From 1924 he served as a staff officer with 3rd Division, then with the 7th Division while attached to the War Ministry. In August 1925 he was promoted to *Oberleutnant* before being appointed to the staff of 3rd Cavalry Regiment in October 1931.

In April 1935 he was transferred to the Luftwaffe with the rank of *Major* and served as Air Attaché in the Germany Embassy in Rome. He served briefly as one of Göring's adjutants before being appointed as the Commander of the 1st Group, 153rd Bomber Wing in October 1936. Promoted to *Oberstleutnant* exactly a year later and at the same time was appointed head of Department III, responsible for training personnel within the Luftwaffe. On 1st February 1938 Hoffmann von Waldau was appointed Head of the Training Staff, and in February 1939 was made Head of the Luftwaffe Command Staff. He was now deputy to Göring's chief of staff *Generalmajor* Hans Jeschonnek, and one of the most important men within the Luftwaffe.

Hoffmann von Waldau was an extremely capable officer, he was forthright but personable and described as being wise to the ways of the world. He was one of the very few officers with whom Jeschonnek was on a first name basis. Their relationship was a good one, and Hoffmann von Waldau got on well with Göring – most of the time. However their relationship turned when the United States came into the war. Except for Milch, Hoffmann von Waldau was the only member of the General Staff who recognised the military potential and strength of the United Sates. He was also against the use of the Ju 88 and other aircraft in bombing and was against Hitler's strategy in the use of such aircraft. Eventually because of his opposition and his conflicting attitude towards Göring he lost his job in Berlin and was quickly moved out of the way.

In April 1942 he was named as Air Commander in Africa succeeding *Generalleutnant* Stefan Fröhlich who had been sacked. Hoffmann von Waldau worked well with Rommel and directed his units with great skill. He went on to direct the Luftwaffe with success in support of Rommel's ground troops especially in the Battle of the Gazala Line and at Tobruk. For his success and leadership during this time he was awarded the Knight's Cross on 28th June 1942. On 31st August 1942 he was appointed Commanding General of the 10th Air Corps, now with the rank of *Generalleutnant*, under the command of *Generalfeldmarschall* Kesselring's 2nd Air Fleet in Greece. He was promoted to *General der Flieger* in January 1943 and was made the commander of a unit formed from the 10th Air Corps, he now led the Luftwaffe Command Southeast still in Greece with its headquarters close to Athens.

On 15th May 1943 during an inspection tour Hoffmann von Waldau's aircraft crashed while flying over the Balkans. His body was recovered from the crash near Petric, Macedonia and he was buried in Greece. His body now lies in the German Military Cemetery in Dionyssos-Rapendoza, Grave 1, Row 4, and Plate 7.

Von Waldau as Generalleutnant and commander of the 10th Air Corps in conversation with his superior Generalfeldmarschall Kesselring, Commander-in-Chief of the 2nd Air Fleet in Greece. (Wehrkundearchiv)

Alexander HOLLE
(1898-1978)
Generalleutnant

Knight's Cross: Awarded on 30th December 1942 as *Oberst* and Air Leader North-East and Commander of the 26th Bomber Wing for his skill and leadership.

Ranks:
Gefreiter – 16th November 1915
Fähnrich – 18th July 1916
Leutnant – 27th January 1917
Oberleutnant – 1st April 1925
Hauptmann – 1st February 1933
Major – 1st July 1935
Oberstleutnant – 1st October 1937
Oberst – 1st February 1940
Generalmajor – 1st February 1943
Generalleutnant – 1st January 1944

Awards:
Iron Cross 2nd Class – World War I
Iron Cross 1st Class – World War I
Cross of Honour for Frontline Combatants
Armed Forces Long Service Award 2nd Class
Bar to Iron Cross 2nd Class
Bar to Iron Cross 1st Class
German Cross in Gold – 26th May 1942

Born on 27th February 1898 in Bielefeld, Alexander Holle joined the Imperial Army in November 1915 as a *Gefreiter* with the 13th Infantry Regiment. Later he served as a Balloon Observer and was commissioned as a *Leutnant* in January 1917. When the war finished he remained in the peace-time army of the Reichswehr serving as a Battery Commander with the 7th Artillery Regiment and later with the 4th Heavy Artillery Battalion.

In March 1928 he left the army and took part in the secret pilot training in Russia before re-joining the army in November 1929 as a Company Officer with the 16th Infantry Regiment. Promoted to *Hauptmann* in February 1933 he transferred to the Luftwaffe the following year and was assigned as Chief of Operations to the 1st Air Division. A year later he was appointed advisor to the Inspector of Bombers while attached to the Air Ministry in Berlin. In July 1935 he was promoted to *Major* and appointed Commander of the 1st Group, 163rd Stuka Wing "Immelmann", at the same time he was also appointed airbase Commandant in Breslau.

He was transferred to Königsberg in April 1938 to take up his new appointment as Chief of Staff to the Luftwaffe Command "East Prussia", under *Generalmajor* Alfred Keller. In February 1939 Holle transferred to the 4th Air Corps where he served as Chief of Staff in Düsseldorf before being promoted to *Oberst* and taking part in the invasion of France in May 1940, later he helped with preparations for the invasion of England. He was appointed Commander of the 26th Bomber Wing in October 1941 and was stationed in France, it was whilst with this command that he won the German Cross in Gold and on 30th December he was awarded the Knight's Cross for his lead-

Generalleutnant Alexander Holle as Commanding General of the 4th Air Corps. (Wehrkundearchiv)

Joachim-Friedrich Huth as Oberstleutnant and Commander of the 26th Destroyer Wing "Horst Wessel", 1940. (Wehrkundearchiv)

ership and success in leading the 26th Bomber Wing during its successful bombing mission during the Western Campaign.

On 1st February 1943 Holle was promoted to *Generalmajor* and exactly a month later was appointed Air Leader "North-East" where he commanded the Luftwaffe forces in Oslo. He was transferred to Athens in January 1943 and succeeded *General der Flieger* Otto Hoffmann von Waldau as Commander of the 10th Air Corps. On 28th September 1943 he was appointed Commander of Luftwaffe Command "West", a unit formed in Mannheim-Sandhofen from the 3rd Air Fleet and subordinated to the Air Fleet Reich under the command of *Generaloberst* Hans-Jurgen Stumpff. His last military command was as the Commanding General of the Luftwaffe in Denmark as well as being the Commanding General of the 4th Air Corps now with the rank of *Generalleutnant*.

On 8th May 1945 he surrendered and was interned by the Allies until 8th February 1948 when he returned home to Germany. He lived in retirement at his home in Munich until his death on 16th July 1978.

Joachim-Friedrich HUTH
(1896-1962)
Generalleutnant

Knight's Cross: Awarded on 11th September 1940 as *Oberstleutnant* and Commander of the 26th Destroyer Wing "Horst Wessel".

Ranks:
Leutnant der Reserve – 4th January 1915
Oberleutnant – skipped
Hauptmann – 1st March 1934
Major – 1st October 1936
Oberstleutnant – 1st January 1939
Oberst – 1st November 1940
Generalmajor – 1st April 1943
Generalleutnant – 1st July 1944

Awards:
Iron Cross 2nd Class – World War I
Iron Cross 1st Class – World War I
Royal Prussian Pilot's Badge
Cross of Honour for Frontline Combatants
Armed Forces Long Service Award 4th Class
Combined Pilot's and Observer's Badge
Bar to Iron Cross 2nd Class
Bar to Iron Cross 1st Class
Wehrmacht Daily Report: 19 August 1940

Joachim-Friedrich Huth was born in the town of Neuhof, Osterburg in Sachsen on 31st July 1896, he entered the German Imperial Army as a war volunteer on 13th July 1914. He served with the 58th Infantry Regiment until June 1917, being commissioned as a *Leutnant* in January 1915. In June 1917 he trained as a pilot with the 14th Fighter Squadron, was wounded in battle on 23rd March 1918 and ended the war in hospital. Huth scored one confirmed aerial victory during the war; apparently he shot down an observation balloon northeast of Septsaulz, France on 28th January 1918.

On 9th April 1919 Huth joined the Freikorps "Küttner" and a year later decided to leave the armed forces. He found it difficult to find work as a civilian in the post-war Weimar Republic but nevertheless he found various part-time jobs. In March 1934 he joined the Luftwaffe with the rank of *Hauptmann* and was assigned to the Reich Air Ministry, and was promoted to *Major* in October 1936. In March 1937 he was transferred from the Air Ministry and found himself attached to the 132nd Fighter Wing, in November he was appointed Group Commander in the same unit and by January 1939 had been promoted to *Oberstleutnant*. In February 1939 he was appointed Commander of 1st Group of the 1st Destroyer Wing former at Jüterbog-Damm, here he began his war training.

In December 1939 he was appointed Commander of the 26th Destroyer Wing "Horst Wessel" and took part in the invasion of France. In August a raid across the Channel in England was led by Johannes Fink and escorting his Dornier bombers was Huth who led about sixty Bf 110 twin-engined fighters. However the operation was cancelled at the last minute but Fink's bombers didn't get the recall message and Huth flew his Messerschmitt to try and stop Fink. It didn't work and the target was bombed and Fink lost ten of his bombers. For his role in the victory over France Huth was awarded the Knight's Cross on 11th September 1940. On 1st November he was promoted to *Oberst* and the following day he took command of the Destroyer School in Memmingen, where he trained pilots for combat.

In August 1941 he became Fighter Leader II, when he succeeded *Generalmajor* Theodor Osterkamp. His command was responsible for protecting the area around Le Touguet and covered fifteen miles north up to Boulogne on the French coast. A year later he was appointed Commander of the newly formed 4th Fighter Division in Döberitz under the overall control of *General der Flieger* Josef Kammhuber. In April 1943 Huth

Huth and Göring during an inspection tour in France, July 1940. (Author's collection)

Oberst Joachim-Friedrich Huth as commander of the newly formed 4th Fighter Division, under the overall control of General der Flieger Josef Kammhuber. He is seen here at his headquarters in Döberitz. (Author's collection)

was promoted to *Generalmajor* and his headquarters moved to Paris when he took over command of the 5th Fighter Division. In February 1944 he was transferred to Schleißheim in Austria where he took command of the 7th Fighter Division and in July was promoted to *Generalleutnant* and took command of the 1st Fighter Corps in Treuenbritzen. On 26th January 1945 Huth took over as Commanding General of the 2nd Fighter Corps from its acting Commander *Generalmajor* Karl-Eduard Wilke. However most of its personnel and aircraft had been taken to form the 14th and 15th Air Division, Huth was left with virtually nothing.

On 8th May 1945 he surrendered to the Allies and was taken into captivity, being transferred to the Island Farm Special Camp for prisoners in January 1946 and from there to Camp 99 in August 1946. He was repatriated to Germany on 25th November 1947, and for a time lived quietly. In November 1956 he re-entered the Post-war German Bundeswehr when he joined the Luftwaffe once again. He was given the rank of *Generalmajor* and appointed Commander of the Luftwaffe School at Fürstenfeldbruck. In December 1957 he was appointed Commanding General of Luftwaffe Group South, and promoted to *Generalleutnant* on 31st October 1959. In September 1961 he retired from active service but within a few months he fell ill and died in Koblenz on 27th March 1962.

Max-Josef IBEL
(1896-1981)
Generalmajor

Knight's Cross: Awarded on 22nd August 1940 as *Oberst* and Commander of the 27th Fighter Wing for actions over France.

Ranks:
Fahnenjunker-Gefreiter – 5th July 1915
Fahnenjunker-Unteroffizier – 27th November 1915
Fähnrich – 13th May 1916
Offiziers-Stellvertreter – 6th July 1916
Leutnant – 18th October 1916
Oberleutnant – 31st July 1925
Hauptmann – 1st December 1932
Major – 1st November 1935
Oberstleutnant – 1st June 1938
Oberst – 21st July 1940
Generalmajor – 1st January 1944

Awards:
Iron Cross 2nd Class – World War I
Iron Cross 1st Class – World War I
Royal Bavarian Military Service Cross 4th Class with Swords
Cross of Honour for Frontline Combatants
Armed Forces Long Service Award 2nd Class
Pilot's Badge
Bar to Iron Cross 2nd Class
Bar to Iron Cross 1st Class

Max-Josef Ibel as Generalmajor and commander of the 2nd Fighter Division. (Wehrkundearchiv)

Max-Josef Ibel is credited among others as one of the creators of the Luftwaffe, he was born on 2nd January 1896 in Munich. He entered the Imperial Army as a *Fahnenjunker-Gefreiter* with the 1st Bavarian Pioneer Replacement Battalion on 5th July 1915. In October 1916 he was commissioned as a *Leutnant* and served as Platoon Leader in the 3rd Field Pioneer Company with the 1st Bavarian Army Corps. In April 1918 he was transferred to the 1st Pioneer Replacement Battalion and finished the war with the Reserve Pioneer Flamethrower Regiment on the Western Front. He remained in the army after the war serving in the 1st Pioneer Battalion in Munich until September 1920 when he was appointed company officer with 7th Pioneer Battalion. He retired from the army in July 1928 with the rank of *Oberleutnant*.

In August 1928 he took part in the secret pilot training in Russia and helped with the co-ordination and training of the new pilots who were training ready to join Germany's new air force. In October 1931 he re-entered the army with the rank of *Oberleutnant* and served with his old command, the 7th Pioneer Battalion. In December 1932 he was promoted to *Hauptmann* and two years later he transferred to the Luftwaffe as an instructor at the Fighter School at Schlesißheim. He then transferred to Dortmund in May 1936 where he was attached to the 134th Fighter Wing and in December he was appointed Squadron Commander with the 1st Group, 232nd Fighter Wing under *Major* Bruno Loerzer. Named as commander of the 1st Group, 135th Fighter Wing in March 1937, he was promoted to *Oberstleutnant* in June 1938. He took over as the commander of the 231st Fighter Wing in Bernberg, Saale in May 1939 and by August it had been renamed the 3rd Fighter Wing "Udet" and was using the new Messerschmitt fighter, the Bf 109 to great effect.

In September 1939 Ibel was made Wing Commander of the 27th Fighter Wing, which was formed in Münster-Handorf and went onto fight with distinction during the Battle of France in May 1940. He saw considerable action during the French Campaign as part of the 8th Air Corps, scoring heavily against Allied bombers during the crossing of the Meuse River. Ibel himself managed to score three aerial victories. After the fall of France he was promoted to *Oberst* in July 1940 and awarded the Knight's Cross on 22nd August for his role in the victory over France. He then spent time in Cherbourg and flew briefly during the Battle of Britain. On 13th October he was appointed

Oberst Ibel wearing the Knight's Cross is seen here with his men at their fighter base in Cherbourg during the Battle of Britain. (Wehrkundearchiv)

Commander of the 4th Fighter School in Fürth and in June 1941 was named Fighter Leader 3 with his headquarters on the coast of France near Deauville. In December 1942 he took over as Fighter Leader "West", formed in Chantilly, near Paris and was part of *Generalfeldmarschall* Sperrle's 3rd Air Fleet.

On 1st October 1943 Ibel was appointed Commander of the 2nd Fighter Division, and was promoted to *Generalmajor* in January 1944. In January 1945 he was put on the Reserve list but in February he returned to active duty when he was appointed Inspector for Jet-Employment, being responsible for the training and distribution of pilots capable of flying the new jet powered aircraft. In May 1945 he was captured by U.S. forces and was interned by the British until March 1948 when he returned to Germany. Ibel returned to active duty with the Bundeswehr in October 1957 with the rank of *Brigadegeneral* and was appointed Commander of the 1st Air Defence Division. He remained in military service until his retirement on 30th September 1961. He died at his home in Rheinbach on 19th March 1981.

Hans JESCHONNEK
(1899-1943)
Generaloberst

Knight's Cross: *Generalmajor* Jeschonnek was awarded the Knight's Cross on 27th October 1939 as Chief of the General Staff of the Luftwaffe.

Ranks:
Fähnrich – 10th August 1914
Leutnant – 26th September 1914
Oberleutnant – 1st April 1925
Hauptmann – 1st June 1932
Major – 1st April 1935
Oberstleutnant – 1st April 1937
Oberst – 1st November 1938
Generalmajor – 1st September 1939
Generalleutnant – skipped
General der Flieger – 19th July 1940
Generaloberst – 1st March 1942

Awards:
Knight's Cross of the Royal Prussian Hohenzollern House Order with Swords
Iron Cross 2nd Class – World War I
Iron Cross 1st Class – World War I

Bar to Iron Cross 2nd Class
Bar to Iron Cross 1st Class
Wound Badge in Black – World War I
Cross of Honour for Frontline Combatants
Royal Prussian Pilot's Badge
Armed Forces Long Service Award 1st Class
Pilot's Badge with Diamonds
Combined Pilot's and Observer's Badge in Gold with Diamonds
Romanian Order of the "Michael the Brave" 3rd Class – 7th November 1941
Romanian Order of the "Michael the Brave" 2nd Class – 1st September 1942
Finnish Order of the Cross of Liberty 1st class with Star and Swords – 25th March 1942

The youngest officer to achieve the rank of *Generaloberst* in the Luftwaffe, Hans Jeschonnek was born in Hohensalza, East Prussia, now part of Poland, on 9th April 1899, the son of a schoolmaster. At the age of fifteen he left school and immediately volunteered for active service, he entered the Imperial Army on 10th August 1914 as a *Fähnrich*. He attended cadet school at Gross-Lichterfelde, was commissioned as a *Leutnant* on 26th September 1914, serving as company officer in the 50th Infantry Regiment. Wounded by shrapnel on 6th October 1915, was hospitalized for three weeks, returning to his unit in November. He stayed in the infantry until July 1917 when he underwent pilot training before joining the 40th Fighter Squadron; he managed to score two aerial victories before the Germans surrendered. His eldest brother Paul had been among the group of officers' who were part of the secret air force of the Reichswehr until he was killed in an aircraft crash in 1929. (Jeschonnek's own son, Gert served in the German Navy during World War II later serving with the West Germany Navy.)

In the months after the Armistice Jeschonnek took part in the fighting on the German and Polish border as a pilot with the Border-Protection Flying Squadron, and then with 11th Mounted Regiment. He officially joined the Reichswehr in 1920, becoming an advisor for weapons and equipment. In October 1928 was attached to the office of the Inspector of weapons under *Oberstleutnant* Hellmuth Felmy. On 30th January 1933, the same day the Nazis seized power, Jeschonnek was named as Operations Officer for the State-Secretary of the Reich Air Ministry Erhard Milch. Promoted to *Hauptmann* in June 1932 he remained in the Air Ministry as adjutant to Milch until April 1935 when he was promoted to *Major* and took part in pilot training. He was later appointed Commandant of the air base at Greifswald, and shortly after was promoted to *Oberstleutnant*. It was during this time that Milch tried to have Jeschonnek court-martialled; apparently it was because of the high number of flying accidents at the 3rd Training Group at Greifswald but the charges were later dropped, mainly thanks to Kesselring.

Hans Jeschonnek as General der Flieger wearing the Knight's Cross as Chief of the General Staff of the Luftwaffe. (Author's collection)

Jeschonnek was a true airman, and unlike Göring, he wasn't interested in material things, his home and office were described as Spartan. His wife and daughter seem to have played only a small part in his life, his loyalty was with Hitler and the Nazis, and this made him a very capable General Staff officer but not a very good husband or father. He became a firm advocate of the dive-bomber but opposed the twin-engined bomber. After 1934 he was promoted rapidly. In fact it took him almost seventeen years to advance from the rank of *Leutnant* to *Hauptmann*, but within the next eight years he would be promoted to *Generaloberst*, skipping the rank of *Generalleutnant* on the way.

In October 1937 Jeschonnek was appointed Chief of Department 1, within the Operations Department of the Luftwaffe General Staff; this was followed by his appointment as Chief of the Operations Staff in February 1938. Promoted to *Oberst* in November 1938, this was followed by his promotion ten months later to *Generalmajor* and his appointment as Chief of the General Staff of the Luftwaffe. Jeschonnek found his new position difficult to handle, having to deal with senior generals like Albert Kesselring, Hugo Sperrle, Wolfram von Richthofen and his old enemy Erhard Milch who saw him as a rival for power and felt that he wasn't up to the position he had been appointed mainly due to his young age and lack of experience. His problems didn't end with these generals because it wasn't long before he was having problems with the generals closest to Göring. These included Bruno Loerzer, Paul Koerner, State Secretary for the Four Year Plan, Karl Bodenschatz, Alfred Keller and Göring's adjutants, *Oberst* Bernd von Brauchitsch and *Oberstleutnant* Werner Teske. Göring himself didn't make matters easy when he took advice from these generals and ignoring any such advice from Jeschonnek.

However Jeschonnek maintained his position mainly due to his professionalism and support from Hitler, although his job was getting more difficult as time went on and the pressure was beginning to show. On 1st March 1942 Jeschonnek was promoted to *Generaloberst*, and he became the youngest general in the Luftwaffe to achieve this rank, but within a few short months his career would start to decline. He had always maintained that aircraft production should remain modest and he was totally against stock piling aircraft. When the RAF began to bomb Germany's armament factories and effect the production of aircraft he soon fell out of favour with Göring. Jeschonnek was a handsome, intelligent and very devoted staff officer, but he was possibly the wrong person to pick as Chief of Staff of the Luftwaffe, this needed a man who could stand up to Göring, men who were not afraid of being critical towards the *Reichsmarschall*, generals like Milch and Kesselring – Jeschonnek was mild mannered and would steer clear of any confrontation with almost any officer, especially Göring.

In June 1942 he was summoned to Hitler's headquarters at Rastenburg and that same day the British bombed Cologne. When he arrived the atmosphere was tense and Hitler asked Jeschonnek how many aircraft had taken part in the bombing. Jeschonnek told him about 200 enemy aircraft had bombed Cologne. Hitler then told Jeschonnek that he thought the Luftwaffe must have been asleep all night. Hitler then screamed at Jeschonnek calling him a liar, he said, "... thank goodness I can rely on my Gauleiter."[63] He then told Jeschonnek that the Gauleiter of Cologne, Josef Gröhe[64] had reported that over a thousand bombers had in fact taken part in the bombing. Hitler then screamed again at Jeschonnek about the Luftwaffe failure and asked him, "Where is Göring? Where?"[65]

The bombing of German cities and factories by the allies got worst and so did the relationship between Hitler and his Luftwaffe. However Hitler blamed Göring for its failure's and began to meet with Jeschonnek rather than his *Reichsmarschall* putting even more pressure on the young general. Hitler would criticize the Luftwaffe at every military conference that Jeschonnek attended and he just sat there and took it all. When he met with Göring to update him on what had been said Göring would shout at him too, and being the gentleman he was Jeschonnek would just sit and take it – for a second time.

By 1943 Jeschonnek was a broken man, he was mentally worn out after the criticism he received about his command. After the failure of Stalingrad, when the Luftwaffe failed to supply the besieged 6th Army with food and supplies and where 270,000 soldiers lost their lives, Göring blamed Jeschonnek and *General der Flieger* Hans-Georg von Seidel, for the failure he wanted them both court-martialed. Hitler would not agree, he knew who was to really blame but he never said or did anything about it. Hitler ordered that Göring and Jeschonnek should reconcile their differences, but Jeschonnek knew it was too late and he thought about denouncing Göring, he thought about resigning as Chief of Staff and even contemplated suicide. He applied for a transfer; he wanted to command an Air Fleet.

Jeschonnek, seen here as a Generalmajor, looking over Göring's shoulder during an inspection in France, summer 1940. (Author's collection)

Generaloberst Jeschonnek arrives by plane during a visit to the Western Front in 1942. (Author's collection)

Göring was happy to get rid of him but Hitler wouldn't allow the transfer and told Göring it was out of the question. Göring tried to argue his case and told Hitler how the two men didn't get on. Hitler ordered his *Reichsmarschall* and his Chief of Staff to effect reconciliation and work together, but the new relationship lasted only three weeks. Jeschonnek knew that drastic action was needed.

By June 1943 Jeschonnek was suffering from stomach cramps, the thought of resigning seemed too humiliating, and a working relationship with Göring had vanished. He had to speak to Hitler but couldn't bring himself to do so. On 1st August during air-raids on Hamburg he finally went to speak with Hitler, he told Hitler that he should assume command of the Luftwaffe personally as Führer. Hitler disagreed and told Jeschonnek that he could not bring himself to dismiss one of his oldest comrades. Jeschonnek left and returned to his office, his secretary later said that he looked a broken man, and she became concerned for his well-being. She had remembered hearing Jeschonnek's adjutant, *Major* Werner Leuchtenburg tell her how he had managed on one occasion to get a revolver out of Jeschonnek's hands and had often heard him talking about being buried in East Prussia on the shores of Lake Goldap.

On 17th August 1943 the Americans raided the ball-bearing factories at Schweinfurt and the aircraft plants at Regensburg. They were heavily damaged and to make matters worse this was the first time the enemy had penetrated the air over the Reich in broad daylight. That same afternoon Jeschonnek had a terrible row with Göring over the situation. Jeschonnek left Göring's office and went for a ride in Goldat Lake; he then made his way back to his quarters at Rastenburg, and drank a bottle of champagne with his adjutant. He later learned that the RAF had carried out a raid with more than 500 aircraft on the V-weapons research site at Peenemunde and had caused serious damage.

Early on the morning of 18th August, the Chief of the Operations Branch, General Rudolf Meister reported the full damage of the raid to Jeschonnek. When he left Jeschonnek shot himself. He left a suicide note which said that he could no longer work with Göring and requested that Göring, his adjutants Diesing and von Brauchitsch should not attend his funeral. Jeschonnek was buried with full honors near the Fuhrer headquarters at Rastenburg. The suicide was covered up and it was announced that the Chief of Staff to the Luftwaffe had died due to a stomach hemorrhage – Göring did attend his funeral and laid a wreath on behalf of Hitler. The *Reichsmarschall* had made Jeschonnek the scapegoat for the bombing on Hamburg and under extreme pressure Jeschonnek had collapsed, he had recently buried his father and his brother, and his brother-in-law had been killed in action.

Studio photograph of Hans Jeschonnek as a Generaloberst. (Author's collection)

Hans Jeschonnek's time as Chief of Staff of the Luftwaffe shouldn't be remembered as a complete failure; after all he could only put into practice the orders of his *Reichsmarschall*. But under his leadership the Luftwaffe did play a major role in the downfall of many countries, like Poland, Denmark, Norway, France, Belgium, Luxembourg, the Netherlands, Yugoslavia, Greece and Crete. He also bore very little responsibility for the loss of the Battle of Britain. But he will always be linked to one of Germany's greatest defeats – the loss of the 6th Army at Stalingrad.

Werner JUNCK
(1895-1976)
Generalleutnant

Knight's Cross: Awarded on 9th June 1944 as *Generalmajor* and Commanding General of the 2nd Fighter Corps for actions on the Western front, near Paris.

Ranks:
Gefreiter – 19th August 1914
Leutnant – 30th September 1915
Oberleutnant – 31st May 1923
Hauptmann – 1st July 1934
Major – 1st April 1935
Oberstleutnant – 1st April 1937
Oberst – 1st October 1939
Generalmajor – 1st April 1943
Generalleutnant – 1st December 1944

Awards:
Iron Cross 2nd Class – World War I
Iron Cross 1st Class – World War I
Imperial Pilot's Badge – World War I
Cross of Honour for Frontline Combatants
Armed Forces Long Service Award 4th Class – 1st Class
Bar to Iron Cross 2nd Class
Bar to Iron Cross 1st Class
Pilot's Badge – World War II

Werner Junck as Generalmajor and Commanding General of the 2nd Fighter Corps. (Wehrkundearchiv)

Werner Junck was a fighter ace during the First World War and a senior test pilot for Heinkel in the early-1930s. He was born in Magdeburg on 28th December 1895, and entered the Army as a war volunteer with the 4th Field Artillery Regiment in August 1914. In May 1915 he served with the 72nd Infantry Regiment and was commissioned as a *Leutnant* in September and appointed Company Commander with the 160th Infantry Regiment on the Western Front. Wounded in action on 11th October 1915, he spent almost two months in hospital, returning to the front just before Christmas 1915. In March 1916 he underwent pilot training with the 8th Air Replacement Battalion at Graudenz, and in January 1917, transferred to the 33rd Field Flying Battalion. In February he was made leader of the 8th Fighter Squadron, and shot down his first enemy aircraft on 24th April, and over the next few months he shot down a further two aircraft. He was wounded in July 1918 but returned before then end of the war and scored his fifth and final aerial victory on 3rd November 1918.

When the war ended Junck remained in the army and in January 1919 he served with the 8th Troops Flying Squadron before joining the Border Police at Breig. In May 1920 he transferred to the 8th Motor Transport Unit and in September he served as Company Officer in the 13th Rifle Regiment. In January 1921 he was appointed Battalion adjutant in the 18th Infantry Regiment, still with the rank of *Leutnant*. On 31st May 1923 he retired from active duty and in June he took a job in Columbia to help establish a German Air Transport Company. Junck still wanted to keep in touch with all new developments in flying and in January 1925 he took part in the secret training in Lipezk, Russia, for future fighter pilots in a new German air force. He remained in Lipezk for sometime serving as a fighter leader and trainer, and returned to Germany in 1927. He then took a position as chief pilot with the Albatross Aircraft Works in Berlin, where he helped to test new aircraft. In 1931 he was head hunted by Heinkel and offered the position of chief pilot and Head of the Test Department at their Works in Warnemünde, he leapt at the chance. In August 1932 Junck took part in the International Tourist Plane Contest, an event which was open to any European nation. The contest was for tourist aircraft only, that is aircraft that could carry two or more passengers over set distances and complete these distances in set times. There were many time trials and speed trails which resulted in a final points table. Pilot's entered individually but competed for their country. In 1932 it was organised by Germany and took place in Berlin, teams from six different countries entered: Germany, France, Italy, Poland, Czechoslovakia and Switzerland. Germany won the short take off competition and Junck came sixth, he also took part in the competition in August 1934, and this time it took place in Warsaw and he did reasonably well coming second in two trials and finishing in twelfth overall.

As Heinkel's chief test pilot Junck flew in many new planes and in February 1933 he took the new He 70 for its maiden test flight. It had been built by the company *Rostocker Flugzeugwerker* in Berlin and designed by Ernst Heinkel. It had been ordered by Lufthansa who had wanted a commercial aircraft that was faster than the American passenger and freight plane "Orion". It had been designed with a drop-like fuselage and was made of an aluminium alloy called Duralumin, whereas the wings were made of wood. Because of new processes the rivets were incorporated into the alloy and so the surface became very smooth and so very aerodynamic. It was one of the very first aerodynamically styled aircraft and surpassed the speed of fighter planes of the time. Junck managed to reach a speed of 348.2km per hour with a payload of 500kg.

In July 1934 Junck entered military service with Germany's new Luftwaffe, he was posted to the Air Ministry as a *Hauptmann* and made responsible for all pilot training matters. In April 1935 he was promoted to *Major* and in August was appointed Commander of Air Group Schwerin, and in March 1936 was made Commander of the 1st Air Group in Kitzingen. A year later he was appointed a department head in the Air Ministry and was promoted soon afterwards to *Oberstleutnant*. In August 1938 he succeeded *Oberst* Bruno Loerzer as Commander of 334th Fighter Wing equipped with Ar 68 biplanes and the new Bf 109 fighter. In February 1939 he was made Inspector of Fighters and promoted to *Oberst* in October.

In June 1940 he took over as Fighter Leader 3, in Wiesbaden and then he transferred to Deauville on the French coast. He took part in the Battle for France and then during the Battle of Britain under the command of *Feldmarschall* Sperrle's 3rd Air Fleet. Most of the fighters of the 3rd Air Fleet were placed under the direction of Junck who led a unit comprising of Messerschmitt Bf 109s and Bf 110s from the 2nd and 3rd Fighter Wings and the 2nd Destroyer Wing. Junck's orders were to close with and destroy the Spitfires and Hurricanes of the RAF as they tried to intercept the German bombers. It wasn't long before Junck realised that his aircraft were no match for the RAF pilot's who had at the time better aircraft and had the advantage of being able to spend much longer in the air and thanks to radar were waiting for their German attackers when they arrived. Junck knew that the fight for air superiority over England was lost.

In May 1941 Junck was made leader of a special Command "*Junck*", a squadron formed to help in Iraq against the British. On 8th May Junck arrived in Iraq at the airfield in Mosul where he had about fifty fighters under his command. On 14th May a German delegation arrived at Baghdad to arrange for a formal request from the Rashid Ali Government for German troop intervention in Iraq. However the situation in Baghdad was far from stable and with the forthcoming invasion of Crete planned by Hitler, and German aircraft being needed for the invasion direct involvement in Iraq by Germany faded away. Junck and his command were ordered back to Germany to make ready for the invasion of the Balkans.

In April 1942 Junck was appointed Commander of Fighter Division Centre, having never fired a shot in anger, and by October 1942 this command had been upgraded to the 3rd Fighter Division, with it's headquarters located in Metz. In July 1943 Hitler had ordered the defence of the Reich strengthened and by the autumn there were five fighter divisions in Germany. The 1st was under *Generalmajor* Kurt-Bertram von Döring[66] responsible for the defence of Berlin and Central Germany; the 2nd under *Generalleutnant* Walter Schwaberdissen[67] and the 3rd under Junck which was responsible for the skies over Holland and the Ruhr area.

Junck was appointed Commanding General of the 2nd Fighter Corps on 15th October 1943 having been promoted to *Generalmajor* in April. With his headquarters in Chantilly near Paris, Junck became responsible for the air defence of Paris and the surrounding area. On 9th June 1944 a few days after D-Day, Junck was awarded the Knight's Cross for actions while commanding the 2nd Fighter Corps. In July he was placed on the Reserve List, although promoted to *Generalleutnant* in December 1944 he would never return to active duty, he had officially retired by the end of the year. He was at home when the war finished and spent the next few years living in quiet retirement in Munich until his death on 6th August 1976.

Josef KAMMHUBER
(1896-1986)
General der Flieger

Knight's Cross: Awarded on 9th July 1941 as *Generalmajor* and Commander of the 1st Night Fighter Division, for his leadership skills.

Ranks:
Gefreiter – 21st May 1915
Fahnenjunker-Unteroffizier – 5th September 1915
Fähnrich – 26th October 1916
Leutnant – 10th September 1917
Oberleutnant – skipped
Hauptmann – 1st February 1931
Major – 1st October 1934
Oberstleutnant – 1st October 1936
Oberst – 1st January 1939
Generalmajor – 17th October 1940
Generalleutnant – 1st October 1941
General der Flieger – 1st January 1943

Awards:
Iron Cross 2nd Class – World War I
Iron Cross 1st Class – World War I
Cross of Honour for Frontline Combatants

Armed Forces Long Service Award 1st Class
Bar to Iron Cross 2nd Class
Bar to Iron Cross 1st Class
Pilot's Badge with Diamonds
Combined Pilot's and Observer's Badge in Gold with Diamonds
Royal Bavarian Military Order of Service 4th Class with Swords
Combat Clasp for Bombers and Dive-Bombers
Wehrmacht Daily Report: 10 April 1941; 27 March 1942; 31 March 1942

Josef Kammhuber was the first General of Night Fighters in the Luftwaffe, and the man responsible for the first night-fighter defence system. Born on 19th August 1896 in Burgkirchen, Upper Bavaria the son of a farmer, he volunteered for the army when the war started joining the 3rd Bavarian Engineer Battalion. He experienced eighteen months of trench warfare in the, "hell that was Verdun" where in 1916 ten thousand German and French soldiers lost their lives. After his experiences at Verdun he was promoted to *Leutnant* in September 1917 and appointed Platoon Commander with the 30th Bavarian Infantry Regiment. He remained in the Army after the war staying with the Bavarian Infantry serving as a Platoon Commander, training officer and as Battalion Adjutant. In November 1923 whilst serving in Munich he was a witness to the Munich Putsch, the attempt by Hitler and his followers to take power from the Bavarian government.

From July 1926 until September 1929 he served in various different battalions, either signals or motor transport, and throughout all this time he seems to have not been promoted. In October 1926 he served on the staff of 2nd Division in Stettin and spent three years training under *Oberstleutnant* Paul Hausser. In October 1928 he was transferred to the Troop Office in the War Ministry and in 1930 he was sent to Russia for pilot training in Lipezk and shortly afterwards was promoted to *Hauptmann*. In September 1933 he was transferred to the newly formed Luftwaffe and served under *Oberst* Walther Wever who was in the process of setting up a strategic bomber command, a plan that faded with the death of Wever in June 1936. In October Kammhuber was promoted to *Oberstleutnant*, and in November 1937 was transferred to the Reich Air Ministry where he became in February 1938 Head of the Organisation Staff of the Luftwaffe. At this time Hitler decided to expand the Luftwaffe and started a RM60,000,000,000 expansion program, a huge undertaking. It wasn't long before the German aircraft industry realised they couldn't handle such a program and the Luftwaffe leadership realised that the expansion plan had to be scaled down. A new plan was thought about and was eventually submitted by Kammhuber, it was a plan that he felt the aircraft industry could achieve and would approve. The plan was agreed by Hans Jeschonnek and Hans-Jurgen Stumpff, both senior officers within the Luftwaffe High Command, and a meeting was organised between Kammhuber, Stumpff, Milch and Göring to decide the fine details. Göring stated that they would agree to meet Hitler's own targets, but they would follow Kammhuber's proposal but not tell Hitler.

Generalleutnant Josef Kammhuber as Commanding General of 12th Air Corps. (Wehrkundearchiv)

Kammhuber soon realised what was going on and didn't like it, he didn't want to be party to the political wrangling between Göring, the Luftwaffe High Command and Hitler. He put in a request to transfer to frontline duty and was in January 1939 promoted to *Oberst*. In October his request was granted and he was appointed Chief of the General Staff of 2nd Air Fleet, under *General der Flieger* Hellmuth Felmy[68] in Münster. In July 1940 he was named as the Commander of the 51st Bomber Wing in France, and it was while flying a bombing mission over France that Kammhuber was shot down and interned in a French POW camp. He was soon released after the fall of France and returned to Germany where he assumed the command of 1st Night-Fighter Division and was shortly afterwards promoted to *Generalmajor*.

He went on to organise the German night-fighter units into a chain known as the Kammhuber Line, this was a series of radar stations with overlapping coverage from Denmark to the middle of France, each covering an area about 32km long and

20km wide. Each control centre was known as a *Himmelbett* zone, consisting of a radar with a range of almost 100km, many searchlights spread throughout the area, and one back up night fighters assigned to that area. The RAF bombers which flew into Germany or France had to cross the line at some point, and the radar would direct the searchlight to illuminate the aircraft. Once this had happened the other searchlights could also then pick up the aircraft and the night-fighter aircraft would intercept and shoot down the bombers. However this meant that many searchlights were needed and they were taken from other cities and used for Berlin until many of the *Bürgermeisters* or mayors demanded that they have them back. To aid some of the night fighter aircraft some were fitted with a short-range infrared device known as *Spanner*, but these proved to be useless.

On 9th July 1941 Kammhuber was awarded the Knight's Cross for his leadership skills in leading the night-fighter force in the defence of the Reich. In August he was appointed Commanding General of 12th Air Corps with its headquarters in Zeist, near Utrecht and was subordinated to the Luftwaffe Commander-in-Chief Centre *Generaloberst* Hubert Wiese. Promoted to *Generalleutnant* in October 1941, this followed his promotion to *General der Flieger* at the beginning of 1943. On 15th September he was appointed Commanding General of all Night Fighters and started to push his idea of the Kammhuber Line. However the British had started to find ways in which to defeat it. At the time Bomber Command sent in their aircraft one at a time in order to force the defences to be spread as far apart as possible, this meant that any one aircraft would have to deal with little concentrated anti-aircraft fire. Bomber Command now decided to reorganise their attacks against a single target, they sent all of the bombers in a single stream, carefully positioned to fly right down the middle of *Himmelbett* area. Now the *Himmelbett* centres were facing hundreds of bombers and their success rate dropped almost to nothing. Kammhuber was soon being asked awkward questions and was being looked upon with suspicion by Milch and Göring.

Kammhuber had to find a solution, and his result was the two-prong concept called: "Wild Boar". It had originally been thought up by a day fighter specialist, Hans-Joachim "Hajo" Herrmann,[69] fighters to be sent up and look for the bombers from the light of flares dropped from light bombers, searchlights would illuminate the clouds and so locate the bombers. The Wild Boar force scored most of their success during the bombing of Peenemünde in August 1943. The British bombers had dropped target marker flares over Berlin and most of the night fighter force was sent there. However when it realised what had happened and where the RAF bombers were most of the aircraft were too far away and too slow to intercept the raid. But the much faster Fw 190s being flown by the Wild Boar forces were able to catch them, and as a result twenty-nine of the forty bombers were shot down. Kammhuber went on to press for a new dedicated night-fighter design, eventually selecting the Heinkel He 219 *Uhu* after seeing it demonstrated in 1942. However Milch cancelled the design and a war of words broke out between Kammhuber and Milch, which resulted in the sacking of Kammhuber as General of the Night-Fighters. In November 1943 Kammhuber was appointed Commander of the 5th Air Fleet in Oslo, succeeding *Generaloberst* Stumpff. Here he commanded mostly out-dated aircraft and as a result had little success, he was eventually placed on the Reserve List when he was succeeded by *Generalmajor* Eduard Ritter von Schleich[70] in September 1944.

Kammhuber as General der Flieger and commander of the 5th Air Fleet, and is seen here in Oslo talking to a member of the ground staff. (Wehrkundearchiv)

In February 1945 he returned to active service and was given a grand title of Special Officer for the Combat of Four-

Josef Kammhuber can be seen here during the birthday visit of the West German Chancellor Konrad Adenauer in August 1957. From left to right in civilian uniform is Defence Minister Franz Joseph Strauss, Generalleutnant Adolf Heusinger, Generalleutnant Hans Speidel, Generalleutnant Josef Kammhuber and in front wearing a coat is Konrad Adenauer. (Author's collection)

Engined Enemy Aircraft, which basically meant he was to defend Germany's cities against the ever present Allied aircraft. He had very little aircraft himself and even less fuel, in March he was also made responsible for all jet aircraft within the Reich. These new planes were meant to turn the tide in Germany's favour and because they were fast it was thought they could destroy more aircraft. However they were difficult to fly, dangerous and there were few pilots who could fly them successfully. The Me 262 jet fighter was a great invention and was a truly innovated aircraft, but it came too late for Germany. Kammhuber surrendered to the Americans at the end of the war and went into allied captivity where he stayed until his release in April 1948.

For a time Kammhuber worked as a wine representative in Bavaria, before returning to active service with the Bundeswehr, the West German Armed Forces. In June 1956 he joined the West German Air force with the rank of *Generalleutnant* and became Inspector of the Luftwaffe. In May 1961 he was promoted to full General, finally retiring in September 1962. During his time with the West German Air force he had gained a high reputation with NATO and was honoured with one of their highest awards in August 1961 when he was awarded the Legion of Merit. In fact in 1962 just before he retired he flew a "Starfighter" jet which could reach a height of 8,000 metres in less than sixty seconds. He was an energetic man with above average mental and physical strength for his age. He wrote various books which included a study of day and night fighter tactics and one called, *The Luftwaffe's Struggle against the Allied Bomber Offensive*, something he knew a lot about. He lived in retirement in Munich until his death on 25th January 1986.

Kammhuber as Generalleutnant and Inspector of the West German Luftwaffe in 1958. (Author's collection)

Alfred KELLER
(1882-1974)
Generaloberst

Knight's Cross: Awarded on 24th June 1940 as *General der Flieger* and Commanding General of 4th Air Corps for actions during the French Campaign.

Ranks:
Fahnenjunker – 5th April 1902
Fähnrich – 22nd November 1902
Leutnant – 18th August 1903
Oberleutnant – 18th August 1911
Hauptmann – 8th November 1914
Charakter als Major – 16th January 1920
Oberst – 1st January 1934
Generalmajor – 1st April 1936
Generalleutnant – 1st February 1938
General der Flieger – 1st April 1939
Generaloberst – 19th July 1940

Awards:
Pour le Mérite – 4th December 1917
Knight's Cross of the Royal Prussian Hohenzollern House Order with Swords
Iron Cross 2nd Class – World War I
Iron Cross 1st Class – World War I
Royal Prussian Pilot's Badge
Bar to Iron Cross 2nd Class
Bar to Iron Cross 1st Class
Bavarian Military Merit Order 4th Class with Swords
Bavarian Military Merit Order 4th Class with Crown and Swords
Cross of Honour for Frontline Combatants
Combined Pilot's and Observer's badge in Gold with Diamonds
Pilot's Badge with Diamonds
Grand Duchy of Hessen Bravery Medal
Medal for the Winter Campaign in Russia 1941/1942
Armed Forces Long Service Award 2nd Class

Born on 19th September 1882 in Bochum, Westphalia, Alfred Keller joined the army as a *Fahnenjunker* with 17th Pioneer Battalion in Thorn on 5th April 1902 at the age of nineteen. He was commissioned as a *Leutnant* in August 1903, and appointed company officer with the 17th Pioneer Battalion. In

Alfred Keller in the uniform of a NSFK Korpsführer wearing the Pour le Mérite and Knight's Cross. (Author's collection)

Oberst Alfred Keller wearing the Pour le Mérite as Commander of the 1st Air Division. (Author's collection)

August 1911 he was promoted to *Oberleutnant* and six months later was transferred to the Engineer Inspectorate where he worked on the fortifications in Wilhelmshaven, at the same time he underwent aerial observer training. In 1914 he became a pilot and was stationed at the Air Base at Darmstadt. On 2nd August he was appointed the commander of a Field Aviation Detachment and in November was promoted to *Hauptmann*. In 1916 he was appointed Commander of Field Aviation Battalion 40 and was beginning to make a name for himself as a excellent bomber pilot and commander. On 1st April 1917 he was appointed Commander of a Bomber Wing of the Army High Command 1, known as the "Iron Keller" Bomber Wing. It was while flying with this command that Keller won the *Pour le Mérite* on 4th December 1917. He dropped over 100,000kg of bombs which forced a British retreat to Calais. He then went on to lead a an important raid on Paris on the night of 30/31 January 1918 which caused serious damage and created major panic among the civilians of the city, furthermore his squadron returned without the loss of a single aircraft. Keller was on leave when Germany surrendered.

From December 1918 until April 1923 he was employed as the Head of the Land Service of the German Air Shipping Company in Berlin, taking a leading position with the Junkers Firm. In May 1925 he became leader of the Air Traffic School in Braunschweig where he remained until early 1934 when he returned to the army as an *Oberst*. At the beginning of February he transferred to the Luftwaffe and continued to serve as leader of the Air Traffic School in Braunschweig until May 1934 when he was appointed Commander of 1st Air Division. Appointed Commander of Bomber Wing 154 in July 1934, he was at the same time also appointed Commander of the Military Air Base at Faßberg. He was promoted to *Generalmajor* in April 1936, and eighteen months later was given temporary command of Air District 1, being promoted to *Generalleutnant* in February

Generaloberst Keller shortly after arriving in France for an inspection. (Author's collection)

An interesting photograph of Generaloberst Keller apparently wearing the Knight's Cross with Oakleaves. Keller was never recommended or indeed awarded the Oakleaves and so this photograph is unusual. (Author's collection)

1938. On 1st August he was appointed Commanding General of the Luftwaffe Command in East Prussia, being promoted to *General der Flieger* in April 1939.

He took part in the Western Campaign during the Battle of France after being appointed as Commanding General of 4th Air Corps at the advanced age of fifty-eight. He led his command in action against the British forces at Dunkirk and against the Netherlands and Belgium. For his leadership qualities and in recognition of his success during the campaign in France he was awarded the Knight's Cross in June 1940, followed in July with promotion to *Generaloberst*. He was then stationed back in France with his headquarters located near St. Malo, and was then chosen to be one of the air commanders during the invasion of Russia as Commanding General of 4th Air Corps. He was charged with supporting *Generalfeldmarschall* von Leeb's[71] Army Group North, with his headquarters now located at Norkitten, Insterburg and later at Ostrov in early 1942.

On 26th June 1943 he was put on the Luftwaffe Reserve List but was given a new appointment when he was made *Korpsführer* of the NSFK, the National Socialist Flying Corps, a Para-military organization that maintained schools for pilots, radiomen, glider pilots, paratroopers and was also responsible for the instruction of young Hitler Youth pilots in the defence of the Reich. He remained leader of the NSFK until the end of the war when he was captured by British troops on 2nd May 1945. On 9th January 1946 he was transferred to the Island Farm Special Camp 11 in Bridgend, South Wales, where he remained until October 1947 when he was repatriated to Hamburg. During the post-war years he created the OdR (*Ordensgemeinschaft der Ritterkreuzträger*), an organisation for members who had won the Knight's Cross during World War II and was the Chairman for many years until his death in Berlin in February 1974 at the age of ninety-one.

Ulrich KESSLER
(1894-1983)
General der Flieger

Generalleutnant Ulrich Kessler wearing the Knight's Cross, 1944. (Wehrkundearchiv)

Knight's Cross: Awarded as *Generalleutnant* and Air Leader of the Atlantic on 3rd April 1944, in recognition of his leadership skills.

Ranks:
Fähnrich zur See – 23rd December 1914
Leutnant zur See – 13th July 1916
Oberleutnant zur See – 28th September 1920
Kapitänleutnant – 1st March 1926
Korvettenkapitän – 1st April 1933
Oberstleutnant – 1st April 1935
Oberst – 1st April 1937
Generalmajor – 1st April 1939
Generalleutnant – 1st April 1941
General der Flieger – 1st September 1944

Awards:
Iron Cross 2nd Class – World War I
Iron Cross 1st Class – World War I
Wound Badge in Black – World War I
The Lübeck Cross, 1914
Cross of Honour for Frontline Combatants
Armed Forces Long Service Award 1st Class
Bar to Iron Cross 2nd Class
Bar to Iron Cross 1st Class
German Cross in Gold – 16th February 1942

Born in Danzig-Langfuhr on 3rd November 1894, Ulrich Kessler entered the Imperial German Navy in April 1914 when he attended the Naval Training School at Mürwik. In November he was assigned aboard the Liner "Wittelsbach" and a year later served on the small cruiser "Lübeck" where he continued with his officer training. In July 1916 he was commissioned as a *Leutnant* and took part in flying training with the 2nd Sea-Air Battalion as a pilot near Zeebrügge and then Norderney. He ended the war as a Flying Boat leader, serving with the same unit.

He remained in the Reichsmarine after the war and for a time served with a rifle Division before being assigned to the Reichsmarine Office in February 1919. In September he joined the staff of the Naval Station of the North Sea and in September 1920 was promoted to *Oberleutnant*. In October 1921 he was appointed Watch Officer with 2nd Torpedo Boat Flotilla, where he remained until 1925 when he was appointed adjutant aboard the cruiser "Hamburg". In March 1926 he was promoted to *Kapitänleutnant* and in April 1927 was assigned to the Naval Command as a Group Leader of Flight Affairs. In April 1931 he was appointed a staff officer and in October was assigned as Watch Officer on the Liner "Hessen". In April 1933 he was promoted to *Korvettenkapitän* and appointed advisor to Naval Command in Berlin. He served for a short while as an expert for Naval Aviation with the German Delegation at the Disarmament Conference in Genf, and then as an advisor within the Naval Command.

In September 1933 he transferred to the Luftwaffe where he served for twelve months as a specialist attached to Reich Air Ministry in Berlin. In October 1934 he was appointed commander of the Flying School in Warnemünde and in April 1935 was promoted to *Oberstleutnant*. He spent a year training at the Wehrmacht Academy in Berlin before being appointed commander of the Coastal Air Group now with the rank of *Oberst*. In October 1937 he was appointed Chief of Staff of Air District Command IV under its commander *Generalmajor* Hubert Wiese. He was then assigned to the Luftwaffe General Staff in Berlin and in November 1938 was appointed Commander of 1st Bomber Wing "Hindenburg", with its headquarters in Kolberg. Promoted to *Generalmajor* in April 1939 he went onto see action in Poland in September where he led his Bomber Wing during bombing missions over Warsaw and other cities, using primarily Heinkel He 111 aircraft.

In January 1940 he was appointed Chief of the General Staff of 1st Air Fleet under *Generaloberst* Hans-Jurgen Stumpff in Berlin. He was appointed Chief of Staff of 10th Air Corps, Air Leader of Drontheim and made Chief of training and education within the Luftwaffe in May and June 1940. Promoted to *Generalleutnant* in April 1941 he went onto head the training department within the Air Ministry until February 1942. On 5th February he succeeded *Generalmajor* Wolfgang von Wild[72] as Air Leader "Atlantic"; he wasn't very successful but kept his position due to his friendship with Göring. He came under the command of 3rd Air Fleet, commanded by *Generalfeldmarschall* Sperrle, and he operated with mainly Ju 88 and He 111 aircraft.

In March 1944 Kessler was transferred to Tokyo where he was appointed Chief of the Luftwaffe Liaison Staff. On 8th April 1944 he was awarded the Knight's Cross in recognition of his leadership skills as Air Commander of the Atlantic – the award was probably recommended and endorsed by Göring. In September he was promoted to *General der Flieger* and took over as Air Attaché still in Tokyo at the German Embassy. In March 1945, Kessler who had returned to Germany, was one of the passengers of U-234 which sailed from Kiel harbour with 240 metric tons of cargo for Japan. Also on board with Kessler were two high ranking Japanese generals, Dr. Heinz Schlicke, a German scientist, and an expert on the V-2 rocket. While still sailing the passengers and crew of U-234 heard on the radio that Hitler was dead and war was over, they listened as the new "Reich President" Karl Dönitz ordered the German surrender. The captain of the U-Boat *Leutnant zur See* Heinrich Fehler had to decide what to do, where should they surrender? He decided on America and U-234 set sail for the United States. The two Japanese generals on hearing the news that the U-Boat was sailing to America to surrender decided to commit suicide and both took an overdose of Luminol, a very powerful barbiturate. They were both buried at sea.

On 16th May 1945 U-234 arrived at its destination, Portsmouth, New Hampshire, on arrival Kessler wearing a monocle over one eye surrendered with a smart salute to the highest-ranking U.S. officer on hand. He later bragged to reporters that he'd learned how to accept defeat in style after World War I, and passed the time reading books until his arrival. During his interrogation Kessler stated that he had always intended to get off the submarine at Argentina, how true this was we may never know. Kessler remained in U.S. captivity until his release on 10th May 1947, he returned to Germany and died on 27th March 1983 in Urach.

As for U-234 it was sunk by a torpedo from USS Greenfish during naval trials approximately forty miles northeast of Cape Cod, off the Massachusetts coast on 20th November 1947.

Friedrich KLESS
(1906-1994)
Generalmajor

Knight's Cross: Awarded on 14th October 1940 as *Major* and Commander of the 2nd Group of the 55th Bomber Wing.

Ranks:
Fahnenjunker-Gefreiter – 1st August 1926
Fahnenjunker-Unteroffizier – 1st November 1926
Fähnrich – 1st September 1927
Oberfähnrich – 1st August 1928
Leutnant – 1st December 1928
Oberleutnant – 1st December 1932
Hauptmann – 1st March 1936
Major – 1st June 1940
Oberstleutnant – 1st April 1942
Oberst – 1st April 1943
Generalmajor – 20th April 1945

Awards:
Armed Forces Long Service Award 3rd Class
Iron Cross 2nd Class – World War II
Iron Cross 1st Class – World War II
Combat Clasp for Bombers in Gold
German Cross in Gold – 12th January 1943

Friedrich Kless as a Major wearing the Knight's Cross as commander of the 2nd Group of the 55th Bomber Wing, 1940. (Author's collection)

Born in Bayreuth on 7th October 1906, Friedrich Kless entered the army as a *Fahnenjunker*, or officer cadet in April 1925 and served for the next three years with the infantry. He was commissioned as a *Leutnant* in December 1928 and attended Infantry School before being granted leave to study languages in Russia in June 1933. He returned to Germany in September and was assigned to the Dresden War School and from there he spent a year at the War School in Potsdam training to be an adjutant.

In March 1936 he was promoted to *Hauptmann* and for the next two years he trained as a General Staff officer at the Berlin War Academy. In August 1938 he transferred to the Luftwaffe where he was assigned to the Reich Air Ministry with special duties. In September he joined the staff of the 5th Air Division and two months later he was appointed its Chief of Operations, serving under *Generalleutnant* Ludwig Wolff in Munich. In March 1940 Kless was appointed Chief of Operations to the Close Combat Leader of Area II, taking part in the Battle of France in May 1940, and from June he was attached to the 55th Bomber Wing and although a staff officer he played his part in the victory over France.

Towards the end of July 1940, Kless now newly promoted to *Major* was appointed Commander of the 2nd Group of the 55th Bomber Wing. On 25th September his Bomber Group took part in a heavy attack on the Bristol Aeroplane Company at Filton. His Group which comprised of fifty-eight He 111s and was escorted by fifty-two Bf 110s of the 26th Destroyer Wing, under *Oberstleutnant* Joachim-Friedrich Huth, attacked their target at about 11:45am. The Luftwaffe force wasn't intercepted by RAF fighters until they had left their target although they lost a single He 111 as a result of local anti-aircraft fire. A total of six Luftwaffe aircraft failed to return, in addition two aircraft crashed on return to France. Over Filton and the surrounding area about eighty tonnes of bombs were dropped which resulted in the deaths of 132 people. On 14th October 1940 Kless was awarded the Knight's Cross for his commands success which included the bombing of the aeroplane works at Filton. The Luftwaffe's own magazine *Der Alder* interviewed Kless and soon after the raid on Filton, Kless proclaimed, "... this factory will not produce any more aircraft."

At the end of October 1940 Kless was appointed Chief of Operations to the 4th Air Corps operating on the Eastern Front and in March 1941 he was transferred to the 5th Air Corps. In April 1942 Kless was promoted to *Oberstleutnant* and appointed Head of Operations in Luftwaffe Command East. In February 1943 he was made Chief of Staff to the same unit under *Generaloberst* von Greim and seeing action in Southern Russia. In February 1943 the Luftwaffe Command East was redesignated the 6th Air Fleet and Kless remained as its Chief of Staff until Germany's surrender. Kless was promoted to *Generalmajor* on 20th April 1945, just a few weeks before the end of the war.

Kless as an Oberst and chief-of-staff of the 6th Air Fleet, 1943. (Wehrkundearchiv)

Kless surrendered to U.S. troops on 8th May 1945 and remained in captivity until his release on 22nd December 1947. Friedrich Kless died in Krailling, near Munich on 6th April 1994.

Fritz KOEHLER
(1897-1949)
Generalmajor

Knight's Cross: Awarded on 4th November 1941 as *Oberstleutnant* and Commander 122nd Reconnaissance Group in actions over the Russian Front.

Ranks:
Gefreiter – 12th March 1915
Unteroffizier – 8th May 1915
Vizefeldwebel – 11th May 1915
Leutnant der Reserve – 9th August 1915
Oberleutnant der Reserve – 1st March 1920
Hauptmann – 1st April 1935
Major – 1st August 1937
Oberstleutnant – 1st April 1941
Oberst – 1st September 1942
Generalmajor – 1st August 1944

Awards:
Cross of Honour for Frontline Combatants
Armed Forces Long Service Award 4th Class
Iron Cross 2nd Class
Iron Cross 1st Class
Pilot's Badge

A Luftwaffe General who spent most of his career as a staff officer but did command a frontline reconnaissance unit in Russia with great success. Fritz Koehler was born in Derby, England on 14th November 1897, his family moved to Germany in the early-1900s when Fritz was still very young. He entered the army as a war volunteer with the 19th Ulanen Regiment in August 1914, and in December he was transferred to the 119th Reserve Infantry Regiment where he served on the Western Front. In August 1915 he was commissioned as a *Leutnant* and in April 1916 he trained as a pilot and three months later served as an observer with the 48th Air Battalion. He flew missions over the frontline until January 1918 when he was assigned to a Fighter Squadron School. In February he flew with the 25th and 38th Fighter Squadrons and in October flew with the 9th Single-Seated Combat Squadron until the Armistice and his retirement in December 1918. At the beginning of 1919 Koehler briefly served in the Freikorps before serving as a pilot with the 21st Troop Flying Squadron. He was appointed as a training officer with the Volunteer Unit Wurzbach and was promoted to *Oberleutnant*. He spent the next fifteen years as a civilian and for a time he served as a pilot with a small airmail company.

In April 1935 with the rank of *Hauptmann* Koehler joined the Luftwaffe and after attending a training course he was assigned once again as an observer with the 114th Reconnaissance Group in Münster. He was promoted to *Major* in August 1937, and by April 1938 he had been appointed adjutant with the 3rd Air Division under *Generalmajor* Richard Putzier.[73] At the beginning of World War II Koehler was transferred to the 4th Air Fleet with special duties, but he did not take part in the Polish Campaign. In November 1939 he was assigned as adjutant to *General der Flieger* Ludwig Wolff the Commander of the Air Region Command in Hamburg. A unit that had been originally formed in Hannover but now covered the areas in Mecklenburg, northern Vorpommern and Priegnitz and later areas in Denmark.

In March 1941 Koehler was given his first real frontline command when he was appointed Commander of the 122nd Reconnaissance Group, seeing action during the Western Campaign from his headquarters in Brussels, and then during the war in Russia. For his success in operations against the Soviet air force Koehler was awarded the Knight's Cross on 4th November 1941. His headquarters moved from Orscha to Smolensk and finally to Trapani in December. In September 1942 he was promoted to *Oberst* and left the front line, he was now assigned to the Air Ministry where he served as a department head in the Luftwaffe Personnel Office. He remained in the Air Ministry until the end of the war being promoted to *Generalmajor* in August 1944.

Generalmajor Fritz Koehler wearing the Knight's Cross, awarded in November 1941. (Wehrkundearchiv)

Koehler was captured by U.S. forces in May 1945 and returned to Germany in March 1947, but he was a sick man. On 20th February 1949 Koehler died at his home in Ulm-Söflingen he was fifty-one years old.

Karl KOLLER
(1898-1951)
General der Flieger

Karl Koller as an Oberst wearing the Knight's Cross as Chief of the General Staff of 3rd Air Fleet. (Author's collection)

Knight's Cross: Awarded as *Oberst* and Chief of the General Staff of 3rd Air Fleet on 10th April 1942, in recognition of his role in the support of ground troops on the Eastern Front.

Ranks:
Gefreiter – 4th August 1917
Unteroffizier – 23rd December 1917
Vizefeldwebel – 27th February 1918
Polizei-Oberwachtmeister – 12th February 1920
Polizei-Leutnant – 30th October 1922
Polizei-Oberleutnant – 1st August 1925
Polizei-Hauptmann – 1st January 1933
Hauptmann – 1st August 1935
Major – 1st August 1936
Oberstleutnant – 1st October 1939
Oberst – 1st January 1941
Generalmajor – 1st March 1943
Generalleutnant – 1st December 1943
General der Flieger – 1st November 1944

Awards:
Iron Cross 2nd Class – World War I
Iron Cross 1st Class – World War I
Prussian Aeronautic Club Badge
Royal Bavarian Pilot's Badge
Cross of Honour for Frontline Combatants
Armed Forces Long Service Award 1st Class
Commemorative Medal for 1st October 1938 with Bar "Prague Castle"
Combined Pilot's and Observer's Badge
Pilot's Badge with Diamonds
Combined Pilot & Observers Badge in Gold with Diamonds
Bar to Iron Cross 2nd Class
Bar to Iron Cross 1st Class

Karl Koller was the last Chief of the General Staff of the Luftwaffe, he was born in Glonn a small town near Munich on 22nd February 1898. He joined the German Imperial Army in August 1914 as a war volunteer, and after his training was assigned as a driver with the Bavarian Railway Replacement Battalion, part of the 8th Bavarian Infantry Division. In January 1916 he was transferred to the 1st Air Replacement Battalion at Schleißheim where he trained as a pilot before being assigned to 34th Flying Squadron in April. He then attended various Flying Schools between May and December 1917, before being assigned as a pilot with 273rd Flying Battalion. Promoted to *Unteroffizier* on 23rd December, he was promoted to *Vizefeldwebel* in February 1918 and was transferred to 47th Flying Battalion and soon afterwards flew with the 76th Fighter Squadron on the Western Front. He was taken prisoner by the British in May 1918, and returned to Germany in December 1919.

Discharged from the army in February 1920 he decided to enter the Bavarian State Police and was immediately assigned as a pilot with the 1st Flying Squadron in Schleißheim where he remained until September 1922. In October he was commissioned as a *Leutnant* and was appointed a platoon commander and training leader with the Police in Munich. In 1928 he was made adjutant of a police district in Munich and became responsible for training, he had risen steadily in the rank and by January 1933 was already a *Hauptmann*.

On 1st August 1935 he transferred to the Luftwaffe as an observer trainer in Faßberg, then in November was attached to the Air Ministry in Berlin before being assigned as a squadron leader on a bomber training course in Jüterbog. In August 1936 he was promoted to *Major* and in December was assigned to the Air Ministry once more where he remained for the next twelve months. In January 1938 Koller was appointed Operations Officer with Air District Command 5, in Munich, where he served under its very capable Chief of Staff *Oberst* Maximilian Ritter von Pohl. Re-designated as the 3rd Air Fleet Command in February 1939, Koller continued to serve as Operations Officer and helped with the planned invasion of Britain; although later cancelled he played an important role in the bombing of London. In January 1941 Koller was promoted to *Oberst* and appointed Chief-of-Staff of 3rd Air Fleet under the command of *Generalfeldmarschall* Hugo Sperrle, with the responsibility of supporting the 9th Army in Russia. On 10th April 1942 Koller was awarded the Knight's Cross in recognition of his part in the successful support of the ground troops of the 9th Army.

In March 1943 Koller was promoted to *Generalmajor* and to *Generalleutnant* in December shortly after being appointed Chief of the Luftwaffe Operations Staff, which made him deputy to the Chief of Staff of the Luftwaffe, *General der Flieger* Günther Korten. After the bomb blast at Rastenburg on 20th July 1944, Korten was seriously injured and died two days later. Göring now took this opportunity to get rid of Koller whom he disliked, and replaced him with *Generalmajor* Eckhardt Christian.[74] Now Hitler acted, he had been dissatisfied with Göring's leadership of the Luftwaffe and now with the death of Korten took his opportunity to replace him with an officer he wanted. He told Göring that Koller should replace Korten and left Göring in no doubt that this was his only choice. Göring had to concede, he knew his own position was in jeopardy. (Hitler had tried on a previous occasion to replace Göring with *Generaloberst* von Greim, but he had refused.) So on 19th September 1944 Koller took over as temporary Chief of the General Staff of the Luftwaffe, it was made permanent in November when Koller was promoted to *General der Flieger*.

Koller now tried to reform the Luftwaffe but it had been mismanaged by Göring and others for too long and air superiority over the skies of Europe had been lost a long time ago. Koller explained the problem after the war in his memoirs; he stated that in June 1944 at a conference at Obersalzberg he tried to point out the weakness of Luftwaffe armament industries. He went onto say that the High Command of the Wehrmacht should have supported the Luftwaffe armament program right from the start and he stated quiet frankly, "… that out top military leaders had simply neglected their duty … and they had refused to consider my arguments."[75] Koller was one of Göring's harshest critics, and stated that he felt that the *Reichsmarschall* had no interest in bringing about an atmosphere of cooperation and that he didn't care about the Luftwaffe anymore.

In April 1945 when Hitler had descended to his Berlin Bunker Koller attended his Führer's final birthday on 20th April. Although several high-ranking Nazi leaders abandoned the city that night, including Göring, Koller remained behind in Berlin at another location near Havel. His representative in the Bunker was *Generalmajor* Eckhardt Christian who kept Koller up to date. Koller's last act was to send all his remaining aircraft in support of *SS-Obergruppenführer* Felix Steiner's[76] relief of Berlin. Hitler told Koller on the telephone that he must guarantee with his life that the last man is thrown in. Hitler also told Koller that, "Any commander who holds back his forces will forfeit his life in five hours."[77] However the attack never happened as Steiner was unable to come to the city's defence, he couldn't retreat let alone attack! When Koller was informed by *Generaloberst* Jodl on 23rd April that Hitler intended to stay in Berlin and commit suicide he flew directly to Obersalzberg to inform Göring in person. It was Koller who pushed Göring into sending a telegram to Hitler informing him that because it was apparent that Hitler had lost his freedom of action to conduct the affairs of the Reich he Göring should take over all his offices as deputy according to the 29th June 1941 decree. Of course Hitler was furious and I suspect Koller knew he would be, and Göring was expelled from the Nazi Party and was briefly placed under house arrest at Obersalzberg. Koller was free to leave Berchtesgaden and persuaded Göring to meet him at Fischhorn at Zell am See where U.S. forces arrested them both on 7th May 1945.

Koller remained in Allied captivity until December 1947, he had for a time been imprisoned by the British at Oxford and had been visited by Charles Lindbergh. In 1949 he published his memoirs, *The Last Month*, written from his personal diary; it provided information about Hitler's last days during the Battle of Berlin. Koller later served as the chairman of the *Verband Deutscher Soldaten* in Bavaria. Karl Koller died at home in Glonn on 22nd December 1951; he was fifty-three years old.

Hans KORTE
(1899-1990)
Generalmajor

Knight's Cross: Awarded on 30th September 1944 as *Generalmajor* and Commander of the 2nd Air Division in Russia.

Ranks:
Unteroffizier – 1st March 1918
Fähnrich – 1st September 1922
Oberfähnrich – 1st August 1923
Leutnant – 1st December 1923
Oberleutnant – 1st February 1928
Hauptmann – 1st June 1934
Major – 1st August 1936
Oberstleutnant – 1st February 1939
Oberst – 1st March 1941
Generalmajor – 1st July 1943

Awards:
Iron Cross 2nd Class – World War I
Cross of Honour for Frontline Combatants
Armed Forces Long Service Award 2nd Class
Iron Cross 1st Class – World War II
German Cross in Gold – 1st January 1945
Wehrmacht Daily Report: 20 June 1944

Hans Korte was born in Dannenberg, about fifty-five miles from Hamburg, on 16th December 1899, he entered the army at the age of eighteen in March 1918. He finished his training just a few weeks before the end of the war and on 29th November

1918 left the army having only served for two months as a frontline soldier. In May 1919 he rejoined the army and was attached to the 1st Kurland Mounted Regiment of the Border Protection Police, and in November was made Platoon Leader with the 3rd Infantry Regiment. In June 1920 he joined the 11th Hussar Regiment and trained as an adjutant, in September he was transferred to the 14th Infantry Regiment and served first as an adjutant and then as a signals officer. In September 1922 he was given the rank of *Fähnrich* and trained to be an officer, and in December 1923 Korte was commissioned as a *Leutnant* and appointed a Company Officer.

In October 1933 Korte was serving at the Berlin War Academy as an *Oberleutnant*, and in June 1934 he had been promoted to *Hauptmann*. He transferred to the Luftwaffe in May 1935 and was appointed Chief of Operations to the Air Commander of Dresden, *General der Flieger* Edmund Wachenfeld. He remained in this position until November 1938 when he was transferred to the 225th Bomber Wing where he was made a Group Commander; it was later upgraded to the 51st Bomber Wing. Promoted to *Major* in August 1938, he was transferred to the staff of the Air Ministry at the end of 1939 now with the rank of *Oberstleutnant*. In May 1940 he was assigned to the 55th Bomber Wing and took part in the invasion of France, and in August 1940 Korte took over as Commander of the 55th Bomber Wing, while attached to the 5th Air Corps in Villacoublay, France.

In February 1941 Korte was appointed Chief of Staff to the Air Region Commander Southeast, and was shortly afterwards promoted to the rank of *Oberst*. He went on to serve in Crete in December 1942, and was named as the Commander of the 13th Luftwaffe Field Division stationed at the Gross-Born Area in Pomerania in early 1943 before being sent to the northern sector of the Russia Front. He was promoted to *Generalmajor* in July and by November had been transferred as a staff officer with the 1st Air Fleet under *General der Flieger* Kurt Pflugbeil in Ostrow, on the Eastern Front. In January 1944 he was appointed temporary Commander of the 1st Parachute Division on the Adriatic coastline.

He took over as the Commander of the 2nd Air Division in February 1944 when he succeeded *General der Flieger* Johannes Fink. Korte was the last commander of the Air Division before it was disbanded in September and used to form the Staff of the Commanding General of the Luftwaffe in Italy. In September 1944 Korte was appointed the Commanding General of the Luftwaffe in Greece and on 30th September he was awarded the Knight's Cross in recognition for his leadership skills when he was commanding the 2nd Parachute Division in Russia. In October he lost his command in Greece when he was placed on the Reserve List. In March 1945 he returned to active duty as the Commanding General of the Luftwaffe Staff West and of the Military Police Command and he managed to direct his troops away from the Russian lines and into the western sector of Germany where they surrendered on 8th May. Korte went into British captivity on 9th May where he remained until 31st October 1947 when he returned to Germany. Hans Korte died in Utting am Ammersee near Landsberg am Lech on 8th April 1990.

Hans Korte shortly after being awarded the Knight's Cross as Generalmajor and commander of the 2nd Air Division. (Wehrkundearchiv)

Günther KORTEN
(1898-1944)
Generaloberst

Knight's Cross: Awarded on 3rd May 1941 as *Generalmajor* and Chief of the General Staff of the 4th Air Fleet for actions in the Balkans.

Ranks:
Fahnenjunker-Gefreiter – 1st December 1914
Fahnenjunker-Unteroffizier – 26th March 1915
Fähnrich – 18th August 1915
Leutnant – 18th October 1915
Oberleutnant – 31st July 1925
Hauptmann – 1st October 1931
Major – 1st December 1934

Oberstleutnant – 1st January 1937
Oberst – 1st April 1939
Generalmajor – 19th July 1940
Generalleutnant – 1st August 1942
General der Flieger – 30th January 1943
Generaloberst – 22nd July 1944

Awards:
Iron Cross2nd Class – World War I
Iron Cross1st Class – World War I
Bar to Iron Cross 2nd Class
Bar to Iron Cross 1st Class
Wound Badge in Black – World War I
Cross of Honour for Frontline Combatants
Medal for the Winter Campaign in Russia 1941/1942
Combined Pilot's and Observer's Badge in Gold with Diamonds
Krim Shield
KRETA Commemorative Shield
Armed Forces Long Service Award 1st Class
Commemorative Medal of 1st October 1938
Commemorative Medal of 13th March 1938
Combat Clasp for Destroyers in Gold
Pilot's Badge with Diamonds
German Cross in Gold – 1st February 1943
Wound Badge of 20th July 1944 in Gold – 22nd July 1944
Wehrmacht Daily Report: 12 August 1943

Günther Korten, the man who succeeded Hans Jeschonnek as Chief of Staff of the Luftwaffe, was born on 26th July 1898 in Cologne; after he completed his education he joined the army as a recruit with 34th Field-Artillery Regiment in September 1914. In December he transferred as a company commander with 8th Pioneer Battalion and was commissioned as a *Leutnant* in October 1915. He remained with the same Regiment throughout the war, apart from being transferred for six months to a Signals Battalion with 15th Infantry Division in late 1916.

When the war ended Korten remained with the Reichswehr serving as a company officer with a number of different army battalions. In May 1924 he was appointed adjutant and welfare officer of the 6th Pioneer Battalion before being transferred in November 1927 to the 6th Artillery Regiment. A year later almost to the day, he went to Russia where he took part in secret pilot training along with other future Luftwaffe commanders. At the beginning of 1930 he returned to Berlin where he served on the staff of the 1st Division attached to its photographic office. On 1st November 1934 he transferred to the Luftwaffe, and was appointed as a General Staff Officer with the State Secretary of the Reich Air Ministry, Erhard Milch. He got on well with the State Secretary and was promoted to *Major* in December 1934 and to *Oberstleutnant* in January 1937. He was briefly appointed commander of Reconnaissance Group 122 and at the same time was appointed commander of the air base at Prenzlau.

General der Flieger Günther Korten. (Author's collection)

In October 1937 Korten was appointed a department chief within the Air Ministry and had now come to the attention of Göring who saw him as capable staff officer. Korten's rise within the Luftwaffe now became rapid. He was appointed in March 1938 as Chief of Operations on the staff of the Commanding General of the Luftwaffe in Austria and a month later was appointed Chief of Staff to the Commander himself, *Generalleutnant* Alexander Löhr. In March 1939 he was transferred to 4th Air Fleet as its Chief of Staff where he remained until the end of the year. In April 1939 he had been promoted to *Oberst* and in July 1940 after the fall of France he was promoted to *Generalmajor*, being appointed Chief of the General Staff of 3rd Air Fleet under *Generalfeldmarschall* Hugo Sperrle. In January 1941 he was transferred to 4th Air Fleet where took over as Chief of Staff under *General der Flieger* Löhr. It was while serving in this capacity that he won the Knight's Cross on 3rd May 1941, for bravery and leadership while serving in the Balkans. In August 1942 he was promoted to *Generalleutnant* and given his own command, he was appointed the Commanding General of 1st Air Corps and at the same time was commander of Luftwaffe Command "Don" on the Russian Front. He was appointed briefly as the commander of 1st Air Fleet at the end of June 1943.

Left: Oberst Günther Korten as chief-of-staff to the 4th Air Fleet. (Author's collection) Above: Korten as Generalleutnant and commander of the 1st Air Corps, with his anti-aircraft commander Oberstleutnant Georg Tyroller. Tyroller was awarded the Knight's Cross on 23rd December 1942 as commander of the 84th Flak Battalion, and was later reported as missing in action on 27th April 1945. (Wehrkundearchiv)

On 19th August 1943, the Chief of the General Staff of the Luftwaffe, *Generaloberst* Hans Jeschonnek committed suicide; a replacement had to be found. On 25th August at 2pm Göring introduced Korten to Hitler as the new Chief of the General Staff. Hitler shook hands with him and invited him to sit down he had heard good things of Korten and they discussed new ideas. Korten believed totally in Hitler, although he was against the invasion of Russia he was an advocate of strategic bombing and like Hitler he believed that the answer to Allied bombing raids was to counterattack in the same manner. He also believed in a strong fighter defence for the Reich and immediately on assuming office as Chief of Staff he transferred six fighter squadrons from the Eastern Front to Germany to assist in the defence of the Fatherland. By November he had taken bombers and crews from Russia and transferred them to Germany in order for them to be retrained in strategic bombing against England. These acts impressed Hitler but infuriated Göring who had wanted a man he could control he had put forward *Generaloberst* Ritter von Greim but Hitler had refused the appointment. In fact the week Korten had taken over his new duties the Luftwaffe had won a series of victories against the Americans over the Reich. The Americans had lost sixty bombers and the Luftwaffe had seriously damaged another 138. Hitler was impressed and knew the right man had been appointed. Göring on the other hand disliked his new Chief of Staff and made his life as difficult as he had made Jeschonnek's. Korten was a stronger character than Jeschonnek and had the backing of both Milch and Hitler and remained very much in control of his own office, he also had a strong deputy – the very capable *Generalleutnant* Karl Koller.

On 20th July 1944 Korten attended an important conference at Hitler's headquarters, the Wolfs Liar at Rastenburg in East Prussia. Korten was leaning over the map table and was about four feet from the bomb that had been placed there by *Oberst* Claus von Stauffenberg,[78] when it exploded. Korten was very seriously injured, although the first reports stated he was

Korten seen here talking to Hauptmann Johannes Wiese, a Knight's Cross winner who was later awarded the Oakleaves on 2nd March 1944 as a Major and commander of the 1st Group, 52nd Fighter Wing. (Wehrkundearchiv)

Funeral of Korten on 28th July 1944 at the Battle of Tannenberg Monument. Present at the funeral were many high-ranking Nazi officials including Göring who can be seen giving the eulogy. Seated in the front row are Generalfeldmarschall Wilhelm Keitel, Großadmiral Karl Dönitz, and Generalfeldmarschall Erhard Milch among others. (Author's collection)

only slightly injured, it was revealed that a large splinter from the table had lodged in his abdomen and he had lost a lot of blood. He was taken to the nearby hospital where for two days in terrible pain he hung between life and death, until on the afternoon of 22nd July he died. Hitler promoted him posthumously to *Generaloberst* the same day in recognition of his service. His funeral was attended by many senior generals including Göring, on 28th July at the Battle of Tannenberg Monument.

Korten in his brief time as Chief of Staff of the Luftwaffe had given the Luftwaffe new purpose and although too late he had not been afraid of making serious decisions that went against Göring, unlike Jeschonnek he wasn't afraid of confrontation with the *Reichsmarschall*. However in early 1944 Korten had told *Generalfeldmarschall* Milch that he intended to resign his position as Chief of Staff in August 1944, because he felt he could no longer work with Göring. The bomb at Hitler's headquarters had taken the decision out of his hands.

Hermann LICHTENBERGER
(1892-1959)
Generalmajor

Knight's Cross: Awarded on 12th November 1941 as an *Oberst* and Commander of 104th Flak Regiment.

Ranks:
Unteroffizier – 1st October 1912
Vizefeldwebel – 17th August 1915
Offiziers-Stellvertreter – 20th October 1917
Leutnant – 1st January 1922
Oberleutnant – 1st April 1925
Hauptmann – 1st August 1929
Major – 1st October 1935
Oberstleutnant – 1st April 1938
Oberst – 1st August 1939
Generalmajor – 1st February 1943

Awards:
Iron Cross 2nd Class – 17th June 1917
Royal Bavarian Military Service Cross 2nd Class with Swords
Wound Badge in Black – World War I
Cross of Honour for Frontline Combatants

Armed Forces Long Service Award 1st Class
Commemorative Medal of 1st October 1938
Bar to Iron Cross 2nd Class – 11th June 1940
Iron Cross 1st Class – 27th May 1941

Hermann Lichtenberger served in the German army for almost twenty-four years but had a very brief career in the Luftwaffe due to serious illness. He was born on 20th August 1892 in Germersheim, near Mannheim, and entered the army in October 1911 with the 2nd Bavarian Foot Artillery Regiment. When war broke out he was serving with the 6th Bavarian Reserve Foot Artillery Battalion and spent the whole war on the Western Front with the same battalion, and served the entire war as a non-commissioned officer.

He remained in the army after the armistice staying with the artillery and was finally commissioned as a *Leutnant* in January 1922. In October 1929, now with the rank of *Hauptmann* he served as a military specialist for motor vehicles on the staff of the 7th Transport Battalion. In November 1932 he was made Battery Commander in the 7th Artillery Regiment before being transferred to the Luftwaffe as a *Major* in October 1935. His first appointment was that of Commander of the 3rd Battalion, 8th Flak Regiment, and then with the 18th Flak Regiment in Mannheim. In August 1937 he was appointed Commander of the 88th Motorised Flak Battalion attached to the Condor Legion, in Spain. His expertise in motorised vehicles was much needed in Spain and he made a good impression and was promoted in April 1938 to *Oberstleutnant*. In July 1939 he was transferred to the staff of the Air Region Commander in Nuremberg, and this was followed by his promotion to *Oberst* in August of the same year.

In November 1939 he Commanded the 5th Flak Regiment in Munich, and later transferred to the 104th Flak Regiment in Paris before being sent to Warsaw where he took part in training in readiness for the invasion of Russia. In June 1941 he led his command into central Russia, mostly around the Orel area, supporting the 2nd Panzer Group. It was during this time that Lichtenberger first became ill, and a few days before he was granted sick leave he was awarded the Knight's Cross for his leadership and bravery during the support operations in Russia. On 17th November 1941 he left Russia a very sick man. He remained on the Reserve List until March 1942 when he returned to active service as Inspector of the Anti-Aircraft troops in Holland. In September he was named as the Commander of the 4th Anti-Aircraft Brigade in Munich. On 26th November he was taken ill again and granted further sick leave, the exact nature of his illness is not known but it must have been serious because less than a year later he was retired from active service with the rank of *Generalmajor*.

Lichtenberger spent the rest of the war at home in Germersheim with his family. He died of his illness on 15th January 1959 at the age of only sixty-six.

Oberst Herman Lichtenberger. (Wehrkundearchiv)

The grave of Hermann Lichtenberger, his wife Emilie, and their son who died in 1943. (Author's collection)

Bruno LOERZER
(1891-1960)
Generaloberst

Knight's Cross: Awarded on 29th May 1940, as *Generalleutnant* and Commanding General of 2nd Air Corps for his support of the ground troops during the invasion of France.

Ranks:
Fahnenjunker-Unteroffizier – 9th March 1912
Fähnrich – 22nd May 1912
Leutnant – 27th January 1913
Oberleutnant – 18th April 1916
Hauptmann – 2nd October 1918
Major – skipped
Oberstleutnant – skipped
Oberst – 1st April 1935
Generalmajor – 1st April 1938
Generalleutnant – 1st January 1940
General der Flieger – 19th July 1940
Generaloberst – 16th February 1943
NSFK-Obergruppenführer – 20th April 1944

Awards:
Knight's Cross of the Royal Prussian Hohenzollern House Order with Swords – 1917
Iron Cross 2nd Class – 1st March 1915
Iron Cross 1st Class – 21st March 1916
Honour Goblet for aerial combat – World War I
Pour le Mérite – 12th February 1918
Bar to Iron Cross 2nd Class
Bar to Iron Cross 1st Class
Royal Prussian Pilot's Badge
Wound Badge in Silver – World War I
Cross of Honour for Frontline Combatants
Armed Forces Long Service Award 1st Class
Combined Pilot's and Observer's Badge in Gold with Diamonds
Pilot's Badge with Diamonds
Luftwaffe Cuff-title "Jagdgeschwader Boelcke No.2 1916/1918"
Medal for the Winter Campaign in Russia 1941/1942
Commemorative Medal for 1st October 1938 with Bar "Prague Castle"
Wehrmacht Daily Report: 7 August 1941; 17 June 1942

General der Flieger Bruno Loerzer wearing the Knight's Cross. (Wehrkundearchiv)

An old comrade of Göring's who once served as his squadron commander during the Great War and he was a fighter ace with forty-four victories to his credit, Bruno Loerzer was born on 22nd January 1891 in Berlin. He joined the army as a cadet with the Bavarian Infantry Regiment 112, at the age of seventeen and was accepted into the Military School at Potsdam where he graduated as a *Leutnant* in January 1913. It was during this time that he met Hermann Göring who was also serving as a young officer in the same regiment and the two men became good friends. Loerzer was the first of the two friends to become interested in flying and after attending flying school at Habsheim and Freiburg was accepted into the Flying Corps. He was attached to 3rd Flying Replacement Battalion in Darmstadt at the beginning of the World War I.

During this time his close friend Göring had been causing problems within his regiment and was close to being court-martialled. Loerzer convinced him to join him in the Air Corps, and in October 1914 Göring joined his friend as an observer pilot – it seems his old regiment was glad to see the back of him. For the next seven months Loerzer and Göring flew hundreds of observer missions over enemy lines and were both awarded the Iron Cross 2nd Class on 1st March 1915. However Loerzer wanted more action and in June 1915 he started training as a fighter pilot, training at the Fighter Combat School at Schwerin-Görries. He completed his training in August and was posted to 25th Field Flying Battalion and then later to 203rd Artillery Flying Battalion where he scored his first victory on 21st March 1916. A month later he had been promoted to *Oberleutnant* and his score had risen to five enemy kills. In January 1917 he was appointed commander 26th Fighter Squadron and by the end of the year his score had reached twenty and he had been appointed

commander of Fighter Wing 3. In February 1918 his skill as a pilot was recognised by Germany when he was awarded the highest German award the *Pour le Mérite*. A few days later his squadron shot down twenty-six enemy aircraft without a loss and he received a personal telegram of congratulations from *Generalfeldmarschall* von Hindenburg. Loerzer continued to fly until the end of the war, shooting down more aircraft and ending the war with a total of forty-four victories and the rank of *Hauptmann*.

He remained a flyer after the war, serving with the Baltic Freikorps until March 1920 he then went into retirement. In 1930 after being contacted by his old friend Hermann Göring, Loerzer agreed to come out of retirement and became the leader of the Reichs Union of German Aircraft Owners, and once Hitler had come to power in 1933 he was appointed President of the German Air Sport Association (DLV), becoming Reich Sport Leader. In April 1935 he joined the newly formed Luftwaffe with the rank of *Oberst*, and over the next few years was appointed to many important positions without any real qualifications. His appointments were due to the good-will of his old friend Göring who had been appointed Commander-in-Chief of the new Luftwaffe. In April 1938 Loerzer was promoted to *Generalmajor* and appointed Inspector of Fighters, a post at least he knew something about after being a successful fighter pilot himself during World War I, but aircraft manufacture and new flying techniques he knew little about.

On 1st February 1939 Loerzer was appointed Commander of the 2nd Air Division, this command was upgraded in October to 2nd Air Corps and Loerzer led this command during the invasion of Poland. In January 1940 Loerzer was promoted to *Generalleutnant* and took part in the successful invasion of France, his command was responsible for the bombing of the Sedan area which helped the German breakthrough. His aircraft flew from their base near Calais over to England during the Battle of Britain and if Operation Sea Lion, the invasion of England, had gone ahead it would have been Loerzer who would have been responsible for air cover for the troop landings and for bombing Britain's communication centres. It was for his outstanding contribution during the invasion of France that Loerzer was awarded the Knight's Cross on 29th May 1940, and two months later on 19th July, after the capitulation of France he was promoted to *General der Flieger*.

In the summer of 1941 Loerzer's 2nd Air Corps took part in the invasion of Russia, under the command of Kesselring's 2nd Air Fleet. He was responsible for the air support of Guderian's 2nd Panzer Group and set up a special air support command which became very successful. Loerzer went onto direct the heavy bombing against Soviet supply installations, airfields, and railroads, attacking anything that moved. In doing so he disrupted Soviet troop movements, and as a result the Red Army was not able to launch a rescue of its forces who had been surrounded at Bialystok. In fact the "special air support command", set up by Loerzer had been such a success that *Generaloberst* Alexander Löhr copied it with equal success.

Opposite
Top left: Oberleutnant Bruno Loerzer wearing the Pour le Mérite as the commander 3rd Fighter Squadron in February 1918. (Author's collection)

Top right: General der Flieger Loerzer with Reichsmarschall Hermann Göring his old friend from the World War I days – both wear their Knight's Cross, and Pour le Mérite, with Göring also wearing his Grand Cross. (Author's collection)

Bottom: Generalleutnant Loerzer as the Commanding General of 2nd Air Corps with his staff at his headquarters in France. (Author's collection)

Göring talking to General Bruno Loerzer together with Oberstleutnant Gustav Wilcke, and at right Feldwebel August Grauting who was awarded the Knight's Cross as Platoon Leader in the 16th Infantry Regiment, 29th May 1940. (Author's collection)

Loerzer with Göring and the Italian leader Benito Mussolini in Sicily, 1942. (Wehrkundearchiv)

In October 1941 Loerzer was transferred to Sicily, with his headquarters in Messina, and later he was sent to Italy under the command of *Generalfeldmarschall* Kesselring. In November 1942, Allied forces landed in Algeria and Morocco and this called for the withdrawal of German troops from North Africa, but Hitler after talking to Kesselring, was convinced a bridgehead could be held and the German ground forces could be supported by the Luftwaffe. Kesselring promised Hitler that he could keep the 130,000 German and Italian forces supplied. However there needed to be changes in the Luftwaffe command in the Mediterranean. As a result Göring recalled Loerzer;

even Göring knew that Loerzer wasn't the most successful air corps commander of the Luftwaffe. Göring promoted his old friend to *Generaloberst* in February 1943 and appointed him Chief of the Luftwaffe Personnel Office. Loerzer would now be seen more and more often in the presence of Göring and with Hitler especially at his headquarters at Rastenburg. On 20th December 1944 he was finally placed on the Reserve List, the only position he now held was that of senior leader within the NSFK (National Socialist Flyer's Corps), with the rank of *Obergruppenführer*.

In early 1945 he moved to the Berchtesgaden area where he was captured by American forces. He was sent to a prisoner-of-war camp and in 1947 was moved to Dachau the former concentration camp near Munich. He was asked to be a character witness for Göring at Nuremberg but he refused turning his back on his old friend who had done so much for him during the war. In 1948 he was released from internment and settled in Hamburg, where he died on 22nd August 1960.

Alfons LUCZNY
(1894-1985)
Generalleutnant

Knight's Cross: Awarded on 9th June 1944 as *Generalleutnant* and Commander of the 2nd Flak Division for actions in Russia.

Ranks:
Gefreiter – 16th September 1913
Fähnrich – 19th June 1914
Leutnant – 6th August 1914
Oberleutnant – 18th April 1918
Polizei-Oberleutnant – 30th November 1920
Polizei-Hauptmann – 1st February 1921
Polizei-Major – 6th November 1933
Major – 1st June 1935
Oberstleutnant – 1st March 1937
Oberst – 1st March 1939
Generalmajor – 1st February 1942
Generalleutnant – 1st February 1944

Awards:
Knight's Cross of the Royal Prussian Hohenzollern House Order with Swords – 2nd October 1918
Iron Cross 2nd Class – 22nd November 1914
Iron Cross 1st Class – 4th September 1916
Silesian Eagle Order 1st & 2nd Class – 27th January 1920
Cross of Honour for Frontline Combatants
Armed Forces Long Service Award 1st Class
Bar to Iron Cross 2nd Class – 7th July 1940
Bar to Iron Cross 1st Class – 19th July 1940
Luftwaffe Anti-Aircraft Badge
German Cross in Gold – 29th March 1944
Wehrmacht Daily Report: 10 February 1944

Generalleutnant Alfons Luczy in 1944 as commander of the 2nd Anti-Aircraft Division. (Wehrkundearchiv)

Alfons Luczny was born on 4th June 1894 in Katscher, Upper Silesia and joined the 21st Field Artillery Regiment in September 1913 at the age of nineteen. By August 1914 he had been commissioned as a *Leutnant* and by March 1915 had been appointed Company Leader in the 63rd Infantry Regiment seeing action on the Western Front. At the start of 1917 he joined the 21st Field Artillery Regiment first as a Battery Commander and then as Regimental Adjutant. On 18th April 1918 he was promoted to *Oberleutnant* and appointed Battalion Adjutant, remaining in this post until the end of the war.

He joined the Border Protection Police in Silesia in 1919, and was made *Polizei-Oberleutnant* in November 1920. In July 1923 he transferred to the Protection Police or *Schutzpolizei* in Oppeln and was promoted to *Polizei-Major* in November 1933. His time in the police was uneventful and he wanted a change, so in June 1935 he transferred to the Luftwaffe where he served in the Reich Air Ministry in the office of Hermann Göring. In October he was transferred to Königsberg where he was appointed Battery Commander with 1st Flak Regiment. In October 1936 he was made Commander of the 1st Battalion, 1st Flak Regiment, and was promoted to *Oberstleutnant* in March 1937.

Luczy (left, front row) as a Leutnant in February 1916 with his comrades. At this time he was battalion adjutant with 63rd Infantry Regiment. (Author's collection)

Alfons Luczny with his wife and family in the uniform of Polizei-Hauptmann, 1925. (Author's collection)

From July 1938 until June 1940 Luczny served as Commander of no less than four different Flak Regiments which included the 13th in Leipzig; the 33rd when he succeeded *Generalmajor* Otto-Wilhelm von Renz in October 1939; the 3rd Regiment in Weimar only briefly and then the 6th in Belgium where he served under *Generaloberst* Otto Deßloch's 2nd Flak Corps. On 29th July 1940 he was appointed Commander of the 1st Flak Searchlight Brigade which had been formed in Arnhem and was later enlarged and became the 1st Flak Searchlight Division. It was part of the Night Fighter Corps and was responsible for illuminating the night sky for the German Night Fighters in their hunt for U.S. bombers.

In February 1942 he was promoted to *Generalmajor* and transferred to the British Channel Islands where he served as head of all Luftwaffe troops under the command of the commandant *Generalmajor* Erich Müller.[79] He served in the Channel Islands until October 1943 and then he was appointed Commander of the 2nd Flak Division where he was responsible for supporting Army Group North in Northern Russia. His command had been sent to Russia to replace the 14th Flak Division and it remained in Russia until September 1944 when it was sent to Trier on the Western Front. His command supported the army well and Luczny was promoted to *Generalleutnant* in February 1944 and was awarded the Knight's Cross on 9th June in for his support of the German ground troops in Russia.

Between November and December 1944 Luczny remained at the disposal of the Air Region Command and although re-

Generalmajor Luczy talking to an unknown officer in 1942. (Author's collection)

called to duty at the beginning of 1945 to serve as head of the Wehrmacht Motor Transport Division he played little part in the war effort for Germany. On 8th May 1945 he was taken prisoner by U.S. troops but was handed over to the Russians in December 1945 and remained a prisoner until his release on 9th October 1955. He spent the last thirty years of his life in retirement and died at the age of ninety-one on 12th August 1985 in Einbeck.

Rudolf Meister as a Generalleutnant and Commanding General of 4th Air Corps. (Wehrkundearchiv)

Rudolf MEISTER
(1897-1958)
General der Flieger

Knight's Cross: Awarded on 5th September 1944 as *Generalleutnant* and Commanding General of 4th Air Corps on the Eastern Front.

Ranks:
Gefreiter – 26th September 1914
Fahnenjunker-Unteroffizier – 2nd January 1915
Fähnrich – 3rd February 1915
Leutnant – 22nd March 1915
Oberleutnant – 31st July 1925
Hauptmann – 1st May 1931
Major – 1st May 1935
Oberstleutnant – 1st August 1937
Oberst – 1st August 1940
Generalmajor – 1st September 1942
Generalleutnant – 1st March 1943
General der Flieger – 1st September 1944

Awards:
Iron Cross 2nd Class – World War I
Iron Cross 1st Class – World War I
Knight's Cross of the Royal Prussian Hohenzollern House Order + Swords – 8th November 1918
Royal Prussian Observer's Badge
Wound Badge in Black – World War I
Cross of Honour for Frontline Combatants
Armed Forces Long Service Award 2nd Classes
Bar to Iron Cross 2nd Class
Bar to Iron Cross 1st Class
German Cross in Gold – 30th October 1941
Wound Badge in Silver – World War II

Rudolf Meister spent most of World War II as a staff officer but still managed to win the Knight's Cross as a frontline commander. He was born on 1st August 1897 in Cologne entering the Imperial Army with the 34th Fusilier Regiment in August 1914. He was wounded in November and spent several weeks in hospital, after returning to duty in January 1915 he was wounded again, this time more seriously and he spent five months recovering before returning to his old regiment in September as a *Leutnant*. In December he was appointed Company Officer and in August 1916 he trained as a pilot-observer with the 4th Air Replacement Battalion, and in October he served as an instructor with the Observer School in Stolp.

He remained in the armed forces after the war and serving as an observer with 420th Volunteer Air Battalion before being transferred to the air base at Königsberg. In September 1923 he went on a leadership course and later transferred to the 2nd Artillery Regiment. In July 1925 he was promoted to *Oberleutnant* and soon afterwards was appointed Company Officer with 4th Infantry Regiment. In March 1928 he left the army and was persuaded by friends to take part in the secret flying training in Russia, and he spent almost three years training before returning to Germany in May 1931.

In September 1933 he became an early member of the Luftwaffe and served as a officer attached to the Inspector of Flying Schools and for a time was attached to the Commander-in-Chief of the Luftwaffe's Office. In May 1935 he was promoted to *Major* and in July 1936 he became commander of 124th Air Group at Kassel. In March 1937 he was appointed Chief of Operations on the staff of Air District Command 4 and by August of the same year was promoted to *Oberstleutnant*. In April 1939 Meister was appointed Chief of the training department of the Air Ministry and in December he was transferred to Cologne where he was appointed Chief of Staff of the 1st Air Corps, under *Generaloberst* Ulrich Grauert.

In June 1940 Meister transferred to the Luftwaffe Personnel Office and in August he was promoted to *Oberst* and was appointed Chief of Staff to the 8th Air Corps, under *Feldmarschall* von Richthofen. He was wounded during an air attack near Kalinin, Russia on 13th October 1941. Transferred back to the Luftwaffe Personnel Office in March 1942 he became the acting Chief of the Operations staff. In March 1943 he was promoted to *Generalleutnant* and in June his appointment in the Air Ministry was confirmed by Göring. He now worked closely with Göring's Chief of Staff *Generaloberst* Hans Jeschonnek. The two men got on reasonable well although by the time Meister was appointed to this position Jeschonnek was a broken man and drank heavily, and Meister found himself doing most of the work, even briefing Göring on important issues. Jeschonnnek would later commit suicide – in fact it was Meister who was the last officer to see him alive. On the morning of 18th August 1943 Meister went to see Jeschonnek in his office to report the latest Allied bombing figures, Jeschonnek listened to him in silence and without any emotion. When Meister left Jeschonnek's office the *Generaloberst* shot himself.

In September 1944 Meister was promoted to *General der Flieger* and was appointed Commanding General of the 4th Air Corps and at the same time was made commander of all Luftwaffe forces in Denmark. He was awarded the Knight's Cross for actions on the Eastern Front on 5th September 1944 and few days later he took up his position in Denmark. His last appointment during World War II was as Chief of the Luftwaffe Personnel Department which he headed from December 1944 until the end of the war. He surrendered to the Allies on 8th May 1945 and was released in 1948; Meister died in Hannover 11th September 1958.

Generalfeldmarschall Erhard Milch holding his Marshal's Baton, winter 1942. (Author's collection)

Erhard Alfred Richard Oskar MILCH
(1892-1972)
Generalfeldmarschall

Knight's Cross: Awarded on 4th May 1940 as *Generaloberst* and Commander of 5th Air Fleet and Commander-in-Chief North.

Ranks:
Fähnrich – 18th October 1910
Leutnant – 18th August 1911
Oberleutnant – 18th August 1915
Hauptmann – 18th August 1918
Major – skipped
Oberstleutnant – skipped
Charakter als Oberst – 28th October 1933
Charakter als Generalmajor – 24 March 1934
Charakter als Generalleutnant – 28 March 1935
Charakter als General der Flieger – 30 January 1936
General der Flieger – 20th April 1936
Generaloberst – 1st November 1938
Generalfeldmarschall – 19th July 1940

Awards:
Iron Cross 2nd Class – World War I
Iron Cross 1st Class – World War I
Royal Bavarian Pilots Observers Badge – World War I
Royal Bavarian Pilots Badge –World War I
Cross of Honour for Frontline Combatants
Combined Pilots and Observers Badge in Gold with Diamonds – November 1935
Civil Defence Award 1st & 2nd Class – 20th April 1938
Pilot's Badge with Diamonds
Armed Forces Long Service Award 2nd Class
Luftwaffe Pilots Badge
Bar to the Iron Cross 2nd Class

Bar to the Iron Cross 1st Class
Golden Party Badge of the NSDAP
Commemorative Medal of 13 March 1938
Commemorative Medal of 1 October 1938 without Bar
Commemorative Medal for 1st October 1938 with Bar "Prague Castle"
Return of Memel Commemorative Medal

Erhard Milch was born on 30th March 1892 in Wilhelmshaven; the son of a Jewish naval pharmacist, Anton, who had left the navy in the early 1890s to setup his own pharmacy in Gelsenkirchen with his wife Klara. In the mid-1900s his parents split and the young Erhard was taken to Berlin with his mother where he received a good education.

He volunteered for service with the Imperial Navy in 1910 but was refused entry, probably because of his Jewish ancestry. He joined the German army instead and after attending officer training he was commissioned in 1911 and assigned to 1st Foot Artillery Regiment at Königsberg. He served on both the Eastern and Western Fronts during World War I as a battalion adjutant, an aerial observer, intelligence officer and briefly the commander of 6th Fighter Group, even though he could not yet fly himself. In 1918 he chose to attend the War Academy in Berlin but the war ended before his training had started. He returned home unemployed and disillusioned. He served briefly with the Freikorps and with the police in Königsberg, taking a job with the large firm of Hugo Junkers in 1920. Between late 1921 and December 1925 Milch was the Managing Director of the Junkers Air Commerce Company which became the German Lufthansa, the commercial German airline.

In 1929 Milch became aware of Hitler and what he stood for and more importantly for Milch the hatred that he and the Nazis had for the Jews. Milch quickly decided that it would be prudent to get on the right side of Hitler as soon as he could. In 1932 he offered Hitler an aeroplane free of charge; he was also depositing 1000 Reichmarks into Göring's account every month. In May 1933 Milch was named as Göring's State Secretary for Aviation within the Reich Air Ministry, and soon afterwards Göring's deputy. It was soon very clear why Milch had deposited so much money into Göring's bank account, he needed Göring's help to cover-up his Jewish ancestry, otherwise his career would be over before it had even started!

Göring now began to help, he concluded that Milch's mother had carried an adulterous affair with Baron Hermann

Oberst Milch as Göring's State Secretary for Aviation, 1933. (Author's collection)

Milch as Generalleutnant at his desk in the Air Ministry as Göring's deputy. (Author's collection)

von Bier for many years while still living with her husband but not having martial relations with him; none of her children were therefore Jewish. Based on this story put together by Göring and his men, a birth certificate was re-issued with Bier listed as his father. Milch was now officially declared an "Aryan". Milch now was rapidly promoted, in March 1934 he was promoted to *Generalmajor*; in March 1935 he was promoted to *Generalleutnant*; in January 1936 he was made *General der Flieger*, followed in November 1938 by *Generaloberst* and after the fall of France was one of a number of generals promoted to *Generalfeldmarschall*.

Although Milch would always be grateful to Göring for his help and support, he never really got on with the *Reichsmarschall* and even tried on a number of occasions to ease Göring out of office and try to replace him. When Ernst Udet killed himself Milch took over as the air armaments chief. He cancelled the production of new aircraft and ordered the mass production of various obsolete aircraft which included the Me 110. However aircraft production did begin to rise under the direction Milch, but he seemed more interested in feuding with the Luftwaffe General Staff and continued to plot against Göring. In 1941 Milch had been slow to recognize the potential of the new Me 262 jet fighter, it was in fact Udet who saw its potential but Milch refused to allow its development until it was too late. In 1943 *Generalmajor* Adolf Galland chief of the Luftwaffe fighter arm, flew one of the new jet-aircraft and was very impressed and made his feelings known. Milch respected Galland and ordered the fighter into full production. In August 1943 it was announced that 4,000 fighters would be built per month and Galland wanted 25% of them made into jet fighters. However Milch was unable to meet production figures and his prestige with Hitler began to decline. Milch tried to get back into Hitler's favour by ordering the production of the Fi-103 flying bomb, but after hundreds of wasted man hours and resources the project was abandoned.

Milch now had a new threat; it was Albert Speer the new Minister of Armaments and War Production. Speer was trying to take over Luftwaffe production and Göring wouldn't intervene to help Milch. When Hitler took an interest in the production of the Me 262, wanting them modified and made into bombers Milch promised Hitler he could make these modifications. Hitler believed again in Milch and was expecting large numbers of this new weapon to make an appearance during the Allied invasion on 6th June 1944. However on 23rd May 1944 Hitler found out that Milch had lied to him and no aircraft were ever delivered. Hitler was furious and Göring wasted no time in stripping Milch of his power. On 27th May the entire armaments industry, which included all air production was handed over to the very capable Reichsminister Speer. On 20th June 1944 Göring ordered Milch to resign from the Air Ministry, the next day he did exactly that.

Milch as Generalfeldmarschall wearing the Knight's Cross and holding his ceremonial Marshals Baton shortly after being promoted, July 1940. (Private source)

Milch with SA-Obergruppenführer Johann Heinrich Böhmcker the Burgermeister of Bremen during an inspection tour in 1942. (Author's collection)

Milch as General Inspector of the Luftwaffe on an inspection tour in Bremen. (Author's collection)

Milch still maintained his rank and the office of General Inspector of the Luftwaffe, and he made a number of inspection tours at the front, much to the surprise of Göring who had thought Milch would fade into the background and remain behind a desk. Milch was trying to establish himself again and perhaps regain the respect of Hitler once more. However on 1st October 1944 everything changed, Milch crashed his car and skidded off the road near Arnhem. Milch woke up in hospital, with three broken ribs, and he lay at his home recovering until early 1945. While he was still recovering Göring dismissed him of all his remaining offices and Milch was transferred to the Führer Reserve.

On 30th March 1945, Milch's 53rd birthday Hitler sent him a birthday greeting and the two met for the last time in the Führer Bunker on 21st April, the day after Hitler's own birthday. On 26th April Milch left his home for the last time and headed north, having declined Speer's invitation to join the Dönitz government at Flensburg. He drove right past Soviet tanks with the headlights of his car turned off, miraculously never being stopped. He drove to Sierhagen Castle near Neustadt, on the Baltic coast where he was arrested by British troops on 4th May.

He was imprisoned in the former concentration camp at Dachau where he was kept in a cell in the infamous "Bunker", the cell's were designed for one person but Milch had to share it with former *Generalfeldmarschall*'s Albert Kesselring, Walter von Brauchitsch, *Generaloberst* Nikolaus von Falkenhorst and *General der Infanterie* Alexander von Falkenhausen. Milch had been a witness for Göring during the latter's own trial even though he hated the former *Reichsmarschall*, he hated the allies even more. Eventually Milch was tried himself at Nuremberg as a minor war criminal.

His trial began on 13th November 1946, and he was charged with three counts relating to the deportation of foreigner's for forced labor, and for the torture of Hungarian and Rumanian slave laborer's. During his trial he said, "Since I became a soldier in 1910 my work has been devoted to my German people." He went on to tell the court that when the government had asked him to build up the Luftwaffe he had done so for the German people. He went on to say, "My full effort was dedicated to the air defense of the German homeland." When he was questioned about the use of slave labor in his factories he answered, "… I had nothing to do with the employment of slave labor … I have always made efforts to improve the living conditions of all workers." His final statement to the court was, "I am only interested in one thing – that the German people should, as soon as possible, be relieved of their untold suffering."[80]

Milch was found guilty on two counts and was sentenced to life imprisonment on 17th April 1947. His sentence was later commuted to fifteen years on 31st January 1951, and he was granted parole on 4th June 1954 and released on 28th June the same year. Upon release he settled in Düsseldorf, Germany where he worked as an industrial consultant for the aviation division of Fiat and for the Thyssen Steel Company. He fell ill in 1971 and died on 25th January 1972 in Wuppertal.

Milch talking to a lawyer during his trial at Nuremberg in 1947. (Private source)

Friedrich-Wilhelm MORZIK
(1891-1985)
Generalmajor

Knight's Cross: Awarded on 16th April 1942 as *Oberst* and Air Transport Leader with the General Quartermaster of the Luftwaffe.

Ranks:
Gefreiter – 11th August 1910
Unteroffizier – 15th April 1911
Sergeant – 15th October 1914
Vizefeldwebel – 24th December 1914
Offiziers-Stellvertreter – 12th July 1916
Leutnant – August 1919
Oberleutnant - skipped
Hauptmann – 1st May 1934
Major – 1st June 1935
Oberstleutnant – 1st October 1937
Oberst – 1st June 1940
Generalmajor – 1st October 1943

Awards:
Iron Cross 2nd Class – World War I
Iron Cross 1st Class – World War I
Royal Prussian Pilot's Badge
Honour Goblet for aerial combat
Cross of Honour for Frontline Combatants
Armed Forces Long Service Award 4th Class
Commemorative Medal for 1st October 1938 with Bar "Prague Castle"
Bar to Iron Cross 2nd Class
Bar to Iron Cross 1st Class
Combat Clasp for Transport Fliers in Gold

Oberst Friedrich-Wilhelm Morzik, 1940. (Wehrkundearchiv)

Friedrich-Wilhelm Morzik was a General Staff Officer during most of World War II and his career was unusual in that he rose through the ranks and wasn't an officer cadet. Born on 10th December 1891 in Passenheim, East Prussia he became an NCO trainee at the age of fifteen while still at School. He entered the army in April 1909 and continued with his studies at the Army School in Treptow. In April 1911 he joined the 5th Grenadier Regiment in Danzig as an *Unteroffizier* and when the war started he served as an observer with the 2nd Air Battalion and later with the 17th Air Battalion. He went on to serve as a pilot with the 300th Air Battalion "Pascha" and saw action on both the Eastern and Western Fronts, as well as in Turkey.

In August 1919 he was commissioned as a *Leutnant* and joined the Silesian Air Police in Breslau, and then worked for a time for the Junkers Aircraft Company and became an expert in commercial aviation. From May 1928 he was a flight instructor at the German Aviation School at Braunschweig, and entered the Luftwaffe as a *Hauptmann* and Squadron Commander in Tutow, two years later he served as an advisor with the Inspector for Flight Security in the Air Ministry. In October 1937 he was promoted to *Oberstleutnant* and in April 1938 was appointed Commander of a Special Purpose Combat Group and at the same time was named Air Base Commandant of Fürstenwalde.

At the outbreak of war in September 1939 he was made Commander of the 1st Transport Wing, by October 1941 he had become Air Transport Leader with the General Quartermaster of the Luftwaffe. He was now responsible for the supplying of all ground troops to the Wehrmacht and for the most part did an excellent job. In February 1942 the Russian army had encircled the German 2nd Army Corps, under *General der Infanterie* Walter Graf von Brockdorff-Ahlefeldt,[81] at Demjansk, south of Leningrad, also cut off was the German 16th Army under *Generaloberst* Ernst Busch and part of the 10th Army Corps under *General der Artillerie* Christian Hansen.[82] Trapped in what became known as the Demjansk Pocket was also the 12th, 30th, 32nd, 123rd and 290th Infantry Divisions, as well as the 3rd SS-Division. Hitler ordered the 2nd Corps to hold out until supplies could be sent, and he promised a daily supply of 270 tons. It was down to Morzik to carry out Hitler's orders; his pilots flew an average of ten to fifteen transports per hour into the Pocket, day after day, regardless of fog, blizzards or heavy anti-aircraft fire. The Pocket did have two good airfields at Demjansk and Peski and the weather conditions most of the time weren't too bad, although there was considerable snow on the ground but the supplies promised did reach the troops, but it did use up most of the Luftwaffe's transport capability, as well as much of their bombers.

In March 1942 the German forces in the Demjansk Pocket managed to open a narrow corridor and over several weeks they managed to widen it. On 21st April the German forces broke out of the Pocket, but the battle had taken its toll. Out of the 100,000 men trapped in the Pocket, 3,335 had been killed and over 10,000 wounded. Morzik's transport aircraft had managed to deliver 65,000 tons of supplies, 31,000 fresh troops and had evacuated 36,000 wounded. However the cost was high and Morzik lost 265 of his transport aircraft. There were many awards given out after the success in Demjansk and this included Morzik who was awarded the Knight's Cross on 16th April 1942 for his success in supplying the 2nd Army Corps during the encirclement.

Morzik didn't have anymore successes like Demjansk and after the failure of supplying the 6th Army at Stalingrad he was transferred to other duties. In October 1943 he was however promoted to *Generalmajor* and during the closing stages of the war Morzik was reinstated as Air Transport Chief of the Wehrmacht but had little aircraft to manage. Most of the aircraft that he had at his disposal was used to move troops west away from the advancing Soviets. In May 1945 Morzik was captured by U.S. troops and held in captivity until his release on 30th June 1947.

Friedrich-Wilhelm Morzik died in Freudenstadt, near the German and French border on 17th June 1985, he was ninety-three years old.

Gottlob MÜLLER
(1895-1945)
Generalleutnant

Knight's Cross: Awarded on 8th June 1943 as *Generalmajor* and Commanding General of the Luftwaffe Administrative Command in Tunis for his organisational qualities.

Ranks:
Fahnenjunker-Unteroffizier – 16th September 1914
Fähnrich – 12th November 1914
Offiziers-Stellvertreter – 25th May 1915
Leutnant – 24th June 1915
Oberleutnant – 1st October 1923
Hauptmann – 1st September 1929
Major – 1st September 1934
Oberstleutnant – 1st October 1936
Oberst – 1st January 1939
Generalmajor – 1st November 1941
Generalleutnant – 1st November 1943

Awards:
German Cross in Silver – 22nd April 1943
Iron Cross 2nd Class – World War I
Iron Cross 1st Class – World War I
Royal Bavarian Military Service Cross 4th Class with Swords
Royal Bavarian Pilot's Badge
Wound Badge in Silver – World War I
Royal Prussian Pilot's Badge
Cross of Honour for Frontline Combatants
Armed Forces Long Service Award 2nd Class
Bar to Iron Cross 2nd Class
Bar to Iron Cross 1st Class
Combined Pilot's and Observer's Badge
Commemorative Medal for 1st October 1938 with Bar "Prague Castle"
War Service Cross 2nd Class with Swords
War Service Cross 1st Class with Swords
Luftwaffe Anti-Aircraft Badge

Luftwaffe Ground Assault Badge
AFRIKA Cufftitle
Wehrmacht Daily Report: 18 November 1943

Born on 17th March 1895 in Kitzingen, Gottlob Müller entered the army with the 15th Bavarian Infantry Regiment in August 1914. Commissioned in June 1915 as a *Leutnant* and shortly after being made temporary Company Commander in the 15th Bavarian Infantry Regiment he was wounded and spent several months recovering in hospital. He returned as Company Commander with the same regiment in September 1916 and in October he was wounded again, this time it was serious and he didn't return to frontline duty until April 1917. He transferred to the staff of the Army High Command briefly on his return and then trained as a pilot in Schleißheim in October. In June 1918 he flew as a pilot with the 290th Air Battalion and then with the 79th Fighter Squadron.

When the war ended he joined the Freikorps "*von Epp*" Flying Battalion and in August 1919 he joined the 121st Artillery Air Squadron while a pupil at the Bavarian War Academy. In October he transferred to the Reichswehr air base at Schleißheim and from May 1920 served with the 7th Motor Vehicle Battalion being promoted to *Oberleutnant* in October 1923. He retired from active service in March 1928 and almost immediately took part in the secret pilot training in Russia and was appointed Commander of the Station at Lipezk in February 1932.

Müller re-entered the armed forces in October 1933 when he joined the Luftwaffe and was immediately appointed Commander of the Air Infantry School at Schleißheim – a place he knew well. In September 1934 he was promoted to *Major* and named as a department head in the 5th Air District Command. From March 1937, now with the rank of *Oberstleutnant* he was named as commander of the 3rd Group, 255th Bomber Wing in Memmingen. In January 1939 after a short time serving in the office of the Commander-in-Chief of the Luftwaffe, he was promoted to *Oberst* and made Commander of the bomber, ground-attack and reconnaissance air schools. He was at the same time also appointed Commander of all airports in the region of Belgium and Northern France.

In March 1943 Müller now promoted to *Generalmajor* was appointed to his most senior position of the war. When the allies landed in North Africa the German High Command established a strict command of the airspace and Müller was sent to establish Luftgau Tunis. In his new position he was made responsible for all air activities, he had to acquire the necessary airfields, he needed to make sure that the troops were kept supplied and attend to the demands of the commanders.

Generalleutnant Gottlob Müller wearing the Knight's Cross, and German Cross in Silver, 1944. (Wehrkundearchiv)

Müller was an excellent organiser and well liked by his troops. In spite of all the supply problems in Africa he was able to keep the flying units there adequately supplied and for this he was awarded the Knight's Cross on 8th June 1943. However the region of Tunis fell in July 1943 and Müller was flown out just before it fell.

Müller was promoted to *Generalleutnant* in November 1943 and served as Air Leader of Berlin until the end of 1944 and in January 1945 he was put on the Reserve List. In February 1945 he returned to duty when he was assigned as acting commander of the 3rd Army Corps to serve as air liaison officer. Müller was killed in the final battle for Berlin on 28th April 1945 in Berlin-Spandau.

Hanns-Horst von NECKER
(1903-1979)
Generalmajor

Knight's Cross: Awarded on 24th June 1944 as *Oberst* and Commander of the 2nd Fallschirm Panzer Grenadier Regiment "Hermann Göring" for actions in Italy.

Ranks:
Fahnenjunker – 1st April 1923
Fähnrich – 1st October 1925
Leutnant – 1st December 1926
Oberleutnant – 1st July 1929
Rittmeister – 1st January 1935
Major – 1st January 1940
Oberstleutnant – 1st March 1942
Oberst – 1st January 1943
Generalmajor – 1st January 1945

Awards:
Iron Cross 2nd Class – World War II
Iron Cross 1st Class – World War II
Armed Forces Long Service Award 3rd Class
Bar to Iron Cross 2nd Class
Bar to Iron Cross 1st Class
German Cross in Gold – 24th November 1942
Luftwaffe Ground Assault Badge

Generalmajor Hanns-Horst von Necker wearing the Knight's Cross. (Wehrkundearchiv)

Hanns-Horst von Necker served most of his career with the army apart from the twelve months he spent in the Luftwaffe while attached to the Hermann Göring Division. He was born in Rudolstadt, Germany on 28th August 1903, joining the 16th Cavalry Regiment in April 1923. He was commissioned as a *Leutnant* in December 1926 and from October 1934 he was posted to the War Academy in Berlin.

In July 1936 *Rittmeister* von Necker was attached to the 3rd Panzer Division, known as the "Bear Division" because of its divisional emblem of the Berlin Bear. In January 1937 he was appointed its Chief of Operations officer, serving under *Generalleutnant* Ernst Fessmann[83] and from September 1937 under *Generalleutnant* Leo Geyr von Schweppenburg.[84] In March 1938 the "Bear Division" was transferred to Austria where it took part in the Anschluss, Union with Germany. In April 1938 he was transferred to the 4th Light Division where he served as Chief Supply Officer and in September 1939 took part in the Polish Campaign, and it was here that he won the Iron Cross 2nd Class.

In December 1939 he took over as Chief of Operations with the 9th Panzer Division, and in January 1940 he was promoted to *Major*. In May 1940 he took part in the invasion of the Netherlands and after Dunkirk his division became part of Panzer Group Guderian during the latter stages of the French Campaign. He took part in the Balkans Campaign and went on to see further saw action in both Greece and Yugoslavia. As part of Army Group South he saw action on the Eastern Front in the Ukraine, being promoted to *Oberstleutnant* along the way.

Von Necker was wounded in December 1942 and spent almost two months on the Reserve List before returning to duty in March 1943, having been promoted to *Oberst* in January. In May 1943 he was appointed Chief of Operations with the 16th Army first under *Generalfeldmarschall* Ernst Busch and then from October 1943 under *General der Artillerie* Christian Hansen, and saw action in the Courland area. He then spent several months on the Reserve List once again, returning to active duty in March 1944, having been transferred to the Luftwaffe where he was appointed Commander of the 1st Parachute Panzer Regiment "Hermann Göring". In May the entire division was withdrawn and the plan was that it would be refitted for its planned move to France, however when the allies offensive broke through towards Rome it was rushed to the front where it held off the Allied forces enough to allow the last German troops escape. On the 4th June 1944 it fell back behind the Italian capital, which had been declared an open city to prevent its destruction. The division along with von Necker's command defended bravely against the allied attacks towards

Florence and it was for his part in the defensive battle that von Necker won the Knight's Cross on 24th June 1944. However in July the division was ordered out of the frontline in order to prepare for transport to the Eastern Front. It fought against the Red Army north of Warsaw along with the 5th SS-Panzer Division "Wiking" and the 19th Panzer Division, and they succeeded in destroying the Soviet forces. In September 1944 von Necker was appointed Divisional Commander of the 1st Parachute Panzer Division "HG", and in October fought against the Red Army during the Soviet offensive in East Prussia. It took part in heavy fighting and was sent to Random in January 1945 where it fought hard and was forced to retreat towards Upper Silesia.

In February 1945 von Necker was transferred back to the Army and after nearly two months on the Reserve List he was recalled and appointed Battle Commandant of Swinemünde until he was captured by the British on 8th May, and remained in captivity until June 1947. He died in Bad Münstereifel-Houverath on 27th February 1979.

Georg NEUFFER
(1895-1977)
Generalleutnant

Knight's Cross: Awarded as *Generalmajor* on 1st August 1943 as Commander of the 20th Flak Division for actions in Tunisia.

Ranks:
Fahnenjunker-Unteroffizier – 14th October 1914
Fähnrich – 31st December 1914
Leutnant – 12th August 1915
Oberleutnant – 1st October 1923
Hauptmann – 1st May 1928
Major – 1st March 1935
Oberstleutnant – 1st January 1938
Oberst – 1st August 1939
Generalmajor – 1st December 1941
Generalleutnant – 1st July 1943

Awards:
Iron Cross 2nd Class – 1st April 1916
Iron Cross 1st Class – 20th September 1918
Wound Badge in Black – World War I
Royal Bavarian Military Service Order 4th Class with Swords – 18th December 1917
Cross of Honour for Frontline Combatants
Armed Forces Long Service Award 1st Class
Bar to Iron Cross 2nd Class – 8th May 1940
Bar to Iron Cross 1st Class – 5th June 1940
Luftwaffe Anti-Aircraft Badge – 19th September 1942
AFRIKA Cufftitle
Wehrmacht Daily Report: 11 March 1943

Oberstleutnant Georg Neuffer a Battalion Commander with the 64th Flak Regiment. (Wehrkundearchiv)

Georg Neuffer was a commander who radiated charm and goodwill, he was an intelligent man and described as a good listener. He was born on 18th April 1895 in Steinbach, Roding and entered the army as an *Fahnenjunker* with the 3rd Bavarian Field Artillery Regiment in August 1914. After completing an artillery training course in Jüterbog he returned to his old regiment as Battery Officer, being commissioned as a *Leutnant* in August 1915. Neuffer was transferred to the 22nd Bavarian Field Artillery Regiment before being transferred to a Flak Battalion in Frankfurt. He then trained as a Flak officer and joined the 54th Bavarian Army Flak Battery in February 1918 and ended the war serving in the 3rd Bavarian Field Artillery Regiment.

From July 1920 he attended Officers School and in October he served as a Battery Officer with the 21st Reichswehr Artillery Regiment. Promoted to *Oberleutnant* in October 1923 he spent five months at the Infantry School in Döberitz before being assigned to the Military District Command VII in October 1924. From July 1925 he served in various artillery units and was promoted to *Hauptmann* in May 1928, and in August 1934 he was attached to the Air Defence Command in Döberitz.

He was promoted to *Major* in March 1935 and in October of the same year he was transferred to the Luftwaffe where he was attached to the Flak Artillery School. In November 1936 he was appointed battalion commander with the 8th Flak Regiment in Fürth, and five months later he was sent to Spain as part of the Condor Legion. In January 1938 he was promoted to *Oberstleutnant* and after serving as a Battalion commander with the 64th Flak Regiment he was appointed Commander of the 34th Fortress Flak Battalion in Speyer in June 1938. In November he was appointed commander of the newly formed 14th Flak Regiment in Cologne-Porz before being appointed Chief of Operations on the staff of the President of the Luftwaffe Control Commission *Generaloberst* Günther Rüdel in April 1939. From August until the end of September he briefly served as Chief of Staff of the Air Defence Command of the Ruhr Area, before being assigned as the Chief of Staff of the 2nd Flak Corps, under *Generaloberst* Otto Deßloch which had been formed in Frankfurt from the 6th Air Division. In October 1939 he became Chief of Staff of Air Region Command IV and in December he was promoted to *Generalmajor* before being appointed to the staff of the Field Air Region Command "Moscow" under *General* Fischer in Minsk where he served as his Chief of Staff until April 1942.

Neuffer briefly served as Commander of the 5th Flak Division from 18th April until November 1942, his role was to make sure the division was equipped and ready for its important action in Romania where it was sent to defend the vital Ploesti oilfields. He was transferred to Tunisia in December where he took over Command of the 20th Flak Division. This unit had been formed in Leipzig and transferred to Tunisia where Neuffer took control of all Flak units, which supported the 5th Panzer Army under *General der Artillerie* Heinz Ziegler[85] and from 20th February *Generaloberst* Hans-Jürgen von Arnim.[86] The division provided air defence and ground support during the fierce fighting in Tunisia against the Anglo-American forces. However the Allied forces soon proved too much for the Germans and on 10th May 1943 after the German Mediterranean supply lines were severed by the U.S. and British navies the German forces surrendered. Neuffer was taken prisoner by the British and von Arnim who had led the 5th Panzer Army was captured two days later. Neuffer spent the next four and a half years in captivity, and in August 1943 he was surprised to learn from his British captors that he had been awarded the Knight's Cross for his support of the ground troops during the defensive actions in the Tunisian Bridgehead. It's unclear whether the award was actually presented to Neuffer while in captivity but it was a legal award nevertheless.

Neuffer was released from captivity on 7th October 1947 and returned to Germany, he died on 11th May 1977 in the small town of Soest not far from Dortmund.

Job Odebrecht as General der Flakartillerie wearing the Knight's Cross. (Wehrkundearchiv)

Job Wilhelm ODEBRECHT
(1892-1982)
General der Flakartillerie

Knight's Cross: Awarded on 5th September 1944 as *General der Flakartillerie* and Commanding General of the 2nd Flak Corps for actions on the Russian Front.

Ranks:
Fähnrich zur See – 12th April 1910
Leutnant zur See – 19th September 1912
Oberleutnant zur See – 30th July 1919
Kapitänleutnant – 29th January 1920
Polizei-Oberleutnant – 23rd August 1920
Polizei-Hauptmann – 20th November 1920
Polizei-Major – 11th August 1929
Major – 1st August 1935
Oberstleutnant – 1st September 1935
Oberst – 1st October 1937
Generalmajor – 1st June 1939
Generalleutnant – 1st June 1941
General der Flakartillerie – 1st December 1942

Awards:
Iron Cross 2nd Class – World War I
Iron Cross 1st Class – World War I
Cross of Honour for Frontline Combatants
Armed Forces Long Service Award 1st Class
Commemorative Medal for 1st October 1938 with Bar "Prague Castle"
Commemorative Medal of 13th March 1938
Bar to Iron Cross 2nd Class – 29th May 1940
Bar to Iron Cross 1st Class – 1st July 1940
Wound Badge in Black – 4th July 1940
Anti-Aircraft Badge of the Luftwaffe
German Cross in Gold – 20th October 1942

Job Wilhelm Odebrecht had an amazing career even before World War II began, he served in the Imperial German Navy and his exploits on Lake Tanganyika in February 1916 are credited with the inspiration for the story that became the film "The African Queen", starring Humphrey Bogart and Katherine Hepburn.

Odebrecht was born in Koblenz-Ehrenbreitstein, Southwest Germany, on 25th February 1892, he attended basic training at the Naval School in Mürwik in April 1909, and in May he served on board the ship school *Hertha*. In April 1910 he returned to Mürwik to complete his training in naval artillery and was promoted to *Leutnant zur See* in September 1912. In April 1913 he was posted to German East Africa and served as an observer on the vessel *Möwe*. When World War I started the German forces in Africa were in trouble, they were outnumbered and faced the Belgians in the Congo. In November 1915 the Germans managed to put together two small gun-boats using guns removed from the ship *Königsberg*, and Odebrecht commanded one of them, the *Hedwig von Wissmann*. The Germans needed to know what they faced and so Odebrecht would often slip ashore from his boat on the Belgian side of the lake, disguised as an African, and he walked through the enemy lines unchallenged gathering intelligence, looking around to see what weapons and armour they had and then he would slip back to his boat. On 9th February 1916 his boat was involved in action against two British gun-boats, *Fifi* and *Mimi*. Just as the battle had started there was a strange atmospheric phenomenon the images of the boats were projected into the sky at ten times normal size. The Germans were astonished and fired at these huge targets and almost destroyed both of them until the British scored a lucky hit and Odebrecht and his crew were captured. It is this duel on Lake Tanganyika which is supposed to be the inspiration for the story "The African Queen".

Odebrecht was transferred to Belgium and in July 1919 he managed to escape from his prison and reached Switzerland. There he remained hidden but after four days was found and arrested and was finally returned to Germany in September. In January 1920 he retired from the Navy and entered the army as a company officer with the 17th Volunteer Infantry Regiment, part of the 9th Reichswehr Brigade "*von Lettow-Vorbeck*", who had been his old commander from his navy days. In September 1920 he joined the Security Police and was promoted to *Oberleutnant*, and three months later he was promoted to *Polizei-Hauptmann* and appointed leader of the Protection Police Border Section in the area of West Prussia. For the next fifteen years he served with the police in a number of different units, including Marienburg, Eiche, Berlin, and Charlottenburg; in June 1929 he was appointed an instructor at the police training school in Sensburg and in August was promoted to *Polizei-Major*.

Odebrecht transferred to the Luftwaffe in August 1935 with the rank of *Major* and was attached to the staff of a Flak battalion in Brandenburg, a month later he was appointed commander of the 1st Battalion, 11th Flak Regiment in Königsberg and at the same time was promoted to *Oberstleutnant*. In October 1936 he was made Commander of the 71st Light Flak Battalion and a year later he was promoted to *Oberst* and transferred to the 34th Flak Regiment in Münster as a battalion commander. In April 1938 he succeeded *Oberstleutnant* Walter Feyerabend[87] as commander of the 25th Flak Regiment in Vienna, a unit that had been formed in Ludwigsburg and moved to Austria shortly after the Anschluss. In November 1938 Odebrecht helped to form the 8th Flak Regiment in Vienna and was appointed its first commander, he was promoted to *Generalmajor* in June 1939.

When World War II started Odebrecht was commanding the 5th Flak Division in Frankfurt am Main. In October 1940 he took over as commander of Air Defence Command 6 and became responsible for providing ground air defence for Western Germany. Later he became responsible for defending the skies over Frankfurt, Mannheim and Saarbrücken when his headquarters was moved to Darmstadt. In June 1941 he was promoted to *Generalleutnant* and three months later his command was redesignated 6th Flak Division and Odebrecht remained as commander. His command moved to Upper Silesia where he was made responsible for protecting the area from Soviet bombers. In April 1942 his command was part of the 1st Air Fleet and was given the mission of supporting and protecting Army Group North.

After the Russian counter-offensive in the winter of 1941-1942 the army was in desperate need of reinforcements, and one of the solutions was to create divisions of infantry from the staff of Luftwaffe ground forces. However Göring didn't want any of his troops under the direct command of an army officer so in October 1942 Odebrecht now a *Generalleutnant* was made its commander. He led this new command with distinction and was awarded the German Cross in Gold on 20th October 1942. In November due to his leadership qualities and success he was given command of the 3rd Luftwaffe Field Corps which had been formed in Gorza and was attached to the 18th Army. In December 1942 he was promoted to *General der Flakartillerie* and continued to command his corps when it was renamed the 2nd Air Corps in October 1943 and moved headquarters to Minsk. His unit fought hard and brave during the Russian Offensive and on 5th September 1944 his competence and skill was recognised when he was awarded the Knight's Cross. However this didn't stop the Soviet onslaught and he made his last desperate defence of the Oder River in March 1945 in support of the 9th Army.

On 8th May 1945 Odebrecht surrendered to the Americans, he was however soon released and returned to Germany in April 1946. He lived in quiet retirement in the city of Bad Homburg in southwest Germany. He had a unique military career and served with distinction in both world wars, he died at the age of ninety on 20th November 1982.

Theodor OSTERKAMP (1892-1975) *Generalleutnant*

Knight's Cross: Awarded as *Generalmajor* on 22nd August 1940, as Commander of all fighter pilots within the 1st Air Fleet during the Battle of Britain.

Ranks:
Leutnant der Reserve – 13th July 1916
Oberleutnant – skipped
Hauptmann – 1st August 1933
Major – 1st April 1934
Oberstleutnant – 1st April 1937
Oberst – 1st October 1939
Generalmajor – 19th July 1940
Generalleutnant – 1st August 1942

Awards:
Knight's Cross of the Royal Prussian Hohenzollern House Order with Swords
Pour le Mérite – 2nd September 1918
Iron Cross 2nd Class – World War I
Iron Cross 1st Class – World War I
Naval Pilot's Badge – World War I
Baltic Cross 1st & 2nd Classes
Cross of Honour for Frontline Combatants
Armed Forces Long Service Award 4th Class
Combined Pilot's and Observer's Badge
Bar to Iron Cross 2nd Class
Bar to Iron Cross 1st Class
AFRIKA Cufftitle

Major Theodor Osterkamp wearing his Pour le Mérite as Squadron Commander in the Fighter Wing "Richthofen". (Wehrkundearchiv)

Theodor Osterkamp was an ace of both World Wars, and during the First World War he flew alongside Oswald Boelcke and Manfred von Richthofen the Red Baron. Born in Düren-Rölsdorf, Germany on 15th April 1892 he entered military service with the Imperial Navy in August 1914, after the army rejected him because of health reasons. He saw action on the Western Front in 1915 and served with the 2nd Naval Flying Battalion in Flanders. In July 1916 he was commissioned as a *Leutnant* and went onto serve as an Observer, and became the first German pilot to fly to England on a reconnaissance mission. In March 1917 he briefly joined the pilot training school in Putzig and in October he took over as commander of the 2nd Naval Field Fighter Squadron. Osterkamp scored a total of thirty-two aerial victories during the war, his first in April 1917 was over Ostkerke, Belgium, the second in May 1917 was off the coast of Ostend, and by August 1918 he had shot down twenty British and French aircraft. He was praised for his skill by Manfred von Richthofen, the famous Red Baron and in September 1918 he was awarded the *Pour le Mérite* in recognition of his aerial achievements. He became the navy's highest scoring ace of World War I.

In January 1919 Osterkamp was serving with the 1st Guards Reserve Division, however by January 1920 he had retired from military service and spent the next six years in and out of various jobs but was still interested in flying. In the early 1930s he joined a flying team that was getting ready to take part in the International Tourist Plane Challenge which took place every year, he took part in 1932 and 1934. In August 1933 he entered the newly formed Luftwaffe and was one of the first pilots to join, he was instrumental in its conception and helped to set up the very first Fighter School.

In April 1934 he was promoted to *Major* and exactly a year later he was appointed a Squadron Commander in the Fighter Wing "Richthofen". Promoted to *Oberstleutnant* in April 1937 he took over as Commander of the Fighter School in Werneuchen and at the same time was appointed Commander of the 4th Group of Fighter Wing 132. In early September 1939 he helped to create the 51st Fighter Wing and became its first Commander, the unit was formed in Münster and trained with the Messerschmitt Bf 109 fighter. He led his Wing during the invasion of France in May 1940 and during the Battle of Britain. He claimed four victories during the French Campaign which included his first of World War II on 12th May when he shot down a Dutch Fokker twin-engine fighter near Soesterburg. He went on to shoot down another three, of which two were Hurricanes these however were never confirmed kills and didn't count towards his total. On 13th July 1940 he shot down his second confirmed aircraft a Spitfire flying over Dover; this was followed shortly by another British fighter. He rose rapidly in the ranks and by October 1939 had been promoted to *Oberst* and after the victory over France he was promoted to *Generalmajor*. On 22nd August 1940 he was awarded the Knight's Cross for his efforts and success against the enemy and in recognition of his skill in forming the 51st Fighter Wing which went on to achieve many victories against enemy fighters.

He was briefly appointed Fighter Leader (*Jagdfliegerführer I*), of the area around Stade, Germany before being made Fighter Leader II in January 1941, being responsible for the area of the Channel around Le Tourquet, Boulogne and Calais. In August 1941 he was transferred to North Africa where he became responsible for all fighter aircraft in that region until April 1942 when he was relieved of his command and placed on the Reserve List. In July 1942 he returned to duty as a fighter trainer commander serving in Berlin and he was promoted to *Generalleutnant* in August and in November his command was transferred to Vienna. In February he was placed at the disposal of the Luftwaffe High Command and served briefly as Fighter Leader in Sicily until June 1943 when he relinquished his command to *Generalleutnant* Adolf Galland.

Osterkamp went on to hold a number of staff positions with various training units before being appointed Inspector of the Luftwaffe Ground Organisation. He became rather vocal in his comments regarding the Luftwaffe High Command and was reprimanded on a number of occasions for his outspokenness. In March 1944 he fell ill, probably his nerves and was sent to the Nursing Hospital in Oberschreiberau-Rupprechtssteg where he remained until early December. Finally due to ill-health and for his criticisms no doubt, he was retired from the Luftwaffe and spent the rest of the war at home. Osterkamp was no Nazi but he was a patriotic commander who saw the benefit in a strong fighter force and like Galland and Mölders wanted recognition and support from Göring during the war. He was almost worshipped by his men who called him "Uncle Theo" and was credited with thirty-eight aerial victories of which thirty-two were achieved during World War I. Theodor Osterkamp died on 2nd January 1975 at Baden-Baden at the age of eighty-two.

Theodor Osterkamp standing next to Werner Mölders with Günther Lützow next to him, and Adolf Galland on the extreme left. Both Mölders and Lützow would be killed during the war. (Wehrkundearchiv)

Hermann Lukas PLOCHER
(1901-1980)
Generalleutnant

Knight's Cross: Awarded as *Generalmajor* and Commander of the 4th Air Division on 22nd November 1943 for operations on the Eastern Front.

Ranks:
Fähnrich 1st October 1921
Oberfähnrich – 1st October 1922
Leutnant – 1st December 1922
Oberleutnant – 1st August 1927
Hauptmann – 1st April 1934
Major – 1st August 1936
Oberstleutnant – 1st March 1938
Oberst – 1st August 1940
Generalmajor – 1st March 1943
Generalleutnant – 1st July 1944

Awards:
Iron Cross 2nd Class – 17th May 1940
Iron Cross 1st Class – 5th June 1940
Spanish Cross in Gold with Swords
Combined Pilot's and Observer's Badge
German Cross in Gold – 9th April 1942
Medal for the Winter Campaign in Russia 1941/1942
Armed Forces Long Service Award 2nd Class

Hermann Plocher as a Generalmajor and commander of the 4th Air Division. (Author's collection)

Plocher as an Oberst in the Spanish Armed Forces during his time as chief-of-staff of the Condor Legion during the Spanish Civil War. (Private source)

Born on 5th January 1901 in Stuttgart Hermann Plocher joined the Infantry at the age of seventeen in November 1918, missing the war by weeks. He stayed in the army serving in the 25th Reichswehr Regiment and in October 1920 he entered the Infantry School in Munich where he trained to become an officer. On 1st December 1922 he was commissioned as a *Leutnant* and was appointed Platoon Commander with the 13th Infantry Regiment. He was promoted to *Oberleutnant* in August 1927 and became a sports flier with the army, learning to fly gliders for army sporting events. In May 1928 he was chosen to take part in the secret pilot training course in Lipezk, Russia and on his return he was assigned to an army weapons technology course in Berlin.

In July 1935 he entered the Luftwaffe with the rank of *Hauptmann* and started training as a General Staff officer, the following month he was attached to the Organisation Department of the Luftwaffe. Promoted to *Major* in August 1936, a year later he was attached to the staff of the Condor Legion, the German force in Spain helping Franco's troops. In October 1937 he was appointed its Chief of Staff seeing service under its three different commanders: *Generalmajor*'s Hugo Sperrle, Helmuth Volkmann[88] and Wolfram von Richthofen. He returned to Germany in February 1939 as an *Oberstleutnant* and found himself attached once again to the Luftwaffe General Staff where he served in the Planning and Mobilization Department.

On 5th January 1940 Plocher was appointed Chief of Staff of the 5th Air Corps serving under *General der Flieger* Ritter von Greim. Its headquarters were at first in Gersthofen where it made ready for action and then in November 1941 it was transferred to Brussels. It was to be used as a mine-laying corps, but this was cancelled and half of the staff was sent to Mariupol and the other half, which included Plocher, was transferred to the Eastern Front. In April 1942 the corps was renamed Luftwaffe Command East and saw action in Smolensk. In October Plocher briefly took command of the 1st Air Division from *Generalleutnant* Alfred Schlemm and then in February 1943 he took over as commander of the 19th Luftwaffe Field Division and was made responsible for its training. Plocher was promoted to *Generalmajor* in March and the following month the division was transferred to France. In July Plocher took over as commander of the 4th Air Division where he once again saw action on the Eastern Front near Smolensk.

On 26th August 1943 Plocher succeeded *Generalmajor* Karl Koller as Chief of Staff of the 3rd Air Fleet under the command of *Generalfeldmarschall* Hugo Sperrle and later under *Generaloberst* Otto Deßloch. The 3rd Air Fleet's headquarters in August 1943 was in Paris and its job was to defend occupied Europe from the Allies. On 22nd November Plocher was awarded the Knight's Cross in recognition of his leadership skills when commanding the 4th Air Division on the Eastern Front. In April 1944 his command moved its headquarters to Arlon and continued its defensive position. But under the command of such a vain and indolent general like Sperrle the 3rd Air Fleet had no chance of defeating the U.S. and British air forces that had begun to pave the way for the invasion of Europe. In June 1944 it had less that 890 aircraft at its disposal of which only 500 were serviceable. Plocher had no influence over Sperrle who acted like an ill-tempered child at times shouting orders at his subordinates and expecting Plocher to make sure they were carried out. Plocher noticed that things were greatly improved when Deßloch took over command but it was just too late – the invasion had started and the allies weren't far way from having total air superiority over the skies of Europe.

Plocher took over as Commander of the 6th *Fallschirmjäger* Division in October 1944 after being promoted to *Generalleutnant* and in July his command was transferred to Meppel in Holland for refitting. In December he took part in the offensive at Arnhem and helped to defeat the British forces there. In March 1945 as part of the 1st *Fallschirmjäger* Army his command fought hard against the British in their attempt to stop them from crossing the Rhine. He surrendered to the Canadians near Zutphen, the Netherlands on 8th May 1945, and was handed over to the British who in turn handed him over to the Americans where he spent almost two years in an American internment camp.

Plocher returned to Germany in June 1945 and entered the West German Luftwaffe with the rank of *Generalmajor* and served in Karlsruhe. In April 1957 he was appointed Chief of Operations on the staff of the Deputy Inspector of the Luftwaffe, two years later he was made Air Leader North in Münster. In February 1961 he was made acting Commanding General of the Luftwaffe Group South, but he became ill towards the end of the year and was granted leave in December, a week later he retired. Plocher was a member of the Knight's Cross Award Association and he had convinced them that he had been awarded the Oakleaves on 8th May 1945, however although the award recommendation was processed to the point of signature, the award was never officially approved and therefore never actually awarded. Hermann Plocher died in Calw, Württemburg on 8th December 1980.

Generalleutnant Plocher wearing the Knight's Cross as chief-of-staff of the 3rd Air Fleet, a position he found insufferable due to the lack of leadership from its commander Generalfeldmarschall Hugo Sperrle. (Wehrkundearchiv)

Ranks:
Fähnrich – 20th May 1913
Leutnant – 1st August 1914
Oberleutnant – 14th December 1917
Hauptmann – 1st June 1924
Major – 1st October 1932
Oberstleutnant – 1st March 1935
Oberst – 1st April 1936
Generalmajor – 1st January 1939
Generalleutnant – 1st August 1940
General der Flieger – 1st February 1942

Awards:
Knight's Cross of the Bavarian Order of Max Joseph – 28th August 1914
Iron Cross 2nd Class – World War I
Iron Cross 1st Class – World War I
Wound Badge in Black – World War I

Maximilian Ritter von POHL (1893-1951) *General der Flieger*

Knight's Cross: Awarded on 15th June 1944 as *General der Flieger* and Commanding General of the German Luftwaffe in Central Italy and Commander of the Close-Combat Corps of the 2nd Air Fleet.

Cross of Honour for Frontline Combatants
Bar to Iron Cross 2nd Class
Bar to Iron Cross 1st Class
Armed Forces Long Service Award 1st Class
Anti-Aircraft Badge of the Luftwaffe
German Cross in Gold – 7th February 1944
Wehrmacht Daily Report: 5 June 1944

Maximilian Ritter von Pohl was born in Munich on 15th April 1893, from a family with a military tradition dating back years. The young Pohl was destined to join the army and in October 1912 he joined the artillery, serving in the 7th Bavarian Field Artillery Regiment. He served as an officer candidate and was commissioned as a *Leutnant* in August 1914, and went on to serve as a battery commander, an ordnance officer and a regimental commander. He won the Iron Cross 1st and 2nd Classes and the Knight's Cross of the Bavarian Order of Max Joseph in August 1914, one of the highest awards of World War I. When the war ended von Pohl joined the famous Freikorps "von Epp" in April 1919 where he stayed until he joined the 7th Artillery Regiment in May 1920. He transferred to the War Ministry in Berlin in February 1921 where he served as an auxiliary advisor in the office of the Inspectorate of Artillery. In June 1924 he was promoted to *Hauptman* and in March 1930 he was made a battery commander with the 5th Artillery Regiment and two years later he was promoted to the rank of *Major*.

In April 1935 von Pohl transferred to the Luftwaffe with the rank of *Oberstleutnant* and served in the Air Ministry as a staff officer until October 1937. He was transferred to Munich to take over as Chief of Staff of Air District I, and in January 1939 von Pohl was promoted to *Generalmajor* and the following month he was appointed Chief of Staff to *Generalfeldmarschall* Hugo Sperrle, commander of the 3rd Air Fleet during the Polish Campaign. In June 1940 the 3rd Air Fleet was transferred and von Pohl was appointed Chief Liaison Officer between the Luftwaffe and the Italian air force. Promoted to *Generalleutnant* in August von Pohl moved his office to Rome when he was appointed Air Attaché at the German Embassy. At the same time he served as the German Commander of the Luftwaffe with the High Command of the Royal Italian Air Force, he was now in control of all Luftwaffe forces in occupied Italy.

Promoted to *General der Flieger* on 1st February 1942, von Pohl remained in Rome until August 1943 when he was appointed commander of all flak units in the South. In February he returned to Rome as Commanding General of the German Luftwaffe in Central Italy, a post he held until the end of the war. Whilst in this command he was investigated by *Reichsleiter* Martin Bormann, the Nazi Party Chairman and the man closest to Hitler politically and who hated both Göring and Himmler and would do anything to try and sabotage their career or create some scandal and inform Hitler. Bormann found that von Pohl was having an affair with his female dietician and Bormann's spies reported back that many of von Pohl's officers spent hours swimming or sunbathing with their secretaries when they

General der Flieger Maximilian Ritter von Pohl, 1944. (Wehrkundearchiv)

Pohl watches flak units as Commanding General of the German Luftwaffe in central Italy, 1944. (Author's collection)

should have been working. However Göring managed to keep Bormann at bay and gave von Pohl some advice regarding his men sunbathing; he said they should be more discreet! Von Pohl was awarded the Knight's Cross on 15th June 1944 for his leadership of the Close-Combat Corps of the 2nd Air Fleet while in Italy. In November he succeeded von Richthofen as Commanding General of the Luftwaffe in Italy after the *Feldmarschall* retired due to health problems.

In April 1945 Pohl was one of the key figures in the Italian surrender along with Higher SS and Police Leader *SS-Obergruppenführer* Karl Wolff,[89] Gauleiter Franz Hofer[90] and *Generaloberst* Heinrich von Vietinghoff-Scheel. These senior officers knew it was senseless to continue the fight and they wanted to save Italy from further bombing and to make sure that the German troops in Italy could surrender to the Western Allies and not the Russians. They knew the Allies would only agree to unconditional surrender, *SS-Obergruppenführer* Wolff knew this after Himmler's failure to secure peace with the Western Powers, leaving out Russia, was rejected. On 23rd April the most senior Germans in Italy, Wolff, Hofer and von Pohl agreed to unconditional surrender. On 29th April the surrender document was signed and a cease-fire was set for 14:00 hours on 2nd May 1945 – the war in Italy was over.

Von Pohl, Wolff, and Hofer were all taken prisoner by the Americans on the day of the cease-fire and spent the next two years in captivity. Pohl died in Pöcking am Starnberger See on 26th July 1951 at the age of just fifty-eight.

General der Flieger von Pohl at his headquarters in Rome during his time as Commanding General of the German Luftwaffe in Italy. (Author's collection)

Johann RAITHEL
(1897-1961)
Generalleutnant

Knight's Cross: Awarded on 17th October 1941 as *Oberst* and Commander of the 77th Bomber Wing for actions over Russia.

Ranks:
Gefreiter – 1st May 1915
Fähnrich – 11th October 1915
Leutnant – 11th March 1916
Oberleutnant – 1st April 1925
Hauptmann – 1st April 1931
Major – 1st December 1934
Oberstleutnant – 1st January 1937
Oberst – 1st April 1939
Generalmajor – 1st April 1942
Generalleutnant – 1st January 1945

Awards:
Iron Cross 2nd Class – World War I
Iron Cross 1st Class – World War I
Royal Bavarian Pilot's Badge
Royal Bavarian Military Service Order 4th Class with Swords

Oberstleutnant Johann Raithel as Inspector of Fighters in 1937. (Wehrkundearchiv)

Wound Badge in Silver – World War I
Royal Prussian Flier's Commemorative Badge
Cross of Honour for Frontline Combatants
Armed Forces Long Service Award 1st Class
Bar to Iron Cross 2nd Class
Bar to Iron Cross 1st Class

Born on 11th March 1897 in Munich Johann Raithel entered the army in June 1915 as a war volunteer with the 1st Bavarian Foot Artillery Regiment. He was wounded in October 1914 and spent two months away from the frontline recovering. In June 1915 he attended an officer training course and was commissioned as a *Leutnant* on 11th March 1916. He served as a Platoon Leader with the 23rd Bavarian Infantry Regiment until July 1916 when he started training as a pilot with the 1st Bavarian Flying Replacement Battalion. In July 1917 he qualified as a fighter pilot and spent the rest of the war attached to the army air corps but seeing little action.

Raithel remained in the armed forces after the war and served in the 20th Infantry Regiment for almost ten years. In October 1929 he attended Technical College where he studied engineering, passing his engineer degree in April 1934. He served from October 1931 until April 1934 with the 9th Mounted Regiment and was for a time assigned to the Army Weapons Office in the War Ministry. In May 1934 he transferred to the Luftwaffe as a *Hauptmann* and was assigned to the Fighter Wing "Richthofen". Promoted to *Major* in December 1934 he was made Squadron Commander and this was followed by his appointment as Group Commander in March 1935. In July 1936 he was appointed Inspector of Fighters and in January 1937 was promoted to *Oberstleutnant*. In May 1938 he became Air Attaché at the Embassy in Sofia and he remained there until shortly after the beginning of World War II.

In August 1940 now promoted to *Oberst* he was appointed Commander of the 77th Bomber Wing when he succeeded *Generalmajor* Heinz-Hellmuth von Wühlisch.[91] He went on to see action in France, East Prussia, Russia and Italy; it was for action in Russia that he won the Knight's Cross on 17th October 1941. In April 1942 he was promoted to *Generalmajor* and transferred to the Air Ministry where he became General of the Troop Technology Department where new weapons were evaluated and tested before going into production. In June 1944 he served as a liaison officer with Air Fleet Reich and the 5th Army Corps but saw little action and finally retired from active duty in February 1945, but not before he had been promoted to *Generalleutant* in January.

Raithel went into Allied captivity in May 1945 and was released two years later and returned home to Hamburg where he died on 29th January 1961.

Knight's Cross winner Generalleutnant Heino von Rantzau as commander of 2nd Flak Division. (Wehrkundearchiv)

Heino von RANTZAU
(1894-1946)
Generalleutnant

Knight's Cross: Awarded on 29th August 1943 as *Generalleutnant* and Commander of 2nd Flak Division.

Ranks:
Leutnant – 22nd March 1913
Oberleutnant – 20th September 1918
Rittmeister – 1st March 1927
Major – 1st October 1934
Oberstleutnant – 1st April 1937
Oberst – 1st April 1939
Generalmajor – 1st April 1942
Generalleutnant – 1st June 1943

Awards:
Iron Cross 2nd Class – World War I
Iron Cross 1st Class – World War I
The Hanseatic Cross – World War I
Grand Duchy of Mecklenburg-Schwerin Military Service Cross 1st & 2nd Classes
Wound Badge in Black – World War I
Cross of Honour for Frontline Combatants
Armed Forces Long Service Award 1st Class
Bar to Iron Cross 2nd Class – 17th May 1940
Bar to Iron Cross 1st Class – 28th July 1940
Luftwaffe Anti-Aircraft Badge
Medal for the Winter Campaign in Russia 1941/1942
German Cross in Gold – 24th December 1942

Heino von Rantzau was born in Karlsruhe on 8th March 1894, he was from a military family and was well educated. He joined the army with the rank of *Leutnant* at the age of nineteen in March 1913, serving as a Battery Officer with the 60th Field Artillery Regiment. In November 1914 until the end of the war he served as Adjutant with the 9th Artillery Regiment seeing action on the Western Front where he was wounded by shrapnel and he won the Iron Cross 1st and 2nd Classes. Von Rantzau remained in the army after the war and retained the rank of *Oberleutnant*, he then served as an adjutant in a number of different regiments and in October 1926 was appointed Platoon Leader with the 2nd Artillery Regiment, and the following year Rantzau was promoted to *Rittmeister*. He then commanded two different transport battalions before joining the Luftwaffe with the rank of *Major* in April 1935.

In October 1935 he was appointed commander of the 1st Battalion, 6th Flak Regiment in Osdorf, Northern Germany, and was promoted to *Oberstleutnant* in April 1937. In July 1938 he was made Commander of the 43rd Flak Regiment in Dessau-Kochstedt, near Leipzig where he remained as its commander until July 1940. Von Rantzau was promoted to *Oberst* in April 1939, and was appointed commander of the 4th Flak Brigade operating from the Channel Coast near the town of Cambrai in readiness for Operation Sealion, the invasion of England. When the invasion was called off by Hitler the 4th Flak Brigade remained in France until 1941 when it was transferred to Stuttgart. However von Rantzau had been transferred in December 1940 and took over as commander of the 2nd Searchlight Brigade which had been formed by the Night Fighter Command in northern Germany. It was moved to Arnhem a few months later and was upgraded to divisional strength in August 1941, and in July 1942 it was disbanded and its units were absorbed by the 2nd Night Fighter Division. For his efforts in protecting ground troops during his time as commander of the 2nd Flak Division von Rantzau was awarded the Knight's Cross on 29th August 1943.

Promoted to *Generalmajor* in April 1942 and to *Generalleutnant* in June 1943 von Rantzau was appointed Inspector of Flak Artillery "East" in October 1943. In early 1944 he was made General of Flak Artillery with the Air Region Command XI, Hamburg and was made responsible for the protection of the skies over northern Germany. On 20th March 1945 he took over from the acting commander of the 3rd Flak Corps *Oberst* Werner von Kistowski, and led this unit during the heavy fighting in the Ruhr Pocket where the division was finally destroyed in April. On 18th April von Rantzau surrendered to U.S. forces and was taken prisoner, he spent eighteen months in captivity where he died on 2nd November 1946, he is buried in Allendorf in the War Grave Cemetery.

Hans-Joachim RATH
(1894-1968)
Generalmajor

Knight's Cross: Awarded as *Oberst* and commander of the 4th Bomber Wing "General Wever" on 9th May 1942, for actions over Russia.

Ranks:
Leutnant – 22nd March 1914
Charakter als Oberleutnant – 31st December 1920
Oberleutnant a.D. – 1st October 1924
Hauptmann – 1st January 1934
Major – 1st September 1935

Generalmajor Hans-Joachim Rath as commander of the 1st Air School Division in Göppingen. (Wehrkundearchiv)

Oberstleutnant – 1st October 1937
Oberst – 1st June 1940
Generalmajor – 1st December 1943

Awards:
Wound Badge in Black – World War I
Iron Cross 2nd Class
Iron Cross 1st Class
Armed Forces Long Service Award 1st Class
German Cross in Gold – 5th January 1942
Combat Clasp for Bombers in Gold

Hans-Joachim Rath was born on 11th December 1894 in Berlin, and entered the Imperial German Army as a *Leutnant* with the 32nd Infantry Regiment in March 1914. A few months after the beginning of the First World War he was injured and hospitalised, and spent five months recovering, he returned to duty in March 1915. Once recovered he was assigned to the Berlin-Lichterfelde Cadet Institute as a teacher and from there he took part in pilot training with the 1st Flying Replacement Regiment and then as a pilot with the 5th Combat Wing. For the next two years Rath served as a pilot in various squadrons seeing action over the skies of France.

After the Armistice he took a position with the Peace Commission and at the end of 1920 he retired from the army. In October 1924 he re-joined the army and started training in weapons and a year later he took part in the secret flying course in Russia for future pilots of the Luftwaffe. From April 1928 until March 1933 he served in various staff positions in the War Ministry, and a year later he transferred to the Luftwaffe with the rank of *Hauptmann*. He was then assigned to various training courses and in April 1935 he was sent to the Bomber Flying School in Lechfeld. In June Rath became leader of a squadron in Giebelstadt and in September he was promoted to *Major*. In May 1936 he was appointed adjutant with the Air District Command 3 serving under *General der Flieger* Edmund Wachenfeld and from June 1937 under *General der Flieger* Albert Kesselring.

Rath was briefly made Group Leader on the staff of Luftwaffe Command 2 in July 1938, then he was appointed to the position of commander of the 1st Group, 4th Bomber Wing in November 1939 under *Oberst* Martin Fiebig. Rath now promoted to *Oberstleutnant* took over the command of the 4th Bomber Wing "General Wever" on 23rd May 1940. In June he was promoted to *Oberst* and after the success against the bombing of Rotterdam his command took part in raids against targets in England. The 4th Bomber Wing continued to fly missions over England until September 1941 when it was relocated to Korowje Selo in Russia. His wing flew many missions over Soviet territory and in mid-1942 was deployed to Central Russia where it saw heavy action. It was for his success and leadership during this difficult time that Rath was awarded the Knight's Cross on 9th May 1942. In June he took over as the commander of the Bomber Flying School at Thorn. In October he was transferred to the Mediterranean, to Tunisia where he was appointed Air Leader Gabes, an important area on the coast. In March 1943 Rath was transferred to Crete where he continued his success as Air Leader Crete with his headquarters in Heraklion, he was subordinated to Luftwaffe Command South-East under *General der Flieger* Hoffmann von Waldau and later under *General der Flieger* Martin Fiebig.

Rath was transferred in October 1943 and took over briefly as commander of the 2nd Air Training Division and in November he was made commander of the 1st Air School Division in Göppingen. The division had been formed from staff of the 2nd Air Training Division and later moved its headquarters to Kempten a town approximately forty-five miles from Munich. It came under the control of the 10th Air Fleet and in May 1945 its commander General Stefan Föhlich ordered its surrender. Rath was taken prisoner on the 8th May 1945 and remained in captivity until June 1947. Hans-Joachim Rath died on 10th May 1968 in Bad Neuenhar.

Hans RAUCH
(1899-1958)
Generalmajor

Knight's Cross: Awarded as *Oberst* and commander of 41st Flak Regiment (mot) on 6th December 1944 for actions in Germany in defence of the Reich.

Ranks:
Obermatrose – 28th March 1917
Bootsmaat – 2nd July 1917
Fähnrich zur See – 17th September 1917
Oberfähnrich zur See – 3rd March 1918
Leutnant zur See der Reserve – 28th September 1919
Leutnant zur See – 10th January 1920
Oberleutnant zur See – 1st May 1921
Kapitänleutnant – 1st January 1922
Korvettenkapitän – 30th November 1934
Hauptmann – 1st October 1935
Major – 8th January 1937
Oberstleutnant – 1st June 1939
Oberst – 1st January 1942
Generalmajor – 30th January 1945

Awards:
Iron Cross 2nd Class – World War I
Cross of Honour for Frontline Combatants
Armed Forces Long Service Award 2nd Class
Commemorative Medal for 1st October 1938
Bar to the Iron Cross 2nd Class
Iron Cross 1st Class
Anti-Aircraft Badge
Medal for the Winter Campaign in Russia 1941/1942
Ground Assault Badge of the Luftwaffe

German Cross in Gold – 15th April 1944
Kurland Cufftitle

Hans Rauch was born on 1st March 1899 in Rothwasser, Görlitz, he entered the Imperial Navy in October 1916 at the age of seventeen. He attended the Naval School at Mürwik and served as a cadet on board the School Ship *Freya* until he was transferred to the Liner *Schlesien* in March 1917. In January 1918 he attended an artillery course on board the *Kaiserin Augusta* and in May he was transferred to the Liner *Hannover* where he saw action and won the Iron Cross 2nd Class.

At the wars end Rauch entered the Reserves and volunteered for service in the 1st Naval Brigade *von Rhoden* in February 1919. He then served with the 29th Reichswehr Infantry Regiment before returning to the active rank of *Leutnant zur See* in January 1920. From July he served with a number of naval minesweeping flotillas and coastal defence battalions reaching the rank of *Kapitänleutnant* in January 1930. In September 1933 he was appointed Watch Officer aboard the Liner *Schleswig-Holstein* and in December 1934 he transferred to the Luftwaffe and was attached to the Office of the Inspector of Flak Artillery in Berlin.

In October 1935 Rauch was promoted to the rank of *Hauptmann* and appointed Battery Leader with 10th Flak Regiment in Dresden. In January 1936 he was promoted to *Major* and transferred to the 1st Battalion, 19th Flak Regiment stationed in Cologne, and in November 1937 he supervised the formation of the 14th Flak Regiment. He became an advisor with the Air Region Commander of Sector XI in Hannover in July 1938 and in May 1939 he was appointed Battery commander with the 26th Flak Regiment and was promoted to *Oberstleutnant* the following month.

Shortly after the outbreak of World War II Rauch was appointed commander of the 1st Battalion, 26th Flak Regiment. Rauch moved from Bremen to the Saarbrücken area and in November 1939 he moved to Bitburg where he saw action in France in May 1940 where he supported the 7th Army Corps. In April 1941 Rauch was named as the Commander of the 31st Flak Regiment and was posted to Russia while serving under the 2nd Flak Division supporting Army Group North. By January 1942 Rauch had been promoted to *Oberst* and in April the same year he was appointed commander of the 31st Flak Regiment and became responsible for defending the skies over Königsberg, East Prussia. In May 1942 he was taken ill and spent the next five months recovering while on the Reserve List. In October he returned to active duty as the commander of the 41st Flak Regiment (mot), on the Russian Front under the 2nd Flak Division, supporting Army Group North. In November 1944 Rauch returned to Germany with the 41st Flak Regiment as part of the 6th Flak Division under *Generalleutant* Werner Anton. On 6th December 1944 he was awarded the Knight's Cross for his leadership and support while commanding his regiment in the defence of the Reich.

Oberst Hans Rauch. (Wehrkundearchiv)

In early 1945 Rauch was promoted to *Generalmajor* and his command was transferred to the Courland area where it took part in the heavy fighting against Soviet troops. It was almost destroyed in May 1945 and it was here that Rauch surrendered to Soviet troops. He remained in Soviet captivity until August 1948 when he returned to Germany. Hans Rauch died on 22nd August 1958 in Traben-Trarbach, he was only fifty-nine years old.

Richard Eduard REIMANN
(1892-1970)
General der Flakartillerie

Knight's Cross: Awarded on 3rd April 1943 as *Generalmajor* and Commander of the 18th Flak Division for his personal bravery during actions in Russia.

Ranks:
Fahnenjunker-Unteroffizier – 27th January 1912
Fähnrich – 18th August 1912

Leutnant – skipped
Oberleutnant – 16th June 1913
Hauptmann – 1st February 1927
Major – 1st October 1934
Oberstleutnant – 20th April 1937
Oberst – 1st April 1939
Generalmajor – 20th April 1941
Generalleutnant – 15th March 1943
General der Flakartillerie – 2nd August 1944

Awards:
Iron Cross 2nd Class – 24th September 1914
Iron Cross 1st Class – 5th January 1920
Royal Prussian Rescue Medal
Wound Badge in Black – World War I
Cross of Honour for Frontline Combatants
Armed Forces Long Service Award 1st Class
Bar to Iron Cross 2nd Class – 12th October 1939
Bar to Iron Cross 1st Class – 15th June 1940
Luftwaffe Parachutist Badge
German Cross in Gold – 1st August 1942
Medal for the Winter Campaign in Russia 1941/1942
Wehrmacht Daily Report: 24 August 1944

Generalleutnant Richard Reimann wearing the Knight's Cross as commander of the 18th Flak Division. (Wehrkundearchiv)

Born on 2nd November 1892 in Minden, Wesfalen, Richard Eduard Reimann entered the army with the 43rd Field Artillery Regiment in December 1911. In January 1912 he was made *Fahnenjunker-Unteroffizier* and after attending the War School in Metz he was appointed a battery officer. He was serving with the 43rd Field Artillery Regiment, with the rank of *Oberleutnant*, when war broke out. He was wounded in September 1914, but soon returned to duty. In September 1915 he joined a motor transport battalion in Schöneberg, and a few weeks later he joined the Balloon Defence Cannon School at Ostend. In June 1916 he became a gun leader with the 89th Flak unit and he ended the war attached to an artillery unit.

Reimann stayed with the army after the war and he volunteered for the Guards Cavalry Rifle Division in January 1919. He was briefly attached to a Freikorps unit before being transferred in October 1919, to the office of the Inspector of Weapons and Equipment in the War Ministry. He then served with the 7th Artillery Regiment and in June 1920 he joined the Freikorps once again. From October 1920 until January 1923 Reimann served with the artillery until he once again was transferred to the War Ministry where he remained until May 1928. In June 1929 he joined the artillery once again and from September was appointed an anti-aircraft instructor. He went onto help develop anti-aircraft weapons, and became an expert in ballistic and munitions and was transferred to the Army Weapons Office in the War Ministry, and was promoted to *Hauptmann* in February 1927 and *Major* in October 1934.

In April 1935 Reimann transferred to the Luftwaffe, and after serving in the Air Ministry he was appointed Commander of the Instructional Battalion of the anti-aircraft School in Wustrow. At the beginning of World War II Reimann became Commander of the 8th Flak Regiment when he succeeded *Generalmajor* Job Odebrecht in October 1939. He had been promoted to *Oberst* in April 1939 and commanded this unit during the Polish Campaign and in May he saw action in Denmark. He was appointed commander of all anti-aircraft artillery schools in June 1940 and in April 1941 Reimann was promoted to *Generalmajor*. In December he took over as Commander of the 1st Flak Corps when he succeeded *Generalmajor* von Axthelm. He commanded this unit during the Russian Campaign, with his headquarters located in Bohnkaly near Brest-Litovsk, in support of the 2nd Panzer Group.

On 20th April 1942 Reimann was given the task of forming the 18th Flak Division which was formed the 2nd Flak Corps in Smolensk and covered the area of Army Group Centre. Reimann was given explicit orders; he was to move his headquarters to Lipitzy where he was to support the northern sector of Army Group Centre. In early 1943 the 18th Flak Division arrived to take over and Reimann was ordered to support the 9th Army and the 3rd Panzer Army in the areas surrounding Vyasma and

Rzhev. Reimann's troops did their job well, despite suffering heavy casualties and he was awarded the Knight's Cross on 3rd April 1943 for his leadership and bravery during the heavy fighting.

On 1st October 1943 Reimann took up what would be his last military command of the war, he was appointed Commanding General of the 1st Flak Corps. He was involved in the heavy fighting in the Crimea and in May 1944 he lost the 9th Flak Division from his command when it was totally destroyed by Soviet forces. In August 1944 Reimann, who had been promoted to *General der Flakartillerie*, now came under the command of *Generaloberst* von Greim's 6th Air Fleet and in October the 1st Flak Corps moved its headquarters to Cracow in Poland. The Soviet onslaught was heavy and in March 1945 Reimann was fighting in Smirschitz and elements of the 1st Flak Corps were made responsible for supporting the 17th Army, 1st Panzer Army and the 4th Panzer Army in Schweidnitz. By May 1945 Reimann's Corps located at its new headquarters at Königgrätz in Czechoslovakia had suffered heavy casualties and was running out of fuel, food and ammunition. On 8th May 1945 Reimann surrendered to Soviet troops and spent the next ten years in a prison camp. He was finally released in October 1955 and returned home, where he lived in retirement in Bad Gastein, Austria, until his death on 28th October 1970

Generalmajor Franz Reuß as commander of 4th Air Division. (Wehrkundearchiv)

Franz REUß
(1904-1992)
Generalmajor

Knight's Cross: Awarded on 18th July 1944 as *Generalmajor* and Commander of 4th Air Division for actions on the Eastern Front.

Ranks:
Polizei-Schütze – 24th March 1920
Polizei-Leutnant – 1st June 1925
Polizei Oberleutnant – 1st January 1929
Polizei-Hauptmann – 1st January 1935
Rittmeister – 1st October 1935
Major – 1st April 1939
Oberstleutnant – 1st April 1941
Oberst – 1st December 1942
Generalmajor – 1st June 1944

Awards:
Iron Cross 2nd Class – World War II
Iron Cross 1st Class – World War II
Armed Forces Long Service Award 2nd Class
Combat Clasp for Bombers in Gold
German Cross in Gold – 21st August 1942
Wound Badge in Silver

Born in Augsburg, Southern Germany, about fifty miles northwest of Munich, on 17th April 1904, Franz Reuß volunteered for service in the 1st Bavarian Rifle Regiment. Three years later he entered the Bavarian State Police and became a *Leutnant* in June 1925. In October 1935 he transferred to the army and was immediately accepted as an officer candidate and was assigned to the War School in Munich. In January 1936 newly promoted to *Rittmeister* Reuss was appointed a Company Commander with the 18th Mounted Regiment and in July of the same year he was transferred to the Army War Academy in Berlin to train as a staff officer.

In August 1938 he transferred to the Luftwaffe and began his pilot training. In April 1939 he was promoted to *Major* and made Squadron Leader with the 53rd Bomber Wing, under the command of *Oberst* Philipp Zoch.[92] In February 1940 Reuss was Group Commander in the 76th Bomber Wing flying Dorniers out of Nidda, Germany. In May 1940 his unit was transferred to Bonn-Hangelar and took part in the invasion of France, by June his headquarters had moved into France itself, now situated about twenty-two miles northwest of Paris.

Reuss who had been badly wounded during a bombing mission in June spent several weeks in hospital before returning to light duties when he was transferred to the Berlin Air War Academy in October 1940. In February 1941 he was appointed Chief of Operations to the 5th Air Fleet, serving under its commander *Generaloberst* Hans-Jurgen Stumpff, and seeing action in Norway. It was a brief appointment and by April he had been transferred to the 4th Air Corps as Chief of Operations under *Generalleutnant* Kurt Pflugbeil and saw further action in Northern France on the coast near St. Malo. In May 1942 Reuss was transferred to the Eastern Front where he became Commander of a Close-Combat Group, while still attached to the 4th Air Corps and saw action during the battles around Kharkov and in September he was awarded the German Cross in Gold in recognition of his leadership during these battles.

In November 1942 Reuss was transferred to the 2nd Luftwaffe Field Corps as Chief of the General Staff under the command of *General der Flieger* Alfred Schlemm. The 2nd Luftwaffe Corps was attached to Group Chevallerie part of the LIX Army Corps and from February 1943 was attached to the 3rd Panzer Army in Russia. In April 1943 he was appointed commander of the 4th Air Division when he succeeded *Generalleutnant* Hermann Plocher. He saw action in Orscha and Minsk on the Eastern Front and was promoted to *Generalmajor* in June 1944. On 18th July he was awarded the Knight's Cross for his actions during the heavy fighting against Soviet troops near Vilna. He transferred to Poland in August, but his Corps was forced to retreat in November to Angerburg, East Prussia. In February 1945 his division had moved to a defensive position near Frankfurt and two months later Reuss was captured by Allied forces and his command was taken over by *Generalmajor* Klaus-Siegfried Uebe. Reuss returned to Germany in January 1947. His post-war activities are unknown at this time and there is no evidence that Reuss ever went on to serve with the Bundeswehr. He died in Munich on 5th June 1992 at the age of eighty-eight.

Herbert Joachim Karl Walter RIECKHOFF
(1898-1948)
Generalleutnant

Knight's Cross: Awarded as *Oberst* and Commander of the 2nd Bomber Wing on 5th July 1941 for actions on the Eastern Front.

Ranks:
Unteroffizier – 1st October 1915
Fähnrich – 22nd March 1916
Leutnant – 8th July 1916
Polizei-Leutnant – 12th August 1920
Polizei-Oberleutnant – 1st October 1923
Polizei-Hauptmann – 1st June 1926
Hauptmann – 1st June 1934

Generalmajor Herbert Rieckhoff wearing the Knight's Cross. (Wehrkundearchiv)

Major – 1st September 1935
Oberstleutnant – 1st February 1938
Oberst – 19th August 1940
Generalmajor – 1st March 1943
Generalleutnant – 1st July 1944

Awards:
Iron Cross 2nd Class – World War I
Iron Cross 1st Class – World War I
Wound Badge in Black – 1917
Armed Forces Long Service Award 3rd Class
Cross of Honour for Frontline Combatants
Air Crew Badge – 3rd April 1935
Combat Clasp for Bombers in Gold
German Cross in Gold – 27th July 1943
Finnish Order of the Cross of Liberty, 1st Class with Swords – 8th January 1944

Herbert Rieckhoff was born on 25th December 1898 in Berlin and entered the Imperial Army with the 1st Replacement Sea Battalion in Kiel in January 1915. He was transferred to the

1st Battalion, 69th Infantry Regiment in August 1915 and in October he was promoted to *Unteroffizier*. He went onto serve with various regiments for the next few months and on 15th May 1916 he was wounded and spent four months in hospital recovering. In September 1916 Rieckhoff returned to active duty with the 69th Infantry Regiment with the rank of *Leutnant*. In February 1917 he was wounded again but returned to active duty two months later as a company commander with his old regiment. In June his wound had become infected, but he made a full recovery rejoining his unit in August 1917. He joined the Observer School in Thorn in February 1918 and underwent flight training , again wounded in August, he returned to flying at the front a few months before Germany's surrender.

Rieckhoff remained with the army after the war and continued to fly but became ill again and decided in March 1920 to retire. In August 1920 he entered the Protection Police in Stettin and served as a platoon commander with the rank of *Polizei-Leutnant*. He continued his training as a police officer joining the 8th Alarm Unit in August 1921 and the Air Surveillance Service in Upper Stettin in March 1922. Promoted to *Polizei-Oberleutnant* in October 1923 he went on to serve as an instructor at the Police School in Hannover. He continued to serve with the police in Stettin until June 1926 when he was promoted to *Polizei-Hauptmann* and transferred as a department head with the State Police in Thuringia.

In June 1934 Rieckhoff transferred to the Luftwaffe with the rank of *Hauptmann* and was appointed Commander of the Luftwaffe Schools in Berlin. Promoted to Major in September 1935 and to *Oberstleutnant* in February 1938, he became a General Staff Officer at about the same time. In April he was appointed a staff officer with the 2nd Air Fleet and in June 1940 while under the command of *General der Flieger* Kesselring he saw action during the French Campaign. He took over as Commander of the 30th Bomber Wing in Aalbourg-West and from September it operated out of Eindhoven. On 21st October 1940 Rieckhoff took command of the 2nd Bomber Wing when he succeeded *Generalmajor* Johannes Fink, seeing action over the skies of France and England. In March 1941 Rieckhoff along with the 2nd Bomber Wing was transferred to Vienna, and the following month his command was one of the first bomber wings to take part in the invasion of Greece. In June his command was transferred to Russia where again his command took part in some of the very first aerial attacks. For his success and leadership during the early stages of the invasion of Russia he was awarded the Knight's Cross on 5th July 1941.

Rieckhoff was appointed Chief of Staff to the commander of the 1st Air Fleet *Generaloberst* Alfred Keller on 13th October 1941, with its headquarters in Germany until February 1942 when it was transferred to Ostrow on the Eastern Front. On 23rd February 1943 Rieckhoff succeeded *Oberst* Thorsten Christ as Air Leader 1 in Pleskau in Russia and the following month he was promoted to *Generalmajor* and by the end of the year his command was transferred to Baranowicze. In January 1944 he was appointed commander of the Air War Academy

Probably taken at Rieckhoff's headquarters in Russia: (front left) Oberst Wolf-Dietrich Wilcke Knight's Cross with Oakleaves and Swords holder, Generalmajor Herbert Rieckhoff, Oberstleutnant Hans Trautloft and Stabsingenieur Dreyer. (Author's collection)

in Berlin-Gatow and while in this position he was promoted to *Generalleutnant* in July 1944. His last military command was that of Commanding General of Air Region V in Stuttgart, formed from the staff of Air Region Command West France. His command covered the areas near Württemberg and Baden and the adjacent territory in France. In April 1945 Rieckhoff decided that it would be better to give up the territory that was still under German control to the Air Region Command VII. It wasn't a popular decision with the Luftwaffe High Command and consequently Rieckhoff spent the remainder of the war on the Reserve List and surrendered to the Allies in May 1945. He remained in captivity until March 1948 when he returned to Germany, he died eight months later on 30th November.

Ernst-August ROTH
(1898-1975)
Generalleutnant

Knight's Cross: Awarded on 6th November 1943 as *Generalmajor* and Air Leader North for actions in Norway.

Ranks:
Seekadett – 3rd January 1916
Fähnrich zur See – 12th October 1916
Leutnant zur See – 17th March 1918
Oberleutnant zur See – 1st April 1922
Charakter als Kapitänleutnant – 31st March 1928
Kapitänleutnant – 1st January 1934
Hauptmann – 3rd January 1934
Major – 1st January 1935
Oberstleutnant – 1st March 1937
Oberst – 1st June 1939
Generalmajor – 1st August 1942
Generalleutnant – 1st January 1945

Awards:
Naval Pilot's Badge – World War I
Commemorative Badge for Naval Pilot's and Observer's – World War I
Cross of Honour for Frontline Combatants
Armed Forces Long Service Award 1st Class
Iron Cross 1st Class
Bar to Iron Cross 2nd Class
German Cross in Gold – 13th November 1941
Wehrmacht Daily Report: 27 August 1943

Ernst-August Roth was born in Potsdam on 19th April 1898, he entered naval service as a cadet on board the School-Ship *Freya* in January 1916. After completing flying training he became a pilot serving with the 2nd Sea Flying Battalion and shortly after the end of the war he joined the 12th Sea Artillery Battalion stationed in Wangerooge, a small island off the coast of northern Germany. He had been commissioned in March 1918 as a *Leutnant zur See* and the following month he was promoted again, ending the war as an *Oberleutnant*.

Roth remained with the Navy after the armistice and served in a number of naval battalions including coastal defence and as an flying advisor with the Naval Station in the North Sea. In September 1927 he was appointed Watch Officer on the Battleship *Schlesien*, until March 1928 when he retired from the navy. In April he was employed by the navy as a civilian, with honorary rank of *Kapitänleutnant*, and was named chief test pilot at Travemünde part of the Reichs Federation of German Aviation Industry. On 16th November 1931 the navy employed him as an air defence consultant with the Navy Command, and in January 1934 the navy reactivated his rank of *Kapitänleutnant*. Three days later he transferred to the ranks of the Luftwaffe with the rank of *Hauptmann* and became a consultant and department head for the Land and Sea Ground Organisation, part of the Reich Air Ministry.

In January 1935 Roth was promoted to *Major* and in July 1936 he was transferred to Parow where he was appointed commander of the local flying school. In March 1937 he was promoted to *Oberstleutnant* and by June 1939 he had been promoted to *Oberst* and took over as the Air Transport commander attached to the 10th Air Corps. He served under *Generalleutnant* Hans Geisler and took part in the invasion of Denmark and Norway in April and May 1940. He helped to organise the mass airlift, in fact the first in history, of over 500 transport aircraft who dropped paratroopers to seize vital airfields and bridges. It was a great success. In August 1940 Roth was transferred to France where he took command of the 28th Bomber Wing, based in Bordeaux and equipped with He 111 bombers. His Bomber Wing was transferred to Nantes in December and then to Brest-Litovsk on the Eastern Front in July 1941. In December he transferred to France where he was appointed commander of the 26th Bomber Wing based in Beauvais, and in January 1942 his Wing was moved to Aalborg-West in Denmark and from there it moved to Stavanger-Sola in Norway. It was here

Generalmajor Ernst-August Roth. (Wehrkundearchiv)

that he took part in anti-shipping strikes against the Aryic convoys sailing to and from Murmansk and Archangel in the Soviet Union. In August Roth transferred to Grosseto in Italy and shortly afterwards was promoted to *Generalmajor*.

In February 1943 Roth returned to Norway where he was appointed Air Leader North and continued to inflict heavy losses on Allied shipping, and was awarded the Knight's Cross on 6th November 1943 for his part in the success of the operation. He remained in Norway until August 1944 when he was put on the Reserve List and placed at the disposal of the Luftwaffe High Command. On 10th October he was recalled to active duty when he was appointed Commanding General of the Luftwaffe in Norway after succeeding *Generalmajor* Eduard *Ritter* von Schleich. However despite his impressive title, the Luftwaffe in Norway consisted of about 140 aircraft of which most were transport planes, of which less than 100 were serviceable. The bulk of the Luftwaffe forces in Norway consisted of anti-aircraft and support troops as well as the 14th Luftwaffe Field Division, now under the command of the army. On New Years Day 1945 Roth was promoted to *Generalleutnant* but a simple promotion made no difference Roth knew the war was almost over. However it lasted longer than most for Roth who wasn't captured by the Allies until the 6th June 1945 when he was arrested by British troops. He spent almost three years in different prison camps finally ending up in Adelheide Camp, near Delmenhorst in December 1947, a prison camp less than five miles from Bremen.

Roth was released on 15th March 1948 and spent the rest of his life in retirement with his wife, Berta. Ernst-August Roth died on 26th September 1975 in Ahrensburg, Germany.

Günther SACHS
(1903-1962)
Generalmajor

Knight's Cross: Awarded as *Generalmajor* as Commander of 18th Flak Division on 24th January 1945 for actions on the Eastern Front.

Ranks:
Gefreiter – 14th August 1922
Unteroffizier – 15th November 1922
Fähnrich – 1st September 1923
Oberfähnrich – 20th August 1924
Leutnant – 1st December 1924
Oberlieutnant – 1st April 1928
Hauptmann – 1st July 1934
Major – 1st April 1937
Oberstleutnant – 1st September 1940
Oberst – 1st April 1942
Generalmajor – 1st December 1944

Awards:
Observer's Badge – 24th September 1935
Armed Forces Long Service Award 2nd Class
Iron Cross 2nd Class – 27th April 1940
Iron Cross 1st Class – 9th April 1940
Luftwaffe Anti-Aircraft Badge – 4th August 1942
Medal for the Winter Campaign in Russia 1941/1942
German Cross in Gold – 3rd January 1944
Wehrmacht Daily Report: 10 March 1945

Born near Hannover in the town of Springe on 4th May 1903 Günther Sachs was only fifteen years old when World War I ended. When he was seventeen he volunteered to join the Reichsheer, the 100,000 man army allowed by the allies under the terms of the Versailles Treaty. Sachs joined the 6th Artillery Regiment becoming an officer candidate in August 1922, and the following month he was sent to the infantry and artillery schools in Munich and Jüterbog. Once he had completed his officer training he was commissioned as a *Leutnant* and returned to the 6th Artillery Regiment in October 1924. In March 1925 he served with the Photography Office in the 6th Division and in October 1928 he returned to Jüterbog to take part in a motor transport artillery course. Between December 1928 and April 1935 he attended various courses which included camouflage, artillery, officers and even a gas protection course.

Generalmajor Günther Sachs as commander of 18th Flak Division. (Wehrkundearchiv)

Sachs was transferred to the Luftwaffe on 1st April 1935, with the rank of *Hauptmann*, and after attending an Observers training course in Braunschweig he joined the General Staff as an advisor on anti aircraft training. In April 1937 Sachs was promoted to *Major* and in November 1938 was appointed Commander of the 1st Battalion, 22nd Flak Regiment, in Döberitz under *Oberst* Karl Soeldner. Sachs was assigned to the staff of the Air Region Command XI in May 1939, and just before the beginning of World War II, in September 1939, he was appointed its Chief of Operations in Hannover, and later in Hamburg under *Generalleutnant* Ludwig Wolff.[93]

On 24th May 1940 Sachs was transferred to the staff of the Air Region Command Belgium and Northern France where he served as Chief of Operations. He served under *Generalmajor* Fritz Lob at its headquarters in Brussels. Later he served under *Generalleutnant* Kurt Pflugbeil when Lob was killed in an air crash. Sachs was promoted to *Oberstleutnant* in September 1940 and a month later he took over as Chief of Staff to the Air Region Command VIII in Breslau, responsible for the General Government area of Poland. On 16th December 1940 Sachs was transferred to Hamburg and was attached to the staff of

Air Region Command XI under *General der Flieger* Ludwig Wolff, covering the area around Denmark.

On 22nd January 1942 Sachs was transferred to the Eastern Front where he took command of the 6th Flak Regiment, part of the 12th Flak Division. In April 1942 his unit came under the command of Generalmajor Reimann's 18th Flak Division and helped to support Army Group Centre during the battles near Smolensk. Sachs was transferred again in November and was appointed Chief of Staff to *Generalleutnant* Job Odebrecht the commander of the 3rd Luftwaffe Field Corps, and saw action in Gorza, near Sosnowyy Bor in the area around Leningrad while attached to the 18th Army. Sachs remained with the 3rd Field Corps until its withdrawal in October 1943 when it was redesignated the 2nd Flak Corps.

Towards the end of October 1943 Sachs returned as Chief of Staff to the Air Region Command VIII under *General der Flieger* Walter Somme,[94] covering the northern half of Poland, with its headquarters in Crackow. Sachs was appointed Commander of the 10th Motorised Flak Brigade in February 1944 when he succeeded *Generalmajor* Adolf Wolff and was responsible for the protection of Army Group Centre near the areas of Brest and Baranovitschi from February until April when the brigade was reorganised and moved to Warsaw. In September it transferred to East Prussia where it was attached to the 27th Flak Division in Lötzen, an area near Dresden under the command of *Generalleutnant* Walter Kathmann.[95] Between March and June 1944 Sachs was made temporary commander of the 12th Flak Division while its permanent commander *Generalleutnant* Werner Prellberg was on leave. At this time it was attached to the 2nd Army and also saw action in the area near Baranovitschi where it was almost destroyed in June 1944.

On 2nd October 1944 Sachs was appointed Commander of the 18th Motorised Flak Division which had in June 1944 been withdrawn to East Prussia where it was supporting the 4th Army and the 3rd Panzer Army. Its mission was to support the northern wing of Army Group Centre from Vyasma to Rzher. It did a good job and Sachs was praised by his superiors. The division suffered heavy casualties though when the Soviet summer offensive of 1944 smashed Army Group Centre and almost destroyed the 9th Army, the 18th Flak Division managed to withdraw across Lithuania and Poland and back into East Prussia. On 21st January 1945 Sachs took control of all the flak units in East Prussia and in the Heiligenbeil Pocket which included the 16th Flak Brigade, 87th, 116th and the 125th Flak Regiments. On 24th January Sachs was awarded the Knight's Cross for his skilful leadership during the withdrawal, his skill had managed to save the lives of hundreds of troops. On 1st March 1945 Sachs moved his headquarters to Stuthenen, now under the control of Luftwaffe Command East Prussia and Sachs took over as commander a few days later. By the 3rd May the 18th Flak Division had been isolated on the Hela Peninsula; however it took some of the last ships out of East Prussia and surrendered to the Western Allies in Schleswig, North-Western Germany. On 8th May Sachs himself surrendered to the British in Schleswig and remained in captivity until his release on 25th February 1948. He spent the remaining years of his life in Venice where he died on 15th July 1962 at the age of fifty-nine.

Richard SCHIMPF
(1897-1972)
Generalleutnant

Knight's Cross: Awarded on 6th October 1944 as *Generalleutnant* and Commander of the 3rd Fallschirmjäger Division for actions during the breakout from the Falaise Pocket in Normandy.

Ranks:
Fahnenjunker – 11th February 1915
Leutnant – 1st March 1916
Oberleutnant – 1st April 1925
Hauptmann – 1st April 1932

Richard Schimpf as Generalleutnant and commander of the 3rd Fallschirmjäger Division. (Wehrkundearchiv)

Major – 1st April 1935
Oberstleutnant – 1st April 1937
Oberst – 1st October 1939
Generalmajor – 18th March 1943
Generalleutnant – 1st August 1943

Awards:
Iron Cross 2nd Class – World War I
Iron Cross 1st Class – World War I
Medal for the Winter Campaign in Russia 1941/1942
Bar to Iron Cross 2nd Class
Bar to Iron Cross 1st Class
Royal Bavarian Military Service Order 4th Class with Swords
Cross of Honour for Frontline Combatants
Armed Forces Long Service Award 1st Class
German Cross in Gold – 26th August 1944
Wound Badge in Silver – 1944
Wehrmacht Daily Report: 19 June 1944

Richard Schimpf was born in Eggenfeld, Bavaria on 16th May 1897, he joined the 9th Royal Bavarian Infantry Regiment as a *Fahnenjunker* in February 1915, serving with the same regiment throughout World War I. He saw action on the Western Front serving as a platoon leader, company leader and as battalion adjutant; in March 1916 he was commissioned as a *Leutnant*. After the war he remained in the army and served as a platoon leader with the 45th Regiment, 23rd Reichswehr Brigade.

After training as a pilot in April 1925 and after being promoted to *Oberleutnant* he began his training as a General Staff officer. In September he joined the staff of the 7th Military District in Munich and for a time served as a photographic officer, later serving with the Scientific Research and Testing Institute in Lipezk. In October 1930 he transferred to the Army Weapons Office and began studying engineering at the Berlin-Charlottenburg Technical College. Promoted to *Hauptmann* in April 1932, Schimpf passed his exams on 31st January 1935 and was awarded a diploma in engineering.

In February 1935 he transferred to the Luftwaffe and was assigned to the Reich Air Ministry until April when he was promoted to *Major* and appointed Squadron Commander with the Air Reconnaissance Group in Münster. In March 1936 he was assigned once again to the Air Ministry where he took over as head of the Aerial Photography and Survey Section. Promoted to *Oberstleutnant* a year later Schimpf held the rank of *Oberst* when he was appointed Operations Officer on the staff of the Luftwaffe General assigned to Army Group A, under *Generaloberst* Gerd von Rundstedt. Here he saw action during the invasion of France and the Low Countries in May and June 1940. After the fall of France he returned to the Air Ministry and in November he became Chief of Staff of the 4th Air Fleet in Vienna under *General der Flieger* Alexander Löhr.

In January 1941 Schimpf was transferred to the General Government in Poland where he was appointed Chief of Staff of Air Region Command VIII, with its headquarters in Breslau under *Generalleutnant* Bernard Waber. In December Air Region Command "Kiev" was formed in Southern Russia with its headquarters in Kharkov. Waber and Schmipf were appointed as it's first commander and Chief of Staff respectively and they were soon engaged in heavy action with strong Soviet forces. In September 1942 Schimpf was given the leadership of the Luftwaffe Field Division "Meindl", a regiment put together from excess Luftwaffe The regiment was made from formed staff of *Generalmajor* Eugen Meindl's 1st Parachute Landing Assault Regiment. It was the first divisional seized Luftwaffe field formation and comprised of a signals battalion, five Luftwaffe field regiments and a ski battalion. In October it was divided into two separate divisions, the 21st and 22nd Luftwaffe Field Divisions. Schimpf was named as the commander of the 21st Division and was sent into combat at the end of the year to the northern section of the Eastern Front, there he was responsible for defending the area near Staraja-Russa for more than a year. In January 1943 it absorbed the Luftwaffe Field Jäger Regiment and soon became a three regiment division with nine infantry battalions and this made it the largest of the Luftwaffe Field Divisions. Schimpf was promoted to *Generalmajor* in March 1943 and to *Generalleutnant* in August, by October his command had been taken over by the army and in November Schimpf handed his command over to *Generalmajor* Rudolf-Eduard Licht[96] and went on the Reserve List.

On 17th February 1944 Schimpf returned to active service when he was appointed commander of the 3rd Fallschirmjäger Division. In May he was placed at the disposal of *Generaloberst* Eugen Dollmann's[97] 7th Army in France. After the Allies landed in Normandy on 6th June the 2nd Fallschirmjäger Corps, 3rd Fallschirmjäger Division and the 17th SS-Panzer Grenadier Division "Götz von Berlichingen" were deployed from Brittany to counter the American forces in the area of St. Lô. The 2nd Fallschirmjäger Corps under General Meindl remained heavily engaged with U.S. forces for the next two months, and the German 5th Panzer Army and 7th Army were almost completely encircled at Falasie by the advancing American and Anglo forces. Meindl's forces however managed to hold open a narrow corridor that allowed thousands of German troops to escape. On 20th August 1944 Schimpf was severely wounded in the leg during the breakout from the Falaise Pocket and had to be carried out by his men. In recognition for his efforts in trying to get the most of his troops out of the Pocket Schimpf was awarded the Knight's Cross on 6th October 1944, his command was taken over personally by the crops commander General Meindl who was himself severely wounded during the breakout.

In early January 1945 Schimpf returned to command the 3rd Fallschirmjäger Division after recovering from his wounds, taking over from its caretaker commander *Generalmajor* Walter Wadehn. Schimpf was now serving under *General der Panzertruppe* Hasso von Manteuffel's[98] 5th Panzer Army, and was engaged in delaying the Allied advance. His division now faced the American offensive which had been launched on 28th January its aim to crack the West Wall or Siegfried Line and drive into the Eifel Region. On 1st March the U.S. 12th Army Group resumed its offensive, a two-pronged advance to clear the southern Rhineland up the Rhine River, the U.S. 1st Army advanced on Cologne while the U.S. 3rd Army under General Patton cleared the Eifel to the south. Schimpf was not allowed to breakout or fall back, Hitler had made it clear there would be no retreat. On 8th March Schimpf was captured near Bad Godesberg along with most of his troops.

Generalleutnant Schimpf remained in Allied captivity until December 1947 when he returned home. He entered the Bundeswehr in 1957 and joined the West German air force, serving as a *Generalmajor* and commander of Military District III, until his retirement in July 1962. Richard Schimpf died on 30th December 1972 in Düsseldorf.

Alfred SCHLEMM
(1894-1986)
General der Fallschirmtruppe

Knight's Cross: Awarded on 11th June 1944 as *General der Flieger* and Commanding General of 1st Parachute Corps.

Ranks:
Fahnenjunker – 8th March 1913
Fähnrich – 20th October 1913
Leutnant – 19th June 1914
Oberleutnant – 16th September 1917
Hauptmann – 1st June 1925
Major – 1st June 1934
Oberstleutnant – 1st September 1935
Oberst – 1st February 1938
Generalmajor – 1st June 1940
Generalleutnant – 1st June 1942
General der Flieger – 30th January 1943
General der Fallschirmtruppe – 4th November 1944

Awards:
Knight's Cross of the Royal Prussian Hohenzollern House Order with Swords – 15th October 1918
Iron Cross 2nd Class – World War I
Iron Cross 1st Class – World War I
Wound Badge in Black – World War I
Bar to Iron Cross 2nd Class – 10th August 1940
Bar to Iron Cross 1st Class – 22nd June 1941
Cross of Honour for Frontline Combatants
Armed Forces Long Service Award 1st Class
Luftwaffe Ground Combat Badge
German Cross in Gold – 4th August 1942
KRETA Cuff-title
Wehrmacht Daily Report: 29 May 1944

General der Flieger Alfred Schlemm as Commanding General of 1st Fallschirmjäger Corps. (Wehrkundearchiv)

Alfred Schlemm wasn't your typical Prussian general, he was about five feet, eight inches tall, stocky, with a large nose and a Slavic face. He was born into an Evangelical middle-class family in Rudolstadt, Thüringen on 18th December 1894, and entered military service as an *Fahnenjunker* in March 1913. After attending War School in Danzig he was commissioned as a *Leutnant* in June 1914 and joined the 56th Field Artillery Regiment where he remained until the end of the war, serving as platoon leader, battery commander and he was promoted in September 1917 to *Oberleutnant*.

Schlemm remained in the army after the war and in October 1919 he joined the staff of the artillery commander of the 5th Reichswehr Brigade. A year later he served with the 3rd Prussian Artillery Regiment and in January 1921 he was transferred to the staff of Military District III in Berlin. He returned to the 3rd Prussian Artillery Regiment in October 1922 as a platoon leader before being transferred to the Reich Defence Ministry in October 1924. He served as a staff officer for the next ten years, in the Army Department of the Troop Office, a department responsible for internal and external army matters such as border patrols, troop employment and organisation, as well as military transport, mapping and charting. In June 1934 Schlemm was promoted to *Major* and in October he was appointed Operations Officer on the staff of the Military District in Berlin before being assigned to the Armed Forces Academy two years later.

Schlemm transferred to the Luftwaffe in February 1938, with the rank of *Oberst* and was assigned to the General Staff and in October 1939 he was transferred to Luftgau XI in Hannover. In December 1940, now with the rank of *Generalmajor*, Schlemm was appointed Chief of Staff of the XI Air Corps, under the command of *General der Flieger* Kurt Student. After the conquest of Yugoslavia and Greece in April 1941, the Germans prepared for "Operation Mercury", the airborne invasion of Crete. On 20th May 1941 the XI Air Corps dropped two massive waves of paratroopers and glider troops from *Generalleutnant* Wilhelm Süssmann's[99] 7th Air Division onto the island. Student's forces captured their objectives despite determined resistance and heavy losses. On 1st June the British forces left on the island surrendered, the conquest of Crete was over.

In February 1942 Schlemm was briefly attached to the staff of *Generaloberst* von Richthofen, the commander of the VIII Air Corps on the Eastern Front. On 12th February Schlemm was made commander of Battle Group *Schlemm*, a formation assigned to the XXXX Panzer Corps where it saw action on the Eastern Front. In June Schlemm was promoted to *Generalleutnant* and made commander of the 1st Air Division, with its headquarters at Dugino where he was responsible for all Luftwaffe air and ground support units under *General der Flieger* von Greim's Luftwaffe Command East.

Schlemm was appointed Commanding General of the II Luftwaffe Field Corps in October 1942, taking control of the 2nd, 3rd, 4th and 6th Luftwaffe Field Divisions in Russia. His corps held the line from south Nevel to the Dvina River east of Vitebsk under the 3rd Panzer Army. In February 1943, shortly after being promoted to *General der Flieger*, Schlemm took part in Operation "Kugelblitz" (Ball Lightning) against the partisan region of Surazh Rayon. On 6th October the 2nd Luftwaffe Field Division was attacked by two Russian armies and crushed, many of the inexperienced troops ran away, this resulted in a ten mile rip in the German lines and the capture of Nevel. In November Schlemm's Corps lost its four divisions to the LIII and IX Army Corps and began transferring to Italy.

In January 1944 it was redesignated the I Fallschirm Corps and Schlemm took control of over 24,000 troops in the area around Rome. Within forty-eight hours of taking command Schlemm's corps received new orders to respond immediately to the Allied beachhead at Anzio. Schlemm led his command against the British and American forces for three days until *Generaloberst* Eberhard von Mackensen[100] the Commander-in-Chief of the 14th Army took over. On 11th June 1944 Schlemm was awarded the Knight's Cross for his energetic and resourceful leadership during the Battle of Anzio. In November he was appointed Commander-in-Chief of the 1st Fallschirm Army with the rank of *General der Fallschirmtruppe* and was engaged in fierce fighting against British and Canadian troops on the Maas and Waal Rivers. By now Schlemm's command consisted of a collection of under strength troops and small Battle Groups as well as the II Fallschirm Corps and the LXXXVI Army Corps, but they still had the will to fight but lacked equipment.

On 8th February 1945 the Canadian 1st Army launched an offensive to clear German forces between the Maas and Rhine Rivers. It was near the Nijmegan area that the Anglo-Canadian forces met with fierce opposition from Schlemm's infantry entrenched in the West Wall positions of the Reichswald. Schlemm attacked the Allied forces in some of the fiercest fighting of the war. Schlemm maintained an unbroken front; he suffered heavy losses, until the advance of the American 9th Army over the Roer condensed Schlemm's forces into a small bridgehead on the west bank of the Rhine. Schlemm had other worries too, Hitler had issued one of his *Führer Orders* he stated that the German commanders would need his explicit permission before even one soldier or one piece of equipment could be evacuated from the west bank to the east. Hitler also made it clear that the bridges across the Rhine were to be destroyed before they could fall into the hands of the Allies; one directive advised that anyone who failed to do so in time would be executed. But he added, anyone who blew up a bridge too soon would also be executed! So any commander who had a bridge in his area of command had to decide precisely the right moment to blow up his bridge. Schlemm, whose forces represented the heaviest concentration of German strength on the west bank later told an American interrogator: "Since I had nine bridges in my area, I could see my hopes for a long life rapidly dwindling."[101]

On 7th March Schlemm began to destroy the bridges in his area. By 9th March seven of the nine bridges in his area had been destroyed; only two at Wesel remained. Schlemm had set up a special bridge command with a team of officers at each bridge with demolition teams linked by radio and linked to Schlemm's headquarters so he could personally give the order to demolish. Schlemm knew because of Hitler's precise orders not to blow a bridge up too late or too early, timing was everything. Throughout the night of 9th March Schlemm got the last of troops and his armour across the Rhine. At 7am on 10th March British troops now in control of Xanten heard the roar of two huge explosions off to the east; Schlemm had blown up the two remaining bridges. Schlemm was later to say that it was the best way he knew of announcing the end of the battle. On 21st March Schlemm's headquarters took a direct hit from Allied bombers and Schlemm was wounded and taken to hospital. Two days later Field Marshal Montgomery's 21st Army Group supported by airborne landings crossed the Rhine and attacked the sector held by the 1st Fallschirm Army. After leaving hospital Schlemm surrendered to British forces on 8th May 1945.

In July 1947 Schlemm was sent to the Island Farm Special Camp and in October he was transferred to a holding camp in Hamburg via Southampton on board the ship *El Nil*. In March 1948 Schlemm was released from British captivity and returned home. Alfred Schlemm died on 24th January 1986 in Ahlten near Hannover.

Joseph "Beppo" SCHMID
(1901-1956)
Generalleutnant

Generalleutnant Joseph "Beppo" Schmid. (Wehrkundearchiv)

Knight's Cross: Awarded as *Generalmajor* and Commander of a detachment of the Luftwaffe Division "Hermann Göring" while in Tunisia on 21st May 1943.

Ranks:
Fähnrich – 1st August 1923
Oberfähnrich – 24th September 1924
Leutnant – 1st December 1924
Oberleutnant – 1st July 1928
Hauptmann – 1st July 1934
Major – 1st August 1936
Oberstleutnant – 1st November 1938
Oberst – 19th July 1940
Generalmajor – 1st March 1943
Generalleutnant – 1st July 1944

Awards:
Blood Order of the N.S.D.A.P.
Iron Cross 2nd Class - World War II
Iron Cross 1st Class – World War II
Armed Forces Long Service Award 2nd Class
AFRIKA Cufftitle

Josef Schmid served during World War II as an intelligence officer, a staff officer and as a front-line commander and it has to be said with little success. According to Adolf Galland he was "a washout", and *Generalfeldmarschall* Erhard Milch described him as "a man who trimmed his sails to the wind, for fear of Göring."[102] Schmid was born on 24th September 1901 in Göggingen near Augsberg and entered military service as a member of von Epps Freikorps in February 1919.

Schmid was a very early member of the Nazi Party and took part in the unsuccessful Beer Hall Putsch of November 1923 and was subsequently awarded the Blood Order. He joined the Reichsheer in April 1921 as an officer candidate or *Fähnrich* with the 19th Infantry Regiment. He was commissioned as a *Leutnant* in December 1924 and after completing a course at the Munich War School he was appointed a Platoon Leader with 21st Infantry Regiment. In October 1933 now with the rank of *Oberleutnant* he entered the War Academy in Berlin and started his training as a staff officer with the General Staff.

Schmid transferred to the Luftwaffe in July 1935 with the rank of *Hauptmann* and was assigned to the General Staff. He was promoted to *Major* in August 1936 and he became chief of the Military Intelligence Branch in April 1939, where he remained until November 1942. During his time with the intelligence branch he did nothing to upgrade or improve its low quality, in fact he probably did more damage himself. Unlike most other intelligence officers who would overstate the strength of the enemy, Schmid consistently underestimated their strength. He reported to Hitler and the High Command regularly regarding the production capacity of the British Royal Air Force, the Russian and the United States air force, underestimating their capabilities. In fact it was his optimistic views and underestimating that contributed to Germany's loss of the Battle of Britain. His reports the following year also led the Luftwaffe leadership to believe that it would face a much easier mission when it invaded the Soviet Union. It was only through Göring's help and support that Schmid wasn't sacked. *Feldmarschall* Milch, the Air Minister certainly wanted him sacked and said of Schmid, "… he wasn't an airman and didn't understand the significance of the reports he received."[103] In fact at the time of the invasion of Russia Schmid placed the strength of the Soviet Air Force at 8000 aircraft of which he said 6,000 were located in the far east of Russia. In fact the Soviets had over 10,000 aircraft in the western area alone.

In October 1942 he was finally replaced and was made commander of Battle Group Schmid, attached to the Panzer Division "Hermann Göring", in Tunisia. He wasn't a great success as a commander and he was flown out of the Tunisian pocket at the very last moment on the personal orders of his friend *Reichsmarschall* Göring. In January 1943 Schmid commanded a detachment of the "Hermann Göring" Division once again, this time in Africa and in March he was promoted to *Generalmajor*. On 21st May 1943 he was awarded the Knight's Cross in recognition of his command during heavy fighting in Africa, no doubt the award came after a recommendation from Göring! In September Schmid took over as Commanding General of the 1st Fighter Corps with his headquarters in Brunswick-Querum, Central Germany, later being moved to Treuenbritzen. In July 1944 he was promoted to *Generalleutnant* and appointed Commander of Luftwaffe Command West in Limburg. In April 1945 he took control of the entire Southwest of Germany, responsible for a huge area under the command of the 6th Air Fleet. It seems incomprehensible that a man like Schmid who wasn't rated by his peers or the officers who served with him could be promoted to such a senior level and be given such a command. It was only through the backing and support of Göring that Schmid rose to such a level.

Apprehended by the Allies on 27th April 1945 Schmid was taken prisoner and held in British captivity until April 1948. Thereafter he lived in Augsberg and wrote a paper for the U.S. Air Forces German Historical Monograph Project in Karlsruhe. Josef Schmid died at the age of fifty-five on 30th August 1956 at home in Augsberg.

August Schmidt as General der Flakartillerie and Commander of Air Region Command VI in Münster. (Wehrkundearchiv)

August SCHMIDT
(1883-1955)
General der Flakartillerie

Knight's Cross: Awarded on 11th February 1945 as *General der Flakartillerie* and Commanding General of Air Region VI, Münster.

Ranks:
Fahnenjunker-Unteroffizier – 27th January 1902
Fähnrich – 17th May 1902
Leutnant – 27th January 1903
Oberleutnant – 27th January 1911
Hauptmann – 8th October 1914
Major – 30th June 1922
Oberstleutnant – skipped
Oberst – 1st March 1935
Generalmajor – 1st January 1939
Generalleutnant – 1st January 1940
General der Flakartillerie – 1st July 1941

Awards:
Iron Cross 2nd Class – 17th September 1914
Iron Cross 1st Class – 14th March 1917
Knight's Cross of the Royal Prussian Hohenzollern House Order with Swords – 12th April 1917
Grand Duchy of Mecklenburg-Schwerin War Service Cross 2nd Class – 16th December 1914
Schaumburg-Lippe Cross for True Loyal Service – 10th June 1915
Knight's Cross First Class of the Order of the Zähringen Lion with Oakleaves and Swords – 8th September 1917
Armed Forces Long Service Award 1st Class
Cross of Honour for Frontline Combatants
Wound Badge in Black – World War I
Bar to Iron Cross 2nd Class – 1st October 1939
Bar to Iron Cross 1st Class – 21st May 1940
German Cross in Gold – 15th December 1943

August Schmidt was born on 1st February 1883 in Hildesheim, he entered military service with the artillery in October 1901 as an officer cadet. In January 1903 he was commissioned as a *Leutnant* and spent time at the Artillery School in Spandau before joining the 10th Artillery Regiment as a battery officer in February 1909. At the outbreak of World War One he was still serving with the same regiment and was promoted to Hauptman in October 1914. In December of the following year he was appointed adjutant with the 19th Reserve Infantry Regiment and later served as Operations Officer with the 28th Infantry Division. He ended the war on the Western Front as part of the General Staff of the 10th Reserve Corps. Schmidt remained in

General der Flakartillerie Schmidt visiting one of the Luftwaffe commands under his control as Commanding General of Luftgau VI, probably in late 1942. (Author's collection)

the army after the war serving with his old regiment until March 1919 when he was transferred to the Reichswehr. He spent the next three years as a staff officer and in June 1922 he retired from active service. He took a job as a farmer in Schleching, Bavaria for the next four years and later he became a member of the German Farmers Union in Berlin, and in June 1930 he took the same position in Kassel.

In June 1934 he returned to the army with the reactivated rank of *Oberst* and was assigned to the War Ministry as a staff officer. In April 1936 he took a position as an instructor at the Air War Academy in Berlin and in May he transferred to the Luftwaffe. He took a course as a bomber commander in September 1936 and in April 1937 he was appointed Commander of Flak Artillery with Air Region I, Königsberg. On 1st November 1937 Schmidt was appointed commander of Air Region Command VI which had been formed in Münster from the 10th Air Region and was responsible for the areas around Westfalen, Aachen, Düsseldorf, Cologne, Osnabrück and Kassel. From May during the Western Campaign it covered the areas to the Aerschot-Dinant Line in France and took over the Eupen-Malmedy area in Belgium. Schmidt was responsible for a large area as well as being responsible for over 25 large Luftwaffe units which included the 4th, 7th and 22nd Flak Divisions and the 2nd, 6th and 10th Flak Brigades. Schmidt was one of the most successful Air Region commanders, he remained in the same position for almost eight years and on 11th February 1945 he was awarded the Knight's Cross in recognition of his support and leadership.

In April 1945 his command was disbanded and some troops of his former command were used to form the Special Purpose Flak Corps which operated in Northern Germany and controlled the 5th Flak Division which was one of the last units to use the V-weapons. On 8th May 1945 Schmidt was captured by British troops and found himself being accused of war crimes. In October 1947 a British Military Court in Hamburg sentenced him to life imprisonment, the charge was the murder of Allied airmen who had landed in his area of command. It was said some had been killed by civilians and others handed over to the Gestapo. However the evidence was weak and his defence appealed and the sentence was reduced to ten years. In November 1950 Schimdt was released due to health reasons and returned home to Rotenburg, Hannover where he died on 23rd November 1955.

Karl-Heinrich SCHULZ
(1906-1986)
Generalmajor

Knight's Cross: Awarded on 9th June 1944 as *Generalmajor* and Chief of the General Staff of 4th Air Fleet.

Ranks:
Fähnrich zur See – 1st April 1926
Leutnant zur See – 1st October 1928

Generalmajor Karl-Heinrich Schulz wearing the Knight's Cross as Chief of the General Staff of 4th Air Fleet. (Wehrkundearchiv)

Oberleutnant zur See – 1st July 1930
Kapitänleutnant – 1st April 1935
Hauptmann – 1st October 1935
Major – 1st December 1938
Major i.G. – 1st June 1939
Oberstleutnant – 1st September 1941
Oberst – 1st August 1942
Generalmajor – 1st May 1944

Awards:
Armed Forces Long Service Award 3rd Class
Iron Cross 2nd Class – 1940
Iron Cross 1st Class – 1940
German Cross in Gold – 15th July 1942

Born on 6th May 1906 in Wilhelmshaven, Karl Heinrich Schulz entered the Navy in April 1924, and trained aboard the School Ship *Niobe*. After attending the Naval School at Mürwik he became an officer candidate with the 2nd Battalion of the Ships Cadre Division in the Baltic Sea. In January 1928 he served aboard the Liner *Hessen* and in October he was commissioned as a *Leutnant zur See* and transferred to the Survey Ship *Me-*

teor. He was promoted to *Oberleutnant* zur See in July 1930 and in September 1932 he served with the Naval Station on the Baltic Sea. In October 1935, shortly after being promoted to *Kapitänleutnant* he transferred to the Luftwaffe as an adjutant with the Inspector of the air reserves.

In April 1936 *Hauptmann* Schulz was made leader of the 2nd Air Course at the Navigation School Brandis and then he was appointed Squadron Commander with the 1st Coastal Reconnaissance Squadron and at the same time was made Air Base Commandant Nest. In February 1938 he was appointed a General Staff Officer with the Inspector of the Luftwaffe and shortly after he was promoted to the rank of *Major*. A year later he was assigned as Chief of Training Affairs with the Air Ministry in Berlin and in June was promoted to *Oberstleutnant*.

At the beginning of World War II he was named as Chief of Operations of the Air Region Command VI, Münster under its commander *Generalmajor* August Schmidt. In June 1940 Schulz was given what would become his only frontline command of the war, he was made commander of 126th Bomber Group succeeding *Hauptmann* Gerd Stein. However the command was short lived when he was shot down in July 1940 while on a bombing mission over France. He returned to duty a few months later and was briefly assigned to the 22nd Air Training Regiment in Warsaw before returning to duty as a staff officer. On 16th October 1940 Schulz was assigned to the 2nd Air Fleet where he would remain for the rest of war serving in various capacities. He was named as Department Head in the General Staff until September 1942 during which time he was promoted to *Oberst*. In October 1942 he was appointed Senior Quartermaster of the 4th Air Fleet under *Feldmarschall* von Richthofen. He continued to serve with the 4th Air Fleet seeing action on the Eastern Front in Jasionsk, Kremenez, Winniysa, Nikolayer, Poltava, Mariupol, Jessentuki and finally in Rostov, and was named Chief of Staff in February 1945 after being promoted to *Generalmajor*. On 9th June 1944 Schulz was awarded the Knight's Cross for his part in the heavy fighting in the Caucasus.

In December 1944 Schulz was one of three judges during a court martial in Oslo of a young Luftwaffe officer who was accused of failing to prevent the sinking of the Battleship Tirpitz on 12th November 1944. Heinrich Ehrler had been the commander of twelve Fw 190 fighters, he had been ordered to intercept a squadron of RAF bombers who had been sent to sink the Tirpitz. At this time the target was unknown and because of conflicting messages being sent to Ehrler as to the location of the RAF bombers he and his squadron failed to intercept the bombers. When it was clear that their target was the Tirpitz it was too late, and when the fighters finally reached the target area they could do nothing to prevent the battleship from being sunk. Prosecuting Ehrler was *Generalmajor* Dr. Ernst Reuter who accused Ehrler of not understanding the seriousness of the attack and having been too preoccupied with achieving his 200th aerial victory. As a result of the hearing Erhler was sentenced to death, however this was commuted to three years imprisonment when Ehrler made an appeal.

Schulz was named as the last Chief of the Luftwaffe Operations Staff after succeeding *Generalmajor* Eckhardt Christian on 23rd April 1945. It was an important title but the Luftwaffe had virtually disappeared, there were hardly any aircraft flying at that time and most troops under his command were either retreating or had already surrendered. On 6th May 1945 Schulz surrendered to Allied forces and spent the next two and half years in captivity, being was released on 23rd December 1947. Karl-Heinrich Schulz died in Dießen, Ammersee on 28th July 1986.

Carl-August SCHUMACHER
(1896-1967)
Generalmajor

Knight's Cross: Awarded on 21st July 1940 as *Oberstleutnant* and Wing Commander of 1st Fighter Wing.

Ranks:
Fähnrich zur See – 1st October 1916
Leutnant zur See – 17th March 1918
Oberleutnant – 1st March 1933
Hauptmann – 1st October 1933
Major – 1st August 1936
Oberstleutnant – 1st March 1939
Oberst – 19th July 1940
Generalmajor – 1st January 1944

Awards:
Iron Cross 2nd Class – World War I
Iron Cross 1st Class – World War I
Armed Forces Long Service Award 3rd Class
Cross of Honour for Frontline Combatants
Pilots Badge

Carl-August Schumacher was born on 19th February 1896 in Rheine, Steinfurt and entered the army as a war volunteer with the 7th Field Artillery Regiment in August 1914. In February 1915 he was transferred to the 43rd Field Artillery and transferred to the Navy as a cadet in January 1916. He trained as an observer and radio-operator with the 1st Sea Flying Battalion from July until October 1917, and then served as a pilot with various flying stations. In March 1918 he was commissioned as a *Leutnant* and in May he served on the ship *"Answald"* as an observation officer and ended the war as a pilot with a battle squadron in the Baltic Sea area.

He retired from active service when the war ended and tried to find work as a civilian. In March 1933 he entered the Luftwaffe with the rank of *Oberleutnant*, serving on the staff of the German Commercial Flying School in Berlin. In May 1934 he became an inspector for flying schools and after an infantry course in Döberitz in October 1934 he was assigned as a company commander with the 16th Air Battalion in Holtenau. In July 1936 he was appointed as a Squadron Commander with the Sea Air Base at Jever, part of the 136th Fighter Group and in August he was promoted to *Major*. In April 1939, now an *Oberstleutnant*, he took over as commander of 2nd Group, 77th Fighter Wing that had been formed in Pilsen and operated with the new Bf 109 fighter.

In March 1939 Schumacher was appointed commander of the 1st Fighter Wing which had been formed in Jever, north-west Germany. It was successful in defending the German coastal areas against British bombers in late 1939, and Schumacher himself shot down a Wellington bomber on 18th December and a Blenheim the following week. In April 1940 Schumacher took part in the invasion of Denmark, Norway and France in May. He was promoted to *Oberst* in July 1940 and was awarded the Knight's Cross on 21st July for the success of the campaign in France and the Low Countries. He had by the end of the campaign shot down a total of thirty-eight aircraft. In April 1941 Schumacher became the Fighter Leader of Norway, and he remained in this position for almost two years.

In May 1943 Schumacher was made head of a special command unit in Romania and here he was made responsible for the training of the Royal Romanian Air Force. He ran a three month course for 150 Romanian pilots, showing them how to fly the Bf 109 fighter aircraft and he trained them in the techniques of a Luftwaffe fighter pilot. In August 1943 the U.S. air force launched an attack on Ploesti and some of the Romanian trainee pilots were scrambled, but they failed to claim one victory. As a result by February 1944 this training unit was disbanded and the personnel were used to form the 1st Romanian Air Corps.

On the first day of 1944 Schumacher was promoted to *Generalmajor* and in April he was appointed to the staff of the Air Region Command XI in Hamburg. In October he was granted sick leave but at the end of January 1945 he returned to head the Operations Staff of the Luftwaffe High Command where he remained until the end of the war. Schumacher surrendered to U.S. troops on 8th May 1945, and remained in captivity until his release in April 1947. He spent his final years in Bad Godesberg where he died on 22nd May 1967.

Generalmajor Carl-August Schumacher. (Wehrkundearchiv)

Günther SCHWARTZKOPFF
(1898-1940)
Generalmajor

Knight's Cross: Awarded posthumously as *Oberst* and Wing Commander of 77th Stuka Wing on 24th November 1940 for actions during the French Campaign.

Ranks:
Fahnenjunker – 2nd October 1914
Fähnrich – 14th July 1915
Leutnant – 30th September 1915
Oberleutnant – 1st April 1925
Hauptmann – 1st February 1932
Major – 1st July 1935
Oberstleutnant – 1st October 1937
Oberst – 1st April 1940
Generalmajor – 28th June 1944 (posthumously)

Awards:
Iron Cross 2nd Class – World War I
Iron Cross1st Class – World War I
Knight's Cross of the Royal Prussian Hohenzollern House Order with Swords
Royal Prussian Pilot's Badge
Wound Badge in Silver – World War I
Cross of Honour for Frontline Combatants
Armed Forces Long Service Award 1st Class
Bar to Iron Cross 2nd Class
Bar to Iron Cross 1st Class

Günter Schwartzkopff was born on 5th August 1898 in Forbach, Posen in Germany (now part of Poland), he entered the army as a *Fahnenjunker* with the infantry in October 1914. Commissioned as a *Leutnant* in September 1915, he served with the 47th

Infantry Regiment until August 1916 when he decided to train as a pilot with the 8th Air Replacement Battalion. In January 1917 he officially became a pilot with the 4th Air Battalion and later with the 13th Battalion, seeing action on the Western front until the end of the war. Schwartzkopff remained in the armed forces after the Armistice and served as a technical officer at the air base at Paderborn. In October 1920 he was transferred as a platoon leader to the 6th Infantry Regiment. In April 1925 Schwartzkopff was promoted to *Oberleutnant* and in March 1928 he was assigned as Welfare Officer with the staff of the 1st Battalion of the 6th Infantry Regiment. In October he joined the 2nd Division and two years later he was transferred back to the 6th Infantry Regiment as a company officer.

Promoted to *Hauptmann* in February 1932 Schwartzkopff transferred to the Luftwaffe Personnel Department in September 1933. In October he was assigned as an instructor at the Pilot School in Neuruppin and in December 1934 he took a similar position in Celle. In April 1935 he was made commander of the Air School at Celle as well as airbase commander, and in July he was promoted to *Major*. He was appointed Group Commander of the 165th Bomber Wing in October 1936 and flew with the Condor Legion in Spain, where he gained valuable experience. A year later he took over as commander of the Stuka Instruction Wing in Barth, Schweinfurt where he directed the training of the first Stuka units.

In May 1939, now with the rank of *Oberstleutnant*, Schwartzkopff was appointed commander of the 77th Stuka Wing, a unit he had helped to form. Its first headquarters were in Breslau-Schögarten and from August 1939 they operated out of Neudorf and then from Cologne in September. He saw action during the Polish Campaign and took part in the invasion of France and the Low Countries in May 1940. On the fourth day of the campaign Schwartzkopff was shot down by ground fire over Belleville-et-Chatillon-Sur-Bar south-east of Le Chesne, France and was killed. He had been flying ground support missions while supporting Guderian's tanks who were fighting the strong French counterattack near Sedan. In recognition of his support and leadership which led to the victory over France Schwartzkopff was posthumously awarded the Knight's Cross on 24th November 1940 and almost four years later he was promoted to *Generalmajor*. Schwartzkopff now rests in the German Military Cemetery at Noyes Pont, Maugis in France, Block 4, and grave #3970.

Hugo SPERRLE (1885-1953) *Generalfeldmarschall*

Knight's Cross: Awarded on 17th May 1940 as *General der Flieger* and Commander of 3rd Air Fleet and Commander-in-Chief West, for his support of Guderian's panzers during the British forced evacuation at Dunkirk.

Günther Schwartzkopff as an Oberstleutnant during which time he was the Commander of the 77th Stuka Wing. (Wehrkundearchiv)

Ranks:
Fahnenjunker – 6th July 1903
Fähnrich – 25th February 1904
Leutnant – 18th October 1904
Oberleutnant – 18th October 1912
Hauptmann – 28th November 1914
Major – 1st October 1926
Oberstleutnant – 1st February 1931
Oberst – 1st August 1933
Generalmajor – 1st October 1935
Generalleutnant – 1st April 1937
General der Flieger – 1st November 1937
Generaloberst – skipped
Generalfeldmarschall – 19th July 1940

Awards:
Knight's Cross of the Royal Prussian Hohenzollern House Order with Swords – 31st March 1917
Iron Cross 2nd Class – World War I
Iron Cross 1st Class – World War I
Knight's Cross of the Royal Württemberg Military order of merit – 21st June 1915

Knight's Cross 1st Class of the Royal Württemberg Friedrich Order with Swords – 21st June 1917
Russian Honour Cross 3rd Class with the Crown and Swords
Royal Prussian Pilots Badge
Royal Prussian Observers Badge
Wound Badge in Black – World War I
Cross of Honour for Frontline Combatants
Armed Forces Long Service Award 1st Class
Medal for the Spanish Campaign 1936-1939 (Spanish)
Cross of the War Cross (Spanish)
Royal Spanish Pilots Badge (Spanish)
Military Individual Medal of Spain with Diamonds
Pilot's Badge with Diamonds
Combined Pilots and Observers Badge in Gold with Diamonds – 1st November 1937
Spanish Cross with Swords in Gold with Diamonds – 4th June 1939
Bar to Iron Cross 2nd Class
Bar to Iron Cross 1st Class
Wehrmacht Daily Report: 5 October 1940; 15 November 1940; 20 November 1940; 9 April 1941; 13 February 1942; 15 February 1942

Hitler called him, "one of my most brutal looking generals."[104] Hugo Sperrle was born on 7th February 1885 in Ludwigsburg, Württemberg, the son of Johann Sperrle a brewer. He joined the Imperial Army as *Fahnenjunker* on 6th July 1903 serving with 126th Infantry Regiment, attached to the 14th Army Corps. He was commissioned in October 1904 and six years later served as adjutant of 2nd Battalion before attending the War Academy and trained as a flyer. He was promoted to *Oberleutnant* in October 1912, and by the outbreak of the war he had been promoted to *Hauptmann*.

During World War I he specialized in aerial reconnaissance serving with 4th Field Flying Detachment as an aerial observer before undergoing pilot training. He went on to lead the 42nd and 60th Field Flying detachments and the 13th Field Flying Wing, before assuming command of the Air Observers School

Hugo Sperrle wearing the Knight's Cross and displaying the rank insignia of a Luftwaffe Generalfeldmarschall. (Author's collection)

Sperrle in the uniform of a General in the Spanish armed forces, seen here during a ceremony in Berlin. Directly in front of Sperrle is Generaloberst Wilhelm Keitel, and next to him Generaloberst Walther von Brauchitsch, Commander-in-Chief of the German Army, 1938. (Author's collection)

at Cologne. In December 1915 when returning from a night flight his plane crashed and Sperrle suffered facial injuries, but it wasn't serious and he returned to duty in February 1916. By the end of the war he was the officer-in-charge of all flying units attached to the 7th Army on the Western Front, while still a *Hauptmann*.

When the war ended Sperrle found himself unemployed and at a loss, until he joined the Lüttwitz Freikorps where he commanded its aviation detachment. In 1919 he was one of the 180 former aviators who were allowed to return to duty in the new officer corps of the new Reichsheer. In October 1920 he was appointed military adviser on the staff of Military District Command 5 (Wehrkreis V) in Stuttgart where he remained until February 1924. In March he was transferred to Berlin where he spent the next five years attached to the War Ministry as a staff officer, being promoted to *Major* in October 1926. In 1928 he traveled to Russia where he underwent secret advanced flight training at the German airbase at Lipetsk. On 1st February 1929 he took over as commander 3rd Battalion, 14th Infantry Regiment in Baden, and was promoted to *Oberstleutnant* in February 1931. In August 1933 he was promoted to *Oberst* and in October of the same year was appointed commander of 8th Infantry Regiment, this would be his last army command.

On 1st April 1934 Sperrle joined the new Luftwaffe and was immediately appointed commander of the 1st Air Division responsible for the area in and around Berlin. Sperrle would play a major role in the emergence of the Luftwaffe when Hitler decided to expand it defying the terms of the Versailles Treaty. In October 1935 Sperrle was promoted to *Generalmajor* and appointed Commanding General of Air District V which covered Munich. In 1936 General Franco of Spain asked Hitler for his help in his fight in the civil war, Hitler agreed and sent twenty Ju 52 transport aircraft with German aircrews. In late October it was decided that the German troops in Spain should be commanded by a Luftwaffe officer and on 6th November 1936 Sperrle became commander of what became known as the Condor Legion during the Spanish Civil War.

On 15th November Sperrle led an attack himself that destroyed the Republican naval base at Cartagena and forced the enemy fleet to put to sea and escape destruction. He was also responsible for a plan that should have ended the war within months had it not been for the incompetence of the Italian army. At Guernica it was Sperrle's aircraft that attacked and killed hundreds of Spanish civilians, probably the first war crime committed by German troops. Promoted to *Generalleutnant* in March 1937, Sperrle was summoned to Berlin in late October and handed over the command of the Condor Legion to *Generalmajor* Helmuth von Volkmann. When Sperrle returned to Germany he was treated like a hero and on 1st November 1937 he was promoted to *General der Flieger*.

In February 1938 Sperrle was ready for his new command, he now commanded the 3rd Air Fleet with its headquarters in Munich, responsible for all Luftwaffe units, bases and operations in southern Germany. Sperrle took part in the occupation of Austria in 1938 and after the Anschluss took the leading role in the bombing demonstrations aimed at intimating Czechoslovakia into giving up the Sudetenland. It worked and in October the Sudetenland was signed over to Hitler without a fight. Next came the complete occupation of Czechoslovakia and again Sperrle took a vital role in this too. During the invasion of Poland his command was responsible for supporting *Generaloberst* von Leeb's Army Group C.

Right: General der Flieger Hellmuth Volkmann who from November 1937 until October 1938 was the commander of the Condor Legion in Spain after Sperrle. He went on to command the Luftwaffe War Academy in Berlin in April 1939, and in May 1940 transferred to the army and took over as commander of the 94th Infantry Division. Volkmann was seriously wounded in a car accident on 4th August 1940 and died in hospital two weeks later. (Wehrkundearchiv)

Below: Sperrle sitting at his desk in Paris as the commander of the 3rd Air Fleet in August 1940. (Author's collection)

During the invasion of France in 1940 Sperrle supported von Rundstedt's Army Group with great effect, later supporting General Guderian's panzers during the breakthrough at Sedan which led to the British forced evacuation at Dunkirk, and for this he was awarded the Knight's Cross by Hitler on 18th May 1940. After the fall of France he was one of only three generals in the Luftwaffe to be promoted to the rank of *Generalfeldmarschall* in a ceremony on 19th July 1940. Although Sperrle was never a party member he was loyal to Hitler, but his advice about the up and coming war with Britain was ignored. Sperrle had a major part in the invasion plan against Britain, and played a major role in the Battle of Britain. His 3rd Air Fleet was stationed in France and was responsible for the attack on the RAF fighter bases in eastern England. During a meeting with Göring and Kesselring in The Hague in September 1940, Sperrle warned Göring that the only way to win the Battle of Britain was the total destruction of fighter command. Göring however wanted to concentrate on bombing London, he felt like Hitler that the British would surrender rather than see their beloved cities destroyed. Sperrle's arguments were ignored, he

During a tour of inspection somewhere in France, Sperrle takes time to talk to two Luftwaffe anti-aircraft gunners. (Author's collection)

A monocled Sperrle during a visit to the front in 1941. This photo clearly shows the shoulder and collar insignia of a Luftwaffe Generalfeldmarschall. (Author's collection)

Below: Sperrle reviews troops in France in 1942. (Author's collection)

left the meeting disgruntled and surprised by the decision, and he knew that both Hitler and Göring had totally underestimated RAF Fighter Command. In October the Luftwaffe was defeated over the skies of England and the invasion of England was cancelled, Sperrle had been proved correct.

In May 1941 Sperrle's command was transferred from France to Poland, where he was appointed as Air Fleet Commander for the entire Western Front. When Operation Barbarossa, the invasion of Russia was announced Sperrle returned to France. While most of the Luftwaffe was fighting the Soviets in a bloody confrontation Sperrle's command was somewhat easier, he began to enjoy himself. His headquarters was in Paris and he was often seen in the bars, clubs and casinos of Deauville. He neglected his duties and could be described, like Göring as lazy, spending most of his time concentrating on enjoying himself. In March 1943 the RAF bombed Berlin and 35,000 people lost their homes, and Sperrle was ordered by Hitler to send his air division to bomb London. His aircraft flew across the channel with 100 tons of bombs to drop on London, however only twelve tonnes fell on target and Hitler flew into a rage, and he was still ranting about Sperrle a week later.

This episode didn't help Sperrle with his own feelings about the way the war was being run; in fact he became more and more disillusioned with Hitler's and Göring's conduct of the war. He became unproductive and his interest in gourmet food and fine wines began to take its toll. He began to drink and gamble like never before and became completely disinterested with his command. When he did turn up at his headquarters he was difficult to work with and his prejudice against women in the service grew to ridiculous proportions. Germany had a shortage of workers and so more and more women were being employed, in the armaments factories and within the Wehrmacht as secretaries, when Sperrle rang the operator and a female voice answered him he would throw down the phone and scream in anger.

In June 1944 when the Allies broke out of the Normandy bridgehead, most of the Luftwaffe under the command of Sperrle simply packed up and headed east. Hitler accused them of running away and held Sperrle responsible, calling him a coward. This seems to have been a little harsh since Sperrle's command had been stripped of nearly all of its aircraft and fuel, but it has to be said that Sperrle didn't react to the Allied landings in Normandy until it was too late. On 19th August Sperrle was inevitably relieved of his command and replaced with *Generaloberst* Otto Deßloch.

Sperrle was captured in Southern Germany by U.S. forces on 8th May 1945, and held at Nuremberg to face war crimes charges. His trial started on 30th December 1947, and it was thought that the man responsible for the bombing of Coventry and London would be charged with the death's of some 40,000 people. In fact the bombings were never mentioned during his trial and Sperrle was only charged with forcing Russian prisoners-of-war to build military facilities, which under the Geneva Convention was illegal. On 27th October 1948 Sperrle was acquitted of all charges, the prosecution said it was due to lack of evidence. He was officially de-nazified on 9th June 1949 and returned to his home in Munich where he died a bitter man on 2nd April 1953, he was buried four days later.

Sperrle talks with Major Helmut Wick who was awarded the Knight's Cross with Oakleaves as commander of the 1st Group, 2nd Fighter Wing "Richthofen". Credited with fifty-six victories in 168 combat missions, Wick was killed on 28th November 1940 when his aircraft was shot down over the English Channel near the Isle of Wight. (Author's collection)

Hans-Jurgen STUMPFF
(1889-1968)
Generaloberst

Knight's Cross: Awarded on 18th September 1941 as *Generaloberst* and Commander of 5th Air Fleet, for his efforts in the bombing against the Russians in Murmansk.

Ranks:
Fahnenjunker-Gefreiter – 2nd September 1907
Fahnenjunker-Unteroffizier – 21st November 1907
Fähnrich – 27th January 1908
Leutnant – 19th November 1908
Oberleutnant – 24th December 1914
Hauptmann – 18th August 1916
Major – 1st July 1927
Oberstleutnant – 1st October 1931
Oberst – 1st April 1934
Generalmajor – 1st April 1936
Genieralleutnant – 1st August 1937
General der Flieger – 1st November 1938
Generaloberst – 19th July 1940

Awards:
Iron Cross 2nd Class – World War I
Iron Cross 1st Class – World War I
The Hanseatic Cross, 1914
The Lübeck Cross, 1914
The Anhalt Friedrich Cross, 1914
Wound Badge in Black – World War I
Cross of Honour for Frontline Combatants
Royal Bavarian Military Service Order 4th Class with Swords
Imperial and Royal Austrian Order of the Iron Crown 3rd Class with War Decoration
Armed Forces Long Service Award 1st Class
Pilot's Badge with Diamonds
Combined Pilot's and Observer's Badge in Gold with Diamonds
Medal for the Winter Campaign in Russia 1941/1942
Commemorative Medal for 1st October 1938 with Bar "Prague Castle"
Commemorative Medal of 13th March 1938
Bar to Iron Cross 2nd Class
Bar to Iron Cross 1st Class
Wehrmacht Daily Report: 10 April 1941; 30 May 1942; 24 August 1943

One of the lesser known Luftwaffe generals of World War II, he was one of the very few to emerge from the war with a completely clean record as far as Hitler and the Allies were concerned. Hans-Jurgen Stumpff was born on 15th June 1889 in Kolberg; he was the second son of an infantry officer Max Stumpff and Kaete Bodenstein also born in Kolberg. In April

Generaloberst Hans-Jurgen Stumpff. (Wehrkundearchiv)

1908, shortly after Stumpff left school he joined the army as a *Fahnenjunker* with 12th Grenadier Regiment and was commissioned as a *Leutnant* in November 1908. In October 1912 he was appointed adjutant to 12th Grenadier Regiment, was wounded at Mons during action against British troops in the early part of the First World War. Once recovered he returned to active service as an *Oberleutnant* with 254th Reserve Infantry Regiment. In August 1916 he was promoted to *Hauptmann* and began his training as a General Staff Officer in November, where he remained until after the armistice.

He stayed on in the Reichswehr serving as adjutant to the Troop Office within the War Ministry until September 1922 when he was appointed Company Commander in the 8th Infantry Regiment. In February 1927 he was appointed to a staff position within the Army Command and was promoted to the rank of *Major* six months later. In the next six years he served in important staff positions and was again promoted, when Hitler came to power in 1933 and transferred to the Luftwaffe Personnel Office, taking over as its head two years later. He was very successful in this position and Kesselring referred to Stumpff as the man who was responsible for the construction of the officers' corps of the Luftwaffe, and said that, "... he had become a real father to the NCOs and men under his care."[105]

In 1937 Stumpff visited England three times, the first time he met with officials from the Royal Air Force and in May he was part of an official delegation, which included *Generalfeldmarschall* von Blomberg, who had been invited to the Coronation of King George VI. In June shortly after the visit Stumpff was appointed Chief of the General Staff of the Luftwaffe, succeeding Kesselring. In October during his final visit to England he was accompanied by Generals Erhard Milch and Ernst Udet, they had been invited by the British Aviation Minister Lord Swinton to view the aircraft of the RAF. Stumpff spoke with Lord Swinton's Chief of Staff Sir Cyril Newall at length and was greatly impressed by the skill of the RAF pilots.

In 1938 the Luftwaffe General Staff was reorganized and Stumpff found himself working closely with the State Secretary Erhard Milch, neither of them got on well with each other. Stumpff was highly regarded by Göring and Kesselring, but Milch didn't get on with either of these men and argued constantly with Stumpff. Although Stumpff was a veteran Staff officer and was a good administrator he was unsuited for this post and knew it, he saw his appointment as a stopgap and wanted a field command. In January 1939 he was succeeded as Chief of the General Staff by Hans Jeschonnek, and was appointed Chief of the Air Defense.

In January 1940 he briefly commanded the 1st Air Fleet before being appointed as commander of the 5th Air Fleet seeing action during the French campaign and the Battle of Britain. His Air Fleet was used mainly to support Kesselring's 2nd Air Fleet and Sperrle's 3rd Air Fleet, and after the fall of France in June 1940 he was promoted to *Generaloberst* going onto take a leading role during the invasions of Norway and Denmark. Stumpff became a very successful Air Fleet commander and his stay in the North was long, his headquarters were at first in Oslo and later moved to Kemi in Finland. From June 1941 until November 1943 he was mainly concerned with the northern

Stumpff in conversation with Generaloberst Eduard Dietl the first recipient of the Knight's Cross with Oakleaves, awarded on 19th July 1940. Dietl commanded the 20th Mountain Army from June 1942 until his death in an aircraft crash in June 1944. Dietl was posthumously awarded the Swords in July 1944. (Wehrkundearchiv)

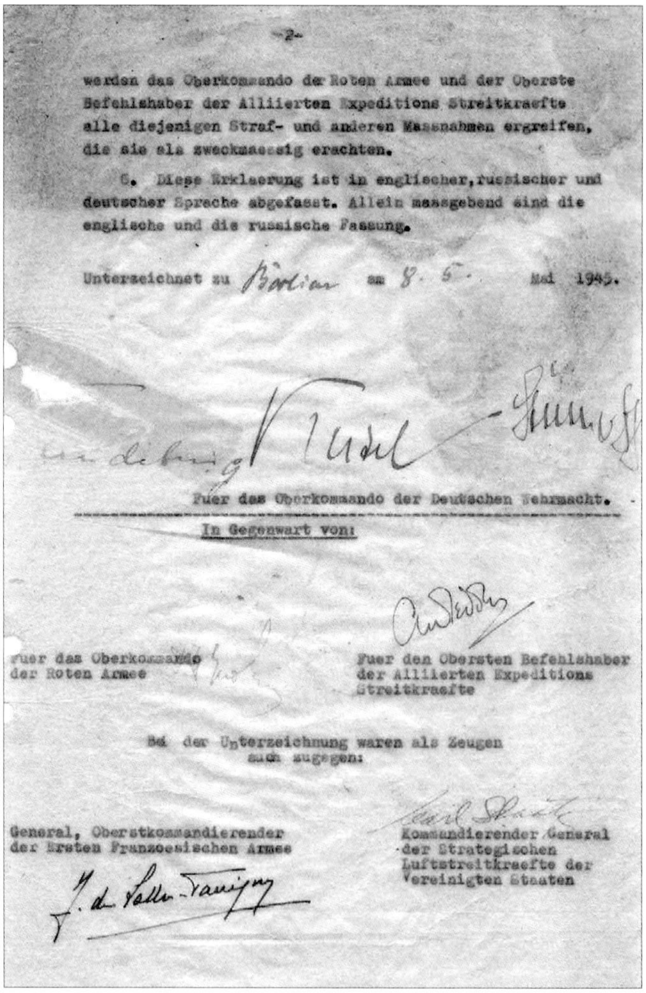

-2-

werden das Oberkommando der Roten Armee und der Oberste Befehlshaber der Alliierten Expeditions Streitkraefte alle diejenigen Straf- und anderen Massnahmen ergreifen, die sie als zweckmaessig erachten.

6. Diese Erklaerung ist in englischer, russischer und deutscher Sprache abgefasst. Allein massgebend sind die englische und die russische Fassung.

Unterzeichnet zu Berlin am 8. 5. Mai 1945.

Fuer das Oberkommando der Deutschen Wehrmacht.

In Gegenwart von:

Fuer das Oberkommando der Roten Armee

Fuer den Obersten Befehlshaber der Alliierten Expeditions Streitkraefte

Bei der Unterzeichnung waren als Zeugen auch zugegen:

General, Oberstkommandierender der Ersten Franzoesischen Armee

Kommandierender General der Strategischen Luftstreitkraefte der Vereinigten Staaten

The surrender document signed by Stumpff on behalf of the Luftwaffe, von Friedeburg on behalf of the German navy, and Generalfeldmarschall Keitel on behalf of the German armed forces. (Private source)

front and supported the Finnish and German troops against the Russians. In September 1941 he was awarded the Knight's Cross for his successful bombing campaign against Murmansk and the Russian railways.

Stumpff was appointed Commander of Air Fleet Reich in January 1944, and was made responsible for the air defence of Germany. He took on this responsibility with great skill and enthusiasm even though Germany was heading for defeat. In the autumn of 1944, mainly due to the efforts of Milch and Armaments Minister Albert Speer, the production of fighter aircraft and jet fighters reached its peak and Stumpff was allocated extra aircraft. However due to the fuel shortages and the lack of trained pilots the extra aircraft more often than not stayed on the ground. By the summer of 1944 the Luftwaffe were losing 300 aircraft a week to the Allies and by February 1945 Berlin had endured as many as forty heavy air raids.

On 8th May Stumpff was named as the Chief of the General Staff of the Luftwaffe in the new Dönitz government and because Göring had been dismissed by Hitler in April and the new Commander-in-Chief *Generalfeldmarschall* von Greim had been badly injured and was in American custody, Stumpff was also appointed acting Commander-in-Chief of the Luftwaffe. At 00:16 hours on 9th May 1945 in Berlin-Karlshorst the surrender of Germany was signed, and one of the signatories was *Generaloberst* Hans-Jurgen Stumpff who as the Luftwaffe representative signed the document along with *Generalfeldmarschall* Wilhelm Keitel and *Generaladmiral* Hans-Georg von Friedeburg[106] the new head of the German Kriegsmarine. Stumpff was then arrested and taken to Nuremberg where he was a witness and where he met up with Milch, Sperrle and Kesselring. In 1946 he was tried by a British Military Court in Hamburg, the charges were that he had failed to protect Allied airmen shot down over Germany from acts of violence committed by the civilian population. On 18th October 1947 he was found not guilty and acquitted of all charges. He lived in retirement in Frankfurt am Main until his death on 9th March 1968.

Knight's Cross winner Generalleutnant Alfred Sturm. (Wehrkundearchiv)

Alfred STURM
(1888-1962)
Generalleutnant

Knight's Cross: Awarded on 9th July 1941 as *Oberst* and commander of 2nd Fallschirmjäger Regiment for actions during the invasion of Crete.

Ranks:
Vizefeldwebel – 1st August 1913
Offiziers-Stellvertreter – 1st January 1915
Leutnant – 5th June 1919
Oberleutnant – 15th January 1921
Hauptmann – 1st March 1926
Major – 21st April 1935
Oberstleutnant – 2nd August 1936
Oberst – 1st October 1938
Generalmajor – 1st August 1941
Generalleutnant – 1st August 1943

Awards:
Iron Cross 2nd Class – 18th June 1916
Iron Cross 1st Class – 17th January 1917
Wound Badge in Black – World War I
Royal Prussian Pilot's Badge
Honour Goblet for aerial combat
Cross of Honour for Frontline Combatants
Armed Forces Long Service Award 1st Class
Bar to Iron Cross 2nd Class – 28th October 1940
Bar to Iron Cross 1st Class – 25th June 1941
KRETA Cuff-title
Wehrmacht Daily Report: 9 June 1941

Born on 23rd August 1888 in Saarbrücken, Alfred Sturm entered army service as a pupil at the NCO School in Bieberich on

17th October 1905. He entered World War I as a *Vizefeldwebel* serving with the 144th Infantry Regiment on the Western Front. Wounded in January 1915, he soon recovered and began training as a pilot with the 4th Flying Replacement Battalion, ending the war with the 89th Fighter Squadron.

Sturm remained in the army after the war and served with 144th Infantry Regiment and was commissioned as a *Leutnant* in June 1919. He served with the Reich War Ministry before being promoted to *Oberleutnant* and assigned as company officer in the 8th Infantry Regiment in April 1921. Promoted to *Hauptmann* in March 1926 he left the infantry two years later to begin his pilot training in Russia. In August 1930 he returned to the army serving with his old regiment and in October 1933 he transferred to the Luftwaffe where he served as a staff officer until December when he transferred to the Fighter Air School in Schleißheim. Sturm was appointed commander of the Air School in Magdeburg in January 1935 and was promoted to *Major* three months later. From January 1936 until March 1939 Sturm served as the Air Base Commander at Detmold, in October 1938 he was promoted to *Oberst* and soon afterwards was appointed commander of the 72nd Air Training Regiment. He then served in the Air Ministry until June 1940 when he was posted to the Wittstock Parachute School where, although fifty-two years old, he underwent tough parachute training.

In July 1940 he was appointed commander of the 2nd Fallschirmjäger Regiment and he took part in the aerial invasion of Crete in May 1941. On the second day of the invasion Sturm was taken prisoner by the British but a few days later he was free when the British surrendered. On 20th May he became acting commander of the 7th Air Division after its commander *Generalleutnant* Wilhelm Süßmann had been killed. For his bravery and leadership during the successful invasion of Crete Sturm was awarded the Knight's Cross on 9th July 1941. In October Sturm, now promoted to *Generalmajor*, was transferred to Stalino in Russia where he was sent to the Leningrad area to fight with Army Group North's 18th Army. For the next two months the Soviets fought against the Fallschirmjäger regiments, but without success, and in December the Fallschirmjäger were sent back to Germany to rest. Then within a few weeks the 2nd Fallschirmjäger Regiment with Sturm still leading them, along with units of the anti-tank and machine gun battalions were sent to the Ukraine to bolster Army Group South. This force was named Battle Group Sturm and it defended a sector along the River Mius near the town of Charzysk through the winter of 1941 and into early 1942 with little success.

Sturm was transferred from the Eastern Front to command the Ground Combat Schools of the Luftwaffe in October 1942, and he remained at this post until January 1945. In August 1943 he was promoted to *Generalleutnant* and in March 1944 he briefly commanded a Battle Group. In January 1945 Sturm was named Head of the Wehrmacht Motor Transport Service, a transport service with little or no petrol and very few vehicles. For the last weeks of the war he commanded a battle group again and on 23rd April 1945 he was captured by Allied troops and held in captivity without charge until June 1947. Sturm died on 8th March 1962 in Detmold, at the age of seventy-three.

Alfred Sturm shortly after being awarded the Knight's Cross as Generalmajor and Wing Commander of 77th Bomber Wing for actions over France. (Wehrkundearchiv)

Wolf von STUTTERHEIM
(1893-1940)
Generalmajor

Knight's Cross: Awarded on 4th July 1940 as *Generalmajor* and Wing Commander of 77th Bomber Wing for actions over France.

Ranks:
Fähnrich – 23rd October 1913
Leutnant – 19th June 1914
Oberleutnant – 16th September 1917
Hauptmann – skipped

Major – 1st July 1935
Oberstleutnant – 1st October 1936
Oberst – 1st January 1939
Charakter als Generalmajor – 27th August 1939

Awards:

Knight's Cross of the Royal Prussian Hohenzollern House Order with Swords – 31st October 1916
Iron Cross 2nd Class – World War I
Iron Cross 1st Class – World War I
Pour le Mérite – 27th August 1918
Wound Badge in Silver - World War I
Wound Badge in Gold – World War I
Armed Forces Long Service Award 3rd Class
Bar to Iron Cross 2nd Class
Bar to Iron Cross 1st Class
Wound Badge in Gold - World War II

A highly decorated soldier of both world wars who had his career during World War II cut short after a fatal air crash. Wolf von Stutterheim was born on 17th January 1893 in Königsberg, East Prussia and entered the Imperial Army in April 1912 serving with the 1st Kaiser Alexander Guards Grenadier Regiment as an officer cadet. In June 1914 he won his commission and was made a platoon leader, he was wounded at the front on 6th September and hospitalised, returning to his regiment in mid October. On New Years Eve 1914 he was wounded again but soon returned to the front as adjutant of a Fusilier Battalion, attached to his old regiment. In May 1915 he was wounded for the third time, and in July he was wounded once again, returning to duty in early August, however by the end of the month he was in hospital after a shell exploded near him injuring him for the fifth time. He returned to his old regiment as battalion adjutant and was promoted to *Oberleutnant* in September 1917.

When the war was over Stutterheim remained in the peace time army with his old regiment. On Christmas Eve 1918 he fell from his horse and fractured his skull, it was a serious injury and he remained in hospital for almost twelve months, he returned to light duties but in May 1920 he retired from military service. For the next three years Stutterheim spent in a sanatorium

Wolf von Stutterheim wearing his Pour le Mérite in the uniform of a Major while attached to the Air Ministry in 1935. (Wehrkundearchiv)

Von Stutterheim was severely wounded in June 1940 after his aircraft was hit by gunfire and crashed in France. He spent many weeks in hospital and never fully recovered. He died in December 1940 and was given a full military funeral. (Author's collection)

and once he felt well enough he travelled to Munich where he studied Forest Sciences at university. In July 1927 he became a junior lawyer in the Forestry Service and spent the next eight years in various positions within the service.

On 1st July 1935 Stutterheim returned to active duty with the rank of *Major* serving with the new Luftwaffe. He was assigned to the Air Ministry at first and then given flying training in Magdeburg. On 28th June 1936 Stutterheim was severely injured during an air-crash and spent almost eighteen months in hospital. Promoted to *Oberstleutnant* in October 1936, he soon recovered and was assigned to various staff positions before being transferred to the 152nd Bomber Wing in November 1938. In January 1939 he took over command of the 4th Group of the Bomber Wing and was promoted to *Oberst*.

During the invasion of Poland Stutterheim commanded the 77th Bomber Wing which had been formed in Prague and from October was flying out of Düsseldorf. His wing was equipped with Dornier Do 17 bombers and they attacked primarily airfields, ammunition dumps, troops, anti-aircraft guns and any targets of opportunity. In May 1940 his Wing took part in the invasion of France and was again very successful, however on 15th June Stutterheims' aircraft was hit during aerial combat over France and he was severely wounded. While recovering in a Berlin hospital he was notified that he had been awarded the Knight's Cross for his actions over France, the award was officially rendered on 4th July 1940. The wounds he received were very serious and it was unlikely that he would return to any type of frontline duty again. On the morning of 3rd December 1940 Stutterheim died, he was given a full military funeral and was made an honorary *Generalmajor*.

Otto Sydow wearing his German Cross in Gold. (Wehrkundearchiv)

Otto SYDOW
(1896-1970)
Generalmajor

Knight's Cross: Awarded as *Generalmajor* and commander of 20th Flak Division on 28th February 1945 for actions while in defence of the Reich.

Ranks:
Gefreiter der Reserve – 1st March 1915
Unteroffizier der Reserve – 9th August 1915
Vizefeldwebel der Reserve – 2nd February 1917
Leutnant der Reserve – 12th November 1917
Polizei-Oberwachtmeister – 20th November 1920
Polizei-Leutnant – 22nd November 1921
Polizei-Oberleutnant – 1st April 1925
Polizei-Hauptmann – 1st April 1932
Hauptmann – 1st October 1935
Major – 1st April 1936
Oberstleutnant – 1st February 1939
Oberst – 1st April 1941
Generalmajor – 1st April 1944

Awards:
Iron Cross 2nd Class – 7th March 1917
Wound Badge in Black – 9th July 1918
Cross of Honour for Frontline Combatants
Armed Forces Long Service Award 2nd Class
Commemorative Medal for 1st October 1938 with Bar "Prague Castle"
Medal for the Winter Campaign in Russia 1941/1942
Bar to Iron Cross 2nd Class – 4th December 1940
Iron Cross 1st Class – 25th August 1941
Luftwaffe Anti-Aircraft Badge – 12th December 1941
German Cross in Gold – 24th September 1942

Otto Sydow was born on 1st February 1896 in Rosemarsow, Demmin he entered the Imperial Army as a war volunteer with the Replacement Battalion, 42nd Infantry Regiment in September 1914. He transferred to the 10th Infantry Regiment in November and was wounded shortly afterwards and spent time in hospital in Karlsruhe. Sydow was made an *Unteroffizier* in the Reserves in August 1915 and a year later he was appointed a Platoon Leader with the 10th Infantry Regiment. He remained with this regiment throughout the war and was commissioned as a *Leutnant* der Reserve in November 1917.

When the war finished Sydow joined the Protection Police in Schneidemühl and by April 1925 he had risen to the rank of *Polizei-Oberleutnant*. In January 1931 he had transferred to Berlin and in April 1932 he was promoted to *Polizei-Hauptmann*. In May 1933 he was made a company commander with the Police Battalion Wecke, the state police named after its World War I commander *Major* Walther Wecke, and under the command of Hermann Göring. In 1934 Göring handed over control of the Prussian State Police to Himmler and this became the Gestapo. He kept control of his own police battalions and renamed them the State Police "General Göring" and when Göring was made commander of the Luftwaffe he took his police battalions with him and Sydow transferred to these new formations in October 1935 with the rank of *Hauptmann*. He remained with the "General Göring" Regiment until January 1939 when with the rank of *Major* and was made commander of the 3rd Battalion, 1st *Fallschirmjäger* Regiment.

Promoted to *Oberstleutnant* in February 1939 Sydow was transferred to Berlin in May 1940 where he joined the staff of Air Region Command III, under the command of *Generalmajor* Gerhard Hoffmann.[107] In June he took over as commander of 1st Battalion, 22nd Flak Regiment and saw action during the invasion of France under *Oberstleutnant* Georg von Gylderfeldt.[108] He remained in France until early 1941 when he returned to Germany as commander of 1st Battalion, 52nd Flak Regiment with its headquarters in Magdeburg under the command of *Oberstleutnant* Adolf Wolf. In April he was promoted to *Oberst* and transferred to Munich where he took command of the 125th Flak Regiment later seeing action in Russia while supporting the 9th Army.

In July 1943 Sydow was appointed Inspector of Flak Artillery while attached to the Luftwaffe Command Southeast in Greece under the command of *General der Flieger* Martin Fiebig. On 1st October 1943 Sydow was asked to reform the 20th Flak Division which had previously been in action in Tunisia under *Generalleutnant* Georg Neuffler until its capture in May 1943. Sydow led his new command in Belgrade where he encountered tough opposition and took part in some fierce fighting. Promoted to *Generalmajor* in April 1944, by late October the division had started to withdraw from the Balkans along with most of Hitler's Wehrmacht. Sydow now took command of the 1st Flak Division in Berlin and became responsible for defending the Reich's capital against very heavy Allied bomber attacks. For his leadership and courage during the defence of the Reich Sydow was awarded the Knight's Cross on 28th February 1945. During the last few weeks of the war he was under the command of *General der Artillerie* Helmuth Weidling's[109] LVI Panzer Corps where it fought as a ground unit. On 2nd May 1945 almost the entire Panzer Corps including the 1st Flak Division and Sydow surrendered to the Red Army. He spent the next ten years in Soviet captivity and was finally released on 8th October 1955. General Weidling never saw Germany again he died in a Soviet prison camp in November 1955. Otto Sydow died in Diepholz, Germany on 24th June 1970.

Ernst UDET
(1896-1941)
Generaloberst

Knight's Cross: *General der Flieger* Udet was awarded the Knight's Cross on 4th July 1940 as Chief of the Planning department within the Reich Air Ministry and as Inspector of Fighters.

Ranks:
Gefreiter der Reserve – 21st September 1915
Unteroffizier der Reserve – 28th November 1915
Vizefeldwebel der Reserve – 13th March 1916
Offiziers-Stellvertreter – 5th November 1916

Ernst Udet in the uniform of a Generaloberst wearing the Pour le Mérite and Knight's Cross. (Author's collection)

Leutnant der Reserve – 22nd January 1917
Oberleutnant der Reserve – 14th September 1918
Oberstleutnant – 1st June 1934
Oberst – 1st June 1935
Generalmajor – 1st April 1937
Generalleutnant – 1st November 1938
General der Flieger – 1st April 1940
Generaloberst – 19th July 1940

Awards:
Knight's Cross of the Royal Prussian Hohenzollern House Order with Swords – 13th November 1917
Iron Cross 2nd Class – 24th September 1915
Iron Cross 1st Class – 20th March 1916
Pour le Mérite – 9th April 1918
Bar to Iron Cross 2nd Class
Bar to Iron Cross 1st Class
Royal Prussian Pilot's Badge
Honour Goblet for aerial combat – 17th August 1916
Royal Wurttemberg Service Cross with Swords – 4th November 1916
The Hanseatic Cross, 1914 – 17th September 1918
The Lübeck Cross, 1914 – 24th August 1918
Wound Badge in Silver – World War I
Cross of Honour for Frontline Combatants
Pilot's Badge with Diamonds
Combined Pilot's and Observer's Badge in Gold with Diamonds
Armed Forces Long Service Award 4th Class

Oberst Udet seen here on his 40th birthday as Inspector of Fighters, April 1936. (Author's collection)

Ernst Udet was one of the saddest figures of the Third Reich, he had gained fame during the Great War as a gifted fighter pilot and was credited with sixty-two victories, second only to the famed Red Baron. He was born on 26th April 1896 in Frankfurt am Main, after attending school in Munich he volunteered for active duty in August 1914, joining the 26th Reserve Infantry Division as a dispatch rider. He wanted to be a pilot but was too young for pilot training so his father Adolf Udet paid for him to learn to fly privately. He was discharged from the ranks of the Reserves and rejoined as an enlisted man with 9th Flying Detachment on 15th June 1915, and went on to serve on the western front.

Udet flew as an observer and was awarded the Iron Cross 2nd Class for bravery in the Vosges area. In November 1915 he was promoted to *Unteroffizier* and transferred to 68th Field Flying Detachment in Flanders as a fighter pilot. He scored his first victory on 18th March 1916, his second victory came in October, and after scoring his fifth victory he became an official ace on 24th April 1917. On 5th August now commissioned as a *Leutnant* he was named commander of the 37th Fighter Squadron and he now began to score more victories. On 18th February 1918 he scored his 20th victory when he shot down a Sopwith Camel near Zandvoorde. Offered command of the 11th Fighter Squadron, part of the Fighter Wing led by Manfred von Richthofen, "The Red Baron", he led this unit for the rest of the war scoring another forty-two victories. When von Richthofen was killed in action everyone assumed Udet would become the new commander but instead *Hauptmann* Hermann Göring was named as his replacement. At first Udet didn't like the man who had taken what he felt was his rightful place as commander of this famous Fighter Wing, but they soon became good friends.

After the World War Udet returned to Munich where he worked for Gustav Otto as an mechanic. On Sundays he worked for a POW relief organization by putting on exhibition dogfights against Robert Ritter von Greim, until he crashed his plane. He survived but with only one aircraft and no hope of getting a replacement dogfights were impossible. Udet then went back to work as a pilot for the Rumpler Works which had started an air service flying between Vienna and Munich. Udet couldn't get on with civilian life, and when the Allied Control Commission took away his aircraft he worked in the construction of sports aircraft until 1925. He then moved to Brazil where he worked as a stunt pilot and didn't return to Germany until early 1933.

Udet wasn't keen to join the Luftwaffe but Göring convinced him to join which he did in June 1934 with the rank of *Oberst*. His promotion was rapid. His first appointment was on 10th February 1936 when he succeeded his old friend von Greim as Inspector of Fighters and Dive-Bombers. Four months later he succeeded *Generalmajor* Wilhelm Wimmer as Chief of the Technical Office of the Luftwaffe which later became the Office for Supply and Procurement. On 1st February 1939 Udet, now a *Generalleutnant* was appointed *Generalluftzeugmeister*, a title Göring had come up with, he was Chief of air armament of the Luftwaffe, a post that reduced Milch's power, something Göring had planned. Göring now had a very good friend in the second most important position in the Luftwaffe, but Udet lacked the skill and experience for such a position. Udet disliked regular working hours, and hated to be tied to a desk, and he had the wrong attitude for a tough important assignment. Udet took drugs, drank to extreme and his lack of ability meant the Technical Office was already out of control by early 1939. However because of Göring's lack of interest in any of his subordinate's offices and the fact that it took time for aircraft to be planned, tested and for production to start there was little or no warning of Udet's failures until it was too late. When Udet and Göring did meet they talked more about the old days as fighter pilots in the Great War than anything else.

Udet trusted the wrong people and surrounded himself with friends and chose people for their personality rather than for their capability to do the job. His Chief of Staff *Generalmajor* August Plocher was incompetent. His chief engineer Ruolf Lucht was inexperienced and his head of technical planning *General-Ingenieur* Günther Tschersisch was far more interested in aircraft development than actual production, which he neglected. Udet began to make mistakes, selecting the wrong aircraft which he had said were capable of succeeding current models, when in fact they were already out of date or hadn't been tested sufficiently. The Me 109 was perhaps the exception this became a very successful fighter, but the Ju 87, the Stuka dive-bomber, although had some success was slow and had many problems. Other aircraft had so many problems they were complete failures like the Me 210, the He 177 and the Ju 88. On 30th September 1938 Göring ordered that the Ju 88 go into production despite the fact that it had not been fully tested, as a result by the time World War II started not one aircraft had been delivered. It was soon taken out of service for good. Because of Udet and his department Germany had no modern bomber in service until 1942.

When war broke out in 1939 Udet was taken by surprise he was very uneasy about Great Britain declaring war on Germany, perhaps he had seen them as a potential ally. However when France fell he was overjoyed and exclaimed to his staff that all their plans could be thrown away, "We don't need them any longer!,"[110] he had thought the war was already over. During the celebrations after the fall of France Udet was promoted to *Generaloberst* and he celebrated for several days, drinking and taking drugs. However things were going to get worse as it became obvious that RAF were far stronger and had superior fighters, and had a big advantage of being able to stay in the air for longer periods. During the Battle of Britain Udet's department failures were made public to the world, it was obvious to everyone that Germany had fallen behind the allies in military aviation technology. To gain it quickly Udet made a gamble and ordered the He 177 into mass production, despite the negative test results. As a result other aircraft including the He 111

Generalmajor August Plocher, Udet's incompetent chief-of-staff, chief engineer Ruolf Lucht, and his head of technical planning General-Ingenieur Günther Tschersisch. (Wehrkundearchiv)

Generaloberst Ernst Udet at the height of his power. (Author's collection)

Above and below: Udet during happier times in front of the special train that Göring used as his mobile headquarters, and in conversation with the man he called the "Iron Man". (Author' collection)

had to be taken out of production to make way for this new aircraft. To change mass production of one aircraft to another so suddenly caused many problems, it wasn't until 1941 that production could actually start. It was a complete failure and 1,446 were manufactured only thirty-three were ever delivered for service in late 1942. Another failure was the Me 210 put into production by Udet and later cancelled by Milch when it became apparent that the aircraft was a death-trap.

By the end of 1940 Udet's health went into steep decline, he had a buzzing in his ears, and bleeding from his lungs and gums. He booked himself into a sanatorium in the Black Forest but only stayed a few days because he was convinced Milch wanted to take away his department. It wasn't long before Hitler started to question Göring and demanded to know why the Luftwaffe production schedules had fallen so far behind. Göring then turned on Udet and they had their first argument. In June 1941 Göring had a meeting with Milch, he ordered the State Secretary to step up mass production in all sectors and at all levels of armament. Milch was given full powers over all aircraft manufacture but Göring stopped short of actually replacing Udet with Milch. Göring however still cared about his old friend and in August 1941 advised him to take a holiday. He even invited Udet to spend time at his hunting lodge, but Udet had lost all interest in hunting and on 25th August he checked himself in at the Black Forest sanatorium once again. He did not return to work for several weeks. When he did finally return in October he found that his department had been completely reorganized, key members of his staff, including Generals Ploch and Tschersisch had been replaced.

On 15th November General Ploch visited Udet while on leave from the eastern front. He told him about the mass murder of the Jews. Udet was very upset. Ploch later said that Udet looked a broken man and drank heavily. In fact when Ploch left Udet drank two bottles of cognac and telephoned his mistress and told her he couldn't take anymore and was going to shoot himself. He said that he wanted to say goodbye to her and he told her, "… they are after me!" She was still trying to talk him out of it when he pulled the trigger. He left a suicide note to Göring and written across the wall above his bed in red was written, "Iron Man, why have you forsaken me".

Udet's suicide was hushed up and the Air Ministry issued a communiqué: "While testing a new weapon on 17th November 1941, the Director of air armament Generaloberst Ernst Udet suffered such a grave accident that he died of his injuries … The Führer has ordered a state funeral."[111]

Every Luftwaffe building in the Reich flew its flags at half-mast on the day of Udet's funeral. Almost every holder of the Knight's Cross attended, and every high ranking Luftwaffe officer attended; Hitler attended although he didn't speak. Göring was the last to appear, dressed in red-brown boots, light-grey uniform and gold braid. He spoke with emotion, "I can only say I have lost my friend."[112]

Ernst Udet is perhaps best known for the man who was responsible for the mass production of the Ju 87, the Stuka dive-bomber and it was Udet who came up with the idea of fixing the Stuka with a screaming siren that made the sound of its dive far more frightening, giving it a greatly enhanced psychological effect on soldiers and civilians alike. It should also be said that apart from Göring, it was Udet who was responsible for the early decline of the Luftwaffe, something it never fully recovered from.

The last resting place of Generaloberst Ernst Udet. (Private source)

Klaus Siegfried UEBE
(1900-1968)
Generalmajor

Knight's Cross: Awarded as *Generalmajor* and Chief of the General Staff of 1st Air Fleet on 9th June 1944 for actions in Russia.

Ranks:
Gefreiter – 18th July 1924
Unteroffizier – 1st November 1924
Fähnrich – 1st October 1925
Leutnant – 1st December 1926
Oberleutnant – 1st November 1929
Hauptmann – 1st July 1934
Hauptmann i.G. – 20th April 1938
Major i.G. – 1st October 1938
Oberstleutnant i.G. – 1st August 1941
Oberst i.G. – 1st July 1942
Generalmajor – 1st January 1944

Awards:
Iron Cross 2nd Class – World War II
Iron Cross 1st Class – World War II
Armed Forces Long Service Award 3rd Class
German Cross in Gold – 29th December 1942
Wehrmacht Daily Report: 10 March 1945

Klaus Uebe was born in Kammin, Pommern on 1st May 1900 and on leaving school he entered the 25th Reserve Infantry Regiment in June 1918, a few months before the end of the war. Uebe had to leave the army soon after Germany's surrender and like many others found it difficult to find work, but in February 1923 he re-entered the army with the infantry, as an officer candidate. He spent the next few months on various training courses and in December 1926 he was commissioned as a *Leutnant*, and two years later he was appointed adjutant with the 18th Infantry Regiment.

In May 1931 Uebe was accepted into the Flying School at Böblingen and undertook secret flying training and observer training. In October 1933 he entered the Luftwaffe with the rank of *Oberleutnant* and served at the Observer School in Braunschweig. In July 1934 he was made adjutant of the Bomber Wing "Boelcke" and promoted to Hauptman on the same day. In November 1935 he was assigned to the Reich Air Ministry as an advisor in the training and development department in Berlin. In October 1938 he was promoted to *Major* and took various staff positions within the Air Ministry, and a year later he was appointed Chief of Operations on the staff of the Chief of the Air Defence.

Uebe was appointed commander of the 3rd Group, 2nd Bomber Wing in September 1940 when he took over from *Major* Adolf Fuchs. He took part in "Eagle Day", the attack on England in preparation for the invasion. On 7th September he led his Group when it raided the London Docks, in fact the aerial bombardment of London continued throughout the night, as 660 tonnes of bombs and thousands of incendiaries rained down on the British capital. Over the next few weeks Uebe flew more missions out of Camrai, near Lille, and continued to bomb England, raids were expanded to Southampton, Brighton, Eastbourne, Canterbury, Yarmouth and Norwich.

In April 1941 Uebe was transferred to the 2nd Air Fleet to act as liaison officer between *Generalfeldmarschall* Kesselring and the commander of Army Group Centre *Generalfeldmarschall* von Bock. He established good relations between the two during the preparations for the invasion of the Soviet Union and in August Uebe was promoted to *Oberstleutnant* and made Chief of Operations with the 2nd Air Fleet who continued to support von Bocks Army Group on the Eastern Front during the attack on Moscow. In January 1942 the 2nd Air Fleet moved to Italy where it established its headquarters in Frascati near Rome, and where Uebe served until March 1942 when he was transferred to the 8th Air Corps as Chief of Staff under *Generalmajor* Martin Fiebig, seeing action in Smolensk.

In October 1942 he took over as Chief of Staff of Luftwaffe Command Don under *Generaloberst* Günther Korten in Kharkov supporting Army Group Don. In August 1943 he was transferred as Chief of Staff to the 1st Air Fleet near Ostrow under *General der Flieger* Kurt Pflugbeil. He continued to see heavy action against the Soviet forces and for his part in successfully supporting the ground troops in their offensive actions he was awarded the Knight's Cross on 9th June 1944. In December he became the last commander of the 4th Air Division in Frankfurt and helped to defend the Reich. Uebe took over as the Commanding General of the Luftwaffe Command East Prussia in January 1945 and he remained as commander until he surrendered to the British on 8th May 1945. He remained in Allied captivity until June 1947, and returned to Germany where he died on 5th February 1968 in Bad Godesberg.

Top: Generalmajor Klaus Uebe. (Wehrkundearchiv)

Bottom: Oberstleutnant Georg Tyroller with Oberst Klaus Uebe in the background. (Wehrkundearchiv)

Oskar VORBRUGG
(1902-1946)
Generalmajor

Oskar Vorbrugg as a Hauptmann during his time as an advisor for training of anti-aircraft artillery with the Luftwaffe General Staff, 1936. (Wehrkundearchiv)

Knight's Cross: Awarded on 9th June 1944 as *Oberst* and commander of 21st Flak Regiment for his part in the defence of Bobruisk.

Ranks:
Oberkanonier – 1st November 1921
Gefreiter – 1st September 1923
Fahnenjunker-Unteroffizier – 1st November 1924
Fähnrich – 1st October 1925
Oberfähnrich – 1st August 1926
Leutnant – 1st December 1926
Oberleutnant – 1st June 1929
Hauptmann – 1st January 1935
Major – 1st June 1938
Oberstleutnant – 1st July 1941
Oberst – 1st January 1943
Generalmajor – 25th February 1945

Awards:
Armed Forces Long Service Award 2nd Class
Iron Cross 2nd Class – 20th May 1940
Iron Cross 1st Class – 11th July 1940
Luftwaffe Anti-Aircraft Badge – 26th March 1943
German Cross in Gold – 27th October 1943
Pilot's Badge – 13th September 1937

Born on 11th July 1902 in Fürth, Oskar Vorbrugg left school and joined Germany's peace time army in May 1919. In August he entered the artillery with the 24th Regiment and by January 1921 he was an officer candidate with the 7th Artillery Regiment. After attending Infantry and Artillery School he was commissioned as a *Leutnant* in December 1926 and was assigned once again to the 7th Artillery Regiment as a battery officer.

In April 1935 he transferred with the rank of *Hauptmann* to the Luftwaffe and began his pilot training at the Air War Academy in Berlin. He was attached to a flying squadron in Cottbus in October 1935 and six months later was an advisor for training of anti-aircraft artillery with the Luftwaffe General Staff. In May he was transferred to the 1st Squadron, 254th Bomber Wing, and in June 1938 Vorbrugg was promoted to the rank of *Major*. In November he was appointed commander of 2nd Battalion, 24th Flak Regiment under *Oberst* Gaston von Chaulin-Egersberg[113] in Essen and later in Düsseldorf.

In February 1940 Vorbrugg was made Chief of Operations with the 2nd Flak Corps, which had been formed in Frankfurt in October 1939, and was now under the command *Generalmajor* Otto Deßloch. In Early 1940 it had been transferred to München-Gladbach where it took control of three Flak regiments the 103rd, 201st and the 202nd and was subordinated to 2nd Air Fleet. Here it supported Army Group B during the invasion of France and in March 1941 it moved to Grunau, Berlin in preparation for the attack on Russia. Vorbrugg was transferred in June 1941 as Chief of Operations with Air Region Command Holland, under *Generalleutnant* Hans Siburg[114] in Amsterdam, during which time he was promoted to *Oberstleutnant*. He became Chief of Staff to *Generalmajor* Rudolf Toussaint, the Wehrmacht Commander in Bohemia and Moravia (Czechoslovakia) in October 1941.

He was transferred to the Eastern Front in December 1942 as commander of the 21st Flak Regiment, part of 12th Flak Division and he fought at Spass-Demensk, Bryansk, Orel, Kursk, during the retreat to the Dneiper in 1943, part of Operation Bagration. In 1944 he also took part in the defence of Bobruisk and was awarded the Knight's Cross in recognition of his leadership on 9th June 1944. On 30th October 1944, now promoted to *Oberst*, Vorbrugg took command of the 23rd Flak Division in support of the 9th Army in the Warsaw-Radom-Posen area. In February 1945 he was promoted to *Generalmajor* and briefly commanded the 10th Flak Division when its commander *Generalmajor* Franz Engel[115] was on leave. His last command came on 10th February when he took over as commander of 25th Flak Division during the defence in the Brescia-Bergamo-Trient area, and after the collapse of Army Group South-West he surrendered along with his command to British troops on 2nd May 1945.

Whilst being held in Rimini, Italy by the British Vorbrugg was killed in an accident on 21st May 1946, he was forty-three years old.

A studio portrait of Generaloberst Hubert Weise taken shortly after his promotion. (Eric Stahel)

Hubert WEISE
(1884-1950)
Generaloberst

Knight's Cross: Awarded on 24th June 1940 as *General der Flakartillerie* and Commanding General of 1st Flak Corps, for his part in the fall of France.

Ranks:
Fahnenjunker – 27th September 1904
Fähnrich – 18th May 1905
Leutnant – 27th January 1906
Oberleutnant – 19th July 1913
Hauptmann – 27th January 1915
Major – 1st July 1927
Oberstleutnant – 1st December 1931
Oberst – 1st April 1934
Generalmajor – 1st August 1936
Generalleutnant – 1st April 1938
General der Flakartillerie – 25th October 1939
Generaloberst – 19th July 1940

Awards:
Iron Cross 2nd Class – September 1914
Iron Cross 1st Class – 1915
Wound Badge in Silver– September 1914
Knight's Cross of the Saxony Order of Albert with Swords
Cross of Honour for Frontline Combatants
Armed Forces Long Service Award 1st Class
Bar to Iron Cross 2nd Class – 2nd October 1939
Bar to Iron Cross 1st Class – 17th May 1940
German Cross in Gold – 14th January 1944

Hubert Weise was born in Erfurt on 22nd December 1884, after attending secondary school he joined the 75th Field Artillery Regiment in September 1904. In April 1905 he attended Military School at Danzig and won his commission in January 1907. He then spent almost three years at the Military Technical Academy in Berlin before being assigned to 7th Field Artillery Regiment at the beginning of World War I. On 13th September 1914 he was severely wounded when a shell exploded and fragments hit him in the head and almost blew off his left hand. Shortly afterwards while recovering in hospital he was awarded the Iron Cross 2nd Class and the Wound Badge in Silver. In February 1915, shortly after being promoted to *Hauptmann*, he was assigned to 64th Reserve Field Artillery Regiment and was appointed as a battalion commander. He saw heavy action on the Eastern Front where he was awarded the Iron Cross 1st Class. In December 1915 he served as adjutant of 79th Field Artillery Brigade before becoming a General Staff Officer with 3rd Reserve Corps. He ended the war as an intelligence officer while still attached to the General Staff of the same unit.

After the Armistice he remained in the Reichswehr and joined the Volunteer *Landesjägerkorps Maerker* as a battery commander. This unit had been formed from former members of 214th Infantry Division by General Ludwig von Maerker and was one of the first Freikorps units to be recognised by the government. Other notable members were *SS-Obergruppenführer* Reinhard Heydrich,[116] *SS-Obergruppenführer* Karl von Eberstein,[117] *Generaloberst* Hermann Hoth[118] and *General der Panzertruppe* Fridolin von Senger among others. For the next few years he served as a battery chief in various different units without really distinguishing himself. In February 1927 he took the position of training advisor with the Inspector of Artillery while attached to Reich War Ministry and was promoted in July 1927 to *Major*. In December 1931 he was promoted to *Oberstleutnant* and by April was made an *Oberst* appointed commander of 3rd Transport Battalion in Berlin. In early 1935 he joined the Luftwaffe and was appointed Chief of Staff to the Inspector of Anti-aircraft Artillery and became responsible for the air protection of the Reich. In August 1936 he was promoted to *Generalmajor* and appointed commander of Luftgau IV. In April 1938 he was promoted to *Generalleutnant* and appointed commander of Luftgau III, which covered the area of the Reich capital.

At the beginning of World War II Weise was appointed Commanding General of the 1st Flak Corps assigned in May 1940 to the Western Front. After his promotion to *General der Flakartillerie* in October 1939 he was soon promoted again after the fall of France to *Generaloberst* and was awarded the Knight's Cross for his part in the victory. From March 1942 until December 1943 he was the Commander of the Air defences and the anti-aircraft expert of the Reich. In March 1944 he was assigned as the chief of the anti-aircraft technical office with the Air Ministry, an appointment he saw as a demotion. He had been outspoken against the regime and had spoken against the more radical generals within the Luftwaffe and after the failed assassination attempt on Hitler he knew he was being watched and knew he had been sidelined. It didn't help when he ordered the removal of all anti-aircraft guns from Hamburg to Italy only two days before the first heavy RAF raid on the city.

His last appointment came in January 1945 when he was made Special Plenipotentiary of the Commander-in-Chief of the Luftwaffe for the Defence of hostile weapons, a grand title but he had little power and almost nobody under his command. In fact the defence of the Reich in Berlin was almost non-existent, only elderly troops and boys from the Hitler Youth! In May 1945 he decided it was time to leave Berlin and on 16th May he was captured by U.S. forces. He spent two years in an American prison and was released in July 1947 and returned home to his wife. He died at home on 14th February 1950 at the age of sixty-five in Bad Kohlgrub, Upper Bavaria.

Hubert Weise wearing the Knight's Cross during which time he was chief of the anti-aircraft technical office with the Air Ministry. (Author's collection)

Paul WEITKUS
(1898-1974)
Generalmajor

Knight's Cross: Awarded on 18th September 1941 as *Oberstleutnant* and Commander of 53rd Bomber Wing "Legion Condor" for actions over Russia.

Ranks:
Leutnant der Reserve – 21st September 1918
Polizei-Oberwachtmeister – 1st June 1921
Polizei-Leutnant – 24th December 1923
Polizei-Oberleutnant – 29th April 1927
Polizei-Hauptmann – 19th December 1933
Hauptmann – 1st August 1935
Major – 1st April 1936
Oberstleutnant – 1st June 1939
Oberst – 1st February 1942
Generalmajor – 30th January 1945

Awards:
Iron Cross 2nd Class
Iron Cross 1st Class
Armed Forces Long Service Award 3rd Class
Cross of Honour for Frontline Combatants
Combat Clasp for Bombers in Gold

Paul Weitkus was born on 17th October 1898 in Miswalde, East Prussia and joined the 150th Infantry Regiment as a war recruit in November 1916. He was commissioned as a *Leutnant* a few months before the end of the war and remained in the infantry for a time before joining the Freikorps Hülsen in March 1920, he finally left the army in March 1920.

In June 1921 Weitkus joined the Police in Potsdam and was promoted to *Polizei-Leutnant* in December 1923 and at the same time was made a platoon leader. In May 1927, now with the rank of *Polizei-Oberleutnant* Weitkus was transferred to the Police School in Spandau as an instructor and by December 1933 he had become a senior instructor with the rank of *Polizei-Hauptmann*. In August 1935 he transferred to the Luftwaffe where he was appointed as an instructor with the Luftwaffe Sports School again in Spandau, Berlin.

By October 1937 Weitkus had been promoted to *Major* and was assigned to the Air Ministry and was appointed Group Commander of 257th Bomber Wing in March 1938. In February 1939 he took over as commander of the 3rd Group, 2nd Bomber Wing and was promoted to *Oberstleutnant* in June. He took part during in the invasion of Poland where he won the Iron Cross 2nd Class and in May 1940 he saw action during the invasion of France and won the Iron Cross 1st Class. After the defeat of France he took part in the preparations for the invasion of Britain and later when this was called off he took part in the bombing campaign of Britain's cities. Weitkus took over as commander of the 53rd Bomber Wing "Legion Condor" in December 1940 and flew the He 111 during the invasion of Russia. He saw action over the skies of Radom, Minsk, Orscha, Schatalowka-Ost and many other towns and was very successful during the early stages of the campaign. On 18th September 1941 he was awarded the Knight's Cross for his leadership and success during the campaign. Promoted to *Oberst* in February 1942 Weitkus remained commander of the 53rd Bomber Wing until June 1944 when he took over from *Generalmajor* Walter Hagen as Air Leader Albania.

Weitkus was promoted to *Generalmajor* at the end of January 1945 and in March he took command of all Air Fleet Troops of the 4th Air Fleet, this was to be his last military command of the war. On 8th May 1945 he was captured and remained in Allied captivity for almost two years. He returned home in early 1947 where he worked in civilian life until his retirement. Paul Weitkus died in Arnsberg on 9th November 1974, he was seventy-six.

Paul Weitkus as an Oberst and commander of the 53rd Bomber Wing. (Wehrkundearchiv)

Gustav WILKE
(1898-1977)
Generalleutnant

Knight's Cross: Awarded as *Oberstleutnant* and Commander of Battle Group 11 on 29th May 1940 for actions during the French Campaign.

Ranks:
Fahnenjunker-Gefreiter – 2nd July 1917
Fahnenjunker-Unteroffizier – 8th July 1917
Fähnrich – 16th October 1917
Leutnant – 27th January 1918
Oberleutnant – 1st February 1927
Hauptmann – 1st April 1934
Major – 1st March 1937
Oberstleutnant – 1st November 1939
Oberst – 1st March 1942
Generalmajor – 20th April 1943
Generalleutnant – 1st May 1944

Awards:
Iron Cross 2nd Class – World War I
Iron Cross 1st Class – World War II
Pilots Badge
Bar to the Iron Cross 2nd Class
Armed Forces Long Service Award 2nd Class
Large Glider Pilot's Badge

Gustav Wilke was born in Deutsch Eylau on 6th March 1898, and at the age of eighteen he joined the army and was attached to the 4th Grenadier Regiment as an officer cadet. After completing various infantry courses he was commissioned as a *Leutnant* in January 1918 and was assigned as a Company Commander

Generalmajor Gustav Wilke. (Eric Stahel)

Gustav Wilke as an Oberstleutnant wearing the Knight's Cross as commander of Battle Group 11 during the French Campaign, May 1940. (Wehrkundearchiv)

to the 425th Infantry Regiment. He remained in the army until October 1919 and spending a few years unemployed he rejoined the military as an officer with the 2nd Infantry Regiment. Promoted to *Oberleutnant* in February 1927 he was transferred to the 2nd Infantry Regiment in October 1929 and by April 1934 he had been promoted to *Hauptmann*.

Wilke entered the Luftwaffe on 1st October 1935 and joined the flying school at Perleberg, and in October 1938 he joined the 23rd Flying Training Regiment. Promoted to *Oberstleutnant* in late 1939 he became Group Commander in the Air Landing Wing at Lippstadt. It was while leading this wing that he was awarded the Knight's Cross on 29th May 1940 for his leadership during the French Campaign. In September Wilke was made Commander of 1st Instruction Wing when its original commander Alfred Bülowius had been wounded and captured when his aircraft crashed, and during the time Bülowius was a prisoner of the French Wilke remained as commander seeing further action over France.

In September 1941 he worked closely with the Messerschmitt Company during the construction and development of the large glider transport aircraft. He became the Luftwaffe Special Representative, reporting back to Göring and Milch on the progress of the work. Three large transport gliders were made by Messerschmitt the Me 321, Me 329 and the Me 323 or *Gigant* (giant) which was put into production and widely used by the end of 1941 to great effect.

In May 1942, now promoted to *Oberst* Wilke was transferred to the Eastern Front where he was given command of the Luftwaffe Regiment "Wilke", and in September he returned to Germany to take charge of a new unit, the 1st Luftwaffe Field Division which had been formed in Königsberg, East Prussia from the 10th Air Regiment and consisted of four battalions, an anti-tank battalion; an artillery battalion; a flak battalion; a bicycle battalion and an engineer company. The division completed its training in late 1942 and was sent to Russia as part of Army Group North. Wilke led it into battle in the Lake Ilmen area and from December 1942 until October 1943 he was responsible for defending a sector near Nogorod.

Wilke was promoted to *Generalmajor* in April 1943 and towards the end of the year he was appointed commander of the 2nd *Fallschirmjäger* Division shortly after it had been transferred to Russia. While under the command of the XXXXII Army Corps its 6th Regiment was almost wiped out. It was down to the strength of 3,200 men by January 1944, but the division was still holding a front thirteen miles long. In April 1944 Wilke was made commander of the 5th *Fallschirmjäger* Division and a month later he was promoted to *Generalleutnant*. In June his Division was engaged in the fighting around the Normandy area and later was trapped in the Falaise Pocket. However in July before his command was completely encircled *SS-Oberstgruppenführer* Paul Hausser, the commander of the 7th Army listed the division as destroyed. The remnants of Wilkes' command were placed under the command of the 275th Infantry Division. As for Wilkes he managed to escape before the encirclement, leading his own Battle Group out of the area and to safety.

Towards the end of September 1944 Wilke was ordered to form the 9th *Fallschirmjäger* Division but this order was delayed shortly afterwards and then cancelled. However in December Wilke formed the division in the Stettin area, and although called the *Fallschirmjäger* Division it had very few paratroopers in it and so became a *Fallschirmjäger* unit by name only. Wilke led it during some fierce fighting at Stargard, at Stettin and at the Küstrin Bridgehead area in Pomerania. In March 1945 Wilke was succeeded by *General der Fallschirmtruppe* Bruno Brauer, after being ordered to form another Division, the 10th *Fallschirmjäger* Division in Austria. Wilke arrived in Graz on 10th March and hastily put together his new unit which included detachments from the 1st and 4th *Fallschirmjäger* Division, and also included about 4,000 troops from four air warfare schools. In fact this new unit never reached divisional strength and never reached more than battle group strength. It fought bravely against the Russians in the Danube Valley before being transferred to Czechoslovakia in the last desperate days of the war. Wilke surrendered with his command in Iglau in May 1945. He was finally released from captivity in July 1947 and returned home to his family. He died in Oberstdorf on 14th March 1977.

Adolf WOLF
(1899-1973)
Generalmajor

Generalmajor Adolf Wolf seen wearing the Knight's Cross, and German Cross in Gold in 1944 as commander of the 18th Motorised Flak Division. (Wehrkundearchiv)

Knight's Cross: Awarded on 10th July 1944 as *Oberstleutnant* and commander 1st Battalion, 64th Flak Regiment for actions in France.

Ranks:
Gefreiter – 10th September 1917
Fahnenjunker-Unteroffizier – 10th February 1918
Fähnrich – 16th July 1918
Leutnant – 27th September 1918
Polizei-Leutnant – 11th June 1920
Polizei-Oberleutnant – 24th May 1924
Polizei-Hauptmann – 26th March 1929
Hauptmann – 1st May 1935
Major – 1st April 1937
Oberstleutnant – 1st December 1939
Oberst – 1st March 1942
Generalmajor – 1st April 1944

Awards:
Iron Cross 2nd Class – 22nd August 1918
Iron Cross 1st Class – 17th December 1920
Brunswick War Service Cross 2nd Class – 10th May 1919
Wound Badge in Black – 14th June 1919
Cross of Honour for Frontline Combatants
Armed Forces Long Service Award 2nd Class
German Riders Badge in Bronze
Reich Sports Badge in Silver
Austrian War Commemorative Medal with Swords
Bar to Iron Cross 2nd Class
Bar to Iron Cross 1st Class
Luftwaffe Anti-Aircraft Badge – 5th November 1941

Luftwaffe Ground Assault Badge – 5th December 1942
German Cross in Gold – 10th July 1944

Adolf Wolf was born in Braunschweig on 23rd May 1899 and once he was old enough he took part in military training for the army in May 1915 at the age of sixteen. In April 1917 he graduated from the Kaiser Wilhelm Gymnasium in Hanover and in June he joined the Infantry as an Officer Cadet. After attending officer training school and serving as a Platoon Leader with the 164th Infantry Regiment he won the Iron Cross 2nd Class in 1918 and was commissioned as a *Leutnant* shortly after. In the last days of the war he was injured and spent almost six months in hospital while in a prisoner of war camp in France where he remained until April 1920. In June he entered the Prussian Police as a *Leutnant* and soon became a department head when he was promoted to *Oberleutnant* in May 1924. He went onto to serve as an adjutant with the Protection Police in Hannover and as a section leader being promoted to *Hauptmann* in May 1924. Later he commanded a police unit in Dusiberg-Hamborn and then he was appointed a battalion commander with the State Police in Sensburg.

On 1st October 1935 Wolf transferred to the Luftwaffe and was appointed as company leader with the 12th Company of the Luftwaffe Regiment "General Göring". Promoted to *Major* in April 1937 he became a battalion commander with the 64th Flak Regiment where he saw action in Poland in September 1939. In June 1940, now with the rank of *Oberstleutnant*, Wolf took part in the French Campaign. At this time the German advance had been in the direction of the English Channel and they had exposed their own flanks and the French were trying to advance on the Germans objective the Abbeville Bridgehead. However the Germans only had the 2nd Infantry Division and the 57th Infantry Division against a strong armoured French force, but a unit hastily formed under the commander of Wolf was on its way to help. Battle Group "Wolf" moved into position with its two heavy batteries and managed to secure the Abbeville Bridgehead and push back the French forces. Wolf fought against strong opposition and in doing so this allowed the German panzer troops to advance and secure victory and for this Wolf was awarded the Knight's Cross.

Towards the end of June 1940 Wolf was appointed commander of the 52nd Flak Regiment stationed in Berlin, waiting to be refitted, at the same time he was assigned as commander of Flak Group North-West Berlin being made responsible for the areas of Magdeburg and Mannheim-Ludwigshafen. In July 1941 he took command of the 49th Flak Regiment and became responsible for the defence of North-West Berlin. Wolf was promoted to *Oberst* in March 1942 and towards the end of 1943 he was briefly the commander of the 10th Motorised Flak Brigade in Russia supporting Army Group Centre. In February 1944 Wolf took over command of the 18th Motorised Flak Division and suffered heavy casualties during the summer offensive when Army Group centre had been smashed and the 9th Army had been virtually destroyed along with the 3rd Panzer Army. Wolf managed to lead his command across Lithuania and Poland and into East Prussia. Promoted to *Generalmajor* in April 1944, Wolf now took command of the 13th Flak Division where he fought in the ground battles at Le Mans, Strasbourg and Kolmar.

Oberstleutnant Adolf Wolf shortly after being awarded the Knight's Cross on 10th July 1944 as commander of the 1st Battalion, 64th Flak Regiment for actions in France. (Wehrkundearchiv)

From January 1945 he controlled thirty-seven heavy flak batteries, twenty-six medium and light batteries and a barrage balloon battery. In February he supported the 19th Army and the following month he gave up the remnants of his unit to the 28th Flak Division and his staff moved to Czechoslovakia. Shortly after the death of Hitler he moved his headquarters West and Wolf surrendered with his troops to the Americans on 8th May.

Wolf remained in American captivity until June 1945 when he was handed over to the British who interned him until February 1948. In December 1948 he was given permission to return to his family in Bayreuth which was in the American zone. His wife had survived the war but he had lost two of his three sons, the eldest had been killed in October 1944 and his second son was killed in March 1945 as an officer cadet in the "Hermann Göring" Division, only his youngest son survived. From 1952 until 1972 Wolf was the Chairman of the city Association for Physical Exercise and took a leading role in the German Olympic Society. In early 1973 he was taken ill and on 11th March he died at home in Bayreuth.

Alwin WOLZ
(1897-1978)
Generalmajor

Oberst Alwin Wolz wearing the Knight's Cross that he won during action in North Africa in June 1943. (Wehrkundearchiv)

Knight's Cross: Awarded on 10th June 1943 as *Oberst* and commander 135th Flak Regiment in North Africa.

Ranks:
Fahnenjunker-Gefreiter – 1st August 1916
Fahnenjunker-Unteroffizier – 16th September 1916
Fähnrich – 25th November 1916
Leutnant – 25th June 1917
Polizei-Leutnant – 24th November 1919
Polizei-Oberleutnant – 23rd April 1924
Polizei-Hauptmann – 21st November 1932
Hauptmann – 1st September 1935
Major – 1st August 1936
Oberstleutnant – 1st March 1939
Oberst – 1st July 1941
Generalmajor – 1st August 1944

Awards:
Iron Cross 2nd Class – World War I
Iron Cross 1st Class – World War I
Royal Bavarian Military Service Cross 4th Class with Swords
Wound Badge in Black – World War I
Cross of Honour for Frontline Combatants
Armed Forces Long Service Award 2nd Class
Bar to Iron Cross 2nd Class
Bar to Iron Cross 1st Class
German Cross in Gold – 21st August 1942
Italian Silver Medal for Bravery – 1st November 1942
Luftwaffe Ground Assault Badge
AFRIKA Cufftitle

Born on 22nd September 1897 in Windsfeld, Gunzenhausen, Alwin Wolz is credited with setting up the wars first flak front in North Africa in May 1942. He joined the Wilhelmshaven Replacement Naval Battalion as a volunteer on 1st August 1915 at the age of seventeen. He was made an officer candidate in August 1916 after transferring to the 5th Bavarian Infantry Regiment where he remained until the end of the war. In June 1917 he was commissioned as a *Leutnant* and won both the Iron Cross 1st and 2nd Classes, as well as various high Bavarian awards.

In April 1919 he joined the Freikorps in Bamberg as a Platoon Leader and later joined the 46th Reichswehr Infantry Regiment and later the 5th Bavarian Infantry Regiment. In November he joined the Bavarian State Police with the rank of *Polizei-Leutnant*. He went onto serve in Nuremberg and trained as a motor vehicle officer and in November 1923 was made Transport Battalion Leader in Regensburg. Promoted to *Polizei-Oberleutnant* in April 1924 and to *Polizei-Hauptmann* in November 1932 he was made leader of the 2nd Police Unit in Ludwigshafen in April 1933.

In September 1935 he transferred to the Luftwaffe with the rank of *Hauptmann* and was assigned to the Luftwaffe officer training school at Berlin-Gatow. In 1936 he was transferred to Munich where he was made commander of the 5th Flak Regiment. Promoted to *Major* in August and two months later he was appointed commander of the Searchlight Battery of the 25th Flak Regiment in Ludwigsberg. In March 1939 he was promoted to *Oberstleutnant* and appointed Commander of the 25th Flak Regiment seeing action later with this unit in France, where he was very successful during the fighting near the Maginot Line.

After seeing action in France Wolz served in various flak units and in July 1941 was promoted to *Oberst* and took command of the 135th Flak Regiment as well as being made Flak Leader with Rommel's Panzer Army Afrika in February 1942. On 27th May Rommel launched "Operation Venezia", the plan to encircle the Gazala Line near Tobruk. The 15th Panzer Division attacked the British and chased them across the dessert when the British 2nd Armoured Division along with the 1st Tank Brigade attacked the Germans from behind. At this time General Nehring, the commander of the Africa Corps along with Wolz was observing the action when Rommel arrived and wanted to know why Wolz hadn't engaged the British with his 88mm flak guns. Wolz then decided to take action and organised his 88mm guns into a line facing the fast approaching British armour. Nehring formed seven of the 88s into a battle group and ordered Wolz to take command of the unit. Wolz now positioned the guns 150 metres apart and lined them up. The British were vastly superior in numbers but the 88's range and penetration gave them the edge. The British tanks began to open fire and charged towards the line of 88s, when the range decreased to 1,200 metres Wolz gave the order to fire. When the battle was over twenty-five British armoured cars had been destroyed or knocked out of action. Wolz went onto score more victories with his 88s and during the withdrawal southwest of El Agareb his unit destroyed fifty enemy tanks.

In May 1943 Wolz left North Africa and briefly commanded the 10th Flak Brigade in Hannover succeeding *Generalmajor* Friedrich Römer.[119] In June he was awarded the Knight's Cross for his leadership and success during combat in North Africa. In May 1944 he was made commander of the 3rd Flak Division in Hamburg but during the first few weeks of his command the unit was almost destroyed by Allied air raids. Promoted to *Generalmajor* in August, and he became Battle Commandant of Hamburg from April 1945. His old division was now commanded by *Generalmajor* Otto Stange[120] but came under his authority as part of Battle Commandant of Hamburg. Wolz surrendered to the British on 4th May 1945 when he handed over the city to Brigadier John Spurling at the City Hall.

Wolz remained in British captivity until July 1947 and returned to Germany once released. Alwin Wolz died on 15th September 1978 in Vaterstetten near Munich.

APPENDICES

Rank Equivalents

Luftwaffe	***United States Army***	***British Army***
Reichsmarschall	N/A	N/A
Generalfeldmarschall	5 Star General	Field Marshal
Generaloberst	N/A	N/A
General der —	4 Star General	General
Generalleutnant	3 Star General	Lieutenant-General
Generalmajor	2 Star General	Major-General
N/A	1 Star General	Brigadier
Oberst	Colonel	Colonel
Oberstleutnant	Lieutenant Colonel	Lieutenant Colonel
Major	Major	Major
Hauptmann	Captain	Captain
Oberleutnant	1st Lieutenant	Lieutenant
Leutnant	2nd Lieutenant	2nd Lieutenant
Stabsfeldwebel	Sergeant Major	Sergeant Major
Oberfeldwebel	Master Sergeant	Master Sergeant
Feldwebel	Technical Sergeant	Staff Sergeant
Unteroffizier	Sergeant	Sergeant
Hauptgefreiter	N/A	N/A
Obergefreiter	Corporal	Corporal
Gefreiter	Private First Class	Lance Corporal
Flieger	Private	Private
Fähnenjunker	–	Officer Cadet

Fähnrich – Officer Candidate. A soldier who served in the ranks, first as a junior non-commissioned officer then with the rank of *Feldwebel* or *Unteroffizier*. The end goal is to create an officer.

Oberfähnrich – as above but serving in the ranks as an *Oberfeldwebel*.

The following tables show various statistics relating to the Luftwaffe Generals in this book.

The twenty youngest generals of the Luftwaffe.
The age is taken from when they were promoted to the rank of *Generalmajor*.

Dietrich Peltz 29
Adolf Galland..30
Hubertus Hitschhold 32
Ulrich Diesing..33
Walter Storp 34
Heinrich Trettner..36
Hans Kroh 37
Karl-Heinrich Schulz 37
Walter Grabmann 38
Friedrich Kless 38
Karl-Lothar Schulz...38
Hermann Göring 40
Martin Harlinghausen 40
Hans Jeschonnek 40
Franz Reuss 40
Hans Seidemann..40
Ernst Udet 40
Ludwig Heilmann 41
Günther Korten 41
Erhard Milch 41

The twenty oldest generals of the Luftwaffe.
The age is taken from when they were promoted to the rank of *Generalmajor*.

August Schmidt..54
Alfred Keller 53
Gotthard Frantz 53
Alfred Sturm 52
Bernhard Ramcke..52
Hubert Weise 51
Rainer Stahel 51
Friedrich-Wilhelm Morzik 51
Walter von Hippel 51
Hugo Sperrle 50
Hermann Lichtenberger 50
Stefan Fröhlich..50
Karl Angerstein 50
Alexander Löhr 49
Otto Deßloch 49
Alfred Bülowius 49
Otto Sydow 48
Ludwig Schulz 48
Richard Reimann 48

The average age of a general in the Luftwaffe was forty-five.

Age and date of death of the twenty oldest Luftwaffe generals who won the Knight's Cross.

Kurt Andersen	9th January 2003	104
Heinrich Trettner	18th September 2006	98
Karl Angerstein	20th September 1985	94
Friedrich-Wilhelm Morzik	17th June 1985	94
Alfred Keller	11th February 1974	91
Alfons Luczny	12th August 1985	91
Alfred Schlemm	24th January 1986	91
Hans Korte	8th April 1990	90
Job Odebrecht	20th November 1982	90
Josef Kammhuber	25th January 1986	89
Stefan Fröhlich	2nd October 1978	88
Ulrich Kessler	27th March 1983	88
Franz Reuss	5th June 1992	88
Kurt Student	1st July 1978	88
Gerhard Conrad	28th May 1982	87
Otto Deßloch	13th May 1977	87
Friedrich Kless	6th April 1994	87
Dietrich Peltz	10th August 2001	87
Wolfgang Pickert	19th July 1984	87
Johannes Fink	1st June 1981	86

Twenty Luftwaffe generals with their death dates – in order of most recent.

Heinrich Trettner	18th September 2006
Kurt Andersen	9th January 2003
Dietrich Peltz	10th August 2001
Adolf Galland	9th February 1996
Friedrich Kless	6th April 1994
Walter Grabmann	11th July 1992
Franz Reuss	5th June 1992
Hans Korte	8th April 1990
Karl-Heinrich Schulz	28th July 1986
Martin Harlinghausen	23rd March 1986
Josef Kammhuber	25th January 1986
Alfred Schlemm	24th January 1985
Karl Angerstein	20th September 1985
Alfons Luczny	12th August 1985
Friedrich-Wilhelm Morzik	17th June 1985
Wolfgang Pickert	19th July 1984
Ulrich Kessler	27th March 1983
Wilhelm Schmalz	15th March 1983
Job Odebrecht	20th November 1982
Gerhard Conrad	28th May 1982

Youngest Luftwaffe Knight's Cross winners – their age at the time of the award.

Dietrich Peltz 26
Adolf Galland..28
Hubertus Hitschhold 28
Walter Storp 30
Ulrich Diesing..31
Heinrich Trettner..32
Friedrich Kless...33
Karl-Lothar Schulz...33
Walter Grabmann 34
Hans Kroh 34
Erich Walther 36
Ludwig Heilmann 37
Martin Harlinghausen 38
Karl-Heinrich Schulz 38
Oskar Dinort...38
Wilhelm Schmalz..39
Franz Reuss..40
Hanns-Horst von Necker..40
Hans Seidemann...40
Hans Jeschonnek 40

Oldest Luftwaffe Knight's Cross winners with the rank of general.

August Schmidt..62
Kurt Pflugbeil...59
Alfred Keller 57
Gotthard Frantz 55
Hugo Sperrle 55
Hubert Weise..55
Alexander Löhr 54
Albert Kesselring 53
Job Odebrecht 52
Bernhard Ramcke...52
Hans-Jurgen Stumpff 52
Alfred Sturm 52
Friedrich-Wilhelm Morzik.....................................51
Otto Deßloch..51
Ernst Buffa 51
Maximilian von Pohl..51
Ulrich Grauert 51
Alfons Luczny..50
Stefan Fröhlich...50

Break down of the different general ranks, and how many officers were promoted to that particular rank.

Reichsmarschall...1
Generalfeldmarschall 5
Generaloberst 11
General der Fallschirmtruppe 6
General der Flakartillerie..5
General der Flieger 18
Generalleutnant 30
Generalmajor...39

ENDNOTES

1. The first Knight's Cross winners were presented their awards by Hitler, and there were eleven recipients: *General der Infanterie* Johannes Blaskowitz; *Generalfeldmarschall* Hermann Göring; *Generaloberst* Wilhelm Keitel; *General der Flieger* Albert Kesselring; *General der Artillerie* Günther von Kluge; *General der Artillerie* Georg von Küchler; *Generaloberst* Wilhelm List; *General der Flieger* Alexander Löhr; *Großadmiral* Erich Raeder; *General der Artillerie* Walter von Reichenau and *Generaloberst* Gerd von Rundstedt.

2. Forty Foreign nationals were awarded the Knight's Cross, including: Italo Gariboldi, the Italian Commander of 8th Army on 1st April 1943; Nikolaus Horthy, commander-in-chief of the Hungarian 3rd Army on 10th September 1941; Carl Gustav Emil Mannerheim, commander-in-chief of Finnish Armed Forces and Isoraku Yamamoto, commander-in-chief of the Imperial Japanese Fleet on 27th May 1943.

3. Karl Dönitz – Commander-in-chief of the German Navy (Kriegsmarine) from 1943 until 1945. He was appointed commander-in-chief of U-Boats in 1939, and in January 1943 he succeeded *Großadmiral* Erich Raeder as commander-in-chief of the Kriegsmarine. Named as Hitler's successor on 1st May 1945, and was head of State for twelve days. Arrested in Flensburg in May 1945, he was tried at Nuremberg and sentenced to ten years imprisonment. He was released on 1st October 1956. He died on 24th December 1980 in Aumühle near Hamburg.

4. Franz von Papen – Reich Chancellor in 1932 and Hitler's Deputy Chancellor 1933-1935. He narrowly escaped with his life at the time of the Blood Purge in June 1934. Arrested at the end of the war and tried at Nuremberg but was acquitted on all counts. Later tried as a "Major Offender" and was sentenced to eight years imprisonment in February 1947, but was released in January 1949. He died on 2nd May 1969 in Oberasbach.

5. Hjalmar Schacht – President of the Reichsbank from 1933 until 1939. He was almost Minister of Economics, a position he held from 1934 until 1937. He was the financial architect of Nazi Germany; he was the first Commissioner of the Four Year Plan. In November 1937 he resigned as Minister of Economics and Plenipotentiary-General for the War Economy and was replaced by Walther Funk. He was dismissed as Reichsbank President in January 1939 after a disagreement with Hitler over the outbreak of World War II. After the failure of the July 1944 plot to kill Hitler he was arrested and sent to Ravensbrück and then Flossenburg concentration camps. Freed by the Americans in 1945 he was however arrested and tried at Nuremberg, but was acquitted. He was later sentenced to eight years imprisonment by a de-Nazification court and was released in September 1948. Schacht died on 3rd June 1970 in Munich.

6. Werner von Blomberg – Hitler's Minister for War and his first *Generalfeldmarschall*. A tall impressive looking man, he came from an officer's family. He played a critical role in Hitler's consolidation of power, and he assured Hitler of the army's loyalty after the June 1934 Blood Purge. In 1935 he was appointed commander-in-chief of the Armed Forces (Wehrmacht) and was made *Generalfeldmarschall* in 1936. After a scandal regarding his wife he resigned in February 1938. Von Blomberg died in American detention on 14th March 1946.

7. Werner von Fritsch – Chief of the High Command of the German Army 1934-1938. He was against Hitler's war plans and was a friend of President von Hindenburg. He was totally against the Nazis and the SS and wanted to be an "apolitical soldier" and was against any acts of aggression with Germany's neighbours until at least as he thought Germany was ready. Hitler had to get rid of him and after a sex scandal von Fritsch resigned from the army. He was later recalled to the army in an honorary position as colonel-in-chief of his old regiment (12th Artillery). Von Fritsch died in strange circumstances during the Polish Campaign in 1939; apparently he walked into the field of fire of a Polish machine gunner.

8. Irving, David: *Göring: A Biography*. London: Focal Point, 1989

9. Martin Bormann – Born on 17th June 1900 in Halberstadt, he joined the Party in 1927 and became chief-of-staff to Hitler's Deputy Rudolf Hess in July 1933. He was appointed *Reichsleiter* in October 1933 and made head of the Reich Chancellery in May 1941 after Hess flew to England on a supposed peace mission. He became Hitler's personal secretary in April 1943. He stayed with Hitler in the Bunker in the final days of the Reich, and was instrumental in getting both Göring and Himmler dismissed from the Party. He disappeared at the end of the war, and it wasn't until 1972 that his body was found buried in Berlin (identified as Bormann's in 1973). He had taken poison while trying to escape the city on 2nd May 1945.

10. Harris, Whitney R: *Tyranny on Trial. The Evidence at Nuremberg*. Southern Methodist UP, 1954.

11. Lufthansa – Germany's commercial airline.

12. *Truppenamt* – or "Troop Office" was the cover organization for the German General Staff from 1919 through until 1933 when the General Staff was recreated. This subterfuge was deemed necessary in order for Germany to be seen to meet the requirements of the Versailles Treaty. It completely revised German tactical and strategic doctrine and thereby conserved, re-energized and unified the military thinking and capability of the Reichswehr, later to become the Wehrmacht.

13. Fedor von Bock – *Generalfeldmarschall* who commanded Army Group North during the attack on Poland. In 1940 von Bock led Army Group B in Holland, Belgium and into Western France. He was one of the twelve generals appointed to *Generalfeldmarschall* by Hitler on 19th July 1940. Later von Bock commanded Army Group Centre in Russia, and when the offensive against

Moscow broke down von Bock was dismissed. He was briefly recalled to command Army Group South, but an argument with Hitler resulted in his final sacking in July 1942. Von Bock was killed in an Allied air raid on Schleswig-Holstein on 4th May 1945.

14. Heinrich von Vietinghoff – Extremely capable soldier, who commanded the 5th Panzer Division during the Polish Campaign. He later went onto serve in the Western Campaign when he commanded the XIII Corps and from late September 1940 he led the XXXXVI Panzer Corps in the Balkans and Russia. He was promoted to *Generaloberst* and named Supreme Commander West in early 1945 but was relieved of his command by Kesselring in April. A few days later Vietinghoff surrendered to the Allies. Winner of the Knight's Cross and Oakleaves von Vietinghoff died on 23rd February 1952 in Pfronten.

15. Gerd von Rundstedt – *Generalfeldmarschall* of the German Army during World War II. He held some of the highest field commands in all phases of the war. Von Rundstedt was promoted to field marshal on July 19, 1940 and took part in the planning of Operation Sealion. When the invasion was called off, von Rundstedt took control of occupation forces and was given responsibility to develop the coastal defenses in the Netherlands, Belgium and France. June 1941 von Rundstedt took part in Operation Barbarossa as commander of Army Group South, where he led fifty-two infantry divisions and five Panzer divisions into the Soviet Union. Ultimately he never faced trial, allegedly because of his poor health. He was released in July 1948, and lived in Hanover until his death in February 1953.

16. Kesselring, Albert: *The Memoirs of Field Marshal Kesselring* London: Kimber, 1953.

17. Ewald von Kleist – During the invasion of Poland, Kleist commanded the XXII Panzer Corps. In the Battle of France he commanded Panzergruppe von Kleist, consisting of XLI Panzer Corps and XIX Panzer Corps, the two southernmost armored corps in the drive to the English Channel. During this time he attempted to relieve Guderian of his command after he and his subordinate, Rommel, disobeyed orders to halt their advance to the Channel; the Wehrmacht chief-of-staff, Gerd von Rundstedt, refused to confirm the order, and the Franco-British armies were trapped. In April 1941, Kleist commanded 1st Panzergruppe, comprising XVIII and XL Panzer Corps, which spearheaded the Blitzkrieg-style invasions of Yugoslavia and Greece. With this formation he also participated in the subsequent Operation Barbarossa as part of Army Group South. Kleist was captured by United States forces in 1945. He was sent to communist Yugoslavia to face alleged war crimes charges in 1946. In 1948 he was then extradited to the Soviet Union where he was condemned to a ten-year sentence in 1952 for war crimes and he died in captivity in Vladimir Prison in 1954.

18. Julius Ringel – an Austrian born in German Genera. He commanded the 3rd Mountain Division, 5th Mountain Division, LXIX Army Corps, Wehrkreis XI and the Corps He was also a recipient of the Knight's Cross (13.06.1941) and the Oakleaves (25.10.1943). Ringel died on 10th February 1967 in Bay risch Gmain.

19. Günther von Kluge – Commander of the 4th Army during the Polish Campaign in 1939. Though he opposed the plan to attack westward, he led the Fourth Army in its attack through the Ardennes that culminated in the fall of France. Promoted to *Generalfeldmarschall* in July 1940, he continued to command the Fourth Army in Operation Barbarossa, where he also developed a strained relationship with Heinz Guderian over tactical issues in the advance and accused him of frequent disobedience of Kluge's orders. After von Bock was relieved of his command of Army Group Center in late 1941, Kluge was promoted and led that army group until he was injured in October 1943. On October 27, 1943, Kluge was badly injured when his car overturned on the Minsk-Smolensk road. He was unable to return to duty until July 1944. After his recovery he became commander of the German forces in the West as Gerd von Rundstedt's replacement. He was part of the plot to kill Hitler and committed suicide in August 1944.

20. Ernst Busch – Served under Wilhelm List during the Invasion of Poland of 1939, and the following year he led the German Sixteenth Army during the Western Offensive. Busch took part in Operation Barbarossa and in September 1941 his 16th Army took Demjansk before taking part in the siege of Leningrad. Despite a counterattack by the Red Army, Busch's troops held the line from Staraya Russa to Ostashkov. After a brave defense of his position he was promoted to field marshal. He commanded Army Group Centre in 1943 and 1944 but after the disastrous defeat of June 1944, he was sacked by Hitler early in July 1944 and replaced by GFM Walther Model. Busch was recalled in March 1945 when he became head of Army Group Northwest. Along with Kurt Student and his 1st Parachute Army, Busch had the task of trying to halt the advance of Field Marshal Bernard Montgomery and the Allies into Germany. Busch surrendered to Montgomery on 3rd May, 1945, and died in a prisoner of war camp in Aldershot, England, on 17 July 1945.

21. Werner Kreipe – Born in Hannover in April 1904 Werner Kreipe became Chief of the General Staff of the 1st Air Corps in November 1941 with the rank of *Oberstleutnant*. By August 1944 he had been appointed Chief of the General Staff of the Luftwaffe, and in September 1944 was promoted to *General der Flieger*. Awarded the German Cross in Gold in June 1942, he was captured by the Allies in May 1945 and released in 1947. He died on 7th September 1967 in Badenweiler.

22. Hanna Reitsch – German aviatrix who was once Adolf Hitler's personal pilot, and was the only woman awarded the Iron Cross First Class, and Luftwaffe Diamond Clasp during World War II. Reitsch was the first female to fly a helicopter, fly a rocket plane, fly a jet fighter and fly a glider over the Alps. She set over forty aviation altitude and endurance records during her career, both before and after World War II, and several of her international gliding records are still standing to this day. After leaving Hitler's Bunker for the last time she was soon captured along with von Greim and the two were interviewed together by American military intelligence officers. She was held and interrogated for eighteen months. Her father killed her mother, her sister, and her sister's children, before killing himself during the last days of the war after expulsion by the Polish from their hometown of Hirschberg. Reitsch died in Frankfurt at the age of sixty-seven on 24 August 1979 following a heart attack. She never married.

23. Dr. Ludwig Stumpfegger – In 1945, Stumpfegger started working directly for Hitler in the Führerbunker in Berlin under the direction of Dr. Theodor Morell. At Hitler's request, he administered a cyanide tablet to Blondi, the German shepherd dog which was a gift from Martin Bormann, to see how quickly it worked. Hitler said he wanted to see how quickly the German Army generals would die after taking their cyanide tablets. As the Red Army advanced towards the bunker, some sources claim that he helped Magda Goebbels murder her children before she and her husband Joseph Goebbels committed suicide. After 21:00 on 1 May, Stumpfegger left Führerbunker in a breakout group that included Martin Bormann and Hitler Youth leader Artur Axmann. They emerged from an underground subway tunnel and quickly became disoriented among the ruins and ongoing battle. They walked for a time with some German tanks, but all three were temporarily stunned by an exploding anti-tank shell. Leaving the tanks and the rest of their group, they walked along railway tracks to Lehrter station where Axmann decided to go alone in the opposite direction of his two companions. When he encountered a Red Army patrol, Axmann doubled back and later insisted he had seen the bodies of Bormann and Stumpfegger near the railway switching yard with moonlight clearly illuminating their faces. Their remains have recently been uncovered, and genetically identified. Fragments of glass found in the two men's jawbones, lead to the conclusion that they committed suicide via cyanide capsules.

24. Willibald Utz – Commander 100th Mountain Jäger Regiment when he won the Knight's Cross on 21st June 1941. He ended the war as a *Generalleutnant* and died on 20th April 1954 in Bad Reichenhall.

25. Fridolin von Senger und Etterlin – German general who took part in the French Campaign, and commanded the 17th Panzer Division during the attack on Russia and then took part in the Italian Campaign. On 8th October 1943, he received the command of the XIV Panzer Corps in Italy, and on January 1, 1944, he was promoted *General der Panzertruppen*. During the Battle of Monte Cassino, von Senger und Etterlin was responsible for the very successful defense of the Gustav Line, which included Monte Cassino. The German position was only broken by the Allies in May, 1944. He was one of the generals who opposed the principles of Nazism, but unlike many of his fellow anti-Nazis he was not implicated in the plot to kill Hitler. He was awarded the Knight's Cross with Oakleaves on 5th April 1944 as *General der Panzertruppe* and commanding general of the XIV Panzer Corps. He died on 4th January 1963 in Freiburg.

26. Traugott Herr – An excellent panzer general who was awarded the Knight's Cross with Oakleaves and Swords on 18th December 1944 as *General der Panzertruppe* and commanding general of the LXXVI Panzer Corps. He died on 13th April 1976 in Achterwehr, Schleswig-Holstein.

27. Clemens Graf von Schönborn-Wiesentheid-Borin in Munich in April 1905 Schönborn-Wiesentheid was awarded the Knight's Cross on 21st July 1940, and he was killed in an aircraft crash over Bulgaria on 30th August 1944 as Air Attaché of the German Embassy in Sofia and as Head of the German Luftwaffe Mission in Bulgaria.

28. Joachim von Ribbentrop – Hitler's Foreign Minister from February 1938 until April 1945. Ribbentrop served in the German Army in World War I. He was awarded the Iron Cross for bravery in action and was transferred into the intelligence department, where he was trained by von Papen. An arrogant man who married the daughter of a wealthy grower of champagne grapes. His new wealth inspired him to enter society, and add "von" to his name. Most people considered Ribbentrop incompetent and lazy, but Hitler was impressed by his connections. Ribbentrop negotiated the agreement between Russia and Germany by which these two nations agreed to attack and divide Poland. With the outbreak of World War II came the end of Ribbentrop's career as a diplomat so curry favour with Hitler he encouraged Germany's allies to join the plan to exterminate the Jews. For this he was sentenced to death at Nuremberg in October 1946.

29. Georg-Hans Reinhardt – German panzer general who was awarded the Knight's Cross on 27th October 1939 as commander of the 4th Panzer Division. He was awarded the Oakleaves and later Swords in May 1944 as *Generaloberst* and Commander-in-Chief of the 3rd Panzer Army. He saw action in Poland and Soviet Union and died on 23rd November 1963 in Tegernsee.

30. Erich von dem Bach-Zelewski – He was born on 1st March 1890 in Lauenburg. He went on to become Himmler's Anti-Partisan Chief from October 1942 until November 1944. He ended the war as *SS-Obergruppenführer und General der Polizei* and was awarded the Knight's Cross on 30th September 1944. He was tried for war crimes after the war and was sentenced to four and a half years in 1961. He died in a Munich hospital in March 1972.

31. Oskar Dirlewanger – Commanded the infamous SS-Sturmbrigade Dirlewanger unit made from amnestied Germans convicted of major crimes. Oskar Dirlewanger was an infantry officer in World War I and won both the Iron Cross 2nd Class and the Iron Cross 1st Class. After the end of war he joined different Freikorps and fought in the Ruhr Area, in Saxonia and in June 1921 in Upper Silesia. Between his militant employments he studied at the university in Frankfurt and in the year 1922 he attained a PhD in political science. He joined the NSDAP in 1923, but was eventually expelled. He served in the Condor Legion in the Spanish Civil War from 1936 to 1939 and he was wounded three times. This helped redeem his reputation and with help of the Nazi party his Doctor title was restored by the University of Frankfurt/Main. In June 1945, French occupation forces used Polish soldiers in their service to forcibly bring him to the Altshausen jail. Dirlewanger was beaten and tortured over the next several days. He died from injuries inflicted by the Polish guards on June 4 or 5, 1945.

32. Eduard Dietl – Dietl commanded the German 3rd Mountain Division that participated in the German invasion of Norway on April 9 and 10, 1940. British naval forces led by the battleship HMS Warspite destroyed all ten destroyers that had ferried Dietl's troops to Narvik and managed to recapture the town, but Dietl's mountaineers withdrew into the hills and later retook the town when Britain abandoned her efforts to evict the Germans from Norway due to Nazi aggression on the western front. A convinced Nazi, he was one of Hitler's favorite generals, the first German soldier to receive, on 19 June 1940, the Oakleaves to the Knight's Cross. Dietl subsequently commanded German forces in Norway and Finland and in Eastern Europe and rose to the rank of *Generaloberst*, commanding the 20th Mountain Army on the northern Eastern Front, where the results of the German Arctic campaign were disappointing. On June 23, 1944, Ju 52 aircraft carrying Dietl, *General der Infanterie* Thomas-Emil von Wickede, *General der Gebirgstruppe* Karl Eglseer, *Generalleutnant* Franz Rossi and three other passengers crashed in the vicinity of the small village of Rettenegg, Styria. All on board, including Dietl died.

33. Walter Nehring – During the Invasion of Poland, Nehring served under Heinz Guderian. He later took command of the Afrika Korps in May 1942 and took part in the Battle of Alam Halfa during which he was wounded in an air raid. Between November and December 1942, he commanded the German contingent in Tunisia. After North Africa, Nehring was posted to the Eastern Front where he commanded the XXIV Panzer Corps, and from July to August 1944 the Fourth Panzer Army. In March 1945, just before the end of the war, he was made commander of the 1st Panzer Army. He died on 20th April 1983.

34. Sigmund Wilhelm List – List was born in Oberkirchberg near Ulm, Württemberg, Germany in 1880 and entered the Bavarian Army in 1898 as a cadet. In 1900 he was promoted to *Leutnant* and in 1913 he joined the general staff as a *Hauptmann*. He served as a staff officer in World War I. During 1939 List commanded the German 14th Army in the invasion of Poland. From 1939 to 1941 he commanded the German 12th Army in France and Greece. During 1941 he was commander-in-chief South-East. In July 1942 he was commander-in-chief of Army Group A on the Eastern Front in the Soviet Union. List was captured by the Allies after the war and was charged with war crimes and crimes against humanity in the Hostages Trial at Nuremberg. He was sentenced to life imprisonment in February 1948. List was released from prison in December 1952 officially because of ill health; however, he lived for another nineteen years, dying on August 17, 1971.

35. Dr. Lothar Rendulic – In September 1939 he was Chief of Staff of XVII Army Corps in Poland. In June 1940 he was commander of 14th Infantry Division and saw action in France. Promoted to *General der Infanterie* in December 1942, he was wounded in action on 15th April 1943. He was appointed commander-in-chief of 2nd Panzer Army and in April 1944 he was promoted to *Generaloberst*. He went onto command the 2oth Mountain Army and between January and May 1945 he commanded Army Groups Kurland, North, South and Ostmark. He was awarded the Knight's Cross with Oakleaves and Swords in January 1945. He died on 18th January 1971 Eferding, Austria.

36. Ludwig Beck – Former Chief of the General Staff of the Army from July 1935 until August 1938, when he was sacked. He lived quietly in retirement but became a secret mentor of the older generals and became the recognized head of the anti-Hitler movement. An operation for cancer in 1943 left him a shell of his former self. Beck's failure to act effectively on 20th July 1944 cost him his life. He was offered the privilege of shooting himself but after two failed attempts that merely rendered him unconscious, a sergeant administered the coup de grâce: a pistol shot in the neck shortly after midnight on 20-21 July 1944.

37. Ernst Blauensteiner – Knight's Cross winner as *Oberstleutnant* and chief-of-staff of the 2nd Fallschirmjäger Corps on 29th October 1944. Saw action in the western campaign and was awarded the German Cross in Gold on 5th September 1944. He died on 18th August 1995 in Vienna, Austria.

38. West Wall – The fortified line along Germany's western border, from the Swiss border through the Upper Rhine, the Palatine Forest, and the Saar Territory, up to the area north of Aachen. Also known as the Siegfried Line. Said to be impregnable, the West Wall had an intimidating effect on the Western Powers in 1939-1940. When it was put to the test in 1944-1945 against the Allied invasion, some of the installations turned out to be useless.

39. Hellmuth Bieneck – Born in November 1887 Bieneck served in the infantry and from 1913 he was a pilot during World War I. He joined the Luftwaffe in January 1934 and was made commander of the 4th Air Division in October 1936 and was promoted to *Generalmajor* in 1938. In February 1941 he was made Commanding General of Luftgau II in Posen and in July was promoted to *General der Flieger*. His last wartime command was as Commanding General of Luftgau I in Königsberg. Bieneck went on the Reserve List in August 1944 and never returned to active service. He died in Cologne on 8th March 1972.

40. Fritz Löb – He joined the army in February 1913, mainly as an adjutant with the Infantry. He stayed in the army after the defeat of Germany and trained as a staff officer. He entered the Luftwaffe in April 1934 as a *Major* and serving primarily as a staff officer. He died in an aircraft crash on 22nd June 1940 as *Generalmajor* and Commanding General of Luftgau Belgium-North France.

41. Erich von Manstein – Served the German military as a lifelong professional soldier. During World War II he attained the rank of *Generalfeldmarschall* and

was held in high esteem by his fellow officers as one of the Wehrmacht's best military minds. He was the initiator and one of the planners of the Ardennes Offensive alternative in the invasion of France in 1940. He commanded the failed relief effort at Stalingrad and the Cherkassy pocket evacuation. He was dismissed from service by Hitler in March 1944, due to his frequent clashes with him over military strategy. In 1949, he was brought on trial in Hamburg for war crimes, which convicted him of "Neglecting to protect civilian lives" and for using scorched earth tactics denying vital food supplies to the local population. He was sentenced to eighteen years in prison, which was later reduced to twelve years but only served four years before being released. After release from a British prison in 1953, he became a military advisor for the West German Government. He died on 13th June 1973.

42. Paul-Werner Hozzel – Served during World War II as a Stuka pilot and won the Knight's Cross with Oakleaves on 14th April 1943 as *Oberstleutnant* and Commander 2nd Stuka Wing "Immelmann". He saw action over Poland, Norway, France, England, Balkans, and in Russia. He died on 7th January 1997 in Stuttgart.

43. Otto Wilhelm von Renz – Entered the army in July 1911 and served with the 14th Field Artillery Regiment. He was commissioned as a *Leutnant* in November 1912 and in 1935 he joined the Luftwaffe as a Major. He went onto command the 33rd Flak Regiment in 1938 and in August 1941 he was promoted to *Generalleutnant* and was appointed 9th Flak Division. In July 1944 was appointed commander of the 4th Flak Corps as *General der Flakartillerie*. He was captured by U.S. troops in May 1945 and released two years later. Renz died on 16th January 1968 in Bad Neuenahr.

44. Heinrich Eberbach – Participated in the German Invasion of Poland in September 1939 by leading his Panzer-Regiment 35 into battles near Lodz and into Warsaw. During the 1940 Battle of France, *Oberst* Eberbach supported *General* Manteuffel's offensive across the Meuse River in Flanders then on into Lyon. In June 1941, as commander of the 5.Panzer-Brigade in *Generaloberst* Guderian's XXIV Panzer Corps, Eberbach participated in the German invasion of the Soviet Union. By March 1942 he had been promoted to *Generalmajor* and made commander of the 4th Panzer-Division in Tula, Russia. Later he became commander of the XLVIII Panzer Corps operating near Kiev. In late November 1942 Eberbach was wounded near Stalingrad and hospitalized until February. Shortly thereafter he became Inspector of the Armored Troops in the Home Army, awarded the Knight's Cross and promoted to *Generalleutnant*. In late August 1944 Eberbach urged the immediate retreat of the German forces to escape eastward through the Falaise Gap before Allied forces could entrap them.

45. Paul Hausser – One of the main architects of the Waffen-SS and he was one of only two Waffen-SS officers to reach the rank of *SS-Oberstgruppenführer und Generaloberst der Waffen-SS*, the other being Josef "Sepp" Dietrich. He was awarded the Knight's Cross with Oakleaves and Swords on 26th August 1944 as Commander-in-Chief of the 7th Army. He fought on the Western Front throughout World War II and was adored by his men who called him "Papa" Hausser. He died on 21st December 1972 in Ludwigsburg and his funeral was attended by hundreds of ex-servicemen, many were Waffen-SS.

46. Wilhelm Wimmer – Commissioned as a *Leutnant* in October 1911 and served in 16th Bavarian Infantry Regiment from 1909 until 1914. He entered the Luftwaffe in September 1933 as an *Oberstleutnant*. He served for a time in the Reich Air Ministry and was promoted to *Generalmajor* in April 1936 and to *Generalleutnant* in April 1938. In July he took over command of the 2nd Air Division and in February 1939 he was appointed Commanding General of the Luftwaffe Commando East Prussia and was promoted to *General der Flieger* in October 1939. In August 1940 he became Commanding General of Luftgau Commando Belgium-Northern France. He surrendered in May 1945 and remained in captivity for nearly two years. He died on 15th May 1973 in Garmisch-Partenkirchen.

47. Walther Model – German general and later *Generalfeldmarschall* World War II. He is noted for his defensive battles in the latter half of the war, mostly on the Eastern Front but also in the west, and for his close association with Hitler and Nazism. He has been called the Wehrmacht's best defensive tactician. He saw action during Poland and as commander of the 16th Army during the Battle of France. For Operation Barbarossa, the 3rd Panzer Division was assigned to the XXIV Panzer Corps, itself part of the Second Panzer Group, commanded by Heinz Guderian. The campaign opened on 22 June 1941, with Guderian urging his divisions forward at breakneck speed. He took part during the attack on Moscow and was promoted to *General der Panzertruppe* and was appointed Commander of the XLI Panzer Corps. On 5 July 1943 Model led the northern assault on Kursk during Operation Citadel, a plan which had caused great controversy within the German high command. Günther von Kluge and Erich von Manstein, commanding Army Groups Centre and South respectively, had originally urged that the salient be attacked in May, before the Soviets could prepare their defences. He was awarded the Knight's Cross with Oakleaves, Swords and Diamonds on 17th August 1944 as GFM Commander-in-Chief of Army Group Centre. Model committed suicide on 21st April 1945 near Ratingen.

48. Georg Jauer – Served during World War I and remained with the Reichswehr serving as a staff officer and later branch chief in the Army Personnel office. Later commanded 29th Artillery Regiment; the Grossdeutschland Artillery Regiment; the 25th Panzer Division; 20th Panzer Grenadier Division and the Grossdeutschland Panzer Corps in 1945. He ended the war as a *General der Panzertruppe* and won the Knight's Cross with Oakleaves on 10th February 1945 as *Generalleutnant* and Commander 20th Panzer Grenadier Division. He died on 5th August 1971 in Greven.

49. *Die Wehrmachtberichte 1939-1945 Band 1*. Deutscher Taschenbuch Verlag, 1985.

50. Otto Skorzeny – *SS-Standarenführer* (Colonel), and a special agent under Himmler's direct orders. He was a tough, fearless Austrian, six feet, four inches tall and widely respected. In September 1943, acting on Hitler's direct orders Skorzeny was responsible for rescuing Mussolini from his Italian captors in a dare – devil raid. Landing his special troops in a glider only a few hundred feet from where Mussolini was being held prisoner. He helped quash a possible mutiny after the bomb attempt on Hitler's life in July 1944 and during the Battle of the Bulge he organized English speaking German soldiers dressed in American uniforms to help to misdirect traffic and create mayhem among the U.S. forces. At the end of the war Skorzeny was captured and tried by a U.S. court in 1947 and acquitted. He moved to Spain and became a prosperous businessman; he died in Madrid on 5th July 1975.

51. Gotthard Heinrici – Extremely capable officer with great skill, and perhaps because he didn't have the strong character such as Rommel or Patton he is almost unknown today. He commanded the 16th Panzer Division in Poland and in 1940 he commanded the XXXXIII Panzer Corps and later in 1942 he commanded the 4th Army. His last command was that of commander-in-chief of Army group Vistula. He won the Knight's Cross with Oakleaves and Swords on 3rd March 1945 and ended the war with the rank of *Generaloberst*. He died on 13th December 1971 in Waiblingen.

52. Andreas Nielsen – Born in December 1899 in Flensburg he entered the army in October 1917 as a war volunteer. He was commissioned as a *Leutnant* in 1924 while serving with the 6th Infantry Regiment. He entered the Luftwaffe in July 1935 as a member of the General Staff. He became Chief of the General Staff of the 2nd Air Corps in February 1940 and was promoted to *Oberst* in 1941. From October 1940 he was chief-of-staff of the 5th Air Fleet and in January 1944 he was appointed Commander of the German Luftwaffe in Denmark. Promoted to *Generalleutnant* in July 1944 he ended the war as chief-of-staff of Air Fleet Reich. He died in his hometown of Flensburg on 24th April 1957.

53. Johann Seifert – Entered the Austrian army in August 1908 as an officer cadet, he was commissioned in May 1911. He served during World War I in the infantry and when the war was over he held the rank of *Hauptmann* He stayed in the Austrian army until March 1938 when he transferred to the Luftwaffe with the rank of *Oberstleutnant*. In February 1940 he led the 44th Flak regiment in France and later commanded the 3rd Flak Brigade with the rank of *Generalmajor*. In September 1941 he commanded the 10th Flak Division and in June 1942 he was promoted to *Generalleutnant*. During the last months of the war he served as a Volkssturm commander and surrendered to U.S. troops on in September 1945. He died on 11th November 1978.

54. Friedrich Hirschauer – Joined the army in July 1902 and was commissioned as a *Leutnant* in October 1904. He served during World War I in the artillery and saw action at Verdun in 1916. He stayed in the army after the war and rose to the rank of *Oberst* before being transferred to the Luftwaffe in October

1934. He served from 1938 until 1942 as the Commanding General of Luftgau XVII, Vienna. In August 1942 he was made President of the German National Air Defense League with the rank of *General der Flakartillerie*. He died on 9th December 1979 in Munich.

55. Beevor, Antony: *Crete: The Battle and the Resistance* London: Penguin Books.

55a. Ibid.

56. Wolfgang Falck – German Luftwaffe fighter ace during World War II. He was one of the key organizers of the German night fighter defences. After the war he worked for different U.S. companies like McDonnell-Douglas. He was awarded the Knight's Cross on 1st October 1940 as Major and Commander of the 1st Night Fighter Wing. He died on 13th August 2007.

57. Georg von Kutzleben – Entered the army in March 1905 and was commissioned the following year. He saw action during World War I with the Artillery and rose to the rank of *Hauptmann* before war's end. He remained in the army after the war and transferred to the Luftwaffe in April 1934 as *Oberstleutnant*. He served mostly during World War II as a Flak officer with various commands and saw action in Russia, and ended the war with the rank of *Generalleutnant*. He died on 3rd July 1962 in Coburg.

58. Werner Prellberg – Entered the army in March 1914 as a *Leutnant* and served with the 84th Field Artillery regiment. He remained in the army after the war and in 1933 he moved to the Reich War Ministry where he remained for two years. In April 1935 he transferred to the Luftwaffe with the rank of *Major*. He commanded the 12th Flak Regiment until February 1940, now with the rank of *Oberst*. He went onto command the 3rd and the 7th Flak Brigades and finally ending the war as commander of the 12th Flak Division with the rank of *Generalleutnant*. He died on 15th June 1960 in Wolfenbüttel.

59. Edmund Wachenfeld – Joined the army in 1896 and served throughout World War I and after as a staff officer. He transferred to the Luftwaffe in April 1934 as a *Generalleutnant* and was assigned as Commander of Luftkreis I and later as Commander of Luftkreis III in Dresden. He was promoted to *General der Flieger* in October 1935 and in 1939 he transferred back to the army. He died on 4th December 1958 in Gräfelfing.

60. Günther Rüdel – Joined the army in 1902 and was commissioned in March 1904. He transferred to the Luftwaffe in April 1935 as a *Generalmajor*. He became Inspector of Flak artillery and head of the Air Defense Department with the Air Ministry, and ended the war with the rank of *Generaloberst*. He was awarded the Knight's Cross of the War Merit Cross with Swords in November 1942. In November 1942 he was transferred to the reserves where he remained for the duration of World War II. He died on 22nd April 1950 in Munich.

61. Hans-Georg von Seidel – Entered the army in March 1910, and later served as an Ordnance Officer with 77th Reserve Division as an *Oberleutnant*. From 1917 he served as a staff officer and remained in the army after World War I. He transferred to the Luftwaffe in May 1934 as a *Major*. In April 1938 he was appointed Quartermaster General of the Luftwaffe with the rank of *Oberst*. Promoted to *Generalmajor* in September 1939 and to *Generalleutnant* in July 1940 he went on to command the 10th Air Fleet in 1944 with the rank of *General der Flieger*. He was awarded the Knight's Cross of the War Merit Cross with swords in July 1944. In May he went into British captivity and was released in May 1948, he died in November 1955 in Bad Godesberg.

62. Wilhelm Mayer – Entered the army in July 1905 and served in World War I mainly as a Staff Officer, ending the war as a *Hauptmann*. He remained in the Reichswehr after the war and was transferred to the Luftwaffe in April 1935 as an *Oberst*. From July 1938 until October 1941 he served as the Commanding General of Luftgau IV in Dresden with the rank of *General der Flieger*. He ended the war on the Reserve List and died on 17th July 1950 in Egglkofen, Upper Bavaria.

63. Irving, David: *Göring: A Biography* London: Harper Collins.

64. Josef Grohe – *Gauleiter* of Cologne-Aachen from 1931 until 1945. Born in November 1902, he joined the Nazi Party in 1922. When the French occupied the Rhineland, he was with a Nazi resistance group and was forced to flee to Munich. He held a number of posts in the party becoming a *Gauleiter* in 1931 and later he served as Reich Commissar for occupied Belgium and Northern France. He spent five years in prison after the war and returned to Cologne where he entered the film industry. He died on 27th December 1987 in Cologne-Brück.

65. Irving, David: *Göring: A Biography* London: Harper Collins.

66. Kurt-Bertram von Döring – Entered the army in March 1907 and served as a pilot during World War I. He left the army in February 1920 but returned to military service in June 1934 with the Luftwaffe. He served as a group commander of the "Richthofen" Squadron from June 1934 until February 1936. He went onto command the "Horst Wessel" Wing and later was appointed Inspector of Fighters in December 1940 with the rank of *Generalmajor*. Awarded the German Cross in Gold in December 1942, he was promoted to *Generalleutnant* in November 1941 he served as Commander of 1st and 3rd Fighter Divisions. He surrendered to the Allies in May 1945 and was released in July 1947. Döring died on 9th July 1960 in Kloster Medingen.

67. Walter Schwaberdissen – Served in the army from July 1914 and was commissioned in January 1915, and served as an observer during World War I. He remained in the army after the war and transferred to the Luftwaffe in September 1933 as a *Hauptmann*. He served as a staff officer from 1933 until January 1942 when he took over command of the 2nd Night Fighter Division. He was promoted to *Oberst* in June 1938; *Generalmajor* in August 1940, and *Generalleutnant* in August 1942. In 1944 he was appointed Commanding General of the German Luftwaffe in Denmark and ended the war on the Reserve List. He was released from U.S. captivity in June 1947; he died on 19th February 1989 in Gauting near Munich.

68. Helmuth Felmy – Entered the army in 1904, and was commissioned as a *Leutnant* in August 1905. Served in the air corps during World War I and remained in the armed forces after Germany's defeat. He transferred to the Luftwaffe in November 1933 as an *Oberst*, and served in the Air Ministry. In 1935 he was appointed Commander of Luftkreis VII and in February 1939 he commanded the 2nd Air Fleet. In May 1941 he was made Commander of the Wehrmacht Mission in Iraq, and had by this time been promoted to *General der Flieger*. His last military command of the war was that of Commanding General of the LXVIII Army Corps in 1944 and from December 1944 until May 1945 he commanded the XXXIV Army Corps. He died on 14th December 1965 in Darmstadt.

69. Hans-Joachim Hermann – Luftwaffe bomber pilot, and later a lawyer focusing his activities mostly on the defense of former Nazis and neo-Nazis, deniers of the holocaust and political activists of the far-right. In World War II, he was a high ranking and influential member of the Luftwaffe. He was one of the Luftwaffe's most innovative air tacticians during World War II. Beginning his military career as an infantry officer, he was commissioned in the newly formed Luftwaffe in 1935. He flew bombing missions over Poland, Norway, England, Malta, Greece, and Italy, and in December 1943 he was appointed Luftwaffe Inspector of Aerial Defense. He was awarded the Knight's Cross with Oakleaves and swords on 23rd January 1944 with the rank of Oberst. He was captured by the Russians after the war and was held prisoner for ten years. Back in Germany he studied law and settled in Düsseldorf. Among others, he defended the deniers of the holocaust: Otto Ernst Remer, David Irving and Fred A. Leuchter. He is still alive today.

70. Eduard Ritter von Schleich – Saw action during World War I with the Bavarian Infantry and later during the war he served as a pilot. He won the *Pour le Mérite* during the war on 4th December 1917. He joined the Luftwaffe in April 1935 as a *Major* and was attached to the Air Ministry. He commanded various air schools before being appointed Commander of the Luftgau Kommandos in Norway in January 1944. He was promoted to *Generalmajor* in February 1941 and to *Generalleutnant* in September 1943. He died on 15th November 1947 in Diessem, Ammersee while in American captivity.

71. Wilhelm Ritter von Leeb – German *Generalfeldmarschall* who commanded Army Group C during the invasion of Poland and later in France. He was promoted to GFM after the fall of France in July 1940. In May 1941 he was appointed commander-in-chief of Army Group North and saw action on the eastern front. He was awarded the Knight's Cross on 24th June 1940 as *Generaloberst*. He died on 29th April 1956 in Hohenschwangau.

72. Wolfgang von Wild – Entered the German Imperial Navy in July 1918 and remained in the navy until he transferred to the Luftwaffe in October 1934. In April 1941 he was made Air Leader East and in August was promoted to *Oberst*. He served as Air Transport Leader in Athens from November 1942 and in December he was Air Leader in Sardinia. He was promoted to *Generalmajor* in March 1945 and was taken prisoner by the British in May, and was released in July 1947. He died on 12th May 1964 in Kassel.

73. Richard Putzier – Joined the army in March 1911 and served during World War I as an artillery officer. He transferred to the Luftwaffe in April 1934 and was promoted to *Oberstleutnant* in October. In February 1939 he was appointed commander of the 3rd Air Division with the rank of *Generalmajor*. He was promoted to *Generalleutnant* in January 1941 and *General der Flieger* in July 1942. He was Commanding General of Luftgau I from January 1941, and Commanding General of Luftgau XXVI in Riga from August 1943. Captured by the Allies in July 1945, he died on 17th July 1979 in Hamburg.

74. Eckhardt Christian – He entered the navy in April 1926 and transferred to the Luftwaffe in October 1934 with the rank of *Hauptmann*. He served throughout World War II as a staff officer and was chief-of-staff of the General Staff of the Luftwaffe from February 1939 until March 1940. In February 1943 he married Traudl Junge Hitler's secretary. In September 1944 he was appointed deputy chief of the General Staff of the Luftwaffe and was captured by U.S. forces in May 1945. He ended the war as a *Generalmajor* and died on 3rd January 1985 in Bad Kreuznach.

75. Koller, Karl: *Der letzte Monat. Die Tagebuchaufzeichnungen des ehemaligen chefs des Generalstabes der deutschen Luftwaffe von 14. April bis zum 27 May 1945*. Mannheim: Wohlgemüth.

76. Felix Steiner – Served as frontline officer during World War I and in 1918 he joined the Border Protection units. He left the Reichswehr in 1933 and in 1935 he joined the SS and helped to build it up. He was rapidly promoted and was awarded the Knight's Cross in August 1940 as *SS-Oberführer* and commander SS-Standarte "Deutschland", awarded the Oakleaves as *SS-Gruppenführer* and commander of the SS-Panzer Grenadier Division "Wiking" in December 1942, and was awarded the Swords in August 1944 as *SS-Obergruppenführer* and commanding General of the 3rd SS-Panzer Corps. The last years of his life he spent in Munich and on 12th May 1966 he was found dead in his flat in Munich.

77. O'Donnell, James P.: *The Berlin Bunker*. J.M. Dent.

78. Claus von Stauffenberg – One of the leaders of the Conspiracy against Hitler and the officer who planted the bomb at Hitler's headquarters on 20th July 1944. He was shot on the evening of the 20th July in the courtyard of the War Ministry Building on the order of *General* Fromm.

79. Erich Müller – Commandant of the Channel Islands from May 1941 until September 1943 with the rank of *Generalmajor*.

80. Harris, Whitney R: *Tyranny on Trial. The Evidence at Nuremberg*. Southern Methodist UP.

81. Walter Graf von Brockdorff-Ahlefeldt – Commander of the 2nd Corps from 1940 to 1942 and took part in the defense in the Demjansk Pocket on the northern sector of the Russian front. He was in poor health in 1942 and had to be relieved, He was promoted to *General der Infanterie* in August 1940 and was an anti-Hitler conspirator from 1938, he died in Berlin on 9th May 1943.

82. Christian Hansen – Commander of the 14th Panzer Division during the Polish Campaign and he was promoted to *General der Kavallerie* in 1940 and commanded the LIV Army Corps on the Eastern front from 1941-1943 before taking command of the German Military Mission to Romania in 1943. He was also Military commander of Romania and he was captured in September 1944 and not released until 1955. He won the Knight's Cross on 3rd August 1941 as Commanding General of the 10th Army Corps. He died on 7th August 1972 in Garmisch-Partenkirchen.

83. Ernst Fessmann – Born in 1881 he entered military service in 1900. He spent most of his career as a cavalryman and rose to command the 17th Cavalry Regiment in 1926. He was given command of the rank division by Ludwig Beck as a counterweight to the perceived rashness of Heinz Guderian. He retired as *General der Panzertruppe* in 1937. Recalled to duty when war broke out, he commanded the 267th Infantry Division from 1939 until 1941. He retired again in 1942 and was discharged in 1943. He settled in Pullach and died on 25th October 1962.

84. Leo Geyr von Schweppenburg – German military attaché to London, Brussels and The Hague in the 1930s. He entered the army in 1904 with the 26th Dragoon Regiment. He led the XXIV Motorized Corps in 1940, and the XXXX Panzer Corps in 1942, and the LVII Panzer Corps 1942-1943. He was appointed commander of Panzer Group West, which later became the 5th Panzer Army in October 1943. He was badly wounded by Allied bombers on 9th June 1944 and his chief of staff was killed. He returned to command troops in Normandy in late June 1944 and was relieved of his command by Hitler in early July. He died in Irschenhausen, Upper Bavaria on 27th January 1974.

85. Heinz Ziegler – Born on 19th May 1894 in Darkehmen. In 1939 he was appointed chief-of-staff to Commander in Chief of the Replacement Army, and was appointed Chief of Staff of the XXXXII Army Corps in 1940. He was awarded the Knight's Cross on 16th April 1943 as *Generalleutnant* and Commander of Army Group Ziegler, while attached to the 5th Panzer Army. He was later promoted to *General der Artillerie*, and his last command was as acting commander of the 14th Army in Italy. He died on 21st August 1972 in Göttingen.

86. Hans-Jurgen von Arnim – Commanded the 52nd Infantry Division when World War II broke out and led the 17th Panzer Division from 1940 until June 1941 when he was wounded and replaced by *Ritter* von Weber. He returned to duty and commanded the XXXIX Panzer Corps in Russia before commanding the 5th Panzer Army in Tunisia and later Army Group Afrika in March 1943. He was promoted to *General der Panzertruppe* in October 1941 and to *Generaloberst* in December 1942. He surrendered his army group on 12th May 1943, he was considered a good general but commanding an army exceeded his capabilities.

87. Walter Feyerabend – Entered the army in March 1910 as a *Leutnant* serving mainly with the artillery. He joined the Luftwaffe in April 1935 with the rank of *Major* and was assigned as a Flak commander in Königsberg. Promoted to *Generalmajor* in April 1939 he went onto command the 14th Flak Division in July 1941 and ended the war as a *Generalleutnant*. He died in April 1962 in Detmold.

88. Helmuth Volkmann – He entered the army in 1907 and was commissioned as a *Leutnant* the following year. He transferred to the Luftwaffe in September 1934 and was appointed commander of the Condor Legion in Spain in November 1937 with the rank of *Generalmajor*, being promoted to *Generalleutnant* in April 1938. He commanded the Air War Academy in Berlin from April 1939 and a year later he transferred back to the army with the rank of *General der Artillerie*. On 4th August 1940 he was severely wounded in a car accident and died of his injuries on 21st August in a Berlin hospital.

89. Karl Wolff – Head of Himmler's personal staff and military governor of Northern Italy from 1943 until 1945. He joined the NSDAP in 1931 and rose rapidly in the SS and was soon appointed personal adjutant to Himmler and later head of his staff and liaison officer with Hitler. In 1942 he was promoted to *SS-Obergruppenführer* and in 1943 he was sent to Italy where he controlled the German occupation for the last two years of the war. He opened negotiations with the Allies in Switzerland in 1945 that resulted in the early surrender of Italy. Although he was implicated with the "Final Solution" he was only sentenced to four years imprisonment by a de-Nazification court. Tried again in 1964 and sentenced to fifteen years imprisonment he was released in 1971. Wolff unrepentant became a successful businessman in West Germany until his death on 17th July 1984.

90. Franz Hofer – *Gauleiter* of Tirol from 1938 until 1945. He was imprisoned by the Austrian authorities in 1933 and later released by the Nazis. He fled the country and went to Germany where he remained until after the Anschluss. In 1938 he was reappointed *Gauleiter* and held the post until the end of the war. After the war he lived under a false name, and later lived under his real name until his death in February 1975 in Mülheim.

91. Heinz-Hellmuth von Wühlisch – Saw action during World War I and transferred to the Luftwaffe in April 1934 with the rank of *Major*. He served as a General Staff officer and in January 1941 was appointed chief-of-staff of the 1st Air Fleet as *Generalmajor*. He was promoted to *Generalleutnant* in April 1942 and from December until April 1945 he served as Chief of the General Staff of the Military Commander of the Netherlands. He committed suicide while in allied captivity on 20th September 1947 in Ellecom, the Netherlands.

92. Philipp Zoch – Joined the Luftwaffe in April 1934 as a *Major* and by the start of World War II had risen to the rank of *Oberst*. In September 1939 he was commander of the Luftwaffe with 3rd Army, and in October he held the same position with the 6th Army. In April 940 he became the commander of the Luftwaffe with Army Group D followed by similar positions with Army C and Centre in June 1941. Promoted to *Generalmajor* in April 1940 and to *Generalleutnant* in April 1942 he was captured by U.S. troops in May 1945 and spent just over two years as a prisoner. He died on 24th May 1949 in Wittlich.

93. Ludwig Wolff – Entered the army in May 1904 and served as staff officer during World War I, rising to the rank of *Major* in 1917. He joined the Luftwaffe in March 1934 and continued to serve as a staff officer being promoted to *Generalmajor* in August 1937. In July 1938 he was appointed Commander of the 5th Air Division and a year later he was promoted to *Generalleutnant* and to *General der Flieger* in February 1941. From February 1939 until the end of the war he served as the Commanding General of Luftgau XI in Hannover and later Hamburg. He was awarded the Knight's Cross of the War Merit Cross with Swords in September 1943.

94. Walter Somme – Entered the Luftwaffe in April 1935 and rose to the rank of *General der Flieger* in May 1942 and commanded Luftgau VIII in Breslau from 1941 until 1944. He surrendered to U.S. troops in April 1945 and was released in June 1947 and lived in retirement until his death in Düren on 14th May 1971.

95. Walter Kathmann – Joined the army in August 1914 and saw action during World War I with the artillery. He transferred to the Luftwaffe in April 1935 and joined a Flak unit with the rank of *Major*. Just before the outbreak of war he was made commander of the 3rd Flak Regiment. In May 1940 he was appointed Chief of Staff of Luftgau Kommandos XVII with the rank of *Oberst*. From November 1941 until June 1943 he served as an officer head in the Air Ministry and was promoted to *Generalmajor* in April 1942 and to *Generalleutnant* in June 1944. His last command during World War II was as commander of the 5th Flak Division. He died in Nuremberg on 4th April 1982.

96. Rudolf-Eduard Licht – Joined the infantry in 1911 and remained in the army after World War II. When war broke out he was commanding the 40th Infantry Regiment and later commanded the 17th Rifle Brigade before becoming commander of the 17th Panzer Division. Not the most successful commander of the war he later commanded the 21st Luftwaffe Field Division in 1943 and later the 710th Infantry Division. He wasn't promoted to *Generalleutnant* until 1944.

97. Eugen Dollmann – *SS-Standarenführer* who acted as an interpreter and liaison officer between Hitler and Mussolini and was a close confidante of Heinrich Himmler. He also had Himmler's authority to liaise with the Vatican when necessary. He played an important role in attempting to prevent the Ardeatine Caves massacre in 1944 by seeking an audience with Pope Pius XII and asking for Vatican intervention. He accompanied Mussolini to the Wolf's Lair on 20th July 1944 and witnessed Hitler's outburst and his promised revenge on the conspirators. Dollmann was also a massive influence on Karl Wolff and deserves credit for helping to negotiate the German.

98. Hasso von Manteuffel – *General der Panzertruppe* who took part in the Polish and French Campaigns. He commanded the 3rd Motorcycle Battalion in 1940; 6th Rifle Regiment in 1941-1942; 7th Rifle Brigade in 1942; In 1944 he commanded the elite Großdeutschland Panzer Division before being promoted from a divisional commander to army commander in August 1944. He led the 5th Panzer Army on the Western Front in 1944-1945 during the Battle of the Bulge and later the 3rd Panzer Army during the fighting for Berlin in 1945. He was one of the best German commanders of the war and won the Knight's Cross with Oakleaves, Swords and Diamonds on 18th February 1945. He died on 24th September 1978 in Reith, Austria.

99. Wilhelm Süssmann – Entered the army in October 1909 and was commissioned in June 1911. He left the army in 1919 and joined the police where he stayed until August 1935 when he transferred to the Luftwaffe. In April 1938 with the rank of *Oberst* he served as commander of the 254th Bomber Wing. In May 1939 he became commander of the 55th Bomber Wing and in January 1939 was promoted to *Generalmajor* and in December 1940 he was promoted to *Generalleutnant*. In October 1940 he was appointed commander of the 7th Air Division and saw action in Crete where he was killed on 20th May 1941.

100. Eberhard von Mackensen – Entered the German Army in 1908 as a *Leutnant*. After being wounded in 1915, he was given a staff job. He remained in the Army and by 1934 had risen to the rank of *Oberst*. In 1935, he was appointed chief of staff to the X Army Corps and in 1937 he was given command of a Cavalry Brigade. At the beginning of World War II, he served as the chief of staff of the German 14th Army during the invasion of Poland. He was made chief of staff of the 12th Army and fought in France. In January 1940 he was promoted to *Generalleutnant* and eight months later to *General der Kavallerie*. In January 1941 he was made Commanding General of the III Army Corps, and in November 1942 he commanded the First Panzer Army which he led in the Third Battle of Kharkov in March 1943. Promoted to *Generaloberst* in 1943, he was send to Italy as Commander of the 14th Army which he led until June 1944 when he retired.

101. Time-Life Books: *The Conquests of the Balkans*.

102. Irving, David: *The Rise and Fall of the Luftwaffe: the Life of Field Marshal Erhard Milch*. Boston: Little Brown.

103. ibid.

104. Irving, David: *Hitler's War* London: Focal Point.

105. Kesselring, Albert: *The Memoirs of Field Marshal Kesselring*. London: Kimber.

106. Hans-Georg von Friedeburg – In spite of having a Jewish grandmother, Friedeburg was an ardent supporter of Nazi regime and was shielded by Heinrich Himmler from anti-Jewish persecutions. Appointed Deputy Commander of the German U-Boat fleet in September 1941, he oversaw all U-Boat training and deployment of the U-Boat bases in France. He was promoted to Rear Admiral in 1942, he assumed command of the German U-Boat fleet in February of the following year. He succeeded Karl Dönitz as Commander-in-Chief of the Kriegsmarine when Dönitz became Reichs President upon Hitler's suicide and was promoted to *Generaladmiral* on 1 May 1945. On May 2, Friedeburg officially signed, on behalf of the German Navy, the document declaring the official surrender of the German high command in Northern Europe, including Germany, taking effect at midnight of 8/9 May 1945. Two weeks later, on 23 May 1945, he committed suicide.

107. Gerhard Hoffmann – he joined the army in March 1906 as a *Leutnant* serving mainly as a staff officer. In November 1934 he joined the Luftwaffe and was assigned to the 5th Flak Regiment in October 1936. The following year he became commander of the 12th Flak Regiment with the rank of *Oberst*. He was promoted to *Generalmajor* in June 1939; *Generalleutnant* in June 1941 and in December 1942 he was promoted to *General der Flieger*. In September 1941 he commanded the 4th Flak Division and in March 1942 he commanded the 15th Flak Division. From 1943 until early 1945 he was Commander of Luftgau III in Berlin before going into the Reserves.

108. Georg von Gylderfeldt – Entered the army in January 1916 as a *Gefreiter* and entered the police in June 1920. He transferred to the Luftwaffe in June 1935 with the rank of *Hauptmann*, and was appointed battery commander with a flak unit. He was promoted to *Major* in 1937; *Oberstleutnant* in June 1939; *Oberst* in January 1942 and in January 1945 he was promoted to *Generalmajor*. He commanded various Flak Regiments during World War II including the 22nd (1940); 6th (1940-1941) 104th (1941-1942 and 122nd (1942-1943). Captured by the Allies in May 1945 he was released from captivity in 1947. He died in May 1977.

109. Helmuth Weidling – Officer in the German Army during World War II, and was the last commander of the Berlin Defense Area during the Battle of Berlin, defending the city against Soviet forces and finally surrendering just

before the end of World War II in Europe. He was awarded the Knight's Cross with Oakleaves and Swords on 28th November 1944. He was captured by the Soviets in May 1945 and in February 1952, a Soviet military tribunal in Moscow sentenced him to twenty-five years of imprisonment for not surrendering Berlin sooner. He died in November 1955, KGB records listed the cause of death as, "arterial and cardiac sclerosis along with circulatory collapse."

110. Irving, David: *Göring: A Biography* London: Harper Collins.

111. Ibid.

112. Ibid.

113. Gaston von Chaulin-Egersberg – Entered the army in March 1913 serving in World War I with the 11th Artillery Regiment, and being commissioned in October 1917. He transferred to the Luftwaffe in June 1935 and served as a Flak commander throughout World War II. He was promoted to *Oberst* in February 1939; *Generalmajor* in December 1941 and to *Generalleutnant* in December 1943. In November 1944 he was appointed General of the Flak Arm and his last command of the war was as commander of Luftwaffe troops in Army Group B. He surrendered to U.S. troops in April 1945 and remained a prisoner until February 1947.

114. Hans Siburg – Entered the Navy in April 1912 and transferred to the Luftwaffe in September 1933. In 1936 he was appointed Chief of Operations with of Air District Command VII with the rank of *Oberst*. In November 1938 he was made Commander of 257th Bomber Wing, and in September 1939 he was made Inspector of Air Navigation and he was promoted to *Generalmajor* in January 1939 and *Generalleutnant* in November 1940. In July 1940 he was made Commander of Air Region Holland and in April 1942 he was promoted to *General der Flieger*. He went into British captivity in May 1945 and was released in July 1947.

115. Franz Engel – Entered the Luftwaffe in August 1935 serving in various Flak units before the start of World War II. Promoted to *Oberstleutnant* in February 1939 he was appointed commander of the 100th Flak Regiment in June 1940. He was promoted to *Oberst* in April 1941 and took over as commander of the 10th Flak Division in June 1943, and was promoted to *Generalmajor* in October 1944. He spent ten years in Soviet captivity and was released in October 1955 and went to live in Munich where he died in May 1965.

116. Reinhard Heydrich – Head of the Reich Main Security Office (RSHA) and Deputy Protector of Bohemia-Morvaia (Czechoslovakia). He began his career as a signals officer in the navy and was dismissed for refusing to marry a woman after having a serious relationship with her. In September 1941 Hitler appointed him Deputy Reich Protector of Bohemia and Moravia and was the architect of the "Final Solution". On 29th May 1942 two British-trained Czechs threw a grenade in his open-top car and the blast blew small particles from the seat into Heydrich's body and he developed blood poisoning which killed him. The Nazis destroyed the village of Lidice and executed more than 3,000 people in reprisal.

117. Karl von Eberstein – Served in World War I in the artillery and then with the Freikorps before joining the Nazi Party and the SS in 1929. In September 1931 he served as adjutant to the Quartermaster of the SA High Command. In September he was promoted to *SA-Gruppenführer* and in February 1933 he left the SA to take up a full time role with the SS. He commanded various Allgemeine-SS units that included Abschnitt XVIII, Mitte and Elbe. From April 1937 until October 1941 he served as Police President fro Munich and served in the Bavarian State Ministry of the Interior from October 1942 to April 1945. In April 1945 he was dismissed from all his posts by Martin Bormann for defeatism. He testified at Nuremberg but was never tried; he died on 10th February 1979.

118. Hermann Hoth – Entered the army in 1904 an entered the Cadet Corps at Potsdam and he went onto command an infantry regiment during World War I. In April 1914 he became a General Staff officer with the rank of *Oberleutnant*. During World War II Hoth commanded the 3rd Panzer Group in November 1940 as a *Generaloberst*. In October 1941 he was appointed Commander-in-Chief of the 17th Army and in May 1942 he took over as commander of the 4th Panzer Army. He was awarded the Knight's Cross with Oakleaves and Swords on 15th September 1943. In May 1945 he surrendered to U.S. troops and went into captivity until 1948. Hermann Hoth died on 25th January 1971 in Goslar.

119. Friedrich Römer – Entered the army in August 1914 as a war volunteer with the 7th Field Artillery Regiment. He joined the police after World War I and transferred to the Luftwaffe in June 1935 with the rank of *Major*. He commanded the 36th Flak Regiment (1938-1939); Commander of 201st Flak Regiment (1939-1940); Commander of 8th Flak Regiment (1940-1942); Commander of the XV Flak Brigade (1942-1943 and was Commander of the 22nd Flak Division (1943-1945). He ended the war as *Generalmajor* and was captured in April 1945. He died on 21st June 1970 in Cologne.

120. Otto Stange – Entered the army in October 1910 and wasn't commissioned until December 1922. He joined the Luftwaffe in April 1935 as battery commander in 22nd Flak Battalion. He was promoted to *Major* in October 1936; *Oberstleutnant* in April 1939; *Oberst* in October 1941 and *Generalmajor* in April 1945. His last military command of the war was as commander of the 3rd Flak Division. In May 1945 he surrendered to British troops and remained in captivity until May 1947. He died on 15th October 1980 in Schopfheim, Baden.

BIBLIOGRAPHY

Angolia, John R: *For Führer and Fatherland. Vol: 1* San Jose: Roger James Bender Publishing, 1976.

Angolia, John R: *On the Field of Honor: A History of the Knight's Cross Bearers Volume 1*. San Jose: Roger James Bender Publishing, 1979.

Angolia, John R: *On the Field of Honor: A History of the Knight's Cross Bearers Volume 2*. San Jose: Roger James Bender Publishing, 1980.

Barnett, Correlli (Editor): *Hitler's Generals*. London: Widened & Nicolson, 1989.

Beevor, Antony: *Crete: The Battle and the Resistance* London: Penguin Books, 1992.

Bickers, Richard Townshend: *The Battle of Britain: The greatest battle in the history of air warfare* Guild Publishing, 1990 reprint..

Brett-Smith, Richard: *Hitler's Generals*. London: Osprey, 1976.

Goralski, Robert: *World War II Almanac 1931-1945: A Political and Military Record* London: Hamish Hamilton, 1981.

Gordon, Harold J. Jr. *Hitler and the Beer Hall Putsch*. Princeton: Princeton University, 1972.

Hamilton, Charles: *Leaders and Personalities of the Third Reich Vols: 1 & 2* Roger James Bender Publishing, 1996.

Harris, Whitney R; Tyranny on Trial. The Evidence at Nuremberg. Southern Methodist University Press, 1954..

Hildebrand, Karl Friedrich: *Die Generale der Deutschen Luftwaffe 1935-1945* Osnabruck: Biblio Verlag. Vols: 1 -3, 1991.

Irving, David: *The Rise and Fall of the Luftwaffe: the Life of Field Marshal Erhard Milch*. Boston: Little Brown, 1973.

Irving, David: *Hitler's War* London: Focal Point, 1991.

Keilig, Wolf: *Die Generale des Heeres und die Sanitätsoffizere im Generalsrang*. Dorheim: Podzun-Pallas-Verlag GmbH, 1983.

Kurowski, Franz: *Knight's Cross Holders of the Afrikakorps* Atglen, PA: Schiffer Military, 1996.

Kurowski, Franz: *Knight's Cross Holders of the Fallschirmjäger* Atglen, PA: Schiffer Military, 1995.

Littlejohn, David and Dodkins, C.M. *Orders, Decorations, Medals and Badges of the Third Reich. Volume 1:* Mountain View, California: Roger James Bender Publishing, 1968.

Mitcham, Samuel W: *Hitler's Legions: German Army Order of Battle*. London: Leo Cooper, 1985.

Mitcham, Samuel: *Men of the Luftwaffe*. Novato, CA: Presidio, 1988.

Mitcham, Samuel W: *Eagles of the Third Reich: Hitler's Luftwaffe* London: Guild Publishing, 1988.

Mitcham, Samuel & Gene Muller: *Hitler's Commanders*. London: Leo Cooper, 1992.

Mosley, Leonard: *The Reich Marshal: A Biography of Hermann Goering*. London: Weidenfeld & Nicolson, 1974.

Philpott, Bryan: *History of the German Air Force*. Bison Books, 1986.

Public Record Office: *The Rise and Fall of the German Air Force 1933-1945* Kew: Public Record Office, 2001.

Scherzer, Veit: *Ritterkreuzträger 1939-1945* Scherzers Militaire-Verlag Ranis: Jena, 2005.

Thomas, Franz: *Die Eichenlaubträger 1940-1945 Band 1: A-K*. Osnabrück: Biblio Verlag, 1997.

—: *Die Eichenlaubträger 1940-1945 Band 2: L-Z*. Osnabrück: Biblio Verlag, 1997.

Williamson, Gordon: *The Iron Cross: A History 1813-1957* Blanford Press, 1984.

Williamson, Gordon: *Knight's Cross of the Iron Cross: A History 1939-1945*. Blanford Press, 1987.

Williamson, Gordon: *Luftwaffe Handbook 1935-1945* Sutton Publishing, 2006.